Revision WorkBook

Commercial Law

EDITED BY
P. A. Read LLB, DPA, Barrister

THIRD EDITION

HLT Publications

HLT PUBLICATIONS
200 Greyhound Road, London W14 9RY

First Edition 1990
Reprinted 1991
Second Edition 1992
Reprinted 1992
Third Edition 1994

ISBN 0 7510 0437 5

British Library Cataloguing-in-Publication.

A CIP Catalogue record for this book is available from the British Library.

Printed and bound in Great Britain.

CONTENTS

ACKNOWLEDGEMENT

Some questions used are taken or adapted from past University of London LLB (External) Degree examination papers and our thanks are extended to the University of London for their kind permission to use and publish the questions.

Caveat

The LLB answers are not approved or sanctioned by the University of London and are entirely our responsibility.

They are not intended as 'Model Answers', but rather as Suggested Solutions.

The answers have two fundamental purposes, namely:

a) To provide a detailed example of a suggested solution to an examination question, and

b) To assist students with their research into the subject and to further their understanding and appreciation of the subject of Laws.

INTRODUCTION

This Revision WorkBook has been designed specifically for those studying Commercial Law to undergraduate level. Its coverage is not confined to any one syllabus, but embraces all the major Commercial Law topics to be found in university or polytechnic examinations.

The main chapters are each divided into sections. Each section contains, in its first few pages, brief notes explaining the scope and overall content of the topic covered. There follows in each case a detailed list of Key Points which will assist the student in studying and memorising essential material that he must be familiar with if he is to fully understand the topic. Recent cases and statutes will be listed as necessary. However, on the assumption that the student will already have a textbook/casebook, case law has been kept to a minimum in the introduction and key points in each chapter for the sake of simplicity.

Additionally, in each section there will be a 'question analysis' which will list and compare past examination questions on similar topics in Commercial Law. This will give the student an appreciation of the potential range of questions possible and some idea of variations in wording, different 'formats' in questions and alternative modes of answering techniques.

Each section will end with one or occasionally two typical examination questions, together with a skeleton answer and a full suggested solution. Most of the questions are drawn from University of London LLB External Commercial Law papers 1983-92. It is therefore inevitable that in compiling a list of questions by topic order, not only do the same topics come up several times in different guises, but that there are gaps. Where a topic has never been covered in an examination question, a typical question will have been written specially by the author, together with skeleton answer and solution.

Undoubtedly the main feature of this Revision WorkBook is the inclusion of as many past examination questions as possible. While the use of past questions as a revision aid is certainly not new, it is hoped that the combination of actual past questions from the University of London LLB external course and some specially written problems where there are gaps in examination coverage, will be of assistance to students in achieving a thorough and systematic revision of the subject.

Careful use of the Revision WorkBook will enhance the student's understanding of Commercial Law and enable you to cope with as wide a range of subject matter and variety of question wording as might occur in any Commercial Law examination.

Though this WorkBook is meant to be quite self-contained and questions for which solutions are provided are quoted in full, it is nevertheless true that the 'question analysis' in each chapter may refer to other questions simply by year and number. For this reason it will be helpful if the student acquires, before commencing to use the book, a set of past papers from London University for the years 1983-92 inclusive.

In this revised 1994 edition the final chapter contains the complete June 1993 University of London LLB (External) Commercial Law question paper, followed by suggested solutions to each question. Thus the student will have the opportunity to review a recent examination paper in its entirety, and can, if desired, use this chapter as a mock examination - referring to the suggested solutions only after first having attempted the questions.

Note:

If enquiring about past papers, whether in a library or when ordering them from London University, remember that the title changed from 'Mercantile Law' to its present name of Commercial Law in 1988.

HOW TO STUDY COMMERCIAL LAW

Commercial Law is that division of law which is concerned with the rights and duties of the parties concerned, wherever goods or services are supplied by way of trade.

One immediate problem for the student is that the scope of the subject is not clearly defined. No two authorities cover exactly the same ground in their textbooks, and the syllabuses of universities and polytechnics are not always the same. Indeed some would say it is not a subject as such, but a combination of bits and pieces from other areas of law.

Certainly, to study Commercial Law successfully, the student needs a good working knowledge of basic contract law, sale of goods, agency and so on; all of which can be treated as individual branches of law and have their own standard reference works. It is an advantage also, to have at least a nodding acquaintance with such diverse topics as securities, negotiable instruments, conveyancing, shipping law and many others. Additionally, students need to be able to relate what he reads of the theory of contract, or shipping law, or whatever, to the specific problems of Commercial Law.

Commercial Law is a constantly changing area of law as business practices and the actual physical methods of doing business change. For example, the introduction of telex machines generated case law on offer and acceptance and presumably, any day now, we can expect to see the first case concerning 'fax' machines. In the constant process of updating Commercial Law the rules change frequently with new statutes and cases; but the basic concepts stay the same. It is this basic foundation of rules which underpin the whole structure of Commercial Law with which the student should first become familiar. Since it is a constantly developing area of law, however, new cases come before the courts all the time and the student will find that vigilant reading, not only of standard reference books and law journals, but of business magazines and even the daily press will all help keep him up to date.

It is important to remember that while the proper study of Commercial Law is through the relevant legislation and case law, many problems arising in the day-to-day world of commerce have never been the topic of reported cases. Even when relevant case law does exist, the litigation often does not divide itself into neat areas for study in isolated compartments. Often a case will involve several different issues and be relevant to several different branches of the subject.

The very core of Commercial Law lies rooted in business transactions. All case law arises as a result of disputed transactions and legislation has been introduced primarily to forestall such disputes and provide a set of rules for the transaction of business affairs. Thus, the student will find it almost impossible to understand the subject properly until he has fully grasped the fundamental nature of such transactions. Once he understands who the parties are, who is affected and how, and the function of the various documents involved, then the rules become immediately, more meaningful. A student who can visualise, for example, every stage of shipment of goods, from their arrival at the quayside, loading on board, the voyage, with different possible hazards that may occur, to the ultimate point of delivery, will be much more readily able to understand CIF contracts. The provisions made in such a contract to counter the various problems and conflict of interest that might arise, can then be seen in their true perspective.

While many areas of common law affect business transactions, the basic framework of Commercial Law is, of course, provided by law of contract. While most students studying this subject will be doing so as part of a law degree course or some other legal qualification, Commercial Law is also of interest to those studying, for example, accountancy or business studies. Here, a problem may arise if a student has no background of basic contract law. While it is possible to study Commercial Law, in isolation, as it were, it is not a course of action to be recommended. To attempt to study contractual dealings between businessmen without being familiar with the details of the contract, or understanding the legal implications, will only result in, at best, a superficial grasp of the topic which can be easily lost in a difficult examination and at worst a failure ever to master the topic. For a student not already thoroughly at home in the basics of contract law the first step towards success in Commercial Law must inevitably be to acquire the necessary grounding in the law of contract.

No one would pretend that Commercial Law is an easy subject to master. But its relevance to the modern business world, its constant changes and development, make it an exciting and challenging area of law to concentrate on.

REVISION AND EXAMINATION TECHNIQUE

Whole books have been written on how to study and this brief note makes no pretence at being an infallible guide. In any case, skill in revision and examination techniques is an art best acquired by actual practice.

The more you study, the more you devise your own short cuts for efficient preparation for exams. Unfortunately, it is only when you actually sit the examination that you can see whether your particular method of revision is successful. If it is not, it is an expensive and frustrating way to find out.

While it is true that examination techniques are best learned actually sitting examinations, it is not necessary to wait until the real thing. 'Mock' examinations, tackled under realistic conditions, can be very helpful. Revision aides like this Workbook, not only give some idea of potential questions and possible solutions, but can be used most efficiently by the student as a form of examination rehearsal. For example, select a question and, without looking at the skeleton answer, write out your own. Compare it with the skeleton answer in the Workbook and if you appear to be working along the right lines, then proceed to write a full solution - preferably under simulated examination conditions. Once you have completed your own solution you can see how it tallies with that given in the Workbook.

Or, if you have time, tackle a full quota of four or five questions at once - as a mock examination.

Remember, none of the solutions given is represented as the 'only' solution, nor need the exact sequence be the same - the main aim is to give you guidance as to a possible way of tackling the question and as to presentation of your answer.

Most people who have succeeded in examinations have times when they think: 'If only I had known then, what I know now, I could have done even better.' For that reason it is often helpful to read other people's suggestions and hints for easier revision and any tips they may have for actually sitting the examination - such advice is often prompted by bitter experience!

Often a large number of such recommendations en masse are rather overwhelming. Indeed, some may actually contradict each other. The secret is to use only that advice which applies to you personally and which you think will fit in with your chosen methods of study.

However, remember that recognizing that what is effective is a personal matter does not mean there are no ground rules at all. The most important thing to remember is that in studying for an exam, especially at degree level your success (or lack of it) will be entirely due to your own efforts. The secret of success is to realise at an early stage that it is necessary to create an efficient pattern of study which suits your own character and with which you will feel comfortable.

The short list of *Do's* and *Dont's* below attempts to set out some suggestions which it is hoped most students will find of practical use in planning their revision and tackling examinations.

Do's

Before the examination

i) *Planning ahead*

Plan ahead and make your plans increasingly detailed as you approach the examination date.

Allocate enough time for each topic to be studied. It is better to devise a realistic timetable, to which you have a reasonable chance of keeping, rather than a wildly optimistic schedule which you will abandon at the first opportunity.

ii) *Self-discipline*

Exercise constant self-discipline, especially if studying at home.

iii) *Self-testing*

Constantly test yourself during your course of study, especially once revision starts, both orally and in writing.

iv) *Keeping up-to-date*

Keep up-to-date. While examiners do not require familiarity with changes in the law during the three months prior to the examination, it obviously creates a good impression to show you are acquainted with any recent changes.

Sources that you might look at in order to be up to date include: leading journals such as *Modern Law Review, Law Quarterly Review* and *New Law Journal.* Cumulative indices to law reports such as the *All England Law Reports*, and such sources as the *Law Society's Gazette* and the *Legal Executive Journal* will also be useful.

v) *Past exam papers*

Familiarise yourself with past examination papers; and try at least one 'mock examination' well before the date of the real thing.

At the examination

vi) *Exam paper instruction*

Read the instructions at the examination carefully. While any last minute changes are unlikely - such as the introduction of a compulsory question - it has been known to happen.

vii) *Exam questions*

Read the questions carefully. Analyse problem questions - work out what the examiner wants. **Plan your answer** before you start to write.

viii) *Mark allocations*

Note mark allocations (if any) on the question paper. It is pointless to spend an excessive amount of time in producing a perfect answer to a part of a problem that carries only a tiny percentage of the marks.

ix) Read your answer over, in the last few minutes.

Don'ts

i) *Completing the syllabus*

Don't finish the syllabus too early - constant revision of the same topic leads to stagnation - but *don't* leave revision so late that you have to 'cram'.

If you *are* the sort of person who works better to a deadline - make it a realistic one!

ii) *Learning by rote*

Don't try to learn by rote. In particular, don't try to reproduce model answers by heart. Learn to express the basic concepts in your own words.

iii) *Answering the right question*

Don't answer the question you expect to see! By all means 'problem-spot' before examinations by going over old exam papers but make sure that what the examiner is asking for really does match what you are preparing to write about.

iv) *Keeping calm*

DON'T PANIC!

It may be useful at this juncture to say a few words about the form and structure of your answer in an examination.

The structure of your answer

Almost all examination problems raise more than one legal issue that you are required to deal with. Your answer should:

i) *Identify the issues raised by the question*

This is of crucial importance and gives shape to the whole answer. It indicates to the examiner that you appreciate what he is asking you about.

This is at least as important as actually answering the questions of law raised by that issue.

The issues should be identified in the first paragraph of the answer.

ii) *Deal with those issues one by one as they arise in the course of the problem*

This, of course, is the substance of the answer and where study and revision pays off.

iii) *If the answer to an issue turns on a provision of a statute, CITE that provision briefly, but do not quote in detail from any statute you may be permitted to bring into the examination hall*

Having cited the provision, show how it is relevant to the question.

iv) *If there is no statute, or the meaning of the statute has been interpreted by the courts, CITE the relevant cases*

'Citing cases' does not mean writing down the name of every case that happens to deal with the general topic with which you are concerned and then detailing all the facts you can think of.

You should cite *only* the most relevant cases - there may perhaps only be one. No more facts should be stated than are absolutely essential to establish the relevance of the case. If there is a relevant case, but you cannot remember its name, it is sufficient to refer to it as 'one decided case'.

v) *Whenever a statute or case is cited, the title of statute or the name of the case should be underlined*

This makes the examiner's job much easier because he can see at a glance whether the relevant material has been dealt with, and it will make him more disposed in your favour.

vi) *Having dealt with the relevant issues, summarise your conclusions in such a way that you answer the question*

A question will often say at the end simply 'Advise A', or B, or C, etc. The advice will usually turn on the individual answers to a number of issues. The point made here is that the final paragraph should pull those individual answers together *and actually give the advice required.* For example, it may begin something like: 'The effect of the answer to the issues raised by the question is that one's advice to A is that ...'

vii) Make sure that you have answered all the questions. For example, if the question says, 'advise A, B and C', don't leave C out. But, don't waste time dealing with items you are not asked about.

Note: The Suggested Solutions

At this level there is no one answer, these solutions are suggestions only and, provided you cover the relevant material thoroughly and support your arguments with the proper authority, the exact sequence and form of the answer is really relatively unimportant.

It will be seen that some of the answers are relatively lengthy - perhaps more so than one could realistically hope to complete in an examination. The opportunity has been taken, when appropriate, to develop themes, suggest alternatives and set out additional material to an extent which would not be possible for an examinee facing a strict time limit.

They are not 'model' answers or 'the' solution - (implying that there is only one), and, while they are not written to strict examination time limits, it is anticipated most candidates could achieve something similar, given thorough preparation.

TABLE OF CASES

TABLE OF STATUTES

READING LIST

This is not meant to be in any way an exhaustive list of available textbooks. It will be seen by any student browsing round a library or bookshop that Commercial Law is an area with considerable literature.

This list may however serve as a reminder to the student of some of the works with which he should already (hopefully) have some aquaintance!

ANSON (Ed. Guest) - *Anson's Law of Contract*, Clarendon Press (1984, 26th Ed)

ATIYAH - *Introduction to the Law of Contract*, Oxford Clarendon Law Series (1989, 4th Ed)

BEALE, BISHOP & FURMSTON - *Contract - Cases & Materials*, Butterworth (1990, 2nd Ed)

BOWSTEAD - *Bowstead on Agency*, Sweet & Maxwell (1985, 15th Ed)

BRADGATE & SAVAGE - *Commercial Law*, Butterworths (1991)

CHESHIRE, FIFOOT & FURMSTON - *Cheshire & Fifoot's Law of Contract*, Butterworths (1986, 11th Ed)

CHITTY - *Chitty on Contracts*, Sweet & Maxwell (1983, 25th Ed)

COLLINS - *The Law of Contract*, Weidenfeld & Nicolson (1986)

COOTE - *Exception Clauses*, Sweet & Maxwell (1964)

DE BATTISTA - *Sale of Goods Carried by Sea*, Butterworths (1990)

FRIDMAN - *Fridman's Law of Agency*, Butterworths (1990, 6th Ed)

READING LIST

GOODE	-	*Commercial Law*, Penguin (1982)
		Consumer Credit Law, Butterworths (1989)
MACLEOD	-	*Consumer Sales Law*, Butterworths (1989)
PAYNE & IVAMY	-	*Carriage of Goods by Sea*, Butterworths (1989, 13th Ed)
PITT	-	*Butterworths Commercial Law Handbook*, Butterworths (1989, 1st Ed)
TREITEL	-	*An Outline of the Law of Contract*, Butterworths (1989, 4th Ed)
YATES	-	*Exclusion Clauses in Contracts*, Sweet & Maxwell (1982)

The HLT *Commercial Law Textbook.*
The HLT *Commercial Law Casebook.*

PART 1

SALE OF GOODS

1 INTRODUCTION AND SCOPE OF THE SALE OF GOODS ACT

1.1 Introduction

Until 1893 the law relating to contracts for sale of goods had no special features. It was governed by the ordinary law of contract. In 1893, the first attempt was made to codify the law - the Sale of Goods Act of that year.

The current Act of 1979 is largely a consolidating act re-enacting much of the earlier legislation.

It should be noted, however, that the Act does not purport to be an exhaustive system of law. In particular s62(1) of the Sale of Goods Act 1979 specifically provides that common law, including mercantile law, should apply except where inconsistent with the provisions of the Act.

Students should note that some other legislation: including Factors Act 1889 and Unfair Contract Terms Act 1977 are also relevant to the law of sales of goods.

1.2 Key points

It is important that the student understands the following points:

a) *The overall effect of the Sale of Goods Act*

Remember, the main effect of the original Sale of Goods Act in 1893 was to imply certain terms where a contract between parties was silent.

It was possible for the parties to exclude the provisions of the Act. Increasing criticism of the use of exclusion clauses to block the effectiveness of the legislation resulted ultimately in the Unfair Contract Terms Act 1977 and this Act had the effect of rigidly limiting the use of exclusion clauses. Therefore the overall effect of the Sale of Goods Act 1979 taken in conjunction with the Unfair Contract Terms Act 1977 is that: while certain basic rules are imposed on the parties as to the conduct of the contract of sale; the basic common law of contract on for example, mistake, misrepresentation, duress and fraud, still applies to contracts for sale of goods.

b) *Classification of goods*

Remember, some sections of the Act make different provision for different categories of goods.

Two classifications in particular are important:

i) Specific or unascertained goods

These are treated quite differently by:

ss6-7 which relate to the perishing of goods;

and ss16-18 which relate to the passing of property in goods.

ii) Future and existing goods

Here the distinction is particularly important in relation to the passing of property in the goods under s18.

c) *The contract of sale*

i) The Act defines the terminology of sale, parties and price. In particular:

Section 2 defines it as 'a contract by which the seller transfers or agrees to transfer the property in the goods for a money consideration, called the price'.

ii) A distinction should be made between 'sales' and 'agreements to sell'.

iii) Sale of goods should be distinguished from other similar transactions.

d) *Formation of the contract of sale*

This will be dealt with in more detail in chapter 2.

Remember, the general law of offer and acceptance governs the formation of the contract and the current legislation makes no special requirements for particular formalities in the mode of contract.

e) *Property, risk and title*

This will be dealt with in more detail in chapters 8 and 9.

Suffice for now to be aware of statutory provisions which are relevant and to be aquainted with the standard definition of each term.

1.3 Analysis of questions

Although questions on sale of goods are frequent in past commercial law papers: very few deal with this introductory material.

Some of those questions which follow in other sections (especially chapters 8 and 9) on more specific areas of sale of goods need a good working knowledge of definitive material. Students should look carefully at Q1 of the 1993 paper (see chapter 36).

When questions do occur, like the one following, they tend to be of the straight narrative essay type, often requiring the student to define certain common words or phrases occurring in the standard definitive sections of the Sale of Goods Act.

1.4 Question

Explain the meaning of, and the relationship between the terms 'property', 'risk' and 'title' in the Sale of Goods Act 1979.

University of London LLB Examination
(for External Students) Commercial Law June 1987 Q2

Skeleton solution

- Introduction; reference to relevant part of the Act.
- Definitions; both statutory (as applicable) and as according to circumstances of contract.
- Nemo dat rule.

Suggested solution

Many examinees would have found this question difficult because it touches on a subject which is not clearly dealt with in any of the standard textbooks. The relationship between the three concepts mentioned in the question is made all the more difficult to discuss by the absence of explanation in the Act itself. Never the less, like so many essay questions, if the effect of the sections of the Act dealing with each concept are remembered then it should not be impossible to say something about their meanings and relationship.

'Property', 'risk' and 'title' are not fully defined in the Sale of Goods Act 1979, indeed the only definition to be found is of property and even that does not pretend to be exhaustive (s61(1) Sale of Goods Act 1979). Within the Act the three concepts all arise in Part III which is entitled 'Effects of the Contract' and generally, deals with three different matters:

a) when the buyer becomes the owner;

b) whether the buyer becomes the owner in cases where the seller was not the owner; and

c) the undefined concept of 'risk'.

Property is reserved from describing the passing of ownership from the seller to the buyer. Section 2 recognises that contracts of sale of goods can provide for ownership to pass immediately or at a future date or on the happening of some condition. If ownership is to pass immediately then the contract is one of sale, if it is to pass at a later date or on the happening of some condition then the contract is an agreement to sell. But in all cases, whether or not the seller is the owner, the parties will agree that ownership should pass at some time. In general the Act states that the parties' agreement on the time of passing of ownership will be respected (s16), but it recognises that in many (if not most) sales the parties will not say when ownership passes. Therefore certain rules are laid down in s18 which will be applicable in the absence of express or implied agreement to the contrary. The rules differ according to the other terms of the contract and the nature of the goods: (a) there are rules for specific goods and others for unascertained goods, (b) there are rules where the parties provide that something must be done to the goods by one or other party and others where nothing has to be done to the goods prior to delivery. Detailed discussion of these sets of rules is outside the scope of this essay.

The definition of property in s61(1) as meaning the general property in goods rather than any special property, shows that it is the global aspect of ownership rather than some equitable interest in the goods which is covered by the s18 rules.

Furthermore, it is noticeable that the rules in s18 have two effects: firstly they identify who is the owner at any time in order to see who, prima facie, should bear any loss caused by damage that is done to the goods; and secondly they determine the remedies open to the parties. The first of those matters is what is meant by risk. The risk in goods is the duty of one party to bear the cost of their loss or damage. The prima facie rule, both at common law and under the 1979 Act, is that the owner of goods must bear such costs (s20(1)). But the parties may always agree that ownership shall pass to the buyer on a particular date or on the happening of a particular event and the risk on another, be it before or after he becomes the owner. For example, in '*Romalpa* ' cases the contract invariably provides that property will only pass on full payment, whereas risk passes to the buyer immediately.

In fact risk is used to describe concepts other than the costs of loss or damage. It can be used in cases where the seller is unsure of his rights of ownership to describe the position of a buyer who buys and takes a chance - he bears the risk of the seller not being the owner and, accordingly, must pay for the goods whether or not he becomes owner. This idea of risk is not one covered by the Act, but arises at common law. The Act is concerned, when talking of risk, with loss or damage only.

The incidence of property also dictates the remedies open to the parties to a limited extent. The buyer cannot be sued for the price unless property has passed to him (s49), even if it is his fault that it has not passed (*Colley* v *Overseas Exporters* (1921)). The seller will therefore be obliged to sue for damages for non-acceptance rather than for the price. In relation to third parties who damage the goods, an action will not lie in negligence unless the plaintiff had property rights at the time they were damaged (*The Aliakmon* (1986)). Cases can, therefore, arise where the parties agree that the buyer has to bear the risk of the goods being damaged, but he cannot sue the third party because he did not have property at the time the damage was done.

'Title' also involves concepts of ownership, but is concerned with the question *whether* the buyer has become owner not *when* he became owner. In ss21 to 25 there are rules allowing a buyer to obtain good title even though the person from whom he bought was not the true owner. The buyer's title does not derive from the seller but vests in him by operation of law. In effect, therefore, ownership passes from the true owner to the buyer and the seller is never owner himself.

The rule nemo dat quod non habet prevails unless the buyer can prove that one of the statutory exceptions applies. Where a seller (S) owns goods and sells them to a buyer (B), B will be able to pass ownership by a sale to a third party (T) if he has obtained ownership himself. Conversely if B is not the owner at the time he sells to T then T can only become the owner if one of the nemo dat exceptions applies. Accordingly it is important to know whether property has passed to B in order to be able to appreciate the effect of his sale to T.

Although the Act refers to property and title as apparently different concepts, they are both concerned with ownership. When the seller of goods is their owner the rules on property determine when the buyer becomes owner, and when the seller does not own them the rules on title allow ownership to be vested in the buyer regardless.

2 FORMATION OF THE CONTRACT AND FORMALITIES

2.1 Introduction

Contracts of sale are, as noted in chapter 1, subject to normal rules of contract. Therefore many of the issues relating generally to formation of contract are relevant. It is necessary to show, for instance, that the parties have the requisite intention to create legal relations; that they have reached agreement via the process known as offer and acceptance and that consideration is present. No vitiating elements, such as mistake duress or undue influence should apply.

For details on these points the student should refer to standard textbooks on law of contract.

2.2 Key points

It is important that the student understands the following points:

a) *Formation of the contract*

i) Intention on the part of the parties to create legal relations is more readily inferred in the kind of commercial transactions which are characteristic of sale of goods. See, for example, the recent case of *Kleinwort Benson* v *Malaysian Mining Corpn* (1989) as to intention to create legal relations.

ii) Offer and acceptance may take place in the form of verbal conversations, telephone calls and so on as well as by standard written communications. The recent Scottish case of *Neilson* v *Stewart* (1991) confirms that while uncertainty will render a contract void, ambiguity may be resolved by inference from common law.

iii) Consideration in sale of goods will always be in a particular form: on the one hand the provision of goods; on the other payment of a monetary consideration known as the price.

Section 8 of Sale of Goods Act governs the question of price and in a normal case this will be fixed or readily ascertainable. Occasionally the parties deal together so regularly they do not need to refer specially to the price, they automatically know how to calculate it. Section 8(2) provides that if there is no procedure at all in the contract for determining price, the buyer may pay a 'reasonable' price.

b) *Mistakes*

One common law doctrine of particular importance to sale of goods is mistake. On occasion it is difficult to assess whether, because of mistake, agreement was ever reached between the parties. In construing such cases the courts will take an objective approach.

There can also be difficulties when mistakes arise as to the identity of one of the parties. Almost always, this results from fraud perpetrated by one party against the other. The main issue in such cases is usually whether the question of mistaken identity avoids the contract or renders it completely void.

c) *Duress*

Note that commercial pressures amounting to duress will vitiate a contract. See *Atlas Express* v *Kafco* (1989).

d) *Auction sales*

Section 57 of the Sale of Goods Act deals specifically with sales contracts concluded at auction sales. In fact, the various subsections largely restate the common law position.

Effectively s57 declares what is already known, that each lot put up for sale at an action is presumed to be the subject matter of a different contract. Subsection (2) states that each sale in an auction is only complete when the auctioneer announces it in whatever manner is customary - this means that until the point of the auctioneer's acceptance the usual common law rules relating to revocation apply and the bidder can withdraw his offer.

Also, note that s3 of the Auctions (Bidding Agreements) Act 1969, in seeking to control 'bidding rings' organised by dealers, provides that the seller may treat any contract concluded at an auction, when a bidding ring was in operation, as avoidable and recover goods or compensation for loss suffered.

e) *Formalities*

As noted in chapter 1 there are now no formal requirements for contracts for sale of goods.

Section 4 of the Act provides that contracts may be under seal, written, verbal or a combination of written and verbal or even implied from the parties' conduct.

Remember, however, that certain other statutes may have an effect on contracts for sale of goods depending either on the nature of the 'goods' in question or possibly on how it is intended to pay for the goods.

Thus:

i) a contract for the sale of an interest in land will be covered by the Law of

Property (Miscellaneous Provisions) Act 1989 and will be unenforceable unless in writing and signed by the parties; or

ii) under the Merchant Shipping Act 1894 transfer of a British ship or a share of one must be in writing; or

iii) credit sale agreements must be in writing and comply with the requirements of the Consumer Credit Act 1974.

2.3 Analysis of questions

There have been no questions solely on the topic of formation of contract in any of the past examination papers set by the University of London. But if one looks at Q2 of the 1993 paper (see chapter 36) it may be seen that a knowledge of common law aspects concerning formation (including particularly caveat emptor and misrepresentation) is required. Though in theory such a question would be perfectly valid it would seem examiners steer clear of the topic because it is largely a matter of ordinary common law as applied to contracts for sales of goods. A possible line of approach is suggested below: the main difficulty in answering such a question would be in supplying sufficient information specifically on sale of goods to answer what is effectively a basic contract law question.

2.4 Question

a) Smith and Jones, who have frequently dealt with each other over the past few years agree a sale of 20 tons of animal foodstuffs. No price is mentioned in the contract. Explain how the price might be discovered. Would your answer be any different if they had not previously dealt together?

b) If Smith agrees to sell to Jones 1,000 tons of rice which are at that time in the course of being shipped from Australia and unknown to either party the ship has already sunk with the loss of the cargo. Explain what the consequences would be on the contract of sale.

Skeleton solution

a)
- Formation of contract governed by general rules of offer and acceptance.
- Section 8 SGA governs question of price specifically.
- Section 9 relates to assessment of price by arbitrator.
- What constitutes a 'reasonable' price: s8(2).

b)
- Categories of mistake, res extincta.
- Risk and the perishing of goods: s6, SGA.
- Section 7 and the doctrine of frustration.

Suggested solution

a) The general law of contract as it relates to offer and acceptance will govern the formation of any contract for sale of goods.

Thus, if Smith and Jones have had frequent previous dealings of the same or a similar type their conduct alone may be sufficient to form a contract. Contracts for sale of goods need no special formalities, generally and may be in the form of written, verbal or implicit contracts or a combination of any or all of these.

Should any contract be lacking a vital term, a court may imply whatever is necessary to give business efficacy to the contract and give effect to the parties wishes as construed from the other terms of the contract. However, it should be remembered that if the contract is too vague and too many important questions not covered, the courts may, in common law, decide that the parties showed no intention to enter legal relations and have not reached agreement.

It is important to consider s8 of the Sale of Goods Act which governs the question of price:

Section 8 provides:

i) 'the price in a contract of sale may be fixed by the contract or may be left to be fixed in a manner agreed by the contract, or may be determined by the course of dealing between the parties;

ii) where the price is not determined as mentioned in (i) above, the buyer must pay a reasonable price;

iii) what is a reasonable price is a question of fact depending on the circumstances of each particular case.'

Thus, Smith and Jones' frequent dealings over the past years may give a clear guide as to what the price will be or hour it can be ascertained; as stipulated in (i) above.

Similarly, it is not uncommon for parties to commercial dealings to provide for the price to be fixed by a valuer or arbitrator s9 of the Act makes special provision for damages if this method is agreed on, and one of the parties then prevents the valuer or arbitrator from making an assessment of the price.

If Smith and Jones had had no previous dealings and their contract was silent as to price then s8(2) stipulates that the buyer must pay a 'reasonable' price. To assess reasonableness, the courts would consider each case on its merits and take an objective view of the background facts to the animal foodstuffs market.

b) To all intents and purposes mistakes fall into two main categories: those which prevent the formation of any agreement between the parties and those which, if operative, deprive the agreement which the parties have reached of having any substance.

In the category of mistake known as 'res extincta', the parties form a contract on the basis of a mutual assumption that the subject matter of the contract existed; when in fact it has either never existed at all or has been destroyed.

This type of case is sometimes referred to as a form of 'initial impossibility' to distinguish it from frustration or 'subsequent impossibility'.

In *Couturier* v *Hastie* (1856) a cargo of corn was shipping from the Mediterranean to England. The cargo of the ship was sold in London, both buyer and seller believing the ship to be in transit and the cargo in existence. In fact the cargo had deteriorated so much, the ship's master had already disposed of the cargo *before* the London contract was negotiated.

Court held that the contract was void because as far as these parties were concerned the subject matter had ceased to exist before the time of contracting.

Similarly in *McRae* v *The Commonwealth Disposals Commission* (1951) the plaintiff made a tender to salvage an oil tanker described as lying grounded on a coral reef off Papua. He not only paid £285 for the salvage rights, but went to considerable expense having a vessel adapted, hiring crew etc.

In fact there was no reef and no oil tanker.

Here the courts decided that the contract was not void for initial impossibility but instead that there was a contract between the parties and the contract had been breached. The non-existence of the subject matter entitled the plaintiff to compensation. Note here, that the strong suggestion of fraud or misrepresentation indicates something rather more than a simple mutual mistake, and Smith and Jones' assumption that the rice still exists is more akin to *Couturier* v *Hastie*. Certainly it would seem that the apparent agreement between Smith and Jones is impossible ab initio rather than rendered subsequently impossible or frustrated.

Finally, it should be noted that the Sale of Goods Act itself by s6 specifically covers 'perishing' of goods. By s6, where there is a contract for sale of specific goods and the goods without the knowledge of the seller have perished at the time when the contract is made; then the contract is void.

The question as to whether 1,000 tons of rice can be specific goods then arises. If the rice is already bagged up; or of a particular type it may be considered to be specific. Usually, however, such an item will be part of a much larger cargo and will be unascertained goods at that stage. In such a case the common law will apply.

In either case the contract will be void.

3 TYPES OF OBLIGATION CREATED

3.1 Introduction

In the negotiation of any contract it is likely that, in the early stages of discussion between the parties, a number of claims or statements (either oral or written) will pass between the two. This chapter deals with the question of the legal status of such statements. Several distinct problems arise in particular: should the statement(s) turn out to be incorrect, what remedy will the buyer have and secondly, to what extent anything which passes between the parties at the early stages of negotiation can be deemed to be incorporated into the contract itself.

The common law distinguishes between statements which are called representations and those which become terms of the contract.

A representation is a statement made by one party to another, which while not important enough to constitute a term of the contract; is never the less one of the factors that persuades the other party to enter into the contract. Where a party is induced to make a contract on the basis of an untrue statement of fact, this is known as misrepresentation. While the state of mind of the party making the misrepresentation will not affect the classification of the statement as a representation at all; his motives may be very relevant in determining the type of misrepresentation involved.

In so far as terms of the contract are concerned, common law once rigidly divided these into 'conditions' and 'warranties'. Recently the courts have adopted a more flexible approach and a third category of contractual term must be considered: the 'innominate term' or 'intermediate stipulation' (the two terms are virtually interchangeable). However, note that the Sale of Goods Act itself, in s11(3), distinguishes between a warranty and a condition only. It does not define 'condition' but simply provides for the consequences should a condition be breached. While the SGA does define 'warranty' in s61, the Act does little to guide on the question of whether a particular term should be defined as a condition or a warranty.

3.2 Key points

It is important that the student understands the following:

a) *Representations, misrepresentation*

A representation is a statement of fact made during the course of negotiations which is sufficiently persuasive to induce the other party to make the contract but which does not, itself become part of the contractual terms.

Should the representation prove untrue this is known as misrepresentation. Representations are statements of fact, but not trade 'puffs', statements of opinion, or future intention, or as to law.

Silence can in certain circumstances amount to misrepresentation, particularly in cases where it gives rise to half truths, or when silence distorts a positive representation. Generally, however it should be noted that mere silence is *not* considered to be misrepresentation.

A misrepresentation will normally have no effect unless it is material and it must have induced the other party to enter the contract. Therefore if the plaintiff can be proved to have been unaware of the representation, or to have placed no reliance on it then there will be no liability on the part of the representor.

There are three categories of misrepresentation:

i) fraudulent

ii) negligent

iii) innocent

and the difference between them can be traced to the state of mind and motivation of the representor. The remedies differ according to the type of misrepresentation and the Misrepresentation Act 1967 now largely regulates the form redress will take. An innocent party misled by fraudulent misrepresentation will have the option of either: affirming the contract and suing for damages for the tort of deceit, or rescinding the contract and sue for damages for deceit. *Derry* v *Peek* (1889) 14 App Cas 337 is the leading case on fraudulent misrepresentation.

In the case of negligent misrepresentation s2 of the Misrepresentation Act gives the alternative remedies of affirmation and damages or rescission with damages.

An innocent misrepesentor is blameless and at common law there was no remedy available. Section 2(1) of the Misrepresentation Act provides damages for innocent misrepresentation.

b) *Conditions and warranties*

The term condition is not defined by the Sale of Goods Act, though 'warranty' is.

In common law a condition may be defined as a term so crucial to the contract that non-performance strikes at the very heart of the contract, entitling the other party to treat the contract as not having been performed.

Obviously what is sufficiently fundamental to be called a condition is largely a question of assessing the parties' intentions at the time of making the contract.

Section 11(3) of SGA makes it clear that it will not necessarily depend on the parties' own terminology:

'Whether a stipulation in a contract of sale is a condition, the breach of which may give rise to a right to treat the contract as repudiated, or a warranty, the breach of which may give rise to a claim for damages, but not to a right to reject the goods and treat the contract as repudiated, depends in each case on the construction and a stipulation may be a condition, though called a warranty in the contract.'

Note the final phrases.

Warranty is defined in s61:

'An agreement with reference to goods which are the subject of a contract of sale, but collateral to the main purpose of such a contract ...'

To sum up, a condition is a term of vital importance, whereas a warranty is only of minor significance, in the performance of a contract. This is reflected in the remedies available in each case. (See the later chapters on remedies.)

c) *'Innominate terms' or 'intermediate stipulations'*

A further category was established in three cases:

i) *Hongkong Fir Shipping Co Ltd* v *Kawasaki Kisen Kaisha Ltd* [1962] 1 All ER 474

   in which the concept of an innominate term was introduced;

ii) *Cehave NV* v *Bremer Handelgesellschaft, The Hansa Nord* [1976] 3 All ER 739

   in which the Court of Appeal held that the principle of an innominate term could be applied to sale of goods cases; and

iii) *Reardon Smith Line* v *Hansen-Tangen* [1976] 3 All ER 570

   in which the House of Lords approved the principle first established in *Hongkong Fir*, thereby finally confirming the idea of a term capable of being neither a condition nor a warranty.

The *Hongkong Fir* case based criteria for defining such a term on the effect of breach, but it has since become clear that the nature of the breach can also be taken into account.

Remedies for breach of an innominate term will be either rescission or damages depending on severity.

Remedies generally will be dealt with in chapters 11-14.

d) *Terms of the contract*

If the contract is express as to all terms and no terms fall foul of either statute (for example, the Unfair Contract Terms Act 1977) or common law (for example, a term which is ambiguous) then in theory the Sale of Goods Act will have no application.

In reality there are few contracts which are so detailed and explicit that the SGA will not imply certain terms into the contract.

In the average contract the terms are partly those explicitly stated or written by the parties and partly those which are implied (unless expressly excluded) automatically into any contract for sale of goods by the SGA.

3.3 Analysis of questions

The same comments apply as with chapter 2. There have been *no* questions dealing exclusively with topics mentioned in this chapter, either wholly or partly, since before 1983 in the London University LLB past papers. Again, as with the previous chapter the reason may be that, given the broad extent of the sale of goods syllabus, this is regarded as being more properly a general law of contract subject. A possible question is suggested below which has in fact been taken from the LLB London *Elements of the Law of Contract* papers. In 1990 there *was* a question (quoted below) which dealt in part with matters raised in this chapter but also required the student to discuss aspects of the SGA and potential areas for reform.

3.4 Questions

Question 1

'Whether a breach of contract discharges the contract or not depends upon the nature of the term broken.'

Discuss.

University of London LLB Examination
(for External Students) Elements of the Law of Contract June 1983 Q4

Skeleton solution

- Assumption that breach discharges the contract should be repudiated.
- Classification of contractual terms.
- Criteria for designating conditions (as opposed to warranties).
- Innominate terms.
- Remedies: choice of repudiation or affirmation.

Suggested solution

First, it should be noted that is not primarily an essay about remedies, though obviously the nature of the breach of term will affect remedies available to the innocent party.

Secondly, it must be said that a breach of contract never discharges a contract, no matter what the nature of the term broken. Certain types of breaches may confer on the innocent party an option to terminate the contract, but he is under no obligation to do so and may, if he chooses elect to affirm the contract and keep it in existence: *White & Carter (Councils) Ltd* v *McGregor* (1962). A breach alone can never terminate or discharge a contract: *Howard* v *Pickford Tool Ltd* (1951). It may be that in reality the innocent party has no option but to accept the breach but as a matter of strict law he does have an election: *Decro-Wall International SA* v *Practioners in Marketing Ltd* (1971). With that qualification one now turns to the relevance of the nature of the term broken to the issue of whether or not the innocent party can elect to treat the contract as discharged.

Broadly the position is as follows:

a) if the term broken is a condition the innocent party can terminate irrespective of the degree of loss or damage flowing from the breach: *Bunge Corporation NY* v *Tradax Exports* (1981);

b) if the term broken is a warranty, the remedy is one in damages only;

c) if the term broken is an innominate term or an intermediate stipulation the innocent party can terminate the contract if the actual and prospective consequences of the breach are such as substantially to deprive him of the benefit of the whole of the consideration he bargained to receive under the contract: *Hongkong Fir Shipping Co* v *Kawasaki Kisen Kaisha Ltd* (1962).

Given the differing remedies available it is therefore of prime importance to be able to distinguish between the different types of contractual terms. As, frequently, parties fail comprehensively to classify their various contractual obligations, this has often been a matter for the courts.

A term may be held to be a condition on one of three grounds:

First, it may be a term which has already been so classified by previous judicial decision, eg *The Mihalis Angelos* (1971) and an expected ready - to - load clause in a charterparty.

Secondly, it may be a term prescribed by statute as a condition, eg the various implied terms contained in the Sale of Goods Act 1979 ss12-15.

Thirdly, and most difficult, the parties may have expressly or impliedly agreed that a particular term should be a condition. The court must be satisfied that the parties intended to use that word in its technical legal sense, ie a term which if broken will without more entitle the innocent party to treat the contract as discharged: *L Schuler AG* v *Wickman Machine Tool Sales Ltd* (1974). Where a term described as a 'condition' was held on its true construction to be merely an innominate term. Conversely, even if a term is not called a 'condition', the court may hold that it was the parties' implied intention that it should be, having regard to the nature of the term, eg a stipulation as to time in a charterparty in *Bunge* v *Tradax* (ante). The fact that the contract uses the word 'condition' will not necessarily be decisive, if in the context of the contract it is apparent that the parties never intended that breach should lead to termination: *Lombard North Central plc* v *Butterworth* (1987). If the term is not a condition, unless the parties have expressly agreed that it should be only a warranty, the court will almost certainly hold it to be an innominate term, as was done in *Cehave NV* v *Bremer Handelgesellschaft mbH* (1976) which is also authority for the proposition that innominate terms do form part of the law of the sale of goods, not withstanding the Sale of Goods Act 1979 s11(3) (re-enacting the old s11(1)(c) of the 1893 Act) which appears to contemplate conditions and warranties only.

The courts have increasingly expressed a preference for innominate terms rather than conditions, eg in *Cehave* v *Bremer* and *Reardon Smith Line* v *Hansen-Tangen* (1976), because of the flexibility this permits them in deciding the appropriate remedy in any given case. Against this, in *Bunge* v *Tradax* the House of Lords affirmed the importance of parties to commercial contracts knowing their respective rights at the date of breach and not having to await judicial determination at some considerably later date.

Thus, it is correct that the nature of the term is crucial in determining whether or not the innocent party can treat the contract as discharged by breach. For completeness, there are two other types of breach other than breach of a term, which justifies termination, (a) renunciation, as exemplified by *Hochster* v *De la Tour* (1853); and (b) impossibility of performance due to the act or omission of one party ('frustration by breach') as in *Universal Cargo Carriers Corporation* v *Citati* (1957).

NB: Further details as to Remedies may be found in chapters 11-14.

Question 2

'The implied terms in the Sale of Goods Act 1979 are simply a method - though an incomplete and imperfect one - of endeavouring to ensure that the buyer of goods gets what he pays for. They serve a useful function, albeit no doubt they could be improved upon.'

Do the current implied terms work well? Could they be made better?

University of London LLB Examination
(for External Students) Commercial Law June 1990 Q3

Skeleton solution

- Terms, conditions and warranties - 'inalienable rights'.
- Origins of the present implied terms - caveat emptor.
- The 1979 Sale of Goods Act, implied terms in context.
- Particular advantages of present implied terms.
- Particular disadvantages of present implied terms.
- Recent developments and proposals for the future.
- Suggestions for improvement - conclusion.

Suggested solution

Generally speaking, the courts will not enquire as to the business efficacy of a contract made between two individuals or trading entities unless certain conditions prevail, for example, the intention of the parties is unclear or there was some misrepresentation. It is generally accepted there are three major categories of contractual terms; namely conditions, warranties and innominate terms (sometimes referred to as intermediate stipulations).

To describe these briefly in the same order as above, conditions are vital or major terms which go to the 'root of the contract', breach of which entitles the innocent party to treat the contract as ended and to claim damages. Warranties are subsidiary or minor terms, breach of which entitles the innocent party to damages only. Section 61 of the Sale of Goods Act 1979 defines a warranty as being 'collateral to the main purpose' of the contract.

The third category referred to above - 'innominate' or intermediate terms, originated in their present form from the decision in the *Hongkong Fir Case* (1961) and were affirmed as such in *Bunge* v *Tradax* (1981) by Lord Scarman. An innominate term is one, the effect of non-performance of which the parties expressly (or as is more usual) impliedly agree will depend on the nature and consequences of the breach. Prior to these decisions it was widely thought that terms in a contract could only be conditions or warranties. In *Cehave* v *Bremer* (1975) the doctrine of innominate terms was extended to contracts for the sale of goods where an express term that goods were to be 'shipped in good condition' were in effect an intermediate stipulation.

In contracts for the sale of goods we are primarily concerned with the former categories, namely conditions and warranties; the reason for this being that firstly, where breach of condition is proved the consumer can repudiate the contract (subject to s11(4) in sale of goods cases) even though no actionable misrepresentation is proven or alleged. Secondly, the honest belief of the trader is no defence to an action for damages for breach of condition or warranty unlike the provisions of s2(1) Misrepresentation Act 1967.

The Sale of Goods Act 1893 ss12-15 introduced certain implied terms which benefited the consumer and strengthened rights and remedies against the seller. The Supply of Goods (Implied Terms) Act 1973 amended these in favour of the consumer and The Sale of Goods Act 1979 incorporated the implied terms as ss12-15 also. The statutory rights embodied in these ss12-15 SGA 1979 are generally regarded as 'inalienable' and (in particular the provisions of s12) cannot be contracted out of by the consumer. Some statutory and common law restrictions on contracting out of ss13-15 are dealt with under s6 of the Unfair Contract Terms Act 1977.

The proposition herein is that the implied terms of the Sale of Goods Act 1979 are an 'incomplete and imperfect' method of 'endeavouring to ensure that the buyer of goods gets what he pays for'. In essence this sums up the rationale behind both the 1893 and 1979 Sale of Goods statutes, but it represents an over-simplification of the complex legal draftsmanship and motivation behind these sections. The proposition continues that 'no doubt they could be improved upon'; this belies the longevity (albeit with some slight amendment) of the sections since their introduction in 1893 and the fact that they are substantially the same now as then.

The Sale of Goods Act 1979 does not actually contain a definition of 'condition' but s11(3) explains the term by reference to its legal effect. Conditions are therefore given their usual meaning (ie terms that go to the 'root' of the contract) and are distinguished from warranties by the remedies available for breach; in the case of breach of condition repudiation, rejection of any goods supplied and damages for breach, in the case of a warranty being breached damages for quantifiable loss being the remedy.

Some reference, without undue attention to detail, is necessary to the actual provisions of ss12-15 SGA 1979 in order to consider the proposition that they merely ensure the consumer gets what he pays for and to consider if improvement is possible.

Section 12 SGA 1979 contains an implied condition on the part of the seller that, in the case of a sale, he has a right to sell the goods, and in the case of an agreement to sell he will have such a right at the time the property is to pass. The section also contains implied warranties of freedom from undisclosed encumbrances and the right (s12(2)) to quiet possession of the goods. This applies to all contracts. Section 13 SGA 1979 contains an implied condition in a contract for the sale of goods by description, there is an implied condition that the goods will correspond with the description; and in a contract for the sale of goods by sample as well as description, a condition that the goods must correspond with both (s13(1). Section 13 applies to all contracts as does s12 and not just to sales made by traders to consumers.

Section 14 SGA 1979 applies to sales 'made in the course of a business' by the seller and contains an implied condition that 'goods supplied under such a contract are of merchantable quality' (with the exception of defects specifically drawn to the buyer's attention and defects which examination by the buyer before purchase ought to reveal)'. Additionally, 'where the seller sells goods in the course of a business and the buyer expressly or by implication makes known to the seller any particular purpose for which the goods are being bought, there is an implied condition that goods supplied under the contract are reasonably fit for the purpose ... except ... where the buyer does not rely on the skill or judgement of the seller.' (s14(3) SGA 1979).

Finally s15, SGA 1979 covers sales by sample where there are implied conditions that the bulk shall correspond with the sample in quality and that the buyer shall have reasonable opportunity of checking this; and that the goods shall be free from any defect rendering them unmerchantable which would not be apparent on reasonable examination of the sample.

Taking all these implied terms together it is apparent that a comprehensive protection is afforded to the consumer and that with other related legislation, in particular the UCTA 1977, these rights cannot be overridden or contracted out of. It cannot therefore be realistic to describe the terms as 'incomplete and imperfect'. The parties are free to make the bargain they choose in the way they choose, doctrines such as 'caveat emptor' still apply; as, for example, where examination takes place and defects should be discovered (s14) but the consumer is protected from unscrupulous dealing by the seller and from the ambiguities that inevitably arise in commercial consumer sales.

These sections are inter-related and form a cumulative protection of the consumer's interests. The best example of this being the inter-relationship between ss13 and 14 by examining the case of *Arcos* v *Ronaasen* (1933). Section 14 implies conditions as to the quality and fitness for purpose of goods for a particular purpose. It is of course possible for goods to be of 'merchantable quality' and fit for their purpose within s14 and yet not to correspond with their description under s13. In *Arcos* v *Ronaasen* the buyer ordered a quantity of staves 1/2 inch thick to make cement barrels, the seller knew this purpose. A fractional deviation in size from the buyer's specification was held by the House of Lords to entitle the buyer to reject for breach of s13 even though the goods were merchantable within the contractual specification. The mere fact that the buyer has suffered no damage does not prevent him from rejecting the goods.

The implied terms have not remained static since the 1893 statute; in particular two important modifications have improved them to the advantage of the consumer. The 1973 Supply of Goods (Implied Terms) Act reworded and rearranged the original 1893 s14 and these amendments were incorporated into the 1979 SGA s14. Section 14(1) begins with the statement of the general principle of caveat emptor, then follows the worded implied condition that goods are of merchantable quality s14(2), and finally the reworded condition that goods are fit for their purpose, s14(3).

In particular, s14(3) represents an improved and simplified provision when compared with the old s14(2) because it is no longer limited to sales by description but covers all 'sales in the course of a business' (the latter being defined to include a 'profession, the activities of any government department ... or local or public authority') and s14(3) applies even if the seller has not previously dealt in goods of a similar kind or does not normally deal in such goods.

The present interpretation of s14(3) was established in *Henry Kendall & Sons* v *Wm Lillico & Sons Ltd* (1969) where the House of Lords stressed that where goods are bought for their normal and obvious purpose, then in the absence of anything to the contrary, the implied condition applies although the buyer has done nothing to indicate the purpose for which they are required. Additionally, the old proviso that there was no condition of fitness for purpose if goods were sold under a patent or trade mark has been deleted from the SGA 1979. It had already lost most of its meaning (*Baldry* v *Marshall* (1925)).

Secondly, in 1987 the Law Commission published a report on the sale and supply of goods (Law Comm No 160, Cmnd 137) which proposed certain developments and proposals; chief amongst these being to replace the statutory definition of 'merchantable quality' by one of 'acceptable quality'. The definition of acceptable quality was to consist of two elements; a basic principle that goods sold or supplied under a contract should be such as would be 'acceptable' to a reasonable person and that there should be a list of aspects of 'quality' any of which could be important in a particular case (eg appearance, finish, fitness of goods for all their common purposes, safety, durability and freedom from minor defects). The Law Commission also proposed that a consumer should not lose the right to reject goods merely because he has signed an 'acceptance note'.

The draft Bill that has resulted from these reports and developments may introduce some more balance between the 'fitness for purposes' and what Atiyah describes as 'non functional aspects of merchantability' - but the same author is of the opinion that 'in general it does not seem likely that the changes proposed by the draft Bill will make much difference to the law ... the concept of "acceptable quality" ... has even less genuine meaning than the concept of "merchantable quality" and must be fleshed out by the case law in the various circumstances.' (Atiyah, *Sale of Goods*).

In conclusion then, despite their great age, and the fact that they have remained relatively unchanged, the implied conditions of the SGA 1979 do not appear to be either 'incomplete or imperfect'. Of course their function of ensuring the buyer gets what he pays for is a useful one; the conditions ensure this in a comprehensive fashion by the way they inter-relate with one another and with other supporting statutes. The Law Commission and learned writers appear to concur that they work well in practice and are hard-pushed to improve them.

4 DUTIES OF THE SELLER, I

4.1 Introduction

In this and the following chapter the duties of the seller are discussed.

Most of the law on this topic is implied by various sections of the Sale of Goods Act. The meaning of various terms as provided by SGA will be discussed in the key points following. Prior to the Unfair Contract Terms Act 1977 it was sometimes possible for the parties to exclude the terms implied by SGA. Under s6(1)(a) liability for breaches of obligations under s12 of SGA cannot be excluded or restricted. This is whether or not the parties deal on a 'business' basis.

4.2 Key points

It is important that the student understands the following:

a) *Title*

Section 12 of SGA provides, briefly, that there is an implied condition that the seller has the right to sell the goods, or will have the right to sell them when property is to pass; that the goods are free of encumbrances or charges and that the buyer will enjoy quiet possession of the goods (save in so far as it may be disturbed by the owner or beneficiary of any charge or encumbrance which has been properly disclosed prior to the contract).

If the seller is in breach of s12(1) so that no property in fact passes to the buyer, then there has clearly been a total failure of consideration and the price, if already paid, can be recovered. This is so even if the buyer has enjoyed the goods for some time before the defect in title became apparent - conduct which would normally amount to affirmation of the contract. Section 12(2) - that the goods are free of encumbrances and the buyer is entitled to quiet enjoyment are warranties, however, and the buyer is not entitled to treat the contract as repudiated by reason of breach of s12(2), he can claim damages only.

b) *Delivery*

The term 'delivery' is defined in s61(1) of SGA as:

'the voluntary transfer of possession from one person to another.'

In order to comply with the implied obligations under the Act, a seller must ensure not only that he has title (as outlined above) but also that he complies with conditions as to description, merchantable quality and fitness for purpose in so far as the subject matter is concerned (see chapter 5). In addition he must make sure that he conforms to any *express* contractual terms.

Delivery is not confined to physical transfer of possession, but includes 'constructive' delivery which is symbolic. The fact of delivery may have significance legally for a number of reasons and delivery may be defined differently depending on the circumstances of the case.

Section 27 SGA provides:

'It is the duty of the seller to deliver the goods and of the buyer to accept and pay for them, in accordance with the terms of the contract.'

Thus, acceptance on the part of the buyer is as much a part of the act of delivery as the physical or constructive act of handover; whether or not acceptance has taken place may be of particular importance in, for example, instalment contracts.

See the recent case of *Compagnie Commerciale Sucres et Denrees* v *Czarnikow* (1990) for further guidelines on the meaning of the term 'ready for delivery'.

c) *Quantity*

The seller must send, or have ready for collection by the buyer, the correct quantity of goods.

Section 30 covers not only insufficient, but excessive delivery; the buyer commits a breach of contract by delivery of the wrong quantity regardless of whether it is too little or too much.

Subject only to fractional deviations, this is a strict duty. Only 'microscopic' (*Arcos* v *Ronaasen* [1933] AC 470) differences might be permissible.

Section 30(4) covers cases where goods are delivered mixed with goods of a different type. Note that where goods are delivered but mixed with goods of defective quality as opposed to different type s30 will not apply.

In general the provisions of s30 are such that the buyer has an option of either rejecting the whole of the goods or rejecting the excess only and accepting the rest.

4.3 Analysis of questions

Questions on seller's duties are common but they have tended to be confined to aspects of merchantable quality/fitness for purpose (see chapter 5).

The first question quoted below does cover the question of a seller's duties under s12 as to title (see key points, above) but it covers other topics as well. Section 14 SGA as to merchantable quality and fitness for purpose will be dealt with in chapter 5 and this question should be read with that in mind. There is also more information on title and the passing of property in chapters 8 and 10.

The second question is concerned to a large extent with the seller's duty as to delivery, but it does, as will be seen, cover other topics notably property risk and title, together with buyer's remedies. For that reason, it could be placed equally effectively in Chapters 8 or 9 or in Chapters 13 or 14. It is a very general question and a good working knowledge is required of the whole span of sale of goods. Look also at Q5 in the 1993 paper (chapter 36) which is primarily concerned with a seller's duty to deliver.

4.4 Questions

Question 1

John, George and Mark bought from City Cars Ltd a Ford, a Peugeot and a Comet respectively. All the cars were second-hand. Each contract of sale stated (inter alia) that:

i) in no case would the purchase money be returned;

ii) the car was warranted not to have done more than 10,000 miles;

iii) the car was accepted 'as she lies'; and

iv) the sellers were not liable 'for any breach of any condition or warranty, express or implied'.

All three buyers consult you and you make the following notes:

1) *As to the Ford*

The owner left the car with Dragon Motors Ltd for repair, but they sold it to Staple Motors Ltd in Maidstone Market. Staple Motors Ltd then sold it to City Cars Ltd. A week after he bought it John discovered that it had a faulty clutch, and could not be moved out of first gear.

2) *As to the Peugeot*

Green sold the car to Star Motors Ltd, who gave him a cheque which was dishonoured on presentation. Green informed the police, but in the meanwhile Star Motors Ltd sold it to City Motors Ltd for a sum well below the market price. George discovered that the car had already done 20,000 miles.

3) *As to the Comet*

The car was let out to William under a hire-purchase agreement, but before all the instalments had been paid he sold it to Pearl Motors Ltd, who failed to take steps to find out whether it was on hire-purchase. Pearl Motors Ltd sold it to Henry, who sold it to City Cars Ltd. Mark discovered that no spare parts were available for it as the manufacturers had gone into liquidation three years ago.

Advise John, George and Mark as to the legal position. (None of them wish to keep the cars which they have bought.)

University of London LLB Examination
(for External Students) Commercial Law 1986 Q2

Skeleton solution

- Three unconnected sales - best to deal with each one separately
- Nemo dat rule
- Section 12 sellers' duties as to title
- Section 14 sellers' duties as to merchantable quality/fitness for purpose (see also chapter 5)
- Misrepresentation
- Exclusion clauses (see also chapter 7)
- Remedies - NB: question already states what form of redress the parties want ... rejection. Other potential remedies need not be discussed.

Suggested solution

There are three unconnected sale contracts here which raised different issues and which will, therefore, be considered separately.

a) *The Ford*

John (J) wishes to reject the car and may have two possible reasons for doing so. Firstly, we must consider whether he can reject it for breach of s12(1) of the Sale of Goods Act 1979, and secondly, whether he can reject for breach of s14 of the same Act.

i) Section 12

Section 12(1) provides that it is an implied condition that the seller will have the right to sell the goods at the time when property is to pass. On the facts given whether City Cars Ltd (CC) had the right to sell depends on whether they owned the car at the time of sale. This was a sale of specific goods, so property passed at the time of sale from CC to J (s18 r1 Sale of Goods Act 1979 (SGA)), therefore it was at that time that CC had to have the right to sell. Breach of s12(1) covers greater ground than sales by non-owners, but it is in that context and in that context alone that it must be discussed here (the rule in *Niblett* v *Confectioners Materials* (1921) is irrelevant).

One preliminary point which can be disposed of quickly is the effect of the exclusion clauses contained in the sale contract. By virtue of s6(1) of the Unfair Contract Terms Act 1977, every clause purporting to exclude or limit liability for breach of s12 of the 1979 Act is void, so if a breach of s12 is made out the exclusion clause will not affect J's position in any way.

Now, as to liability. It is necessary to start out with the original owner who left the car with Dragon Motors Ltd (DM) and trace the passage of the goods. Although DM did not have the right to sell the car, the application of any of the exceptions to the rule nemo dat quod non habet would pass title to a subsequent purchaser. Three exceptions to the nemo dat rule fall for discussion: firstly, s2(1) of the Factors Act 1889; secondly, s22 of the Sale of Goods Act 1979 (both of these exceptions arising in connection with the sale from DM to Staple Motors Ltd (Staple); and thirdly, s25(1) of the 1979 Act (in relation to the sale from Staple to CC).

When the car was left with DM it was left for the purpose of repair. Section 2(1) of the 1889 Act will apply to pass good title to Staple if DM were mercantile agents (sce s1 of the 1889 Act and s26 SGA), in possession of the goods with the consent of the owner in their capacity as mercantile agents and they sold in the normal course of business of mercantile agency. There is no evidence given whether DM were mercantile agents, but it is not uncommon for motor dealers to buy or sell as agents on behalf of customers, so it will be assumed that they were mercantile agents. The second criterion for the application of s2(1), however, appears not to have been fulfilled. DM were entrusted with possession with the consent of the true owner, but for the purpose of effecting repairs and this is not the giving of possession to DM in their capacity as mercantile agents (*Pearson* v *Rose & Young* (1951)). Therefore s2(1) of the Factors Act 1889 did not pass good title from the original owner to Staple. On this basis the third criterion does not fall for discussion.

The sale to Staple was in Maidstone Market. Maidstone Market is market overt for the sale of cars (*Bishopsgate Motor Finance* v *Transport Brakes* (1949)), but s22 of the 1979 Act only passes title to a bona fide buyer in market overt without notice, if the sale was between the hours of sunrise and sunset (*Reid* v *MPC* (1973)) and was conducted in accordance with the customs of the market (*Case of Market Overt* (1596)). We are not given enough information to say for say whether Staple did buy in good faith and without notice, nor the time of day at which the sale took place, nor the manner of the transaction. Therefore, if these criteria were fulfilled then Staple would have obtained a good title and would have passed that title on to CC; in which case CC would have had a perfect right to sell.

Staple 'bought' the car whether or not they obtained good title from DM, because the essence of having bought is the agreement that ownership would pass from DM to Staple (s2(1) SGA). Therefore, at the time Staple sold to CC, Staple were buyers in possession with consent of the person who had sold them the goods (DM). This means that CC obtained good title provided Staple sold in a way which would have been in the ordinary course of business had they been mercantile agents (*Newtons of Wembley* v *Williams* (1965)). In other words, provided it was a business-like sale in business hours and at business premises (*Oppenheimer* v *Attenborough* (1908)). Naturally there is a further requirement under s25(1) that CC must have bought in good faith without notice. Again we are given insufficient facts to be able to say whether good title did pass under s25(1), but it seems likely that it did (*Janesich* v *Attenborough* (1910)). If it did, then, again, CC would not have been in breach of s12 when they sold to J because they would have been the owners and entitled to sell.

Finally, had CC not obtained good title from Staple then they could none the less have passed good title themselves under s25(1).

This would not, though, affect J's right to reject the car for breach of s12, because that breach does not depend on J getting title it depends on CC being in a position at the time of sale that no one by lawful process could stop the sale (*Niblett* v *Confectioners Materials* (1921)). Even if CC passed good title to J, had CC not been the owners at the time of the sale they would have been in breach of s12(1) because the true owners could have prevented the sale (*Niblett* v *Confectioners Materials* (1921)).

ii) Section 14

Section 14 of the Sale of Goods Act 1979 lays down two implied conditions in sale contract which may have relevance here. Section 14(2) provides an implied condition that goods sold in the course of a business will be of merchantable quality; which means that they must be reasonably fit for the purpose or purposes for which goods of the kind are commonly bought (s14(6) SGA). Section 14(3) implies a condition that goods must be reasonably fit for the particular purpose of the buyer where he has made known that particular purpose to the seller, has relied on the seller's skill and judgment to provide goods reasonably fit for that particular purpose and has reasonably so relied. On sale of a motor car it is obvious that the buyer wants it to be capable of being driven (*Crowther* v *Shannon Motor Co* (1975)), so there is no problem establishing that J made known his particular purpose to CC. Nor is there any problem in showing that reliance on CC's skill and judgment was reasonable; there is a presumption that where reliance is reasonable, reliance also occurred, and that would avail J here (*Manchester Liners* v *Rea* (1922)). Therefore, if the car was not reasonably fit, then there would be a breach of both s14(2) and s14(3).

Second-hand goods do not have to be as fit for use as new goods, but they must, none the less be reasonably fit second-hand goods in all the circumstances of the case (*Bartlett* v *Sydney Marcus* (1965)).

The normal remedy for such breaches is rejection of the goods and recovery of the price paid (s54 SGA), in addition to damages to compensate for loss of bargain (s51(1) SGA) and, in appropriate cases, other sufficiently foreseeable losses (s54 SGA, the second rule in *Hadley* v *Baxendale* (1854)). From the facts given the only loss suffered by J seems to have been that he paid for a car which was useless, so he can, prima facie, reject the car, recover the price paid and sue for the difference, if any, between the price paid and the value the car would have had if merchantable.

The right to reject will be lost if the car had been accepted within s35(1). There is no evidence that J expressly accepted the car, nor that he acted inconsistently with the ownership of CC. We are not told when he bought the car, but it is assumed that he is still within a reasonable time of the taking of delivery and so can still reject.

The exclusion clauses would be void against J, by virtue of s6(2) of the Unfair Contract Terms Act 1977, because he dealt as a consumer in that CC sold in the course of a business, J bought otherwise than in the course of a business and the car is a type of goods commonly bought for private or consumer use (s12(1) Unfair Contract Terms Act 1977 (UCTA)).

b) *The Peugeot*

We are told that Star Motors Ltd (Star) sold the car to City Motors Ltd; this will be treated as a misprint for City Cars Ltd, otherwise there is no explanation of how the car came into the hands of City Cars Ltd and no advice can be given.

In relation to the Peugeot three issues fall for discussion. Firstly, did Star pass good title to CC under s23 or s25(1); secondly, what is the effect of CC's misstatement of mileage; and thirdly, are CC protected by the exclusion clause from the consequences, if any, of their statement that the car had not travelled more than 10,000 miles?

i) Section 12

The contract of sale between Green and Star was voidable at the instance of Green because of Star's misrepresentation that the cheque would be met (*Phillips* v *Brooks* (1919)). Prior to any possible act of rescission by Green (contacting the police is unlikely to be enough, in any event, to invoke the special, but limited rule in *Car and Universal Finance* v *Caldwell* (1965), Star sold to CC but at a price well below market price. CC would obtain good title under s23 unless they bought in bad faith. There is a presumption against criminality, so the burden of proving bad faith is on the person alleging it. The purchase of goods at an under value is not, of itself, evidence of lack of good faith unless the value is so low as to indicate to the reasonable man that there may be a defect in the seller's title (*Janesich* v *Attenborough* (1910)). Yet again, we are not given enough detail to advise with any degree of certainty whether CC will be looked upon as having bought in bad faith.

If CC did buy in bad faith, then they would not obtain title by virtue of s25(1) either, because that section also has a requirement of good faith. If CC did not obtain good title, then G would be able to reject the car for breach of s12(1), because the circumstances would then be the same as one set of events postulated in relation to the Ford. The right to reject for this breach would exist whether or not G obtained title by virtue of s25(1). As with J's case, the exclusion clause would be ineffective to excuse a breach of s12(1) (s6(1) UCTA).

ii) The mileage

The contract contained a statement that the car was warranted not to have done more than 10,000 miles. Although the word 'warranted' is used, this does not mean that it is a warranty of the contract that the statement of mileage is correct (*Wallis* v *Pratt & Haynes* (1911)). That statement was, in any event a misrepresentation, and coming from an expert would be treated as a term (*Dick Bentley* v *Harold Smith (Motors)* (1965)). The mileage which a car has done is, obviously, a matter of great importance and, therefore the statement is most likely to be a condition. In any event, it would be at least an innominate term, the breach of which has given rise to a very serious event - the car has done twice the stated mileage, and so it would fall to be treated as a condition (*Hongkong Fir* v *Kawasaki Kisen Kaisha* (1962)). The statement could be seen as part of the contractual description of the goods, but it is not clear that this would be the case. If it is not part of the description, then s6 of the Unfair Contract Terms Act 1977 would not apply, and this could have an effect on G's remedy, so it is necessary to consider whether it is part of the description.

The normal remedy for breach of a condition in a sale contract is rejection of the goods, repayment of the purchase price and an award of damages to compensate for loss of bargain and, where appropriate, other losses. As with the case of the Ford there is no evidence to suggest that the right to reject has been lost, so, prima facie, G can reject the car, claim repayment of the price and also obtain damages equivalent to the excess of value that the Peugeot would have had if it had only done 10,000 miles over the contract price.

The exclusion clause here would also be wholly ineffective, because G dealt as a consumer in the same was as did J. If the above conclusion about the applicability of s13 of the 1979 Act is incorrect, then there would have been breach of an express condition and the exclusion clause would have to be reasonable by virtue of s3(2)(a) of the Unfair Contract Terms Act 1977. The reasonableness test is only relevant, however, to the extent that the clause is sufficiently clearly worded to cover the breach which has occurred. Clause (i) must be read contra proferentem and it is possible to give it a very restricted meaning. It could be read as saying that the very same money which had been paid to CC by G would not be refunded; and one could, perhaps by use of the rule in *Clayton's Case* (1816) try to work out whether CC still have that money. Such a reading would not find favour with the courts, these days, following dicta in the House of Lords cases in this area. Exclusion clauses must be given their normal meaning and if that is clear then the clause will be looked at as having that clear effect (*Photo Production* v *Securicor Transport* (1980); *Ailsa Craig Fishing* v *Malvern Shipping* (1983); *George Mitchell Ltd* v *Finney Lock Seeds* (1983). Therefore, it is submitted, clause (i) is sufficiently clear to apply to G. Clause (ii) is not an exclusion clause at all, so is not relevant to the present discussion. Clause (iii) must be read contra proferentem and, it is submitted, would not apply because 'as she lies' relates to quality rather than description (The distinction between quality and description is not easy to draw in many cases, but is the difference between having goods which are the right type of thing, albeit a poor example of the type, and goods which are so defective as to not be the same type of thing at all). In other words it applies to faults in the vehicle, not to the mileage which is specifically asserted in clause (ii) not to exceed 10,000. Clause (iv) is a clear clause applying to the breach here, because there has been breach of an express condition. Therefore, clauses (i) and (iv) must satisfy the reasonableness test.

Clause (i) appears to be unreasonable in that it prevents recovery of the purchase price in any circumstances. The reasonableness test in s11(1) of the Unfair Contract Terms Act 1977 requires it to be asked whether it is reasonable to include the clause in the contract in the first place, not whether it is reasonable to rely on it in the events which have occurred (having regard to the matters set out in Sch 2 UCTA). Because it is a blanket clause covering any breach, no matter how severe, so it would be unreasonable. Clause (iv) likewise would be unreasonable, because it has the effect of negating the very presence of a contract. If there is no liability for breach of any warranty or condition, then G would have no enforceable rights, except for breach of innominate terms. It must be unreasonable to allow a remedy for breach of an innominate term, but not to allow recovery for breach of a condition or, especially, for breach of a warranty.

G is advised that he can reject the car for breach of the express term relating to mileage or, in the alternative, for breach of s13(1). The exclusion clause would be unreasonable (in so far as a claim for breach of an express term could be brought) or void (in relation to s13(1)).

Therefore, he may recover his purchase price and claim damages as mentioned above. Further, he may have the same remedy for breach of s12(1), but there is insufficient evidence to be at all sure on this matter.

c) *The Comet*

Mark (M) has two potential grounds of complaint; there may have been a breach of s12(1) of the Sale of Goods Act 1979 in that CC may not have had the right to sell, and there may be a breach of s14(2) or s14(3), the car being unmerchantable because of the unavailability of spare parts.

i) Section 12

If CC did not own the car at the time they sold it to M, then he can reject it and reclaim the purchase price for breach of s12(1). Whether CC owned it depends on the effect of Part III of the Hire Purchase Act 1964. In the context of M's case this provides (s27 Hire Purchase Act 1964 (HPA)) that where a car is subject to a hire purchase agreement and is sold by the hirer, the first private purchaser in good faith and without notice of the hire agreement (Section 27(3) HPA 1964 requires there to have been no notice of 'the relevant agreement', s29(3) requires there to have been no notice of 'any such agreement'. Section s27(3) contains the preferred meaning of lack of notice: *Barker* v *Bell* (1972)) obtains the title which the creditor under the hire purchase agreement had.

Pearl Motors Ltd (Pearl) were not private purchasers, being trade purchasers (s29(2) HPA 1964); therefore they could not obtain title under Part III. Their good faith, or lack of it, is irrelevant. Henry (H) does not appear on the facts given to be involved in the motor trade, so he would be a private purchaser (s29(2) HPA 1964) and since there is no evidence of lack of good faith on his part would obtain the title of the finance company, whom it is assumed were the owners. The sale from H to CC, therefore, passed a perfect title and CC, therefore, had the right to sell to M. On the facts given there was no breach of s12(1) by CC.

ii) Section 14

As has been stated above a second-hand car does not have to be of as high quality as a new car, but it must be reasonably fit as a second-hand car. The absence of a supplier of spare parts would not, it is submitted, make the car unmerchantable, nor unfit for the buyer's particular purpose, because that would render any sale by a garage of a second-hand car in breach where the manufacturer no longer makes all the parts which may be needed for the car. In any event the absence of spare parts would not, of itself, affect the quality of the car and would, again, be irrelevant to the question of breach of s14(2) or s14(3).

M is advised that on the evidence given he has no remedy against CC.

Question 2

Slimbo manufactures a run of 100 'superwidgets', which he advertises for orders. He agrees to sell 40 to Bill, in Birmingham, who needs them for his business. Slimbo delivers a crate of 40 to a depot owned by Harry, an independent road haulier, for 'delivery to be advised'. Harry later tells Slimbo that he has a delivery to make in Birmingham the following day and Slimbo says, 'You may as well drop off that crate at Bill's if you have time.' On the way to Birmingham, Harry's lorry is involved in an accident, after which it is towed back to Harry's depot, with the crate and its contents damaged.

The next day, Slimbo sell 60 superwidgets to Chloe in Cardiff under a contract providing that he is 'to retain title to the goods until paid for'. Chloe makes a down payment for 30 superwidgets. Since Harry's next delivery is in Cardiff, Slimbo tells him to deliver to Chloe the crate which is at his depot; Harry does this.

Slimbo, who has not received any further orders for superwidgets, then becomes insolvent.

Advise the parties.

University of London LLB Examination
(for External Students) Commercial Law June 1990 Q5

Skeleton solution

- Making a contract, duties of buyer and seller, ownership and risk.
- Delivery to independent carrier, status of carrier in relation to contract, specific goods.
- Separate contracts, different buyers, 'delivery to be advised', property, risk and title.
- Second contract to Chloe, quantity incorrect, conditional contract retention of title clause, damaged goods.
- Remedies of buyer against insolvent seller for non-delivery and damaged goods.

Suggested solution

Slimbo appears to have entered into a contractual arrangement with Bill and Chloe to sell them widgets; we are expressly told that Bill requires the widgets for his business but no mention is made in either case that time is to be of the essence in the delivery thereof. The contract with Bill appears to have resulted from the adverts placed by Slimbo. We are given no information as to how the contract with Chloe is arrived at. The contracts appear to both be 'one off' contracts and do not seem to form part of any instalment contract for sale and delivery. The goods which are the subject of the contract with Bill appear to be 'specific goods' as defined by s61(1) Sale of Goods Act 1979 ie 'goods identified and agreed upon at the time a contract of sale is made'. In Bill's case the goods have been manufactured and advertised for sale; 40 of the 100 manufactured have been set aside from the remainder and delivered to an independent carrier for onward delivery to Bill. Thus they are identified and agreed upon by both parties at the time of the contract.

However, the 60 widgets sold the subsequent day to Chloe are sold under a condition, namely that Slimbo is to retain title to the goods until paid for. Chloe, we are told, has made a down payment for 30 widgets. It may well be that half of Chloe's 60 required widgets are specific goods (as defined above) but it seems more likely that all 60 are merely 'unascertained goods' in that they are not identified and agreed upon at the time of the contract, and they require some act of subsequent appropriation for their identification. By s16 SGA 1979 property in unascertained goods cannot pass until they become ascertained, eg *Re Wait* (1927).

Having determined the nature of the goods under the respective contracts, it is necessary to examine when, if at all, the property as referred to in the SGA 1979 (ie the ownership of the goods) passes to the purchasers and when the risk attached to the goods is passed from seller to buyer. The SGA uses the word title synonymously with 'ownership' and it uses the phrases 'transfer of property' and 'property passes' to denote transfer of ownership. Section 20 SGA provides that risk (of loss of goods from trader to consumer) passes with property, ie risk of loss or damage to goods passed to the consumer when ownership passes to him with three exceptions:

1) the parties may expressly or impliedly agree otherwise;
2) where delivery has been delayed through the fault of one party (the party at fault takes the risk of any loss that might not otherwise have occurred);

3) the party in possession, being a bailee of goods, is liable at common law if he is negligent.

In the case of the 40 widgets sold to Bill, the goods are ascertained; the basic fundamental rule concerning the transfer of property is that property 'in goods passes when the parties intend it to pass' (SGA s17).

However, the contract here appears to be silent as to the parties intention and the circumstances surrounding the contract appear indecisive and complicated by the fact that delivery has been made by Slimbo to Harry (an independent carrier) and on condition 'that delivery is to be advised'. Delivery to an independent carrier is covered by SGA s32(1).

'where in pursuance of a contract of sale the seller is authorised or required to send the goods to the buyer, delivery of goods to a carrier (whether named by the buyer or not), for the purpose of transmission to the buyer is prima facie to be a delivery of the goods to a buyer'.

However, s32(2) covers the situation where the seller makes a contract with an independent carrier on behalf of the buyer "the seller must make such contract with the carrier on behalf of the buyer as may be reasonable, having regard to the nature of the goods and to other circumstances of the case. If the seller omits to do so, and the goods are lost or damaged in the course of transit, the buyer may decline to treat the delivery to the carrier as a delivery to himself, or may hold the seller responsible in damages". See *Thomas Young & Sons* v *Hobson & Partners* (1949).

What constitutes 'delivery' is defined by s61 SGA 'voluntary transfer of possession from one person to another', so where the seller is authorised to send the goods via independent carrier, delivery to the carrier is prima facie. delivery to the consumer s32(1) SGA. Delivery to a carrier does not affect the buyer's rights to examine and reject the goods. Generally speaking, time is not of the essence in contracts for the sale of goods unless a contrary intention can be derived from the terms of contract (see s10 SGA). It may be that Bill who is stated to 'need' the widgets for his business has stipulated delivery time to be of the essence. Usually the place of delivery is the consumer's place of business (SGA s29(2)), the consumer does not have to accept part only of the goods.

Bill is awaiting delivery of the widgets 'to be advised' but as Harry's lorry is damaged he never receives them or is advised of their 'delivery'. So that, even though delivery to a carrier by the seller usually amounts to 'delivery', in this case Slimbo has failed to deliver. Additionally, Bill has not had the opportunity to examine the goods as allowed for in s34 SGA. It would appear therefore that, despite the fact that delivery to a carrier normally amounts to constructive delivery, in this case because delivery is 'to be advised' and it has not been, the property in the goods has not passed from Slimbo to Bill. Section 27 SGA provides that

'it is the duty of the seller to delivery the goods and of the buyer to accept and pay for them, in accordance with the terms of the contract of sale'.

Slimbo is in breach of this obligation to deliver and his subsequent actions disposing of the goods to Chloe, despite their being damaged, compound the breach - accordingly Bill can pursue a claim for damages for breach of the duty to deliver and for breach of contract (see below).

The contract with Chloe appears to be difficult in several respects, not least of them being that she is receiving damaged goods at an amount of 40 from the 60 she has ordered. She has made a down payment for only 30 and Slimbo has inserted a 'reservation of title' clause reserving his rights of disposal over the goods until the goods are fully paid for. Moreover, Chloe has only paid for 30 on a down payment basis whereas she receives 40 (that rightfully belonged to Bill if they had been delivered in good order in accordance with his contract). So the problems Chloe faces are that there has been an 'under' delivery of her contracted amount, unknown to her at delivery the goods are damaged (we are not told how badly). There is a 'reservation of title clause' which may prevent her obtaining title to the goods as against Slimbo's receiver in bankruptcy and lastly, the goods by rights should have gone to Bill.

To Chloe there has been an 'actual' delivery whilst to Bill, it can be argued there has been a 'constructive delivery' in that the goods to complete his contract were delivered to a contractor. It may be that Bill will choose to allege negligence against Harry, the independent carrier; particularly as Harry has damaged goods in his care and in transit to Bill. It would appear that the relationship between Slimbo and Harry may be a contractual contract of agency and Harry appears to be obeying instructions from Slimbo - for example, he delivers the 40 widgets destined for Bill, to Chloe. It could be argued, that on the contrary, Harry is the agent of the buyers herein; and that once goods in a deliverable state are available at Slimbo's premises the latter has discharged the duty imposed upon him by s27 SGA, ie 'It is the duty of the seller to deliver the goods and of the buyer to accept and pay for them.' This would appear to be inconclusive as delivery appears to be conditional upon being 'advised' and Slimbo has transferred the goods to Harry for onward transmission to Bill. 'Delivery' by the seller to the agent of the seller does not amount to delivery to a buyer because the seller is merely sending the goods to his alter ego: *Galbraith and Grant Ltd* v *Block* (1922).

Thus Bill's remedies lie against Slimbo for non-delivery and he will claim damages for this; such damages being a species of damages for breach of contract and the rules for claiming them are set out in SGA s51 - the remedy applies whether or not property has passed to the buyer.

Section 51(1) 'Where the seller wrongfully neglects to deliver the goods ... the buyer may maintain an action against the seller for damages for non-delivery.

(2) The measure of damages is the estimated loss directly and naturally resulting, in the ordinary course of events, from the seller's breach of contract.'

However, as Slimbo is now insolvent this would appear to be a poor option; better that Bill sues the agent (Harry) and joins the seller in the action so that the agent will pay for damage to the goods from his insurance policy and seek an indemnity from the receivers of his principal.

Chloe's contract is the subject of a so-called Romalpa (ie retention of title clause), emanating from *Aluminium Industrie* v *Romalpa Aluminium Ltd* (1976) which is designed to reserve the property in the goods to the seller until the price is paid in full, notwithstanding the goods have been delivered to the buyer. Whilst in the practical sense the goods have been delivered to the premises belonging to Chloe's business, in the legal sense delivery (s27 SGA) has not taken place. She has had no opportunity to inspect the goods and would not want damaged goods. She can therefore reject the goods and claim breach of contract under the same grounds as Bill, with the additional element that goods of insufficient quantity have been taken to her premises in breach of s30(1) SGA 'where the seller delivers to the buyer a quantity of goods less than he contracted to sell, the buyer may reject them.' Moreover, as Slimbo has sold goods in the course of a business s14 SGA implied conditions applies and Chloe can reject the goods as being 'not fit for their purpose' or of 'merchantable quality': *Behrend & Co Ltd* v *Produce Brothers Co Ltd* (1920).

Chloe will obviously have to pursue her claim in priority with other creditors in Slimbo's insolvency, as there is no contractual link between her and Harry and the goods. She cannot pursue the options available to Bill.

5 DUTIES OF THE SELLER, II

5.1 Introduction

It should not be forgotten that the common law rule on the sale of goods was 'caveat emptor' - let the buyer beware.

Sections 13-15 of Sale of Goods Act now imply into virtually all contracts for sale of goods a series of provisions which govern the quality of the subject matter. The possibilities for exclusion of these implied terms are severely curtailed; since the Unfair Contract Terms Act 1977 especially; and the buyer has therefore some degree of statutory protection which lessens the effect of the caveat emptor maxim.

It must also be noted that the parties may have drafted their own express terms; certain types of commercial contract especially now have standard form contracts. These express terms, save in so far as they directly conflict with SGA, will impose extra obligations under the contract, to the parties' duties.

Section 14 of the Act provides that except in so far as provided by ss13-15 or any other enactment there is no implied condition or warranty as to the quality or fitness for purpose of goods supplied under a contract of sale.

Subject to that proviso, however, these three sections in particular establish quite a comprehensive code of implied warranties as to quality and fitness.

Some of s14; in particular subs(2) and (3) only apply where the sale is made in the course of a business; this means that not all sale of goods contracts especially those between private buyers, are protected by the SGA.

5.2 Key points

It is important that the student understands the following:

a) *Terms implied by statute*

   i) Sales by description

      The expression 'sale by description' is not actually defined in the Act. Essentially, however, a sale by description would be when the goods sold and identified verbally or in writing by the seller. This can be further defined by saying that most sales are either cases of description alone, eg: '100 per cent pure wool' or by sample and description; eg: 'Dutch tomatoes, warranted equal to sample'. The mere fact that the buyer sees specific goods, as for example, when buying in a shop, does not necessarily mean this is not sale by description.

Indeed, most authorities are of the opinion that virtually all sales will be 'by description', and possibly the only case which does not come into this category is where the buyer seeks out particular goods and makes it clear he is buying solely for the unique qualities the goods possess.

Section 13 of SGA provides, inter alia:

- where there is a contract of sale of goods by description there is an implied condition that the goods shall comply with the description;
- if the sale is by sample as well as description it is not sufficient if the bulk of the goods corresponds with the sample if the goods do not also correspond with the description.

It is important to note that the description becomes, in effect, a term of the contract and is not merely a representation inducing the buyer into the contract. Since the case of *Ashington Piggeries Ltd* v *Christopher Hill Ltd* [1972] AC 441 it has been recognised that a 'description' will only constitute a term of the contract within the meaning of SGA if it is concerned with identity of the goods, rather than their mere attributes. In reality the two are rather difficult to sever and a test suggested is to look at the essence of the contract and what the parties are trying to achieve and then to assess whether the 'description' is so crucial that if not incorporated the goods sold would be something quite different.

Where there is a breach of s13, the goods received are, in essence, not those contracted for and even slight deviations from the description will probably entitle the buyer to treat the contract as breached and reject the goods. The mere fact that the buyer has suffered no damage does not prevent him rejecting the goods.

(Note that s13 overlaps in part with s30 of SGA which deals with remedies generally. For further details, see chapters 13-14.)

ii) Merchantable quality

The term is now defined by s14(6) to mean 'as fit for the purpose or purposes for which goods of that kind are commonly bought as is reasonable to expect having regard to any description applied to them, the price (if relevant) and all other circumstances.'

It must be borne in mind that 'merchantable quality' does not dictate an absolute standard, thus if buying a second-hand caravan the standard expected would differ according to its age, price and other relevant criteria.

There is a considerable amount of case law as to the interpretation of s14 (indeed *all* the terms implying duties as to quality of the goods) which space does not permit to be dealt with here, but it is clearly established that liability for quality under s14 is strict.

Thus, a seller who supplies goods, which do not comply with the statutory requirements as to merchantability and fitness for purpose as laid down in s14, will be responsible. This is so, even if the defect is one which in the ordinary way of things could not reasonably be expected to be discovered by the seller.

Under the SGA it is the 'goods supplied under a contract of sale' to which the terms relating to quality apply. So, even goods included erroneously along with the goods specified will be affected by s14.

Section 14(2) provides:

'When the seller sells goods in the course of a business, there is an implied condition that the goods supplied under the contract are of merchantable quality, except that there is no such condition:

- as regards defects specifically drawn to the buyer's attention before the contract is made; or
- if the buyer examines the goods before the contract ... as regards defects which that examination ought to reveal.'

Note that as stated earlier in this Section, since this only applies to contracts conducted in the ordinary course of business and because of the effect of the two exceptions there are inevitably contracts made for sale of goods where s14 will not be implicit.

The term 'merchantable quality' has been the subject of litigation on numerous occasions and the student should consult a standard work of reference if he is not familiar with the case law on the subject. The one thing that can be said about the phrase is that it is, today, widely regarded as unsatisfactory, especially in regard to consumer transactions. One particular problem has always been that given the history of mercantile law the phrase clearly relates to 'merchants' and 'trade' is often inapplicable to consumer dealings. It was for this reason that the definition in s14(6) was introduced (see above). Even that creates problems since it is not altogether clear whether this definition is drafted simply to re-state existing law; or whether its introduction was intended to be a completely new approach to the topic.

In *Cehave NV* v *Bremer Handelgesellschaft mbH, The Hansa Nord* [1976] QB 44, Denning stated that he regarded the section (at that time incorporated into Supply of Goods (Implied Terms) Act 1973) as probably the best description of merchantable quality either pre- or post-1973.

iii) Fitness for purpose

Section 14(3) of the SGA provides:

'Where a seller sells goods in the course of a business and the buyer expressly or by implication makes known to the seller ... any particular purpose for which the goods are being bought, there is an implied condition that the goods supplied ... are reasonably fit for that purpose ... except where the circumstances show that the buyer does not rely, or it is unreasonable for him to rely on the skill or judgment of the seller.'

Clearly where an item has an obvious purpose, simply asking for the goods will be regarded as implied notification of the purpose. If goods have more than one function, or the buyer wishes to use goods in some unusual way, then the buyer will be expected to indicate just what he wants to do with the goods. In the case of goods sold in 'specialist' shops, eg a chemist or a pet-shop reliance on special skill and judgment possessed by the seller will be implicit. Note, however, that s14(3) only applies to 'sales in the course of business' and therefore all private sales of goods will be excluded.

There is considerable overlapping between ss14(2) and 14(3). It is perfectly feasible if goods have only one purpose and are unfit for that purpose for the seller to be in breach of both subsections.

iv) Sale by sample

Section 15 of SGA provides that there is a contract of sale by sample, where there is a term, express or implied, in the contract to that effect.

Section 15 like s13 but unlike s14 is not restricted to 'sales in the course of business'.

The section, in its purported definition is obviously rather vague and not of much assistance in defining the concept of sale by sample.

There has been some case law on the subject, probably one of the most helpful definitions was in:

Parker v *Palmer* (1821) 4 B & A 387 in which it was stated:

'A sale by sample is a sale where the seller, expressly or impliedly, promises that the goods sold should answer the description of a small parcel exhibited at the time of the sale.'

Where the section does apply; subs15(2)(a) applies and there is an implied condition that the bulk shall correspond with sample quality; there is also an implied condition under s15(2)(b) that the buyer shall have a reasonable opportunity of comparing the bulk with the sample; and in s15(2)(c) there is an implied condition that goods shall be free from any defect rendering them unmerchantable which would not be apparent on examination of the sample.

It will be recalled, that in a case of sale by sample and by description (s13, ante) there is also an implied condition that goods correspond with both sample and description.

There is considerable overlap between s14(2) and s15(2)(c), for example in a situation where a defect would not be apparent merely from the sample.

Where the defect might have been discovered on a reasonable inspection of the sample; the buyer might possibly still have rights under s14(2) alone.

b) *Other implied terms*

Section 14(4) of SGA provides:

'An implied condition or warranty about quality or fitness for a particular purpose, may be annexed to a contract of sale by usage.'

As it has always been the case in common law, that, should the intentions of the parties in formulating the contractual terms clearly be to include the usual traditions or customs of a particular trade then the courts will give effect to those intentions; then clearly s14(4) adds nothing to pre-existing common law.

5.3 Analysis of questions

A quick look through past commercial law papers from University of London gives the impression that questions on merchantability, fitness for purpose and implied terms as to quality generally; are so common that at least one question on the subject is bound to occur on each paper.

In fact this is not quite true. Looked at more carefully it will be seen that there is only *one* question which covers the topic in isolation.

In most cases, in the examination papers from 1983-93, the topic is raised in combination with something else and sometimes forms only a very small part of the overall answer. Students should not, therefore, rush into answering a question merely because they recognise some element of implicit terms and merchantability/fitness for purpose unless they are equally sure they are familiar with other issues raised in the question.

A favourite combination of topics is ss13-15 linked with the problem of exclusion clauses; this has occurred on no less than four occasions, in 1983, 1986, 1987 and 1988. Another favourite of the examiners is to link implied terms with title and the nemo dat rule; this has occurred at least twice. Or alternatively in a question apparently about CIF contracts (1983 and 1993) or about mail order contracts (1985) the 'subject goods' merchantability or fitness for purpose must be discussed by the student.

Clearly, therefore, in 'question-spotting' the student may anticipate that while it is highly likely that the topic of implied terms as to quality will appear as the subject matter of, at least, one question; it may not be the *sole* topic for discussion.

Note also, that almost all questions are of the problem type. The first question which appears below is perhaps incorrectly described as 'typical' because for years it was the *only* essay type of question to appear. In 1993, for another essay question on an unusual aspect of implied terms, see Q2. The second question to appear below is mainly concerned with implied terms, though other aspects are relevant, especially exclusion clauses (see chapter 7), reservation of title clauses (see chapter 8) and product safety (see chapter 15).

5.4 Questions

Question 1

'In their recent "Report on sale and supply of goods" the Law Commission recognise many of the weaknesses in the present law on merchantable quality, but it is suggested that the new recommendations pose almost as many problems as they solve.' (Brown)

Discuss.

University of London LLB Examination
(for External Students) Commercial Law June 1988 Q3

Skeleton solution

- Introduction, difficulties of definition.
- Present law on merchantability, ss14(2) and 14(6) SGA.
- Definition of merchantability at common law, effect of s14(6), defects of existing law.
- Law Commission's recommendations - problems caused, especially by modern remedies.

Suggested solution

The Law Commission's report on sale and supply of goods made no clear recommendations about how the present statutory definition of merchantability could be changed for the better. It pointed out problems with the present law which had appeared in the cases anyway and suggested several ways in which Parliament could change things for the better. In the end it was faced with the inevitable difficulty in this area, which is that no single definition can be short enough to get through Parliament yet detailed enough to cover all of the hundreds of different cases which come before the courts each year.

The present law on merchantable quality is contained in ss14(2) and 14(6) of the Sale of Goods Act 1979. Section 14(2) states that where a seller sells in the course of a business it is a condition that the goods supplied must be of merchantable quality. Section 14(6) defines merchantable quality as being a quality which is reasonable fit for the purpose or purposes for which goods of the type are commonly supplied. The definition section was first introduced in 1973 (s15(3) Supply of Goods (Implied Terms) Act 1973) and brought into the Sale of Goods Act when it was revised in 1979.

It was felt necessary to enact a definition of merchantable quality because three approaches to merchantability had been adopted by the courts and they were not always compatible. The first approach was of Farwell LJ in *Bristol Tramways etc Carriage Co Ltd* v *Fiat Motors Ltd* (1910). He said that one should ask whether the goods supplied were such that the buyer would accept them as fulfilling the contract if he had examined them fully. By contrast Lord Wright defined unmerchantable goods in *Cammell Laird & Co Ltd* v *Manganese Bronze and Brass Co Ltd* (1934) as goods which are of no use for any purpose for which they would normally be used. The third interpretation was of Dixon J in *Grant* v *Australian Knitting Mills Ltd* (1936), who aid that goods are merchantable if a buyer who is fully acquainted with any defects which may exist would buy them without abatement of price. In *Henry Kendall & Sons* v *William Lillico & Sons Ltd* (1969) the House of Lords did not lay down any single test of merchantability. There was approval to varying degrees of all three of the earlier stated definitions.

The statutory definition was held in *Aswan Engineering Establishment Co* v *Lupdine Ltd* (1987) to reflect the view of Lord Reid in the *Henry Kendall* case, namely that goods are of merchantable quality if they are reasonably fit for at least one of the purposes for which goods of their type are commonly bought. The 'type' is governed by the description given to the goods. The more general the description the greater the risk of the seller supplying goods which are fit for one use but not others, the more precise the description the less scope there is for a variation of acceptance qualities.

There are also general recent cases, mainly concerned with second-hand cars on this question (*Shine* v *General Guarantee Corpn Ltd* (1988); *Business Applications Specialists Ltd* v *Nationwide Credit Corpn* (1988)). The Law Commission's difficulties are amply demonstrated by these cases. In order to be sufficiently flexible to cover all possible factual situations, the definition must be stated in general terms. But any definition which is in general terms runs the risk of being interpreted in different ways, or ambiguously, in different cases. The doctrine of precedent can do little to prevent the courts from adopting whatever approach to merchantability it thinks suitable for a particular case. If the desired approach seems to contradict that of an earlier case, the earlier case can almost always be distinguished on its facts.

There are several difficulties in the present law. For example it is not clear how the buyer of new goods stands where they work but have minor defects, eg if a new car has a defective windscreen wiper, or one of the warning lights on the dashboard does not work. At present either the car is unmerchantable in which case he may reject it or claim damages, or it is merchantable in which case he has no remedy at all, not even in damages for the cost of putting right the problem. Also the appellate courts and the High Court can only give general guidance, but many disputes in this area are litigated in the County Courts and it is inevitable that there is a lack of consistency from court to court on similar facts. A recurrent problem is that of goods which do not maintain their quality of purchase. It has not been decided authoritatively what relevance, if any, durability has to merchantability.

The Law Commission made three suggestions of possible changes to the definitions of merchantability. Firstly they considered imposing a test of 'acceptability' rather than merchantability. This would have the advantage of the legal test bearing, in name at least, some relation to the reality of the buyer's position. The buyer is not always concerned with whether he could market the goods, so 'merchantability' is an inappropriate was to describe his requirements. However, the courts do not approach s14(6) by asking whether the buyer could sell the goods, they ask whether he can use them. To change the name of the seller's duty would not of itself go very far.

Secondly, it was suggested that a best of 'appropriateness' should be adopted - if the goods are reasonably appropriate in all the circumstances, the seller would have complied with the contract. Again this would be a matter of words only. Either of these changes would simply give rise to a flood of litigation with the courts either saying that there is no difference in substance or that there is a difference. But if there is a difference the new statutory definition would be no more precise than that in s14(6) and the difficulties of interpretation encountered with s14(6) would simply be repeated.

The third recommendation was that legislation could expand the present definition of merchantability to give examples of specific matters which render goods unmerchantable. This could cover such matters as durability, safety and the appearance of goods where appearance does not affected their function. This third possibility may go some way towards making the law more understandable to non-lawyers, but would not prevent there being perhaps just as many cases as there are today in which it is not known whether the goods which are actually supplied fall within or outside the new definition. Of course, were a new definition to pretend to be exhaustive it would have to be immensely long. If, though, it only gives a few examples of required qualities in goods, questions will still arise whether those qualities are present in any particular case.

The Commission concentrated their efforts on reviewing remedies available to dissatisfied buyers. The problems which are most commonly encountered with merchantability today arise either because there is a question whether the buyer has rejected the goods or there is a question whether some minor defect is sufficiently serious to amount to a breach of the condition implied by s14(2). The strictness of the doctrine of acceptance and the inflexibility of s14 in implying a condition rather than an innominate term deserve greater priority than revision of the definition of merchantable quality. If the remedies available were flexible enough to allow a damages claim without rejection when the goods are only slightly flawed and also to allow the buyer a reasonable time to discover the defects which actually exist, rather than the present position where he has a reasonable time in which to discover whether the goods are generally acceptable (*Bernstein* v *Pamson Motors (Golders Green) Ltd* (1987)), much of the present litigation may be avoided; but it would not be avoided by tampering with the definition of merchantability itself.

Question 2

Slimbo buys from Adolf a quantity of corn pellets which Adolf has for a number of years imported from Germany and which he supplies to Slimbo on the basis that 'ownership in the goods remains in the supplier until all outstanding liabilities are discharged to the supplier, who is under no liability for the suitability of the goods for any of the purposes to which they may be put.'

Slimbo also buys from Bismak a quantity of Algerian Skanoil which Bismak has imported on Slimbo's instructions. The Skanoil is delivered to Bismak in sealed drums which Bismak delivers to Slimbo unopened. The small print of the accompanying invoice, which Bismak does not read or pass on to Slimbo, states that, once Skanoil is exposed to air, it must be used within five days to avoid deterioration.

Over a period of several months, Slimbo immerses the corn pellets in the Skanoil to produce Kornskam, a product which he retails as animal feedstuff. He sells some of this to Gorby 'on the terms as in my agreement with Adolf'. Gorby feeds some of the Kornskam to his cattle, which develop an allergic reaction to it and go mad, rampaging across and destroying the wheatfield of his neighbour Boris.

Advise Slimbo and Gorby.

University of London LLB Examination
(for External Students) Commercial Law June 1991 Q6

Skeleton solution

Slimbo - Adolf

- Implied terms under ss13-15 SGA, especially s14.
- Purported exclusion clause.
- Effect of UCTA.
- Reservation of title; Romalpa clauses.
- Dealing as businesses; on an equal footing?

Slimbo - Bismak

- Implied terms under s14 SGA.
- Goods defective - or packaging?
- Consumer Protection Act 1987.

Slimbo - Gorby

- Implied terms under s14 SGA.
- Slimbo and Gorby dealing business-consumer.
- Effect of UCTA.

Suggested solution

This is a question best answered by dealing with the main problems separately.

Slimbo's purchase of corn pellets from Adolf

Sections 13-15 of Sale of Goods Act 1979 (SGA) now imply into virtually all contracts for the sale of goods a series of provisions as to quality of the subject matter. It is not clear from the wording of the question whether this is a sale by description, or by sample. Indeed it is not clear whether the corn pellets are in any way faulty either before or after the combination with Skanoil. Finally it is not apparent whether or not Adolf is aware of the intended use to which Slimbo is going to put the pellets. So what, from this somewhat vague scenario, can we advise Slimbo?

Firstly, if the goods were sold by description then s13 SGA will apply. Most authorities are of the opinion that virtually all sales will be by description (save where the goods are unique in some way and sought out by the buyer). Thus if Slimbo contacts Adolf and asks for 'some more of those corn pellets' or 'corn pellets suitable for combining with other substances' or whatever, then this will be a sale by description. Section 13 requires that the goods in bulk comply with description. The same rules by virtue of s15 apply to sale by sample, though we do not know if Slimbo bought on the basis of a sample. *Ashington Piggeries* v *Christopher Hill Ltd* (1972) makes it clear that if the description is so crucial to the contract that if the goods sold do not tally with the description it becomes a different contract, then the description becomes in effect a term of the contract, not merely a representation.

The first thing we need to know therefore is if Slimbo gave Adolf a description of the goods he wanted, or if Adolf described the goods in such a way as to convince Slimbo that these goods were suitable for his purpose. We need to know much the same thing for another purpose too: s14(3) SGA provides: 'Where a seller sells goods in the course of a business, and the buyer expressly or impliedly makes known to the seller ... any particular purpose for which the goods are being bought, there is an implied condition that the goods will be fit for that purpose.' Obviously, whether or not Slimbo mentioned his intention of combining the corn pellets with Skanoil is of crucial importance. Section 14(3) only applies to sales in the course of a business and will not apply if it can be shown that the buyer does not rely on the seller's guidance. Similarly s14(2), which overlaps considerably, requires goods to be of merchantable quality ie fit for the purpose or purposes for which such goods are commonly bought. Again the question arises: is it usual to combine different substances to make cattle food ... is this 'a purpose for which such goods are commonly bought'?

We are told that Adolf supplies the goods on a particular basis: 'that ownership in the goods remains in the supplier until all outstanding liabilities are discharged to the supplier, who is under no liability for the suitability of the goods for any of the purposes to which they may be put.' The first part of this clause is clearly an attempt on Adolf's part to reserve title in the goods until such time as he is paid. Normally property (and consequently risk) passes as and when the goods are delivered regardless of time of payment. Such clauses amending the usual rule are often called 'Romalpa clauses' (*Aluminium Industrie* v *Romalpa* (1976)). Unfortunately what we do not know is whether Slimbo has paid Adolf in full and whether property (and consequently, risk) has now passed from Adolf to Slimbo. The second part of the conditional requirement, the exclusion clause, needs to be looked at carefully. Nowhere in the question does it say whether this is a written clause or an oral one.

The question of incorporation of exclusion clauses is such that a number of possibilities spring to mind. Incorporation by signature is possible, but we do not know if Slimbo has signed any documentation. Previous dealings, if they have consistently been on the same terms, are enough to incorporate a clause: we are told that Adolf has 'for a number of years' imported the corn pellets, but have his contracts always been with Slimbo and always on the same terms? It seems most likely that incorporation, if it has occurred at all, is on the basis that it is conspicuously displayed (*Olley* v *Marlborough Court Hotel* (1949)) on documents that are clearly contractual

(*McCutcheon* v *McBrayne* (1964)). The actual time and method of making the contract is also important (*Levison* v *Patent Steam Carpet Cleaning* (1978)).

But even if the exclusion clause has been incorporated, is it in any case, valid? We must look first at the Unfair Contract Terms Act 1977 (UCTA). Firstly, it is worth noting that s26 exempts international supply contracts. We are told the goods are imported from Germany, but not whether Adolf is actually in Germany and whether the goods form the basis of such an international contract. If this is the case, of course, it does not necessarily mean that the exclusion clause will have no effect, simply that it will not be governed by UCTA. The Act is stated in s1(3) to apply to business contracts and there have been a number of cases defining 'business' (*Davies* v *Sumner* (1984); *R & B Customs Brokers Co* v *UDT* (1988)). It is not entirely clear whether Slimbo is in fact 'in business' on a full time basis. Nevertheless he will for convenience be presumed so to be, as will Adolf. The position would in any event be similar (even if not exactly the same) if he were dealing as a consumer. Only where two individuals deal together will UCTA not apply at all. Section 6(2) provides that exclusion of implied terms as to description, quality, fitness for purpose and correspondence with sample (ss13-15 SGA) is ineffective where one of the parties deals as a consumer. As stated above it will be assumed that Slimbo and Adolf are dealing on an equal business footing. In such cases an exclusion clause may be acceptable if the 'reasonableness' test applies. That test, as set down in s11 and Sched 2 of UCTA, provides similar guidelines to those used in common law prior to the Act's introduction. Such criteria include the relative status of the parties, the availability of the goods, whether other suppliers may use similar exclusion clauses, whether the goods could be insured and so on. Superficially at any rate there seems no glaring reason why the clause should not satisfy the reasonableness test, but there is one point to ponder. The clause reads ... 'no liability' ... and is thus extremely wide. Remember that by s2(1) UCTA in cases of business dealing a party cannot in any way exclude or restrict his liability for death or personal injury, resulting from negligence, to any person, whether that person deals as a consumer or not. Thus the exact scope of the clause will be limited, but otherwise on the basis of the reasonableness test, probably valid.

Finally, despite the foregoing there is no evidence in the question that the corn pellets are in any way faulty; all the pointers indicate that the Skanoil is to blame. It is to this aspect of the question that we shall next proceed.

Slimbo's purchase of Skanoil from Bismak

The same sort of imponderable factors tend to apply as much to this transaction as to the first. Since the question says that Bismak imports the oil 'on Slimbo's instructions' it does not sound as though the contract is an international sale contract. The main problem here appears to be that while the goods are not in themselves faulty, the instructions that go with them are very precise, but, unfortunately, not well communicated. Bismak delivers the drums of oil unopened, but he fails to pass on the accompanying invoice which has on it a warning about exposing Skanoil to air.

It has long been settled that the implied conditions in SGA under s14 as to fitness for purpose and merchantability relate not only to the goods, but also to the container or packaging in which the goods are supplied (*Geddling* v *Marsh* (1920); *Wormell* v *RHM Agricultural (East) Ltd* (1987)). But is a phrase or two incorporated into the small print of the invoice part of the packaging? Certainly there would appear to be nothing on the drums themselves. Any sort of preliminary examination of the oil drums by Slimbo would presumably not reveal this problem; it is not apparent from the drums and Bismak has not drawn it to Slimbo's attention. In disregarding the invoice and throwing it away unread, Bismak may, of course, by the ordinary rules of negligence (see *Donoghue* v *Stevenson* (1932)) be liable in tort to Slimbo and possibly also Gorby.

The main test as to merchantable quality is that quoted in *Kendall* v *Lillico* (1969) in which Lloyd LJ stated:

'To bring s14(2) into operation, a buyer had to show that the goods had been bought by description from a seller dealing with goods of that description. If so ... the goods were required to be of merchantable quality ... the goods did not have to be suitable for every purpose within a range of purposes for which goods were normally bought under that description. It was sufficient that ... they were commercially saleable under that description.'

We do not know what information Slimbo gave to Bismak, only that the oil was imported from Algeria 'on Slimbo's instructions'. Nor do we know what quantity of oil is involved. Obviously oil which cannot be exposed to air for more than five days is not of merchantable quality, especially if it is normally used in fairly small quantities. But a great deal will depend on just what information Slimbo gave Bismak, and also on whether normal usage is to use Skanoil quickly and in large quantities.

Note incidentally that under the Consumer Protection Act 1987 s2(2)(c) that those who import into the EC (the oil is from Algeria) defective products will be liable in tort. The term 'importers' will cover both Bismak and Slimbo.

But is the oil, or more likely its packaging with the lack of any warning label, defective? Or is it the combination of corn pellets and Skanoil that constitutes the problem?

Slimbo's sale of Kornskam to Gorby

Whatever the background of its constituent parts it seems clear that as an animal foodstuff Kornskam is defective. It fails to comply with the implied conditions of s14 as to merchantability or fitness for purpose. We are not told just how Gorby purchases the goods, whether by description or sample or whatever; it seems unlikely that the defect which causes the cattle to go mad would be apparent on any inspection that Gorby might or might not make. The *Ashington Piggeries* case (above) establishes that this is almost certainly a sale by description. Slimbo deals by way of business with Gorby as a consumer and since his contract is on the same terms as that with Adolf the UCTA will presumably apply. Liability as to death and personal injury cannot be excluded (s2(1) UCTA as noted above). The only difference between the two contracts is that Adolf and Slimbo deal on an equal (presumably) business footing; whereas Slimbo and Gorby are on a business-consumer customer footing. In the latter case, since Gorby is dealing as a consumer, or seems to be, exclusion or purported exclusion of, inter alia, s14 as to fitness and merchantability under SGA will be ineffective. Slimbo's attempt to exclude liability for the defective Kornskam as against Gorby will therefore be ineffective. This is of course provided Gorby is not dealing as another business as sometimes happens where large companies manage a farm. If Slimbo and Gorby are on an equal business footing then the 'reasonableness' test, as already mentioned, will be applicable to the clause excluding liability.

Finally note the effect of the case of *Parsons* v *Uttley Ingham* (1978) on likely damages which may be awarded to Gorby.

6 DUTIES OF THE BUYER

6.1 Introduction

Sections 27-37 of SGA deal with the topics of delivery acceptance and payment in performance of a contract.

In particular s27 provides that:

'It is the duty of the seller to deliver the goods and of the buyer to accept and pay for them in accordance with the contract of sale.'

Section 28 goes on to provide that unless otherwise agreed, delivery of the goods and payment of the price are *concurrent conditions*.

6.2 Key points

a) *Duty to pay*

The buyer must pay the price agreed or to be agreed, or a reasonable price (see chapter 2).

The seller is entitled to payment at his place of business at a time expressly or impliedly laid down in the contract.

By s10(1) time of payment is not prima facie 'of the essence', but like provisions as to place or time of delivery this may be changed expressly by the parties.

Section 28, by making payment and delivery concurrent conditions, effectively makes willingness on the part of the buyer to pay the all important element. Thus, if the seller is sued for non-delivery of the goods, the buyer need not prove actual payment, but simply that he was *ready and willing* to pay at the relevant time.

b) *To take delivery*

Though obviously this dovetails with the duty to accept the goods, it is a separate duty.

Taking of delivery is quite distinct in that it is not, as such, to be construed as acceptance.

It may be that, for a number of reasons, having taken delivery the buyer will go on to reject the goods.

Sections 34-35 deal with acceptance; and the legal effect of acceptance is better dealt with in chapters 13 and 14, because once acceptance has taken place the buyer will lose his right to reject the goods.

6.3 Analysis of questions

On its own this is an area of sale of goods too confined and with too little relevant case law or related material to form a satisfactory topic for a question.

For obvious reasons it occurs most frequently in tandem with questions on buyer's remedies, and usually the topic of the buyer's duties requires only minimal reference in an answer.

For a sample of possible examination questions on these topics, please refer to chapters 13 and 14.

7 EXCLUSION OF LIABILITY

7.1 Introduction

While some contracts for sale of goods may be individually negotiated by the parties, it is quite usual in commercial contracts to find the trader using a standard form contract while exclusion clauses are not confined to standard form contracts they are most commonly found there. Standard form contracts have the advantage of being cheap but they have certain inherent disadvantages, one of the main problems being that in drafting the contract the trader way take the opportunity to exclude liability to which he would normally be subject, both under the Sale of Goods Act and common law.

Since the customer is not normally on an equal footing with the trader, there may be a monopoly or near monopoly of the supply of certain goods, the standard form contract may be forced on the unfortunate customer. Obviously in such cases, the use of exclusion clauses is highly undesirable.

Exclusion clauses can take a number of different forms from an all-out effort to exclude any liability for any eventuality to 'limitation clauses' which while they do not try to exclude liability, as such, seek to place an upper limit on the damages a trader will have to pay if he is found to be in breach of the contract.

Over the years the courts have sought to exercise some degree of control over the use of exclusion clauses. More recently, legislation, in particular the Unfair Contract Terms Act 1977, has been introduced to try to achieve the same ends. It should be remembered that judicial control is still of practical importance, partly because the legislation does not cover every type of sale of goods contract and partly because, even where the relevant legislation applies, the criteria of the statutes tend to depend in certain cases on what is fair and reasonable. The courts have given some thought not only as to the meaning of the term 'fair and reasonable', but also as to whether the clause can be considered incorporated into the contract or applicable to the particular situation in hand. Obviously such case law is of particular relevance in applying statutory rules.

7.2 Key points

It is important that the student understands the following points:

a) *Judicial control: incorporation and interpretation*

Whether or not a clause has been incorporated into a contract depends in common law on a number of factors.

It may of course be expressly written into the contract and drawn to the buyers attention specifically; this is the simplest possibility.

Signature of a contract: see *L'Estrange* v *Graucob* [1934] 2 KB 394 usually means that (except in cases of fraud) the party signing will be bound by all the provisions of the contract, including exclusion clauses, regardless of whether he has read them or not.

As was made clear in the above case, there are certain instances where the rule does not apply, especially as in *Curtis* v *Chemical Cleaning and Dyeing Co Ltd* [1951] 1 KB 805 where the effect of the clause has been accidentally or deliberately misrepresented to the signor.

There is also, of course, the doctrine of 'non est factum' to consider, in which the signature has been obtained under the mistaken belief of the consumer that the document is something quite different from what it actually is.

When no document has been signed, or in cases where either there is no written contract at all, or the contract verbally refers to a notice, or ticket or some such display of contractual obligations, then the question of incorporation becomes more difficult.

To determine whether an exclusion clause will have any legal effectiveness a number of questions need to be answered including:

i) Is the document contractual; that is, does the document, notice, ticket or whatever containing the clause form an integral part of the contract?

ii) Has reasonably sufficient notice been given? Each case will depend on individual facts, but the overall effect of this test is to assess whether the consumer had adequate advance notice of the exclusion clause. Certainly notice should be given, preferably before the contract is negotiated, but at the very latest at the time of actually finalising the terms.

iii) Has the clause been incorporated by a course of dealing? Where trader and consumer have dealt with each other before it is possible to argue implicit incorporation of exclusion clauses. However, there are a number of restrictions the practical effect of which is to ensure that it will normally be impossible to show a past history of dealings sufficiently lengthy *and* consistent.

The courts have never looked favourably on exclusion clauses and this is reflected in the fact that they operate a rule of strict construction in interpreting such clauses. They adopt in its application.

Certain types of contract are specifically declared, not to be subject to the Act at all.

Also, the Act is stated in s1(3) to apply, with only a minor exception, to business liability.

Although the term 'business' is stated in s14 to include professional activities and contracts made by central or local government, thereby giving the expression wider connotations than perhaps it would normally have, it does never the less mean that most contracts between private individuals are not covered. Other than s14 above, there is no formal definition of 'business'. Primarily the Act is most concerned to deal with cases where there is inequality of bargaining power between the parties. Thus, where private individuals contract between themselves, exclusion clauses may in principle be upheld (given the common law rules already discussed) and no question of unfairness will arise.

An exclusion clause is essentially one a 'contra preferentem' approach; that is, they will go to some lengths to interpret a clause in a way favourable to the party against whom it was sought to apply the clause.

There is a very great deal of case law on the topics both of incorporation and interpretation. Given that not only are there a small number of contracts not covered by the Unfair Contract Terms Act at all, but also that some of the case law is even now relevant to the interpretation of the Act, the student should make sure he is familiar with the leading cases on the subject.

b) *The Unfair Contract Terms Act 1977*

The ability of the courts to control the use of exclusion clauses was ineffective, largely because constrained as they were to work within the limits of common law, they were always handicapped by the one overriding doctrine of the English law of contract - the notion that freedom of contract should always have priority.

The Unfair Contract Terms Act is restricted that purports to deprive a party to a contract of a remedy that he would otherwise have had for breach.

Under s13 of the Act:

'To the extent that this part of the Act prevents the exclusion or restriction of any liability; it also prevents:

a) making the liability or its enforcement subject to restrictive or onerous conditions

b) excluding or restricting any right or remedy in respect of the liability or subjecting a person to any prejudice in consequence of his pursuing any such right or remedy

c) excluding or restricting rules of evidence or procedure.'

There is a subsection, s13(2), which can create some problems because it provides that an agreement to submit to arbitration is not to be regarded as a true exclusion clause. Usually such clauses are treated as ineffective, however, unless specifically bought to the attention of the consumer and expressly agreed to by him.

The most important and far-reaching provisions of the Act apply where there is a contract between someone in business and a person dealing as a consumer, s12 defines 'dealing as a consumer' where a person

'a) neither makes the contract in the course of a business, nor holds himself out as doing so; and

b) the other party does make the contract in the course of business; and

c) ... the goods ... are of a type ordinarily supplied for private use or consumption.'

Note that s12 specifically excludes buyers in auction sales, or by competitive tender from being classified as 'consumers'. Onus of proof is on the party claiming that a person does not deal as a consumer.

Bear in mind that 'to hold himself out as not doing so' will in the context of this Act make a person something other than a consumer. Thus, to obtain a trade discount card to buy at a reduced price from a wholesaler will mean that the buyer will be deemed to be making the contract 'in the course of business', though he may normally have no links with the business in question. He will *not* be a consumer.

Section 11 of the Act gives some guidelines as to what constitutes an 'unfair' term. It provides:

'In relation to a contract term the requirement for reasonableness for the purposes of this part of the Act is s3 of the Misrepresentation Act 1967 ... is that the term shall have been a fair and reasonable one to be included having regard to the circumstances which were, or reasonably ought to have been known to, or in the contemplation of the parties when the contract was made ...'

For further details as to the question of reasonableness see Key Point (c) following:

Any exclusion or restriction of liability will be rendered void in the following cases:

i) Liability for personal injury or death

   By s2(1) in cases of business liability a party cannot in any way exclude or restrict his liability for death or personal injury resulting from negligence to any person, whether that person deals as a consumer or not.

ii) Guarantees relating to consumer goods

   Section 5(1) provides that in cases of business liability a party cannot by means of a purported 'guarantee' exclude or limit liability for loss or damage arising from defects caused by negligence during manufacture or distribution of the goods. The goods must be in 'consumer use', but this covers all cases where the owner does not use the goods for a purely business purpose; thus, s5(1) may cover goods used for part business/part private use.

iii) Sale of goods and hire purchase contracts

Section 6(1) provides that liability for breach of the terms implied into contracts of sale by SGA 1979 s12 and into hire purchase contracts by the Supply of Goods (Implied Terms) Act 1973 s8 cannot be excluded or restricted; regardless of whether the parties deal 'as consumer' or not.

By s6(2), exclusion of terms implied by ss13-15 of SGA or ss9-11 in Supply of Goods (Implied Terms) Act as to quality of goods is ineffective if the parties deal 'as consumer'.

iv) Supply of goods

Section 7 of UCTA deals with cases other than sale of goods proper. Exchanges, hire purchase pledging and other forms of contract are all covered by s7 which provides that where the parties deal 'as consumer' an attempt to exclude or limit liability; in respect of breach of implied obligations as to quality of goods; will be void.

The overall effect of those sections of the UCTA as listed above is that liability for any breach of term relating to title is impossible to exclude or restrict. Where a party deals 'as consumer' the other party cannot exclude liability for breach of terms relating to quality. Where a party does not deal 'as consumer' such purported exclusions need only satisfy a reasonableness test.

c) *The reasonableness test*

By the UCTA some terms purporting to exclude liability are subject to a reasonableness test as laid down in s11 (see Key Point (b), ante) and Schedule 2 of the Act.

The guidelines as laid down in Schedule 2 owe a great deal to the similar criteria used in common law prior to the introduction of the Act.

The Act imposes the use of the reasonableness test on those terms which are not regarded as unfair per se; but which would possibly deprive one party of his remedies under law if permitted.

The terms made subject to the test include:

i) liability for loss or damage, other than personal injury or death where caused by negligence. Section 2(2) allows exclusions of this type, if reasonable;

ii) s3 cases; concerning the actual performance of the contract. Section 3 covers a number of types of contract, which overlap to some degree; but in particular contracts in the course of business either between two businesses or business and a consumer, especially where the contract is of the standard-form type. It primarily covers exclusions or restrictions of liability where the contract is not substantially performed as intended;

iii) s6(3) covers cases in sale of goods and hire purchase where the party deals otherwise then as a consumer;

iv) s7(3) which lays down similar rules to s6(3)(iii) above; but which is confined to business only contracts;

v) 'indemnity' clauses where one party seeks to limit his liability by requiring the consumer to indemnify himself against the trader's or manufacturer's negligence or breach of contract;

vi) s8 of UCTA amends s3 of the Misrepresentation Act 1967 in such a way as to incorporate into the MA a statutory requirement for reasonableness. The original s3 of MA had a test of reasonableness based on common law criteria; now the statutory test (as contained in s11 and Schedule 2 of UCTA) applies to any clause purporting to exclude or limit liability for misrepresentation;

vii) s9 of UCTA provides that a fundamental breach does not mean that a party can no longer rely on any exclusion clause. The major test is twofold - did the parties anticipate that in the event of a fundamental breach the guilty party might try to use the exclusion clause in question and secondly, is the exclusion clause reasonable?

The test of reasonableness itself as laid out in Schedule 2 bears a strong family resemblance to the test as applied at common law.

The criteria to be taken into account by the court include any or all of the following as relevant:

i) the relative strength of the bargaining positions of the two parties;

ii) whether the customer received an inducement to enter into the contract and to be bound by the exclusion term(s);

iii) whether the customer might have entered into another contract with other persons, but without having to agree to the exclusion clause;

iv) whether the customer knew or ought reasonably to have known of the term, having regard to, inter alia, the custom of the trade and any previous dealings;

v) where the exclusion clause will apply only if some condition is not met with, whether it was reasonable at the time to expect problems with compliance with the condition;

vi) whether the goods were manufactured, processed or adapted to the special orders of the customer.

There have been relatively few reported cases on the Act and the reasonableness test. One reason may no doubt be that in many cases any proceedings are heard in the County Court where there is no formal system of reporting.

Note that the criteria laid down in Schedule 2 are merely intended to be guidelines not an exhaustive list of matters relevant to the test of reasonableness.

Note also that by s11(5) it is for the person claiming that an exclusion or limitation clause satisfies the test of reasonableness to prove it. In other words the court will assume unreasonableness and the burden of proof is on the party relying on the clause to prove to the contrary.

d) *Avoidance of the rules on exclusion clauses*

The UCTA contemplates three possible means by which the Act might be evaded and counters them as follows.

i) Section 4 covers indemnity clauses which could in theory be used to avoid the effects of UCTA by making one party indemnify the other for liability. Section 4 as seen ante, now makes indemnity clauses subject to the reasonableness test.

ii) Section 10 covers the use of secondary contracts by providing:

'A person is not bound by any contract term prejudicing or taking away rights of his which arise under or in connection with ... another contract ...'

Although the intention of s10 is quite clear to prevent a party excluding liability by incorporating the relevant clause(s) in another secondary contract - there are problems with the wording of the section. For one thing s10 uses different terminology from the rest of the Act: talking of 'prejudicing or taking away rights' not to 'excluding' liability. It remains to be seen whether the courts will treat s10 in such a way as to ignore the terminology since, so far the matter has not come before the courts.

iii) Section 27(2) covers cases where it appears that one of the parties at least, has with deliberate avoidance of the UCTA in mind, provided for the contract to be governed, not by English law, but by the laws of a country not subject to UCTA. Note that s27(2) is particularly concerned with intention to evade UCTA and therefore the motives of the party relying on the term taking the contract out of English law are of paramount importance.

7.3 Analysis of questions

There are a number of questions appearing in past London University papers with at least some part devoted to exclusion clauses. Almost inevitably the questions tend to link exclusion clauses with the topic of terms implied by SGA as to fitness and quality generally.

One such question has already been noted which covered in part the question of seller's duties as implied by statute and also the question of whether or not the seller might exclude any or all of these obligations. See also Q6 of the 1991 paper (chapter 5), which is concerned to some extent with exclusion clauses. Perhaps surprisingly, there has never been a question entirely devoted to exclusion of liability.

All the problems have been of the problem type and it is quite common to find that the topic of exclusion clauses occupies only perhaps a quarter or a third of the overall subject matter.

The question quoted below typifies the sort of format often used.

7.4 Question

Charlie, the purchasing officer of the Students' Union of Barnet University, bought and took delivery at the Students' Union of the following goods:

a) A 'second hand' Range Rover from Dodgey Motors Ltd at 20 per cent below the dealer's guide recommended price, for use by members of the Students' Union. It was subsequently discovered that the car would need extensive repairs to make it roadworthy.

b) A piano advertised in the South Totteride Gazette as 'Once owned by Liberace. Present owner redundant and must sell. Price £500 ono'. The advertisement gave a private address at which the goods might be viewed, which was that of Shark. Unknown to Charlie, Shark, following his usual practice, had obtained the piano on sale or return from a dealer. Charlie inspected the piano and agreed to pay £450 for it. Subsequently, Charlie discovered that the piano was merely of a type favoured by Liberace, and worth only £100.

c) A typewriter, priced £195, from White Elephant Ltd, as a birthday present for his fiancee. At the suggestion of the salesman, the goods were invoiced to the Students' Union so that Charlie might get the trade discount. On inspection, the typewriter was found to be jammed solid.

Each of these three sales contracts was made on similar standard forms and contained the following term: 'All conditions, warranties and other terms express or implied, by statute common law or otherwise, are hereby excluded to the extent allowed by law.'

Advise Charlie.

University of London LLB Examination
(for External Students) Commercial Law June 1987 Q1

Skeleton solution

- Implied conditions at to quality of goods s14(2) and (6) in particular; merchantable quality; fitness for purpose etc.
- Misrepresentations.
- Nemo dat rule; s12(1) as to title.
- Exclusion clauses, the Unfair Contract Terms Act 1977, the reasonableness test.
- Charlie as agent.

Suggested solution

a) *The Range Rover*

The Range Rover was bought second - hand and at a reduced price. Although the phrasing of the question is ambiguous it will be assumed that the price paid was 20 per cent below the dealer's guide price for a second - hand Range Rover.

There is an implied condition in contracts of sale that goods sold by persons selling in the course of a business should be of merchantable quality (s14(2) Sale of Goods Act 1979). Merchantable quality means reasonably fit for the purpose or purposes for which goods of the type are commonly brought (s14(6) Sale of Goods Act 1979). In deciding whether goods are of merchantable quality it is necessary to take into consideration all of the circumstances of the sale, including the price paid.

Second - hand goods can be expected to be in poorer condition than new goods, because they have been used already and, therefore, they will have aged somewhat. Nevertheless, a second - hand car should still be roadworthy unless it is sold at such a low price that it is clearly being sold as an unroadworthy vehicle (*Bartlett* v *Sidney Marcus Ltd* (1965)).

On the information given there is nothing to suggest that the Range Rover was reasonably fit for use as a motor vehicle even when sold at a price 20 per cent lower than that recommended for such a vehicle second - hand. Certainly a car should be capable of being driven on the road legally and it appears that the work required to make this one roadworthy would be unreasonably expensive. It was suggested in *Bernstein* v *Pamson Motors (Golders Green) Ltd* (1987) that if repairs could be easily effected then that may mean that the car is merchantable, but this approach was not adopted by the Court of Appeal in *Rogers* v *Parish (Scarborough) Ltd* (1987) and, in any event, would appear not to be relevant here.

The remedy of the Students' Union is to reject the car and claim the repayment of the purchase price. There is no evidence that any consequential loss was suffered. Nor is there any evidence that the right to reject has been lost.

In order to be effective to allow Dodgey Motors Ltd to escape from liability the exclusion clause will have to be reasonable because of s6(3) of the Unfair Contract Terms Act 1977 (the question of reasonableness is discussed in section (d) below).

b) *The piano*

There seem to have been two misstatements in the advertisement: firstly, that the piano was once owned by Liberace; and secondly, that the present owner had been made redundant and was forced to sell. Although Shark had only obtained the piano on sale or return, he still had the right to sell it, and therefore the sale by him to Charlie was not in breach of s12(1) of the Sale of Goods Act 1979 (*Kirkham* v *Attenborough* (1897)). When Shark sold it property passed to him by virtue of s18 r4 and automatically from Shark to Charlie.

That the piano is only worth £100 rather than the £450 paid for it does not of itself give Charlie a remedy, despite a dictum in *Rogers* v *Parish (Scarborough) Ltd* (1987) that a buyer is entitled to value for money. That dictum must be restricted to cases where there is an established second - hand market for the type of goods in question so that the price is an indication of the quality to be expected by the buyer. Certainly where there have been express statements made about the goods which, if true, would justify the price charged then the buyer's remedy, if any, must come from the express statements not the statutory implied term of merchantable quality.

In any event there must be some doubt about whether Shark sold in the course of a business, because he sold from a private address. But given that it is said that Shark followed his normal practice by taking the piano from a dealer on sale or return it may be that he does sell pianos for profit.

The misstatement that the piano was once owned by Liberace was an actionable misrepresentation. It was a statement which could have induced a reasonable man to enter into the contract on the terms agreed (*Hopkins* v *Tanqueray* (1854)) by Charlie and, indeed, it appears that it may have induced him although we are not told whether it in fact had any effect on him. It is not clear from the facts what type of misrepresentation it was, although in the absence of any evidence it should be assumed that it was negligent, and the burden will be on Shark to prove that he had reasonable grounds to believe and did believe that Liberace once owned it (s2(1) Misrepresentation Act 1967). Charlie would be able to rescind the contract or claim damages. The damages would be calculated so as to put him into the position he would have been if the statement had not been made, this would give him £350. If Charlie elects to rescind the contract he would be entitled to the return of his £450. The inspection of the piano would not alter Charlie's rights in this respect because he would not be able to tell from it whether the representation was true.

It is submitted that this first misstatement would not alter the contractual description of the goods sold. Something is part of the description if it forms a substantial ingredient of the identity of the goods sold (*Reardon Smith Line Ltd* v *Hansen-Tangen* (1976)) and the identity of the goods here is 'piano'.

The misstatement that the owner was redundant and had to sell would not give Charlie a remedy because it would not be likely to induce a reasonable man into the contract (*Traill* v *Baring* (1864)), nor does it appear to have affected Charlie.

The exclusion clause would only be enforceable if reasonable, because of s3 of the Misrepresentation Act 1967, the question of reasonableness is discussed in section (d) below.

c) *The typewriter*

The salesman who sold the typewriter to Charlie appears to have acted outside his authority because he acted against the interest of his principal (White Elephant Ltd) when suggesting that Charlie use the Students' Union name to get a discount. The salesman appears to have known that Charlie was not entitled to the discount, but gave that discount anyway. This would prevent property passing to Charlie at all. No exception to the nemo dat rule would apply because Charlie was not acting in good faith. White Elephant Ltd would be entitled to sue either the salesman in contract or conversion for damages or Charlie in conversion for delivery of the typewriter or damages (Fridman on Agency). It is possible, however, that the salesman would be authorised to give such a discount on the basis, perhaps, that he can use his discretion in order to gain goodwill with Charlie which may reap benefits by inducing Charlie in his role as purchasing officer of the Union to buy other goods from White Elephant Ltd later.

On the basis therefore that the contract of sale was valid and was made with Charlie personally rather than with the Union, then there is no doubt that the typewriter was of such a poor condition that it was unmerchantable and, accordingly, in breach of the condition implied by s14(2). It would also be in breach of s14(3) (*Priest* v *Last* (1903)) but there is no additional remedy for that. Provided he has not had the typewriter for longer than a reasonable time, or has not lost the right to reject in any other way, he would be able to reject it and reclaim the price, subject to the effectiveness of the exclusion clause.

The exclusion clause would have to be reasonable to be effective. Section 6(3) of the 1977 Act applies because Charlie acted otherwise than as a consumer in that he held himself out as buying on behalf of the Union (s12 Unfair Contract Terms Act 1977). The question of reasonableness is discussed in section (d) below.

d) *The exclusion clause*

As stated above, the effectiveness of the exclusion clause to exempt the sellers from liability for breach/misrepresentation depends in each case on reasonableness. The reasonableness test requires the court to ask whether the term was a fair and reasonable one to include in the contract, taking into consideration all the circumstances as known to the parties at that time (s11 Unfair Contract Terms Act 1977).

If the clause simply tried to exclude all express and implied terms, then it would not be reasonable because it would effectively make the agreement to sell non-contractual. That it adds that all terms are 'excluded to the extent allowed by law' makes the reasonableness test more difficult to apply. That clause would make sense if reasonableness was to be judged according to whether it is reasonable to rely on the clause bearing in mind how seriously defective the goods are, because it would then be necessary to ask whether it is reasonable for the seller to escape liability for the defects which exist. The problem that arises here, however, is that it is not the law which allows exclusion of liability but the parties who agree exclusion subject to the law setting limits to the effectiveness of their agreement. It is necessary that the parties agree what is being excluded before the 1977 Act can have any effect. It is submitted that as it stands the clause is not sufficiently clear to have any meaning, and therefore is ineffective to exclude any liability of the sellers.

8 PASSING OF PROPERTY

8.1 Introduction

It can often be important to decide the exact point at which property in the goods is transferred from seller to buyer. This question is important for several reasons; a number of consequences may follow the passing of property of which the more important are:

a) unless otherwise agreed the risk of accidental loss or damage to the goods passes to the buyer (this problem will be examined in more detail in chapter 9);

b) the passing of property gives the seller the right to sue for the price;

c) when the property in the goods has passed the buyer can legitimately sell the goods to a third party (and pass good title) even if he has not yet paid the seller;

d) if there is a difference between the passing of property and the physical taking of possession, then the person physically in possession may, despite the fact that he is not the lawful owner, pass good title to an innocent third party taking in good faith (see chapter 10 on transfer of title by a non-owner);

e) if a seller becomes insolvent while the goods are still in his possession the only circumstances in which the buyer can claim the goods are if the property has passed, or if at the court's discretion he is granted specific performance (see chapter 14).

To ascertain exactly when property passes criteria are based largely on whether the goods are specific or unascertained. In chapter 1 the question of terminology was noted.

8.2 Key points

It is important that the student understands the following points:

a) *Types of goods: unascertained, specific*

The basic rule as to unascertained goods is laid down in s16 SGA which states:

'Where there is a contract for sale of unascertained goods, no property in the goods is transferred to the buyer unless and until the goods are ascertained.'

Property will pass only when the goods are 'appropriated' to the contract or 'ascertained by exhaustion', ie a series of sales diminishes the stock of goods to a point where only the amount specified remains. The rule in s16 is not to be depended on, however, because there are one or two cases in which property *has* been held to pass while the goods are unascertained; certainly, this whole area of law is considered unsatisfactory, both in its inconsistencies and in the effect of s16 as applied. The Law Reform Committee is presently collating criticisms and reform suggestions, with a view to pressing for changes in the law.

Or, possibly it will be r5 of s18 SGA which will decide when property in unascertained goods passes.

Section 18 r5(1) provides in part:

'Where there is a contract for sale of unascertained or future goods by description ... and goods are ... unconditionally appropriated to the contract either by the seller with the assent of the buyer or the buyer with the assent of the seller, the property in the goods thereupon passes to the buyer; and the assent may be ... express or implied ... before or after appropriation is made.'

Rule 5, like all the rules of s18, is subject to a contrary intention. It is only one of a series of rules, including those of common law, used for working out the intentions of the parties as to time when property in goods is to pass. There is a very great deal of case law, with which the student should make himself familiar, mainly concerned with the meaning of phrases such as 'unconditional appropriation' or 'implied assent'.

In the case of specific goods it is ss17 and 18 SGA that are relevant. Section 17 provides that:

'... where there is a contract for the sale of specific or ascertained goods the property in them is transferred to the buyer at such time as the parties intend.'

Section 17(2) dictates that for the purpose of ascertaining the parties' intentions the court will consider the terms of the contract, the conduct of the parties and, generally, the background and circumstances of the case.

Section 18 provides that where the contract is silent and gives no help on these matter then:

'unless a different intention appears the following rules apply for ascertaining the intention of the parties as to the time at which property in the goods is to pass to the buyer.'

The five rules incorporated into s18 are to be used unless there is some clear evidence the parties did not wish them to be applied, and in recent years there has been a steady increase in the so-called 'Romalpa clauses' whereby commercial sellers of goods have attempted to ensure they retain property in the goods until payment in full has been made. In particular this is aimed at making sure that, should the buyer become insolvent, the goods do not pass to the insolvent purchaser's creditors because property might have passed under rules in s18. See *Aluminium Industrie BV* v *Romalpa Aluminium Ltd* [1976] 2 All ER 552.

It is not proposed to quote all the rules of s18 here; r5 has already been mentioned in the context of unascertained goods (ante). The student should refer to any textbook for further details.

b) *Reservation of rights of disposal*

Section 19 sets out a number of possible ways in which a seller may reserve a right of disposal over the goods. Probably the most common is that shown in s19(1) where the seller may, by the terms of the contract, specifically reserve the right of disposal until certain conditions (notably to be paid in full) are met.

The 'Romalpa clauses' mentioned in 1.2(a) above are typical of this type of reservation. The Scottish case *Armour* v *Thyssen Edelstahlwerke AG* (1990) recently gave more information as to reservation of title clauses.

c) *Acceptance*

In any cases which do not fall under ss17-19 as previously discussed then s35 provides property must finally pass on acceptance of the goods by the buyer.

A buyer is deemed to have accepted goods where:

i) he indicates to the seller that has accepted or when the goods have been physically delivered, after the buyer has had a reasonable chance to examine them, either:

   - he does any act inconsistent with ownership by the seller; or
   - after a lapse of a reasonable time he keeps the goods, not having said he is rejecting them.

Because acceptance by the buyer means he loses his right to reject the goods; the question of defining the term acceptance will be dealt with again in later chapters dealing with 'Remedies'.

8.3 Analysis of questions

Until two years ago, this was not an area of sale of goods law which attracted a lot of questions in the London University Commercial Law examinations. One of them, Q2 of the 1987 paper, has already been included in chapter 1 as being more relevant to the general question of the terminology of the SGA. The student might, however, now look at it again in the context of this chapter. Two other questions in 1984 and 1985 involved a general round-up of sale of goods law. The pattern of the question is a common one, and in both cases the question of the passing of property and risk occurs. It is, however, only a minor part of the answer expected. In 1992 and then again in 1993 (see Q3) questions appeared on reservation of title clauses. The three questions which appear below require, respectively, a general overview of the law relating to title, risk and property, an account of the passing of title/risk (linked with the right to reject) and a knowledge of Romalpa clauses.

8.4 Questions

Question 1

To what extent does a distinction have to be made between the passing of property in and the transfer of title to goods?

University of London LLB Examination
(for External Students) Commercial Law June 1989 Q2

Skeleton solution

- Terminology - SGA.
- Passing of property - ss16-20 SGA.
- Title - ss21-26 SGA.
- Nemo dat rule.
- Importance of distinction between two concepts.

Suggested solution

The rules relating to the passing of property are dealt with in ss16-20 Sale of Goods Act 1979 (SGA). 'Property' is defined by s61 of the Act as meaning general property in goods, ie it means ownership of goods. The passing of property in goods, therefore, means the transfer of ownership in those goods and this, of course, is the purpose of a contract of sale. A person who has ownership of goods will have the right to deal with the goods in any way he chooses and to prevent anyone else claiming rights over them.

Passing of property under ss16-20 SGA, however, does not have this general effect. The sections are grouped under a sub-heading 'Transfer of property as between seller and buyer'. This suggests, as is in fact the case, that the transfer of property has only a limited effect. Its implications are important in relation to the seller and the buyer but they have virtually no effect on the parties' rights as against outsiders to the contract.

The main effect of property passing is that, by s20 SGA, the risk of accidental loss of or damage to the goods will pass to the buyer. In other words, the risk is borne by the person who has property in the goods. Until property passes, the seller must bear the risk of the goods being accidentally lost or damaged. When property passes according to the provisions of ss16-19 so does the risk.

From the seller's point of view, another reason why it is important to establish whether or not property has passed is that it is only after property in the goods has been transferred to the buyer that the seller can maintain an action for the purchase price of the goods. Whilst property remains in the seller, his action for the buyer's breach of contract can only lie in damages. This means that the seller must try to mitigate his loss by selling elsewhere and that, if there is an available market, the measure of damages will be the difference between the contract price and the available market price regardless of how much less the seller obtained on a re-sale. If the property in the goods has passed, however, the seller has the right to argue that these goods now belong to the buyer and to sue the buyer for the agreed price. There will be no question of the seller having to mitigate.

Apart from this right to sue for the purchase price and the matter of where risk in the goods lies, the question of passing property does not affect the seller's rights. So, for example, if the seller is unpaid he will be able to exercise the right of lien, stoppage and resale even though property in the goods has passed to the buyer. These rights continue even though the buyer is insolvent. The important point from the seller's point of view is that either he has retained physical possession or that the goods are in the hands of a carrier. In these circumstances, even though property, ie ownership, in the goods has passed to the buyer, the buyer's trustee in bankruptcy has no right to claim them for the buyer's estate.

From the buyer's point of view, even though property in the goods has passed to him he will not be entitled to claim the goods until he has paid or tendered the purchase price. In other words, the mere fact that property has passed does not give the buyer the right to possession. It therefore follows that even though the buyer has property, he will have no right to sue the seller in conversion, an action which is based on a right to possession. Nor will he have a right to sue the seller for specific performance of the contract even if the goods are unique. The buyer will have no right to possession until he has paid or tendered the price. Furthermore, if the seller retains physical possession of the goods and sells them to a third party, that third party will obtain goods title and the original buyer will be left with a merely personal right of action against the seller, even though property in the goods had in fact passed to the buyer under the original contract.

In effect, therefore, it can be seen that, although passing of property means passing of ownership, and ownership implies rights which are good against the whole world, in practice the passing of property, with nothing more, affects mainly the personal rights and liabilities of the seller and the buyer inter se. The presumption in ss16-20 SGA appears to be that the seller owns the goods being sold. The question of defective title does not arise. Where there are issues relating to title in the goods, the position will be covered by ss21-26 SGA.

Sections 21-26 SGA deal with cases where a person acquires goods from a seller who does not own these goods. These sections deal with the transfer of title by non-owners. Although only one person can have absolute ownership of goods, a number of persons can have a title in one form or another and these sections give the courts guidance as to which of these people has the best title. The reason for the somewhat artificial distinction between property and title lies in the fact that the English sale of goods does not differentiate between the contract for the sale of goods and the conveyance of ownership in the goods. They both occur in the same transaction. It therefore becomes necessary to draw these artificial distinctions.

The basic rule relating to the transfer of title is nemo dat quod non habet, ie no-one can give what he does not have. In other words, a person without title cannot generally create a good title to anyone else. As a rule, therefore, if a person other than the true owner sells goods, the true owner will remain entitled to immediate possession and will be able to recover the goods from anyone who is holding them without good title, however innocent that person may be.

The difficulty that this principle presents however is that, although the courts protect ownership, commerce requires that in certain circumstances a bona fide purchaser of goods must be able to know that, when he buys these goods, they are his absolutely (Lord Denning in *Bishopsgate Motor Finance Co* v *Transport Brakes Ltd* (1949)). Sections 21-26 provide a number of exceptions to the nemo dat rule. In other words, they describe circumstances where a purchaser can acquire good title to goods even though the seller had no title to transfer.

The distinction between the passing of property and transfer of title, therefore, is an important one to make. They deal with totally different situations which may arise. Sections 16-20 are concerned mainly with allocating the risk of accidental loss or damage as between the true owner and a person who buys the goods from the owner. The question of defective title does not arise. If, however, the seller does not own the goods which have been bought an the true owner seeks to recover them from the buyer ss21-26 will be relevant. These are concerned with the question of title and are designed to effect the compromise between the need to protect ownership and the commercial requirement that, in certain circumstances, a purchaser of goods is entitled to treat those goods as his absolutely, despite any lack of title in the seller.

Question 2

'The buyer wants goods which conform with the contract but, depending upon when risk passes, he may well have to accept non-conforming goods without there being any liability on the seller.'

Discuss.

University of London LLB Examination
(for External Students) Commercial Law June 1992 Q2

Skeleton solution

- Implicit requirement of Sale of Goods Act 1979 as to goods.
- Express requirements.
- Right to reject goods as non-conforming.
- Doctrine of acceptance - ss34-35 Sale of Goods Act 1979.
- Criteria as to when property passes in: unascertained goods, s16; specific goods, s17.
- In both cases the rules in s18 may be important.
- Attempts to explain apparent conflict between passing of property and right to reject.

Suggested solution

In any sale of goods contract, there are, by virtue of the Sale of Goods Act 1979

(SGA), certain implicit requirements as to the nature of the goods. Chief among these are that the goods coincide with their description (s13); that the goods are of merchantable quality and fit for purpose (s14) and, if sold by sample, that the bulk of the goods correspond to the sample (s15). There are also conditions relating to title and quiet enjoyment (s12), and as to quantity (ss30-31), ie whether there are too little or too many goods.

The buyer is entitled to expect goods to conform not only to these implied terms, but also to any additional stipulations that the parties may insert expressly into the contract. If the goods do not conform the buyer may have a number of remedies, chief among them the right to reject.

It should be stated at the outset that the passing of property in the goods does not affect the buyer's right to reject, despite an insinuation to the contrary in the wording of the question. It was formerly the case that under the old s11(1) of the 1893 Sale of Goods Act that the buyer lost the right to reject when property passed to him. It thus became of the utmost importance to ascertain exactly when property passed. But the Misrepresentation Act 1967 amended this provision and the new s11 in the current SGA makes it clear that passing of property is no longer important as a criterion; the right to reject is now lost *only* when the buyer accepts the goods.

We therefore need to examine firstly the doctrine of acceptance and its relevance today to the buyer's right to reject.

The right to reject is now lost only by acceptance of the goods by the buyer. The SGA's main provisions on when the buyer will be deemed to have accepted are contained in ss34 and 35(1). Also note s11(4) which provides, in effect, that once the buyer has accepted the goods, then he will be prevented from rejecting them, whatever breach of contract has been committed by the seller. The right of rejection is not of course the only possible remedy, and the buyer may have other forms of redress for the breach.

Section 34 provides that where goods are delivered to the buyer and he has not previously examined them, he is not deemed to have accepted them until he has had a reasonable opportunity of examining them to ascertain whether they conform to the contract. By s35(1) a buyer is deemed to have accepted the goods when he intimates to the seller that he has accepted, or when he does any act in relation to the goods which is inconsistent with the seller's ownership, or when, after a reasonable lapse of time, he retains the goods without intimating to the seller that he has rejected them.

Obviously there is some degree of conflict between these two sections. The buyer may do some act inconsistent with the ownership of the seller before having had an opportunity of examining the goods. Originally the old SGA made no distinction between the two. In an attempt to resolve the conflict the courts made some heavily criticised decisions (see, for instance, *Hardy* v *Hillerns & Fowler* (1923)). However, s4(2) of the Misrepresentation Act 1967 made the necessary amendments to the SGA to make it clear that s34 is the dominant section. That is, if a buyer apparently accepts by doing some act inconsistent with the rights of the seller, but has not in fact had reasonable opportunity to examine the goods, then s34 applies and he will be held not to have accepted until after the examination of the goods (if that proves satisfactory). Some difficulty has arisen in the interpretation of these two sections and there is a considerable body of case law relating to ss34 and 35(1). For example, what constitutes a 'reasonable opportunity' to examine the goods is defined in *Molling & Co* v *Dean & Son* (1901); the meaning of the phrase 'an act inconsistent with the ownership of the seller has been examined in numerous cases, notably *Kwei Tek Chao* v *British Traders and Shippers* (1954) and *Armaghdown Motors Ltd* v *Gray Motors Ltd* (1962); while 'reasonable lapse of time' was considered in *Lightburn* v *Belmont Sales* (1969) and *Manifatture Tessile Laniera Wooltex* v *Ashley* (1979).

It is not within the scope of this answer to examine the extent of the doctrine of acceptance in more detail. It is sufficient to note that until the point of acceptance the buyer has the right to reject goods which do not conform. This is the case, even if property has already passed. When, then, will property in the goods pass from seller to buyer?

Criteria as to when property passes depends largely on the nature of the goods - whether they are unascertained or specific. The basic rule relating to unascertained goods is laid down in s16 SGA, which effectively provides that not until the goods are ascertained will the property in them pass to the buyer. The rules as to what constitute ascertainment are complex, usually unascertained goods become ascertained when they are 'appropriated to the contract' (Rule 5, s18 SGA). But there are exceptions: some by implication of law, eg ascertainment by exhaustion (*Wait & James* v *Midland Bank* (1926)); and some by operation of certain types of common trade contracts, eg fob and cif contracts. Probably the leading case on appropriation of goods is *Carlos Felderspiel* v *Charles Twigg & Co Ltd* (1957), in which five basic rules were laid down as to the point at which ascertainment of goods and hence passing of property occurs.

As to specific goods ss17 and 18 SGA provide that the time property passes is the time the parties intend it to pass (s17). Examples of s17 intention may be found in cases like *Re Anchor Line* (1937) and *Ward* v *Bignall* (1967). If no intention may be found according to s17, then s18 raises, in a series of rules, presumptions as to the intention of the parties, all of which are rebuttable. In particular, Rule 1 provides that in an unconditional contract, if the goods are in a deliverable state, property passes at the time of making the contract. There are other rules, covering cases when goods must be weighed, measured, etc (property passes when this is complete), and where goods are yet to have something done to them to put them in a deliverable state (property passes when they are deliverable), and where the goods are supplied on 'sale or return' (property passes when the buyer makes it clear, expressly or impliedly, that he has appropriated the goods).

From all of the foregoing it will be apparent that in certain cases although property may have passed in the goods, this does *not* deprive a buyer of a right to judge the goods non-conforming and reject them.

One explanation of this apparent conflict was suggested by Devlin J in *Kwei Tek Chao* (above) who stated that where property passes to a buyer in circumstances where he retains a right to reject, the passing of property is merely conditional. Atiyah has however criticised this view as being a 'circular argument'. His argument is that the seller has a reversionary interest in the goods, that they will be available at the place and in the condition that they were in if rejected. Once accepted, this reversionary right ceases. Obviously there is some degree of difficulty here, if the seller is to part with property in the goods and then apparently be reinvested with title on the buyer's rejection of goods, Atiyah's suggestion and Devlin's seem, each of them, to be valid. No-one seems yet to have found any way of satisfactorily explaining the conflict. But certainly the suggestion in the question is not true and a buyer will have a right to reject non-conforming goods even if property has passed to him. He will retain this right until he can be deemed to have accepted.

Question 3

Slimbo agrees to sell Ben 10,000 gallons of skimmed milk. Ben wants to combine this with other liquids to make animal feedstuff. He has agreed to buy the other liquids from Jack. Pete agrees to sell Ben 50,000 steel strengthening rods, which Ben uses in the manufacture of returnable plastic containers in which the feedstuff is packed for sale to farmers. Slimbo, Jack and Peter each supply their goods under separate contracts containing the following clause:

'Goods are supplied on the understanding that the supplier shall be the legal and equitable owner of the goods until full payment has been received by the supplier for all debts due to the supplier; and any money from the sale of the goods to third parties shall be payable to the supplier.'

Ben sells half of the finished feedstuff to Gerald for £5,000. Gerald pays £2,000 to Ben and delivers a tractor to him (worth £1,500) in lieu of a further £1,000 of the price due, leaving £2,000 still owing.

Ben dies insolvent.

Advise the parties.

University of London LLB Examination
(for External Students) Commercial Law June 1992 Q5

Skeleton solution

- Romalpa clauses.
- Rights under s19 Sale of Goods Act 1979 to reserve title.
- Reservation of title in raw materials; courts' stricter approach.
- Criticisms of reservation of title clauses.
- Section 25(1) Sale of Goods Act 1979. Despite 'nemo dat' rule even if property has not passed to buyer, sub-buyers may obtain valid title.

Suggested solution

Clauses of the type incorporated into the three contracts are known as reservation of title clauses, sometimes as 'Romalpa' clauses, after the leading case on the subject (see below).

Section 19 of the Sale of Goods Act 1979 (SGA) sets out a variety of situations in which the seller in some way reserves a right of disposal over the goods. Section 19(1) provides:

'Where there is a contract of sale for specific goods, or where goods are subsequently appropriated to the contract, the seller may ... reserve the right of appropriation until certain conditions are fulfilled and in such a case, notwithstanding delivery of the goods to the buyer ... the property in the goods does not pass to the buyer until the conditions ... are fulfilled.'

In the case of specific goods the buyer must reserve the right of disposal at the time the contract is made (*Dennant* v *Skinner & Collom* (1948)), but in the case of subsequently ascertained goods reservation may be either at the time of the contract, or at the time the goods are appropriated. It seems most likely in the case of the goods purchased by Ben, none of them are specific, having to be ascertained from much larger stocks. However, even if they are specific - the 'liquids' purchased from Jack, bought by name and weight, or 50,000 steel rods ordered by description direct from the factory perhaps - the clause reserving title is incorporated into the contract which each supplier agrees with Ben. Thus the first requirement of s19(1) would appear to be satisfied, regardless of how one classifies the goods. In truth, the goods are probably, as already noted, future or unascertained goods.

Section 19(1) has frequently been used by the courts to justify protecting the interests of the seller in the event of the buyer's bankruptcy. We are told Ben, the buyer, dies insolvent. If a seller has property in the goods or a right of disposal of the goods he can claim the goods and will not be confined to claiming a dividend on bankruptcy. However, this apparently straightforward rule is complicated by two factors. Firstly, a buyer may still be able to resell to a third party, passing good title under s25(1) of SGA. Secondly, the fact that the goods in question are not to remain in their present state but are raw materials for incorporation into, and packaging of, a finished product means that the courts' approach will be stricter. Both these factors will be discussed in more detail, but it may first be useful to discuss briefly the reservation clause itself.

The leading case is *Aluminium Industrie Vaasen BV* v *Romalpa Aluminium* (1976). The clause in question in that case stated that the seller should be entitled to the proceeds of the sale or resale of goods supplied, and that if the goods were in fact resold and the sub-buyer had not paid, then the seller should be entitled to the book debt owed by the sub-buyer to the buyer. This is very similar to the clause in the problem. The *Romalpa* decision has been much criticised because it enables a seller to create a secret, unregistrable, unnotifiable form of security. Should the buyer become bankrupt before the seller is paid then the seller would be able to reclaim the goods. However, the buyer's other creditors have no way of knowing that property in the goods has been reserved by the seller, so they will be unfairly prejudiced, often receiving only a fraction of what they might have expected to receive on bankruptcy since the buyer's assets will have been considerably reduced. A further criticism has been that *Romalpa* introduced into commercial contracts the idea of equitable tracing, while it is constantly argued (see *Re Wait* (1927)) that equitable doctrines have no place in sale of goods.

Where a clause seeks to reserve title in raw materials, as in this case, the problem is particularly acute. Quite clearly the seller, in reserving title, has no expectation or intention of recovering the goods, but intends purely and simply to take priority over other creditors.

For these reasons, the courts' approach has over the past years been stricter, especially since the advent of the Companies Act 1985. In *E Pfeiffer Weinkellerei-Weineinikauf GmbH* v *Arbuthnot Factors* (1988) the court came to the conclusion that not only had a charge over book debts been created by the reservation clause but that s396(1) of the Companies Act 1985 required such charges to be registered. Since the charge had *not* been registered, the seller's claim would fail. In *Borden (UK) Ltd* v *Scottish Timber Products* (1981) the court held that unless the charge was registered (under the then Companies Act) it would be void as against the company's creditors and liquidator. The courts also look critically at the drafting of such reservation clauses; if such a clause is in any way ambiguous, it will be construed against the seller. In *Tatung (UK) Ltd* v *Galex Telesure* (1989) the clause was detailed and made express provision for the interests that the sellers were to have at various stages of dealing with the goods and was looked on with approval by the courts.

Thus in the problem in hand, it is necessary to judge the reservation clauses on a number of different levels. Can any of the goods be recovered and re-used by the sellers? At least half of the steel rods used in making returnable plastic packs may be recoverable, or are they irretrievably welded together? Certainly the milk and other liquids are presumably now inextricably mixed. Is the clause in each contract absolutely clear? And if a charge over book debts has been created, has it been registered under s396(1) of the Companies Act 1985? It should be noted, however, that with all the criticisms of reservation of title clauses, they are still accepted by the courts, even if their approach is now more stringent. Recent cases such as *Armour* v *Thyssen Edelstahlwerke AG* (1990) make this quite clear.

One final problem remains to be resolved. Only half the finished feedstuff has been sold to Gerald, who still owes £2,000 of the £5,000 price. If the reservation clause stands, can Slimbo, Jack and Peter, each by virtue of their separate contracts, take action against Gerald, either to recover the feedstuffs, or sue for the remainder of the price owing? Reservation of title clauses show that the parties sometimes wish to create the impression of agency, in order to give the sellers a greater degree of security. It is a fictitious situation; the sellers never expect to demand return of the goods and there is nothing approximate to bailment to the buyer, nor do the sellers serve as 'principals' in any sale by the buyer (*Coggs* v *Bernard* (1703)).

It should be noted, however, that even when, by means of the sort of clause quoted in the question, a seller successfully manages to prevent property passing to the buyer that subsequent sub-buyers may, despite the nemo dat rule, obtain valid title by virtue of s25(1) of SGA.

This section reproduces with only minimal alterations s9 of the Factors Act 1889 which provides:

'Where a person having bought ... goods, obtains with the consent of the seller possession of the goods ... the delivery or transfer by that person ... of the goods under any sale, pledge or other disposition thereof to any person receiving ... in good faith and without notice of any lien or other right of the original seller ... has the same effect as if the person making delivery or transfer were a mercantile agent in possession of the goods ... with the consent of the owner.'

The requirements of this section are largely self evident. Ben must have obtained physical possession of the goods and taken them away, in order to turn them into feedstuffs and package it. He has not paid for goods obtained from any of the three sellers. Provided Gerald took in good faith and unaware of the reservation of title clauses insisted on by the sellers, then he will have good title to the goods. The original sellers will of course have redress against the buyer's estate (insolvent though it is), but will not have any rights against the goods themselves. The reservation of title clauses may therefore only be utilised, provided Gerald complies with s25(1) of SGA, against the half of the goods remaining unsold. Ben's estate may of course proceed against Gerald for the amount still outstanding and this will be added to the estate's assets, so the sellers Slimbo, Jack and Peter may benefit indirectly from this.

9 RISK, IMPOSSIBILITY AND FRUSTRATION

9.1 Introduction

In the previous chapter it was noted that one of the reasons why it was important to work out when property passed in goods was because this usually determined at which party's risk the goods were at any given time. The question of risk and the related questions of impossibility of performance and frustration are dealt with below.

Basically the rules relating to risk are applied to determine which of the parties will stand the loss should anything happen to the goods and they be lost or damaged.

The general rule is things which perish do so at the expense of the owner, sometimes expressed as 'res perit domino'.

With regard to the general rules of common law relating to frustration and impossibility, the Sale of Goods Act largely preserves these unaltered but additionally the SGA incorporates extra provisions dealing specifically with problems arising where the goods perish before the property in them passes to the buyer.

9.2 Key points

It is important that the student understands the following:

a) *Risk*

Section 20(1) SGA provides:

'Unless otherwise agreed, the goods remain at the seller's risk until the property in them is transferred to the buyer, but when the property in them is transferred to the buyer the goods are at the buyer's risk whether delivery has been made or not.'

The effect of this section is that where property has passed it is the owner of the goods who will suffer whether or not the goods are, as yet, physically in his possession.

As can be seen the general rule operates 'unless otherwise agreed' and s20(1) can be varied by explicit agreement between the parties or by trade usage. The parties may agree, or it may be customary that, risk will not pass till payment or some other event, or conversely it may be agreed for the risk to pass *before* property passes.

Section 20(2) goes on to provide that the rule in s20(1) is varied in cases where delivery is delayed. It provides that where the delay is at the fault of the buyer or the seller whoever is at fault will have the risk of the goods as regards loss which would not have occurred save for the delay. The party at fault is, it should be noted, liable only for losses due to his delay, not loss which would have occurred anyway. In the latter case the normal rules apply.

b) *Impossibility*

Section 6 SGA provides that, unless otherwise agreed:

'Where there is a contract for the sale of specific goods and the goods without the knowledge of the seller have perished at the time when the contract is made, the contract is void.'

It should be noted that s6 is not strictly a rule about frustration, but simply a statutory provision envisaging the likelihood of antecedent impossibility.

The section is self - explanatory; obviously if A and B agree a contract for the sale of a caravan which has to be fetched from a site 100 miles away and unknown to A the caravan has already been destroyed in a fire, then the contract is void.

Section 6 will not apply to goods which have never existed, it applies only where specific goods perish before the contract is made. The meaning of perished in the context of s6 (and s7, post) has given rise to some difficulty in interpretation. It appears that the goods need not be totally destroyed; it is enough if the goods are so badly damaged as to be useless for the purpose for which sold. Note that s6 is subject to the qualification 'unless otherwise agreed'. It is always open to the parties to make other arrangements.

Note also that in the case of a contract which is severable as to the subject matter, if a part only of the goods perish, then s6 will apply only to that part and the remainder of the (severed) contract will operate normally.

c) *Frustration*

Section 7 provides:

'Where there is an agreement to sell specific goods and subsequently the goods without any fault on the part of buyer or seller, perish before the risk passes to the buyer the agreement is thereby voided.'

There are a number of limitations to this section. For one thing, like s6, it only applies to specific goods. Also the perishing of the goods must be from a cause quite unrelated to the fault of either party. In fact, since the section refers only to 'perishing' that is, in itself, a limitation, as contracts can become frustrated for other reasons (if for example, it suddenly became illegal to deal in the type of goods specified) then the ordinary common law would apply to anything other than the outright destruction or severe damage to goods that 'perishing' implies.

In order for s7 to apply, the goods must perish before risk passes to the buyer, but after the contract has been concluded. Should the parties have agreed for example, as is possible under s18 for risk and property to pass immediately on making the contract, then s7 could have no application.

Note that the section is not subject to the Law Reform (Frustrated Contracts) Act 1943 (see s2(5)(c) of that Act).

In the case of unascertained goods there is no provision in the SGA governing frustration of contract.

It would be difficult, in any case, to see how any form of 'perishing' could arise in the type of situation where unascertained goods form the subject matter of the contract. If the source from which the seller had intended to obtain the goods has ceased to exist, then the seller must obtain the goods from elsewhere. If, however, the contract specified the source as being of fundamental importance (eg a shipment of wine to be harvested from a particular vineyard, and the vines are destroyed by some form of disease) then the position is different and the ordinary common law relating to frustration, including the Law Reform (Frustrated Contracts) Act 1943 will apply.

d) *Seller's bankruptcy*

This is a topic more conveniently dealt with in the chapters on Remedies (following). However, it should be briefly noted here, that if property in the goods has passed to the buyer where the seller becomes bankrupt, then the buyer may claim the goods, regardless of whether he actually has keep in his possession.

The two main exceptions to this rule are that: (i) the goods may remain in the sellers' 'reputed ownership'; and that (ii) the seller may have an unpaid seller's lieu or the right of stoppage in transit over the goods.

9.3 Analysis of questions

No question has been set in the past eleven years by University of London on the topic of impossibility and frustration as such. The observant student will already have noticed some examination questions that in part, require some discussion of 'risk'. In chapter 1 Q2 of the 1987 London University Commercial Law paper required the term to be defined in the context of SGA and the relationship between 'risk' and other concepts, notably 'property' and 'ownership' examined. It would be impossible to discuss the questions in chapter 8 without at least some mention of 'risk'.

It is also quite common to find, as has already been noted, questions on the sale of goods in the University of London papers which require a fairly general approach to the problem of contracts for sale of goods. Often such problems are far ranging in their scope and application and refer to matters of property, title and risk as well as other implied terms. Look at Q3 in 1984 and Q2 in 1985 for examples of this sort of problem. Look, most recently, at Q5 of the 1993 paper (chapter 36), which concerns, inter alia, aspects of risk.

The question below is an example of the sort of question one might expect to find on impossibility and frustration, should an examiner ever confine himself to this rather narrow aspect of sale of goods law.

9.4 Question

a) 'Even if there is a radical change of circumstances a contract is not necessarily frustrated.'

Comment.

b) Larry agrees to purchase from Jason 50 bales of wool 'from wool stored in Jason's barn and sheared from Jason's sheep'.

Twenty of the bales are destroyed when a fire burns the barn down.

Tom agrees to deliver to Harry, who lives 100 miles away, a motor car of a particular make and year. Before the car can be delivered vandals so damage it that it is good only for scrap metal.

Advise Larry and Harry.

Written by Editor

Skeleton solution

a)
- Analysis of the test to decide whether a contract is frustrated or not.
- Definition of 'perishing' in the context of specific goods.
- Frustration as applied to unascertained goods.

b)
- Goods unascertained or not? s6 or s7 or neither.
- Specific goods, definition of perishing, application of ss6 or 7?

Suggested solution

a) Prior to 1863 contractual obligations were regarded as absolute, irrespective of the change in circumstances, *Paradine* v *Jane* (1647). At that date the doctrine of frustration was introduced into English law by the decision in *Taylor* v *Caldwell* (1863), where it was held that a contract for the use of a music hall was frustrated when the building was destroyed by fire. This was said to rest on there being an implied term of the contract that the building should continue to exist, and on it destruction the parties were discharged of further obligations.

The courts have subsequently discarded the implied term approach in favour of the radical change in obligations test, first propounded in the speech of Lord Radcliffe in *Davis Contractors Ltd* v *Fareham Urban District Council* (1956). His Lordship said that 'frustration occurs whenever the law recognises that without default of either party a contractual obligation has become incapable of being performed because the circumstances in which performance is called for would render it a thing radically different from that which was undertaken by the contract. Non haec in foedera veni. It was not this that I promised to do'.

The principle enunciated by Viscount Radcliffe has been approved by two further decisions of the House of Lords, *National Carriers Ltd* v *Panalpina (Northern) Ltd* (1981) and *The Nema* (1982).

Two further points emerge from Viscount Radcliffe's speech. The first is that it is not hardship or inconvenience or material loss itself which calls the principle of frustration into play. The second is that although his Lordship referred to a contractual obligation being 'incapable of being performed' he did not mean that frustration occurs only when the contract is physically impossible of performance. Elsewhere in his speech he refers to such a change in the significance of the obligation that the thing undertaken would, if performed, be a different thing from that contracted for.

Davis v *Fareham* (1956) is itself an illustration of the first point. Delay caused by bad weather and the shortage of labour rendered the contract unprofitable for the appellants, but this did not constitute a frustrating event. Further illustration is afforded by *The Eugenia* (1964) where the closure of the Suez Canal caused delay and considerable additional expense. Lord Denning emphasised the point, saying 'the fact that it has become more onerous or more expensive for one party than he thought is not sufficient to bring about a frustration. It must be more than merely more onerous or more expensive. It must be positively unjust to hold the parties bound.'

The second point, that it is not only physical impossibility that causes frustration, is illustrated by cases such as *Jackson* v *Union Marine Insurance Co Ltd* (1873) and *Krell* v *Henry* (1903). In both these cases physical performance was still possible, but the supervening events had rendered the nature of the contractual obligations fundamentally different.

The question is, therefore, not simply whether there has been a radical change in the circumstances, but whether there has been a radical change in the obligation. Was 'performance ... fundamentally different in a commercial sense?' *Tsakiroglou & Co Ltd* v *Noblee Thorl GmbH* (1962).

Note that, in the case of contracts for sale of specific goods, the Sale of Goods Act, ss6 and 7 make special provision for cases where the goods 'perish'. 'Perish' is itself subject to several interpretative cases, notably *Barrow Lane & Ballard Ltd* v *Phillip Phillips & Co Ltd* (1929). Certainly it would appear that the condition of the goods must be such, that they would be unsaleable under the contract description. Note also that the rules on frustration as set out in s7 only applies to specific goods which have '*perished*'. Should the goods become unsaleable for any other reason the ordinary common law will apply. Since the statutory provisions of SGA do not usually apply to unascertained goods the test as to whether a contract is frustrated will be as set out above.

b) i) The first problem here is to decide whether the goods are unascertained. Though at first sight this would appear to be the case, the fact that the contract stipulates specific wool from specific sheep, presently stored in a specific barn, may alter the position. There is some authority (*Howell* v *Coupland* (1876)) for thinking the goods will be regarded as specific.

Obviously the fact that only 20 of the 50 bales have been destroyed will raise the question as to whether the contract can be treated as frustrated at all.

Larry must be advised that he must resolve these initial questions in order to ascertain his remedies. Should the goods be decided to be specific s7 *may* apply if the goods can be considered 'perished'. In *Sainsbury* v *Street* (1972) it was suggested that where a part, only, of the goods perished the seller may be obliged to offer the remaining goods to the buyer, but that the buyer may not be forced to take them.

Larry's remedies would depend on these factors, bearing in mind that, in the case of specific goods, s7 precludes the application of the Law Reform (Frustrated Contracts) Act 1943 s2(5)(c). Where it applies, s7 discharges both parties from their obligations provided risk has passed and the parties show no clear and express intention to the contrary. All the facts are not known here, but it is assumed that, as in the case of most bulk goods, property and hence risk would not pass until the goods are ascertained and delivered, or in a deliverable state. With goods stored, as here in bales, it is largely an individual question of fact as to when delivery takes place; often delivery is constructive anyway. More importantly the rules of s18 SGA will dictate when property passes and risk is transferred to the buyer.

To sum up: if the goods can be defined as specific, and construed as having perished and if risk has passed then s7 will apply provided the parties do not indicate to the contrary. If one of these factors does not apply; in particular, if the goods are defined as unascertained, then the ordinary common law rules relating to frustration will apply.

ii) Clearly, the car; being defined so closely, can be classified as specific goods. Equally clearly its destruction by vandals who reduce it to scrap metal will bring it within the definition of 'perished' goods.

The only factor left open to doubt is whether the car was destroyed before or after the contract, ie whether ss6 or 7 applies. In truth, it is an academic distinction, since to all practical intents and purposes the two sections are so similar as to have much the same effect.

It should, however, be noted that unlike s6 which covers antecedent impossibility, s7 has more restrictions. It covers, for a start only 'agreements to sell' not immediate sales and it covers only cases where the risk has not already passed. There is no indication as to exactly what arrangements have been made between Tom and Harry, but since the car is 100 miles away they may have made arrangements for the risk to pass before delivery, to cover possible risks during transit. If the risk has already passed to Harry then s7 will not apply and Harry must bear the loss and pay the contract price.

Finally, another problem which may apply here is fault - s7 provides, unlike s6, that if the damage is due to either party's fault then the section will not apply. It therefore needs to be ascertained, in advising Harry, whether the vandalism is due to some act of negligence by Tom.

10 TRANSFER OF TITLE BY A NON-OWNER

10.1 Introduction

Sections 21-26 of the Act deal with transfer of title. The general proposition is that a person cannot give a better title than he himself possesses when he purports to sell goods. This is best expressed in the maxim: nemo dat quod non habet.

Section 21(1) provides:

'Subject to this Act, when goods are sold by a person who is not their owner and who does not sell them under the authority and consent of the owner, the buyer acquires no better title to the goods than the seller had ...'

At one time the only exception to this was sale in market overt, but in response to commercial pressures a steady flow of further exceptions have been introduced both by statute and common law. The most important of the exceptions to the 'nemo dat' rule will be dealt with below.

10.2 Key points

It is important that the student understands the following exceptions to the 'nemo dat' rule:

a) *Estoppel*

This exception is incorporated into s21(1) which ends:

'... unless the owner of the goods is by his conduct precluded from denying the seller's authority to sell.'

Section 21 can only operate to pass title when there has been a sale, if there is merely an agreement to sell then the doctrine of estoppel will not operate. Estoppel is often considered to operate in a number of possible ways, by words, by conduct or by negligence. For example, an owner might indicate to a potential buyer either verbally or by his conduct, that some other person had the right to sell goods for him and then allow the sale to proceed. Or, an owner of goods might by his own negligence, allow a seller of goods to appear as a true owner, or as agent for the owner. In these situations the owner will be estopped from denying the truth of the representations made to the buyer and the buyer will get good title. The nature of estoppel is that it provides a defence to the person in whose favour it operates, so that the owner of the goods, (the person estopped) is not allowed subsequently to deny the truth of what he has represented or allowed to be represented and on which the buyer has relied to his detriment.

The student seeking more information as to the background and operation of the doctrine of estoppel should consult a textbook. The doctrine is complex in its operation and space precludes dealing with it in detail here.

b) *Sale under common law or statutory powers of sale, or under a court order*

Section 21(2)(b) provides that nothing in the SGA affects:

'the validity of any contract of sale under any special common law or statutory powers of sale, or under the order of a court of competent jurisdiction.'

The High Court, for example, has the power to order a sale if the goods are perishable or for some other reason likely to deteriorate quickly.

Similarly, many of the common law powers preserved by the Act are of very ancient origin. For example, an agent of necessity can pass good title, even though he is not the owner. There are four or five statutes which give comparable rights, one example being the Torts (Interference with Goods) Act 1977 which confers a power on bailees to sell goods after due notice has been given.

c) *Sale in market overt*

The concept of market overt is a medieval one, or even older, and this exception to the 'nemo dat' rule is now expressly covered by s22 which provides:

'When goods are sold in market overt, according to the usage of the market, the buyer acquires good title to the goods, provided he buys them in good faith and without notice of any defect or want of title on the part of the seller.'

Market overt means an open, public and properly constituted lawful market, and such markets may originate by ancient charter or modern local authority bye laws. Every shop in the boundary of the City of London is regarded as 'market overt'. The fact that the sale must be according to the 'usage of the market' means inter alia that the goods in the contract must be of a type regularly sold in the market; the sale must take place during the normal hours of the market (usually sunrise to sunset), and the goods must be openly displayed.

It is generally agreed that the concept of market overt is now thoroughly out of date and needs either abolishing or revising.

d) *Sale under a voidable title*

Section 23 provides:

'When a seller of goods has a voidable title to them, but his title has not been avoided at the time of the sale, the buyer acquires good title to the goods, provided he buys in good faith and without notice of the seller's defect of title.'

This section preserves the old common law rule relating to the avoidance of contract: that a party who has the right of avoidance will lose such a right if innocent third parties acquire rights in the goods.

Section 23 presents one major problem: that it is essential to distinguish between contracts which are voidable and those which are actually void. In the latter case s23 will not apply.

The cases in this area of sale of goods mostly involve the purchase of goods by some fraud, where the perpetrator of the fraud disposes of the goods to an innocent (usually) third party.

The real test lies in the intention of the original seller. If his intention was, regardless of the fraud, to deal with, and pass title to, the original buyer then the contract will merely be voidable. If, however, he intended to pass title not to the original buyer, but to someone else, but was defrauded into dealing with the original buyer then the contract will be void.

There are cases which go either way on virtually identical facts and the student should examine some of the leading cases in this area. In particular since *Car and Universal Finance Ltd* v *Caldwell* [1965] 1 QB 525 it has been thought that if a seller in a voidable contract rescinds the contract and takes all reasonable steps to publicise the fact of rescission *before* the fraudulent party resells then s23 will not apply and title will not pass to the third party. If this decision is correct, it has obviously greatly decreased the importance of s23.

e) *Sale by an agent*

Section 62 SGA expressly preserves the common law powers of an agent. The whole topic of agency will be examined further in Part 3; but essentially, the sale by an agent of goods belonging to his principal, will pass good title, provided the agent had 'actual' or 'ostensible' authority to make the sale.

f) *Sale by a mercantile agent*

The concept of a mercantile agent within the meaning of the Factors Act 1889 and the power of sale by such agents has been expressly preserved by s21(2). The Factors Act itself was passed in 1889 to protect third parties dealing with professional or 'mercantile' agents acting in the ordinary course of their business. Such agents would have authority to sell goods or consign goods for sale or to buy goods or to raise money on the security of goods. The Act covers people who in today's language are brokers or dealers.

Section 2(1) of the Factors Act provides:

'where a mercantile agent is with the consent of the owner in possession of goods or the documents of title to goods, any sale pledge or other disposition of the goods made by him ... as mercantile agent shall ... be valid as if he were expressly authorised by the owner ... provided the person taking ... (the goods) ... acts in good faith and has not at the time of the disposition notice that the person making the disposition has not the authority to make the same.'

Thus, a person who entrusts goods of some kind to a mercantile agent for sale, but instructs him to withhold the goods for some weeks until the market price has risen will find that, should the goods be sold prematurely, title will have been conveyed to any innocent third party who takes without notice, and he will not be able to recover the goods.

It will have been noted, that a mercantile agent must be someone who is in a business of some kind, although it has been held that to act on just one occasion in a business capacity will mean that this is to be regarded as being 'in the customary course of business.'

For the purposes of the Factors Act the agent must receive the possession of the goods, or documents of title to the goods and have the owner's consent to this possession. Considerable difficulties have been encountered especially in the courts interpretation of 'consent'. Because the Factors Act was aimed at protecting innocent third parties dealing with mercantile agents, the courts have tended to lean over backwards to imply consent, even where it might be considered to be unreal because of some kind of fraud on the part of the agent. Ultimately, in deciding as between an innocent owner and an innocent buyer the Act has tended to favour the latter and the courts have given effect, wherever possible, to this approach. Generally, therefore, even consent obtained by a trick or fraud is still considered consent for the purposes of this Act.

g) *Sale by a seller in possession*

This exception to the 'nemo dat' rule is contained in s8 of the Factors Act which is reproduced with only minimal changes in s24 SGA which provides:

'Where a person having sold goods, continues, or is in possession of the goods or the documents of title to the goods, the delivery or transfer by that person ... of the goods or documents of title under any sale, pledge or other disposition thereof ... to any person receiving the same in good faith and without notice of the previous sale, shall have the same effect as if the person making the delivery or transfer were expressly authorised by the owner of the goods to make the same.'

Most of the requirements of this section are self - explanatory. A typical example of this sort of situation would be: an owner of a crop of barley (presently stored in his barn) sold it to a buyer and it is agreed that delivery will take place in a month's time.

If, in the meantime, the farmer gets a better offer and sells and *actually delivers* the barley to a new purchaser, provided the new buyer takes it in good faith and without notice he will obtain good title. It goes without saying that the original buyer will have an action against the former for breach of contract, but he will not have a right to the goods themselves.

h) *Sale by a buyer in possession*

In a similar way to the previous key point s25(1) of the SGA reproduces with only minor alterations s9 of the Factors Act. Section 25 provides that:

'Where a person having bought or agreed to buy goods, obtains with the consent of the seller possession of the goods or the documents of title to the goods, the delivery or transfer by that person ... of the goods or documents of title under any sale pledge or other disposition thereof to any person receiving ... in good faith and without notice of any lien or other right of the original seller ... has the same effect as if the person making delivery or transfer were a mercantile agent in possession of the goods ... with the consent of the owner.'

Again, the requirements of this section are largely self-evident. A typical case would be if a true owner agreed to sell goods agreeing that property is to pass not, as is usual on delivery of the goods, but on the happening of payment in full. The buyer, with the seller's consent obtains physical possession of the goods and *takes them away* and then does not pay. If, in the interim, the buyer has sold the goods to a third party who takes in good faith and unaware of the seller's rights then the third party will acquire good title. The original seller will, of course have redress against the original buyer, but he will not have any rights in the goods themselves.

i) *Motor vehicles subject to a hire purchase or conditional sale agreement*

Part III, ss27-29 of the Hire Purchase Act 1964 provides an important exception to the 'nemo dat' rule. The provisions of this Act, which were themselves amended by the 1974 Consumer Credit Act are strictly limited to motor vehicles.

Section 27 provides that where a motor vehicle is held under a hire purchase or conditional sale agreement and the person who has the vehicle sells to a private purchaser (rather than a dealer or finance house) before payment has been completed then subject to certain qualifications the purchaser has good title.

The purchaser *must* be a private individual and he must take in good faith and without notice of the hire purchase or conditional sale agreement. If the vehicle is disposed of to a dealer or finance house then no title will pass but if the dealer or finance house then disposes of the goods to a private purchaser who takes in good faith and without notice then under s27(3) that private purchaser will acquire good title. This is confined to a first purchaser only, not a whole chain.

There are other similar provisions in s29(1) where a finance company relets a car under a new hire purchase arrangement; once the new hirer has paid the payment instalments he will acquire good title even if, in the interval the true facts have become known. This is of course always subject to his being of good faith and without notice at the time he actually entered the hire purchase contract.

Note: There are, other minor exceptions, which any textbook will deal with, but space means they cannot all be listed here.

10.3 Analysis of questions

A number of questions have occurred which deal with the 'nemo dat' rule; though not all of them require any treatment of any or all of the exceptions listed in this chapter. Question 3 on the 1983 University of London Commercial Law paper covers aspects of 'nemo dat', some exceptions, combining with remedies under the 1977 Torts (Interference with Goods) Act when exceptions to 'nemo dat' may deprive a rightful owner of title. A number of questions, including Q2 of the 1986 paper (as quoted in chapter 4), cover the general pattern of implied terms of SGA: title, nemo dat and other related sale of goods matters. These generalised problems may be slanted in a number of ways according to subject matter, some requiring more attention to one aspect, some to another. In 1988 in Q4 of the University of London's Commercial Law paper, for a change, the topic of nemo dat and its exceptions was linked with some (fairly straightfoward) aspects of agency. Look at Q5, 1991 (quoted below) and compare it with Q6, 1992 (see chapter 15). They have very similar sections on nemo dat and mercantile agents.

The second question quoted below is fairly typical of the sort of approach found in any Commercial Law examination.

10.4 Questions

Question 1

Elmo contracts to sell his motorcycle for £1,000 to Felicity, who pays him a twenty per cent deposit and agrees to pay the rest after the motorcycle has been serviced. Elmo takes the motorcycle to a garage owned by Gillian, who suggests to Elmo that it is worth much more than £1,000. Elmo therefore asks her to see if she can obtain any higher offers for it.

Hilary, another one of Gillian's customers, sees the motorcycle and tells Gillian that she is willing to pay £1,200 on behalf of her husband, Jacko, who is looking for a new machine. She asks Gillian to carry out a complete overhaul, for which she agrees to pay a further £200.

When Gillian finishes the work, Jacko borrows the motorcycle for a week to take Hilary on holiday. Afterwards, he returns it to Gillian for some final adjustments. At the same time as Jacko returns to take final delivery and to pay, Elmo and Felicity arrive at the garage. Each of them also demands it from Gillian.

Advise the parties.

University of London LLB Examination
(for External Students) Commercial Law June 1991 Q5

Skeleton solution

- SGA ss17 & 18; passing of property.
- Mercantile agents, Factors Act 1889.
- Nemo dat rule.

- Exceptions.
- On approval?
- Remedies.

Suggested solution

Under the provisions of the Sale of Goods Act 1979 (SGA), where there is a sale of, or agreement to sell, goods, property in the goods will pass at different times according to the nature of the goods and the intentions of the parties.

In the case of specific goods (in this case Elmo's (E) motorcycle) it is ss17-18 of the SGA which are relevant. Section 17 dictates that where there is such a contract, property passes when the parties intend it to pass, and that intention shall be ascertained by reference to the terms and circumstances of the contract, and also to the various 'rules' in s18. Rule 1 of s18 provides that if there is an unconditional sale of specific goods in a deliverable state then property passes to the buyer at the point when the contract is made, regardless of time of payment or time of delivery. The term 'unconditional' appears to refer to any conditions that might indicate that property is to pass at a particular point. Is the sale in question conditional? There is really nothing to indicate from the wording of the question that either E or Felicity (F) is making the service of the bike and its successful conclusion the point at which property will pass. F does not for example say: 'If you can get that motorbike working, I will buy it.' She has already apparently bought it, and has merely deferred the main payment until after the service. Is the bike in a 'deliverable' state? Rule 2 provides that where the buyer is bound to do something to put the goods in a deliverable state, then property will not pass unless and until he does so. But again, the bike would appear to be in a deliverable state from the beginning; nothing is indicated to the contrary in the question and F does not ask for the bike to be made functional or assembled or painted a different colour or whatever.

On all the evidence, therefore, it seems that property will have passed to F at the point the contract is agreed. The fact that she still has to pay 80 per cent of the price and take delivery from E is immaterial. This being the case she will, of course, be entitled to damages for non delivery under s51 SGA. She might also have a right of action in tort for interference with goods against the others, but it is impossible to get a greater sum of damages in tort and the action in tort is rarely used. If the motorbike had been a museum piece or in some way unique, one might have been tempted to consider the possibility of specific performance, but this seems unlikely in the circumstances, damages providing a perfectly adequate remedy.

Of course if this assessment of the situation is wrong and E and F have made it clear by some means, express or implied, that property is not to pass until payment is complete, or is conditional on servicing of the motorbike to a particular standard, then obviously by the wishes of the parties property in the goods will not have passed to F and she has no real rights, other than the return of her deposit.

Elmo, we are told, takes the motorbike to a garage owned by Gillian (G) and accedes to her suggestion that she try to sell the bike for him. It seems likely that G is what is called a mercantile agent. Such a person will have some business in which he or she customarily sells such goods as are the subject of the dispute and the goods will be in possession of the mercantile agent with the consent of the owner. Such agents are governed by the Factors Act 1889.

There is in sale of goods law a maxim that 'Nemo dat quod non habet' that is to say no one can pass title in property who is not the rightful owner. In theory therefore if F is the rightful owner of the goods, then neither E nor his agent G may pass title to either Hilary (H) or Jacko (J). Section 21(1) of SGA provides ... 'where goods are sold by a person who is not their owner, and without the consent of the owner, the buyer acquires no better title ... than the seller had'. There are however a number of exceptions to this nemo dat rule, devised mainly to protect a buyer who in all good faith purchases goods which belong to someone other than the seller (*Bishopsgate Motor Finance Co* v *Transport Brakes* (1949)). One of the main exceptions is a sale by a mercantile agent and we therefore need to return to G to ascertain whether she is in fact a true mercantile agent under the Factors Act. The main requirements are: there must be a customary course of business, the agent must have usual authority to contract and need not seek specific authority for each act, the agent must be independent not an employee, and finally the agent will have possession of the goods with the consent of the owner. All of the above would seem to apply to G. She has a garage, 'an ordinary course of business'. She has the usual authority attributed to an independent garage owner, she is not an employee of E and she has at least the implied consent of F (whom one presumes to be the owner) in that F has agreed to the servicing. This is of course also true if E is still the owner: *Weiner* v *Harris* (1910) and *Pearson* v *Rose & Young* (1951)). The same considerations apply to the agreement between H and G as between E and F. We are told that H agrees to pay £1,200 and another £200 for an overhaul, but it is apparent from the fact that Jacko turns up 'to pay', that no initial payment is made. Therefore as a mercantile agent G can pass title to H, in an exception to the normal nemo dat rule, but does she? What are the intentions of the parties?

Jacko's act in borrowing the motorcycle for a week might be construed in two ways (note that the very use of the word 'borrowing' is an indication that the bike is not yet his!). First of all, it might be taken as confirmation of H and G's intentions. If property was intended to pass as of the moment of the agreement, regardless of time of delivery or payment, J's arrival to take the bike off for a week might be construed as an act consistent with ownership and thus indicate that property has indeed passed, even though payment has still to be made. Alternatively, however, Jacko's act might just be construed as taking out the bike 'on approval'. Admittedly the words are nowhere used by H in her agreement with G, but had she made a successful overhaul a condition of the sale, subject to satisfactory tests subsequently, this might apply to the transaction. Rule 4 of s18 SGA provides that property does not pass to the buyer until he either signifies his approval or does some act signifying approval. Until such time property remains in the seller or his agent. If such an act signifies approval, of course, property will in any event have passed when he returns it to G for final adjustments, unless these final adjustments too are a part of the approval period, which seems unlikely.

In order for a mercantile agent to pass good title, the buyer(s) must act in good faith and with no notice of the defect in the seller's title. The first indication that H and J appear to have of anything wrong is when all the parties turn up at G's garage together.

We are not told what, if any, document of title exists for the motorbike, or if its absence ought to make H and J suspicious, but unlike car log-books etc, it is unlikely that suspicions would be aroused by a motorbike without documentation.

So, to sum up. It seems that F is the true owner of the bike. Elmo has no further property in the bike. G, however, as a mercantile agent, may pass on property to H and J and it seems from the circumstances that she does do so. In any nemo dat case the question that tends to arise is which of two or more relatively innocent parties (F or H and J) is to suffer. Although it is impossible to satisfy everyone in such cases, F seems to be the one with least to lose and may easily obtain redress whereas if H and J are made to return the bike, then G may not receive money for the work she has done on their behalf. Such a compromise - to allow H and J to keep the bike - seems to be making the best of a complex situation.

Question 2

On 1 April 1984, Simpson, a car dealer, had on his forecourt:

1) a Renault;

2) a Ford; and

3) a Volvo.

A price guide circulating privately among car dealers estimated the value of the vehicles at £5,000, £4,500 and £6,000 respectively.

The following facts are subsequently established:

1) As to the Renault

   The car was left with Simpson on March 22 by Peter, who told him to obtain offers for it within one week. On 3 April, Simpson sold it to Grey for £4,500. He did not hand over the registration book. The book was discovered later in a locked glove compartment.

   Advise Peter's executors.

2) As to the Ford

   On 29 March the car had been sold to Simpson for £4,500 by Horner, another car dealer, 'on approval for 14 days'. On 2 April, Simpson sold it to Edwards for £5,100 'on approval for 14 days'. Edwards returned it to Simpson on 12 April in a damaged condition after using it in a stock car race. On 13 April, Simpson drove it to Horner's premises, and refused to pay him the price.

   Advise Simpson.

3) As to the Volvo

   On 15 March, Baker had left the car with Eversure Motors asking them to repair it.

On 25 March, Eversure Motors sold it to Simpson. Simpson failed to check with HP Information plc, who could have told him that it was the property of Northern Finance plc who had left it to Barker under a hire purchase agreement. On 8 April, which was a Sunday, Simpson sold it to Young, who wanted it partly for use in his business and partly for his own private purposes, for £5,500.

Advise Northern Finance plc.

University of London LLB Examination
(for External Students) Commercial Law 1984 Q3

Skeleton solution

- Nemo dat rule; s21 SGA.
- Simpson as mercantile agent? Estoppel?
- Sale or return; r4 of s18 SGA.
- Part III of Hire Purchase Act 1964 as amm Consumer Credit Act 1974.

Suggested solution

1) *The Renault*

The starting point in advising Peter's executors is to consider the common law maxims, 'nemo dat quod non habet' and 'caveat emptor'. This is to say that at common law a transferor of goods cannot pass a better title to goods than he possesses and 'buyer beware'. These common law notions have now received statutory effect and are to be found in s21 of the Sale of Goods Act 1979 and therefore prima facie Grey will not obtain a good title to the Renault.

There are exceptions to these provisions and it is necessary to consider whether the executors fall foul of these. The first exception is that of agency. It is clear that Simpson did not have actual authority to make the sale but did he have apparent authority? The actual authority he gave was for Simpson to obtain offers for the car for one week from 22 March. Even if that authority extended by consent for longer than one week, it terminated on Peter's death on 2 April, one day before the sale.

In considering his apparent authority it is necessary to consider whether Simpson was acting as a mercantile agent within the meaning of the Factors Act 1889. It matters not that he was only acting for Peter in this one transaction for he can still be a 'mercantile agent': *Weiner* v *Harris* (1910). Section 2(1) of the Factors Act 1889 provides that where a mercantile agent is, with the consent of the owner, in possession of goods or documents of title to goods, any sale made by him when acting in the ordinary course of business of a mercantile agent shall be as valid as if he were expressly authorised by the owner of the goods to make the same, provided that the person taking under the disposition acts in good faith and has not at the time of the disposition notice that the person making the disposition has not authority to make the same. It is clear that Simpson came into possession of the car with the consent of Peter and he came into possession in his capacity as a mercantile agent. I am not informed as to the bona fides of Grey but even presuming that they exist, he will not receive good title under the Factors Act because the sale was not in the ordinary course of business of a mercantile agent in that the car was sold without the registration book and further, although the book was in the car it cannot be said to have been in Simpson's possession with Peter's consent: *Pearson* v *Rose & Young* (1951). Of course, if Peter had consented to Simpson having the book and that consent was not initiated by being obtained by a fraud, then the sale would be valid if the other factors were present.

Assuming that Grey cannot establish title under the Factors Act, it is unlikely that he will be able to raise any estoppel since *Moorgate Mercantile Co Ltd* v *Twitchings* (1976), and further it is unlikely that he will be able to claim that Simpson had 'apparent ownership' of the car as the log book would have shown that this was not the case. Therefore unless he can show that the sale took place in a market within the provisions of s22(1) of the Sale of Goods Act 1979, he will have to return the car to the executors and pursue his remedy against Simpson.

2) *The Ford*

The agreement between Simpson and Horner was not in the true sense a contract for sale or agreement to sell because it was expressed to be 'on approval for 14 days'. The effect of these words by virtue of s18 r4 of the Sale of Goods Act 1979 is that property does not pass to the 'buyer' until he either signifies his approval or does some other act adopting the transaction, or retains the goods without giving notice of rejection, beyond the time fixed for the return of the goods.

Until the property in the goods passes the risk remains with the seller unless a contrary intention is to be found from the agreement. This in effect means that if the goods, in the possession of the buyer are damaged, the seller bears the loss although the buyer does have the usual bailee's duty to take reasonable care of them.

In this matter Simpson took the Ford on approval and so at that stage property did not pass to him and accordingly risk remained with the seller. On 2 April he sold the car 'on approval' to Edwards and again at that stage property could not pass to Edwards by virtue of s18 r4. However, it is arguable that this 'sale' was an act adopting the transaction with Horner and thus passing the property to Simpson because Edwards would be entitled to keep the goods after the period of Simpson's 'approval' had ended. There are no cases on this point and it is likely that this argument would not succeed in the court because at the time of the 'sale by approval' to Edwards property did not pass, nor was it represented that it would pass to him.

If this is the case then Simpson's returning the car within the 14-day period would probably mean that he was not liable for the damage caused. However, as he failed to return the car within the time period the property passes to him in accordance with s18 r4 and he is liable to pay £4,500 for the car. Property did not pass to Edwards as he returned the car within the 14-day period, but he will be liable for the damage to the car because he was in breach of the bailee's duty to take reasonable care of bailed goods by entering it for a stock car race.

3) *The Volvo*

The first question that must be answered in this matter is whether Simpson received a good title to the Volvo. The prima facie position is that Barker did not receive property in the car because he was purchasing on hire purchase and he would not receive property until he had paid all the instalments due and a purchase fee. He could not pass property to Eversure Motors who in turn could not pass it to Simpson. This is an application of the nemo dat non quod habet rule, that is, that a transferor of goods cannot pass a better title to goods than he possesses, see s21 of the Sale of Goods Act 1979.

Simpson will not be able to rely on the Factors Act 1889 as it is clear that Eversure Motors did not get possession of the Volvo with the consent of the owner, as a mercantile agent within that Act. Further, Simpson will not be able to rely on ostensible ownership as it is unlikely that Northern Finance could have given Eversure Motors the indicia of title to the vehicle. Simpson is a car dealer and as such he will not be granted any relief by reason of Part III of the Hire Purchase Act 1964 as amended by the Consumer Credit Act 1974 as he is not a private purchaser even if he only works part-time in the buying and selling of cars: *Stevenson* v *Beverley Bentinck Ltd* (1976).

The only way in which Simpson could claim property in the car would be by showing that the sale to him was in a market overt - s22(1) Sale of Goods Act 1979 - and even then he would have to show that he bought in good faith and without notice of any defect of title. He sold the car for less than a price guide indicated it was worth and this could indicate a lack of good faith, although it is not conclusive. Further, he did not contact HP Information plc which would have informed him of the true state of affairs and it could be held that due to this failure he had 'notice' of the true ownership. This is unlikely in view of the observations made in *Moorgate Mercantile Co Ltd* v *Twitchings* (1976) but is always possible.

The most likely state of affairs is that Simpson did not obtain property in the vehicle and thus it remains to be decided as to whether or not Young obtained such. It is unlikely that he would be able to claim that this was a sale in a market overt because it took place on a Sunday which presumably is not a customary time. Young's only claim is under Part III of the 1964 Act. If he is a trade purchaser he will not be protected and thus it is important to ascertain his business. If he is held to be a private purchaser that is not an end to the matter for he has to show that Barker's 'disposed' of the goods to Eversure Motors. As Baker did not 'dispose' of the goods under a contract of sale or hire purchase Young will not be protected and Northern Finance are entitled to the return of the car.

11 REAL REMEDIES OF THE SELLER

11.1 Introduction

Sections 38-50 of SGA deal with the rights of the seller should things go wrong. It should be noted that a seller may have *real* remedies, ie remedies against the goods themselves or *personal* remedies, ie rights against the buyer personally. Essentially there are three main real remedies: the right of lien, the right of stoppage in transit and the right of resale.

Often the first two remedies will serve as a preliminary procedure to the act of resale since this is what most sellers will have to do in order to recoup their loss.

The remedies themselves have in the past been subject to some confusion largely resulting from ambiguities in the legislation. Case law has clarified some of the more obscure areas and the student should therefore make sure that he is particularly familiar with relevant case law. The remedies only become available when the buyer defaults and the initial problem is to define the terms 'unpaid' in the context of SGA.

11.2 Key points

It is important that the student understands the following:

a) *The meaning of 'unpaid seller'*

Section 38(1) of SGA provides:

'The seller of goods is deemed to be an "unpaid seller" within the meaning of this Act:

a) when the whole of the price has not been paid or tendered;

b) when a bill of exchange or other negotiable instrument which has been received as conditional payment, and the condition on which it was received has not been fulfilled by reason of the dishonour of the instrument or otherwise.'

The effect of s38 if interpreted literally is that a seller may be unpaid if *any part* of the whole price has not been paid or tendered. Even a minimal amount left unpaid, would, strictly speaking, leave the seller 'unpaid'.

Section 38(2) goes on to define seller and explains that the term will include a person representing, or in the position of the seller such as an agent or consignor.

b) *The unpaid seller's right of lien*

Section 39(1)(a) provides for the basic right of lien and ss41-43 dictate the circumstances under which the right of lien must be exercised.

Section 41 provides that an unpaid seller in possession of goods is entitled to keep them:

'a) When the goods have been sold without any stipulation as to credit.

b) When the goods have been sold on credit, but the term of credit has expired.

c) Where the buyer becomes insolvent.'

The goods must actually be in the possession of the seller before a lien can operate. The right of lien is then a right to keep the goods until the whole of the purchase price has been paid or tendered. It should be noted that the seller cannot exercise a right of lien with regard to debts generally owed him by the buyer, but only in regard to non-payment for those specific goods only.

Section 42 dictates that where an unpaid seller has made a part delivery of the goods he can exercise a lien over the remainder, but where there are a number of separate contracts, each contract to be paid for separately, the old case of *Merchant Banking Co* v *Phoenix Bessemer Steel Ltd* (1877) 5 Ch D 205 makes it clear that the right of lien extends to goods unpaid for in the present contract only.

The right of lien may be lost by virtue of a whole host of different circumstances. They include:

i) when the seller ceases to be 'unpaid';

ii) when the seller delivers the goods to a carrier or other bailee for the purpose of delivery to the buyer (but note that he may still have a right of stoppage in transit - see below);

iii) when the buyer, or his agent, lawfully (that is, with the consent of the seller) obtains possession of the goods;

iv) when the buyer gets possession of the documents of title to the goods; s47(2) SGA provides that if this is, lawfully, transferred to a third party who takes in good faith and for valuable consideration, then provided this transfer can be defined as a sale, the unpaid seller's lien is defeated;

v) s47(1) provides that a sale or other disposition of the goods by the buyer, *if consented to by the original seller* will defeat the first seller's right of lien. Note that the seller must consent; merely for the buyer to inform him is not sufficient;

vi) when a seller waives his right of lien; it cannot subsequently be resurrected.

c) *Right of stoppage in transit*

The right of stoppage is conferred in s39(1)(b) and the conditions under which it may be exercised defined in s44 SGA. Note that the right of stoppage is exercisable only where the buyer is insolvent. A definition of insolvency is provided by s61(4) SGA:

'a person is deemed to be insolvent ... if he has either ceased to pay his debts in the ordinary course of business, or he cannot pay his debts as they become due, whether he has committed an act of bankruptcy or not ...'

Though apparently straightforward, defining insolvency can present problems. It is unclear whether the unpaid seller can exercise his right of stoppage on the basis of rumours, for instance. Certainly if the seller wrongly exercises a right of stoppage he may face action from the buyer.

Section 45 SGA deals with the definition of 'in transit' and has clarified much of the ambiguity formerly attaching to this phrase.

Basically goods are in transit when they have passed into the possession of an independent carrier; but this is much oversimplified and the student would be advised to read further to familiarise himself with the concept. Certainly it is usually fairly easy to determine the starting point of transit, but the point where it ends is less easy to predict. Transit does not always mean the goods must be in motion; they might be stored somewhere and still be in transit. Section 46 SGA makes provision as regards the actual methods for 'stoppage'.

An unpaid seller can exercise his rights either by physically taking possession of the goods and thereby preventing transit, or more likely, by notifying the carrier that he is exercising his right of stoppage. If a carrier has been sent a notice of stoppage and he still delivers the goods to the buyer he will be liable for wrongful interference. At the same time, it should also be noted the unpaid seller's right of stoppage may have to take second place to any rights of lien the carrier may have for unpaid freight costs.

d) *Right of resale*

Section 48 SGA governs the unpaid seller's right of resale.

Section 48(2) provides:

'Where an unpaid seller who has exercised his right of lien or stoppage in transit resells the goods, the buyer acquires good title ... as against the original buyer.'

This makes it clear that the right of resale under this subsection cannot be exercised without first asserting either a right of lien, or stoppage in transit.

Section 48(3) provides:

'Where the goods are of a perishable nature or where the unpaid seller gives notice ... of his intention to resell, and the buyer does not within a reasonable time pay or tender the price, the unpaid seller may resell the goods and recover from the original buyer damages for any loss occasioned by his breach of contract.'

This subsection is self explanatory. Essentially with regard to perishable goods it makes time of payment 'of the essence' and allows a seller to treat the contract as repudiated where a buyer delays unreasonably in payment for perishable goods. In the case of goods other than perishable; the service of a notice (as outlined in s48(3) above) on the buyer, informs him that the seller is now making time 'of the essence'. Section 48(4) gives the seller a right of resale if he originally reserved such a right expressly.

Finally, it should be noted that if the seller still has property in the goods or if property has passed to the buyer but he still has possession, he may not need to invoke s48. A power of sale may exist under s24 of SGA. (See 'sale by a seller in possession', chapter 10.)

11.3 Analysis of questions

There have been surprisingly few questions specifically on the real remedies of an unpaid seller. In earlier chapters it has been noted already, that a certain form of problem on sale of goods is quite popular; which demands a knowledge which is fairly superficial of differing aspects of the Sale of Goods Act. Sometimes this may include some brief reference to seller's remedies. The question below is one of the very few to deal with the topic in the University of London's past papers.

11.4 Question

a) How are the rights of an unpaid seller under Part V of the Sale of Goods Act 1979 to be reconciled with his duties under s28 of the Act?

b) Laurie, a London electrical wholesaler, contracts to sell with free delivery at Nottingham, payment to be net cash within one month, goods as follows: on 1 January, 300 personal computers to each of Ben and Cartwright; and, on 15 January, 200 videos to Joe. Laurie despatches the goods by rail to Nottingham and supplies each buyer with a delivery warrant. Within a fortnight, Ben collects his computers from British Rail. On 4 February, Laurie reads in a trade paper that certain (unnamed) Nottingham electrical retailers are unable to pay their debts as they fall due and realises that none of the three buyers has paid him. He immediately instruct British Rail to suspend all further deliveries and telegraphs the buyers that he requires cash before delivery. The next day, Cartwright and Joe present their delivery warrants to British Rail. British Rail immediately advises Laurie of this fact and requires instructions.

   Advise Laurie.

University of London LLB Examination
(for External Students) Commercial Law 1987 Q5

Skeleton solution

a) • Section 28 SGA seller's duty to be ready and willing to give possession.

- Sections 38-48 seller's right to refuse possession - real remedies especially lien, stoppage and re-sale.

b) Laurie's sales:

- remedy under s49 only;
- stoppage in transit;
- no real remedy - Joe not insolvent.

Suggested solution

a) *Seller's duties*

The seller's duty is to deliver goods which comply with the contractual requirements as to description, quality and quantity. Section 28, however, only states the duty to be ready and willing to give possession but makes that duty concurrent with the buyer's duty to be ready and willing to pay the price. The real remedies in ss38-48 allow the seller to refuse to give possession at all, or to delay the giving of possession, depending on the circumstances.

The real remedies are three: a right of lien, a right of stoppage in transit and a right to resell. The third remedy is a consequence of the first two, in other words without exercise of the lien or the right of stoppage the seller is not allowed to resell. The two main remedies are only available when the seller has not been paid, although he is an unpaid seller even if the price has not yet fallen due to be paid. The right of lien can be exercised where the price is due and has not been paid or where the buyer is insolvent regardless of whether the price is due. The buyer is insolvent where he has ceased to pay his debts as they fall due or is incapable of paying them as they fall due (s61(4) Sale of Goods Act 1979).

By definition, once the buyer is insolvent he cannot be ready and willing to pay for the goods, and it follows from that that he cannot comply with his obligation to make payment in return for delivery. We have seen that s28 makes it the seller's duty to be ready and willing to pay and so long as the buyer's duty to be ready and willing it makes sense that the seller should have the right to withhold delivery.

The seller may, of course, be entitled to treat the contract as discharged, but this will only be possible where the buyer's insolvency amounts to a repudiatory breach, which it normally will not do (*Ex parte Chalmers* (1873)). If the buyer has not committed such a breach then the lien allows the seller who is still in physical possession to retain possession unless he waives that right (ss41 and 43 Sale of Goods Act 1979).

Similarly, if the seller has sent the goods by independent carrier to the buyer, he may order the carrier to withhold delivery. This remedy can only be exercised if the buyer is insolvent, but if the price has fallen due and has not been paid then he will be insolvent. The seller can then make time of payment of the essence by giving notice of his intention to resell and if the buyer does not pay within a reasonable time then he will have committed a repudiatory breach and the seller will be entitled to treat the contract as discharged by re-selling and the new buyer will obtain good title as against the insolvent buyer (s48(2) Sale of Goods Act 1979).

In this respect the wording of s28 is rather unfortunate, because it refers to the duties of delivery and payment as concurrent 'conditions'. This does not mean that unreadiness or unwillingness to make payment is always a breach of condition, because if it were the seller would always be entitled to resell on the buyer being unready or unwilling. The use of 'condition' in s28 denotes that the obligations are mutually dependent, not that they are conditions in the way the most important terms implied in ss12 to 15 are conditions.

b) *Laurie's computers*

Laurie has made three contracts of sale, one each to Ben, Cartwright and Joe. It was agreed that payment would not be due on delivery but that the buyers had one month in which to pay. Although it is not entirely clear from the facts given it will be assumed that they had one month from the time of sale. Laurie is an unpaid seller in relation to all three buyers, although only Ben and Cartwright are due to pay already.

Ben has collected his computers but has not paid. Laurie's only remedy is to sue for the price. In the absence of a retention of ownership clause, property would have passed to Ben, at latest when he collected the computers. Laurie is therefore left with no remedy which can be exercised against the goods themselves but must settle for an action under s49. He is entitled to receive the price whether this is more or less than the goods would now be worth on the open market.

Cartwright should have paid by 1 February, because his 300 computers were sold to him on 1 January. The computers are still in the possession of British Rail, however, so Laurie may be able to exercise a remedy against the goods and will not necessarily have to sue Cartwright for money. British Rail is an independent carrier, not the agent of either Laurie or Cartwright. Delivery to a carrier is prima facie delivery to the buyer (s32(1) Sale of Goods Act 1979) but that rule does not prevail for present purposes over British Rail's status as an independent carrier. The fact that British Rail is an independent carrier means that Laurie has lost possession of the goods himself, so he will not be able to exercise a right of lien.

If Laurie is to be able to properly exercise a right of stoppage in transit he must be sure that Cartwright is insolvent. Furthermore, the expiry of the period of credit does not necessarily place Cartwright in repudiatory breach because the duty to pay is an innominate obligation and it would have to be shown that the breach here has been so serious as to go to the root of the contract before his breach would be repudiatory.

It is possible to say that Cartwright has not paid his debts as they fell due, because his debt to Laurie (the price) was due on a certain date (1 February) and was not paid. Therefore, Cartwright is insolvent. Laurie has ordered British Rail not to make delivery, and that is something he was entitled to do (s46(1) Sale of Goods Act 1979). He was also entitled to demand that Cartwright produce cash before the goods are released to him. No notice of intention to resell has been served by Laurie, but there is no evidence that he wishes to resell. The position, therefore, is that Cartwright has committed a non-repudiatory breach and Laurie has properly exercised his right of stoppage in transit. If Cartwright wants the goods he must pay cash as demanded. Laurie may serve a notice of intention to resell which will give Cartwright a reasonable time in which to come up with the money, if he fails to do this then Laurie may resell and the new buyer will obtain good title to the goods as against Cartwright. The contract with Cartwright will then be rescinded (*RV Ward Ltd* v *Bignall* (1967)).

By 4 February Joe's obligation to pay had not yet crystallised, because his purchase was made on 15 January. Therefore, although Laurie is still an unpaid seller so far as Joe is concerned Joe is not insolvent and therefore Laurie has no real remedies against the goods. The order to British Rail not to deliver and their apparent refusal to deliver against the warrant presented by Joe, was a breach by Laurie, which was compounded by the telegraph message he sent demanding payment of cash against the goods. It cannot be said with any certainty whether this breach is repudiatory but the presumption is that time of delivery is of the essence (*Hartley* v *Hymans* (1920)) and there seems to be no reason why that presumption should not apply here. But Joe has waived any right that he may have to treat the contract as discharged because he actually presented his warrant, thereby showing that he was not electing to discharge the contract following receipt of the telegraph message. Laurie, therefore, should countermand his order to British Rail not to deliver to Joe and wait until either he has evidence of Joe's insolvency, rather than mere suspicion, or until 15th and then sue for the price.

12 PERSONAL REMEDIES OF THE SELLER

12.1 Introduction

It was noted in the last chapter that the seller's remedies might be divided into real remedies and personal. Personal remedies are those against the buyer himself rather than to seize or retain or resell the goods. Sections 49-50 SGA lay down two forms of action: an action for the price of the goods sold or an action for damages for non-acceptance of goods. The basic difference between them is that an action for the price of the goods is appropriate where the property in the goods has passed to the buyer; whereas if the property has not passed an action for damages would be the most suitable form of remedy for the seller. Sometimes property will have passed to the buyer, but he refuses to accept the goods and in such cases the seller will have a choice of actions.

12.2 Key points

It is important that the student understands the following:

a) *The action for the price of the goods sold*

Section 49(1) provides that:

'Where, under a contract of sale, the property in goods had passed to the buyer and he wrongfully neglects or refuses to pay ... the seller may maintain an action against him for the price of the goods.'

Section 49(2) goes on to provide one exceptional case when the seller may pursue an action for the price, even though property in the goods has not yet passed. It states:

'Where, under a contract of sale, the price is payable on a certain day, irrespective of delivery, and the buyer wrongfully neglects or refuses to pay ... the seller may maintain an action for the price, even though the property has not passed and the goods have not been appropriated to the contract.'

These two subsections are self-explanatory. It should be noted however that of the two courses of action for the seller to take, the possibility of bringing an action for the price of goods sold is likely to be financially less rewarding. In general there will be a substantial difference between simply claiming the price of goods sold and claiming damages for non-acceptance. The latter sum is invariably larger. If a seller opts for the wrong course of action, for example, if he is unsure of whether property has passed to the buyer or not he may find himself considerably out of pocket.

For example, if he sues for the price of the goods, on the basis that property has passed, he may be wrong. In such a case, his ultimate damages would be reduced because he had not mitigated his loss as obliged to do so.

Alternatively, if he guesses wrong and re-sells or attempts to resell the goods on the basis that property has not passed and it transpires that the buyer has property after all, a court may treat the seller's acts of resale as an acceptance of the buyer's repudiation of the contract. In such a case he will lose his right of action for the price of the goods because the goods will have been held to re-vest in him.

b) *The action for damages for non-acceptance of the goods*

Section 50(1) provides:

'Where the buyer wrongfully neglects or refuses to accept or pay for the goods, the seller may maintain an action for damages for non-acceptance'

which is, in any case, merely a re-statement of what the common law implies anyway. The method of calculating damages is governed by the common law rule in *Hadley* v *Baxendale* (1854) which has been incorporated into the various subsections of s50 SGA. In particular s50(2) provides:

'The measure of damages is the estimated loss, directly and naturally resulting in the ordinary course of events, from the buyer's breach of contract'

and s50(3) goes on:

'where there is an available market for the goods in question, the measure of damages is prima facie to be ascertained by the difference between the contract price and the market or current price at the time or times when the goods ought to have been accepted (or if no time was fixed) at the time of refusal to accept.'

This subsection is largely self-explanatory. Should there be more than one available market, the relevant place is wherever the goods were to be delivered under the contract.

Note that s50 lays down a series of prima facie rules which may be rebutted should there be evidence that the use of s50 rules will not result in a proper assessment of damages. The onus of proof is on the seller to establish the assessment of damages will not be correct. Cases such as *Thompson Ltd* v *Robinson (Gunmakers) Ltd* [1955] Ch 17 and *Charter* v *Sullivan* [1957] 2 QB 117 have established that the courts may be persuaded to set s50 aside if it seems inappropriate in the circumstances. Where s50(3) SGA does apply, the measure of damages is based on a fictitious sale by the seller on the available market. If the seller has in fact resold at a price less than the notional 'available market price' he may find it difficult to convince the courts that he acted reasonably and to recover the difference between the two prices. If he sells at more than the 'available market price' the buyer will almost certainly seek to have damages restricted to the amount of difference between contract and resale prices. 'Available market' was further defined in *Shearson Lehman Hutton* v *McLaine Watson & Co (No 2)* [1990] 3 All ER 723.

12.3 Analysis of questions

Questions as to sellers' personal remedies have occurred several times over the past eleven years in University of London past papers. Almost always, the subject has been combined with some other topic. In 1984 for example, it was necessary to deal in almost equal detail with the remedies of both buyer and seller in order to answer Question 4 appropriately. Again in 1987, Question 3, the two topics were combined. See also Q6 1993. The question quoted below is unusual in that it requires more detail than would normally be the case on the topic of common law damages and associated topics.

Nevertheless it is a useful question to study as it raises a number of issues relevant to seller's personal remedies.

12.4 Question

a) 'The law of contract compensates for damages resulting from the defendant's breach; it does not compensate a plaintiff for damages resulting from his making a bad bargain.' (per Berger J in *Bowlay Logging Ltd* v *Domtar Ltd* [1978] 4 WWR 105, at 117).

   Discuss.

b) In April 1982, Blue agreed to buy from Saul two portable generators priced £5,000 each, for delivery on 1 July 1983. To the knowledge of Saul, Blue required the first generator to power his factory in the event of an electricity cut, and the second for resale. Saul had not delivered either generator by July 1984, when Blue decided to commence an action for damages. The price of a similar generator was £2,500, on 1 July 1983, but has now risen to £5,000. Blue also wishes to claim the following special damage: first £3,500 net profit lost whilst his factory production was halted by a power cut during the winter 1983/84; and second, the £4,000 clear profit he would have made under a contract made in May 1982 to sell a generator of those specifications for delivery in August 1983.

   Advise Blue.

University of London LLB Examination
(for External Students) Commercial Law June 1985 Q4

Skeleton solution

a) • Define question, discuss *Bowlay* case briefly.
   • Commercial law rules as to damages *Hadley* v *Baxendale*.

b) • First generator: time of delivery nature of term breached - available market first head of *Hadley* v *Baxendale.*

  • Second generator - second head of *Hadley* v *Baxendale.*

  • Overall advice.

Suggested solution

a) The *Bowlay Logging* case (1978) concerned with agreed damages clauses, was concerned with the circumstances in which damages will be awarded to compensate for wasted expenditure rather than loss of profit, and it is to this issue that the rest of this answer will be directed.

The general rule in contract is that damages are awarded on a 'loss of bargain' basis. In other words, the courts attempt to put the injured party into the position in which he would have been had the contract been performed properly. The provisions of the Sale of Goods Act 1979 relating to damages stress the loss of bargain measure as being the proper assessment. For example, by virtue of s51(3) the damages payable by the seller who fails to deliver are to be assessed at the difference between the contract price and the available market price at the time the goods should have been delivered. The theory behind this measure is clear. If the goods had been delivered the buyer would have paid the contract price and received goods which were worth the market price at the time of delivery. He could then have sold them, had he so wished, at a profit - his bargain with the seller was that he would make this profit in the capital value of the goods; the failure to deliver prevents this profit being made and therefore the amount of lost profit is the measure of damages. There can be problems in other contexts, however, where it is not easy to assess loss of bargain damages, and it is to these cases that the alternative measure - wasted expenditure - is directed.

The common description of wasted expenditure damages is 'reliance interest' damages. Loss of bargain damages can be put in terms of an interest which is injured, namely the 'expectation interest'. There is sometimes said to be a third type of interest which needs to be protected, the 'restitution interest' (These interests are identified by Fuller and Perdue, 'The Reliance Interest in Contract Damages' (1936) 46 Yale LJ 52 and 373. The restitution interest is not relevant to the problem under consideration here, so no more will be said about it.). These 'interests' are useful analytical tools in that they indicate how the breach of a contract may lead to three different types of loss - it may be that the innocent party has conferred a benefit on the breaker, or he may have spent money preparing to perform the contract, or he may have been expecting to make a profit which he can no longer make (see Fuller and and Perdue at pp53-57). If he has conferred a benefit on the breaker it is reasonable to suggest that the benefit should be repaid; if he has spent money which has been wasted it is reasonable to suggest that he should get it back; if he has failed to make his expected profit it is reasonable to suggest that he receive the profit as an award of damages. In many cases the interests are not separate entities, but are complementary. For example, if A buys a knitting machine in order to set up business selling to B who has promised to buy a certain number of items; the failure of B to honour his part of the bargain will lead to injury to A's reliance interest and his expectation interest - A will have wasted money on a machine and will have lost the expected profits on sale of the knitted items. But to give A the full value of the machine and the full profit would be to allow him to make an additional profit from B's breach, because he would have had to buy the machine in order to make a profit on sale of the end product. It is the overlap of reliance interest and expectation interest which has caused most problems in this area. To use an example given by Fuller and Perdue (see pp74): if a building contractor builds half of a structure and then the property owner tells him to stop one can see his reliance interest being rewarded by damages equalling the amount he spent on the half that he built, and his expectation interest being compensated by payment of the final profits; but a combination of both would be to give double recovery. Had he finished the work he would have spent twice the amount he did spend in order to earn the same expectation interest. The proper measure of damages in such a case is to give the builder the full expectation interest minus the amount of expenditure saved by not having to build the other half of the house. This, in the circumstances is his net expectation interest loss. If we change the example a little, it can be seen how important it is to bear in mind the overall position. Say the builder was to be paid £5,000 by the time the work was stopped; it would be futile to suggest that there is any realism in looking to his reliance interest alone. Clearly in reliance on the promise by the property owner that he would pay £5,000 for the structure the builder incurred expenses, equally clearly the promise of the owner was not kept. But if the promise had been kept, if the contract had not been terminated early, the builder would have spent far in excess of the price of £5,000. Only by considering both his reliance interest and his expectation interest it is possible to reach the proper figure of damage.

It is to this latter sort of case that the words of Berger J in *Bowlay Logging* (1978), were directed. The builder in the revised example, above, made a bad bargain. He had agreed to do work for £5,000 which would cost him more than that to complete. The cause of his loss was not the breach of contract but the bad bargain he made in the first place. It is only if the breach by the owner causes the loss that the builder could recover any damages.

The argument so far has attempted to show that in principle three rules on the award of damages can be identified:

1) If it can be proved that the plaintiff would have made an overall profit on performance of the contract then he should recover that profit.

2) If it can be proved that the plaintiff would have made a loss had the contract been performed then he can only receive damages if the breach has caused him to incur a greater loss.

3) If it cannot be proved what would have happened on performance of the contract, then one must consider whether the plaintiff should receive any damages, and if so how much.

These rules draw on two principles, first that damages should compensate an innocent party affected by the breach by the other party of the contract and second, that it is not satisfactory to consider just reliance interest or just expectation interest. It must be borne in mind that the exact quantification of damages in each of the first two cases will depend on the law's idea of loss, namely non-remote loss as defined in *Hadley* v *Baxendale* (1854) and subsequent cases (see particularly *Victoria* v *Newman Industries* (1949) and *The Heron II* (1969)).

In all cases there is the risk that the innocent party will suffer some remote loss which he can prove but cannot recover.

In some circumstances the law refuses to look at expectation interest because it is too difficult to assess. For example, the rule in *Bain* v *Fothergill* (1874) limits damages to wasted expenditure where the vendor of real property fails to make a good title. The reason is that the value of property is never static and the fluidity of the market could lead to greater difficulties of quantification. *Bain* v *Fothergill* also illustrates that the law will not award expectation interest damages (loss of profit) where that could be an unreasonably high sum bearing in mind the relatively minor nature of the breach. In many ways the law on impossibility and frustration can be justified with similar policy arguments (Fuller and Perdue at pp377-386). In the event of frustration there is no award of damages because as a matter of policy that would be too harsh. It may be that one party would have made a profit had the contract been performed, but he cannot recover from the other party because there is no justice in making someone compensate another for loss outside his own control. *Bain* v *Fothergill* could be seen to be a policy decision limiting damages because any sharp rise in property prices which would have led to the buyer making a profit are not under the control of the vendor, he may pay something, but full loss of profit would not be fair (it must not be forgotten that the rule in *Bain* v *Fothergill* has been criticised, perhaps this just reflects differences of opinion of policy). These special cases apart, the law leans strongly in favour of awarding full compensation.

With this general principle in mind - that full compensation should follow a breach of contract - we must return to the question of whether damages should be awarded when it cannot be proved whether there was a loss of profit or not, and if so, how those damages should be measured. The first matter that must be covered is that of the burden of proof. Normally the plaintiff bears the burden of proving his claim in a civil case (*Abrath* v *NE Railway* (1883)). In a contract case, when considering damages, the plaintiff, clearly, would want to prove the maximum possible figure as his loss. If he cannot prove that he would suffer a loss of profit then, according to this general rule he would be awarded nothing if loss of profit, or expectation interest, were the only possible measure of damages. Therefore the position in English law is that if the plaintiff claims wasted expenditure as his monetary remedy, then the burden of proof is put onto the defendant to prove that in fact the plaintiff would have made a loss overall (*CCC* v *Quadrant Films* (1984)). This rule is based on the premise that the plaintiff always has an unfettered choice between claiming wasted expenditure and claiming loss of profit (*Cullinane* v *British 'Rema'*

Manufacturing (1954)). That the right is unfettered is clear, what is often left obscure in the nature of the plaintiff's right.

The situation may be best summed up by saying that once he has established that there was a breach of contract, the innocent party (the plaintiff) should not suffer a loss at the end of the day; unless the evidence proves he would have made a loss even had the contract been properly performed. Therefore it is for the plaintiff to prove the breach and chose whether to claim for loss of profit or wasted expenditure.

b) *Blue v Saul*

This problem involves two contracts which will be considered separately.

i) For use in power cut

We are told that Blue has commenced an action for damages, but not whether the contract has been terminated. The duty to deliver is a condition of a sale contract at common law, because it is fundamental that the goods are delivered; it is also usually a condition that the goods are delivered at the time agreed (*Hartley* v *Hymans* (1920)). Therefore, in this case Saul committed a breach of condition on failing to deliver on 1 July 1983. Breach of condition does not automatically terminate the contract, however. Instead the innocent party has an option whether to terminate the contract and claim compensation in damages, or leave the contract open, thereby waiving the breach (*Tate & Lyle* v *Hain SS Co* (1936)), though it is important to remember that waiver of the 'breach' is somewhat misleading in that there is still a right to damages, all that is waived is the right to terminate the contract. It has been argued that on breach of condition the contract automatically ends unless the innocent party elects to keep it open, but the courts have not yet taken this approach. Therefore the contract did not automatically terminate when Saul breached the condition, rather it only terminated if Blue elected to terminate it. We are told that Blue only commenced his action for damages in 1984. This gives the impression that he considered the contract still to be open so that Saul could deliver late. If this is correct then the contract did not terminate in July 1983.

The election whether to terminate or keep open a contract on breach of condition must be exercised at the time of breach, therefore the failure to deliver on 1 July 1983 cannot now be a ground for attempting to terminate the contract. But, where a delivery time is agreed but not kept to, the seller is not then absolved from any obligation to deliver, rather he must deliver within a reasonable time, and failure to do so is a separate breach of condition (*Hartley* v *Hymans* (1920)). So, if the delay is so long as to amount to a repudiatory breach Blue could now terminate the contract. The length of delay required before the buyer may terminate the contract is always a matter of fact depending on all the circumstances of the case. The general test can be put in terms of frustration - if the delay would be a frustrating event if it happened without fault, then it is a repudiatory breach when it happens because of the seller's fault (*Borthwick* v *Bunge* (1969)). On the facts given there can be little doubt that the delay is so serious as to be a repudiatory breach. Therefore Blue is now entitled to terminate the contract.

The result of the discussion so far is that damages claimed by Blue will be assessed on the basis that the contract has been terminated. It may make some difference whether the termination occurred on 1 July 1983 or at a later date, and this point will be discussed as it arises.

Blue's first claim is for the loss of a capital asset. It is clear from s51(3) Sale of Goods Act 1979 that the normal measure of damages for failure to deliver is the excess of the available market price over the contract price. The reason for this has already been considered in part (a) of this answer. Two questions arise as to the use of s51 here: the first is whether there was an available market, the second is the time at which available market price should be measured.

The meaning of available market has never been made clear by the courts. The purpose of the available market test is to set a standard for the measure of damages under the first head of *Hadley* v *Baxendale.* If the goods had been delivered to the buyer in compliance with the terms of the contract then he would have paid the contract price and received goods of a certain value. It may be that the actual value of the goods is less than he paid for them, or it may be that their actual value is higher than the contract price, or it may be that the price agreed is an accurate reflection of their value on delivery. The buyer will only be able to claim damages for non-delivery if he can prove that the value on delivery would have exceeded the agreed price. This is the sum payable under the first head of *Hadley* v *Baxendale* because it is the loss which will be incurred in every case where the seller fails to deliver. The available market test aims to lay down a rule for assessing the true value the goods would have had if delivered on time. The theory, then, is simple - available market price is equal to the true value of the goods at the time they should have been delivered. But the difficulty arises when one tries to consider how to measure this value. Various methods have been suggested by the courts, some in cases of non-delivery and some in cases of non-acceptance (because the available market test also arises in s50(3) Sale of Goods Act 1979). Running through all of the definitions is the practical consideration that the innocent buyer who has failed to receive goods he contracted for will usually want to buy similar goods therefore the available market test must bear some relation to whether it was possible for the buyer to buy substitute goods. It has been suggested that there is only an available market if there is a physical place at which goods of the type concerned can be bought and sold (*Dunkirk Colliery* v *Lever* (1878); and see Waters, 'The Concept of Market in the Sale of Goods' (1958) 36 Can BR 360, 373). In other cases the need for a physical location as the market has been said to be irrelevant and that what is important is whether identical goods could have been bought from somewhere by the buyer (*Marshall* v *Nicoll* (1919); *The*

Arpad (1934) and see Waters (pp373-375). At other times, in the context of damages for non-acceptance, it has been said that there is an available market provided the goods which the buyer failed to accept could be sold by the seller (*Thompson* v *Robinson* (1955)), but this argument can only be used in relation to non-delivery if the buyer could buy identical goods, although there are suggestions in *Thompson* v *Robinson* that in cases of non-delivery what is important is whether it was possible for the buyer to buy goods to satisfy his want, they need not be identical.

The time set in s51(3) for assessing available market price is the time at which the goods should have been delivered. In this case that was 1 July 1983, originally, but may have been altered by Blue's waiver of the initial breach. The effect of his waiver would be to substitute 'within a reasonable time' for 'by 1 July 1983' as the time for delivery. Therefore it would appear that available market price should be measured at either the 1 July 1983, or the last day of the reasonable period. The facts given indicate that at no relevant time did the market price of a similar generator exceed £5,000. Therefore if there was an available market the evidence indicates that no damages will be awarded. If there was no available market then the price which Blue would have paid Saul at the date of delivery would have to be found, but the facts given show that a similar model cost £5,000 at most, and this would influence the amount that Blue would be prepared to pay. Therefore it seems that at no relevant time was there an excess of true value over contract price and therefore no damages will be payable under s51 Sale of Goods Act 1979.

If Blue is to recover any damages for the loss of profit during the power cut he must prove that he comes within the second head of *Hadley* v *Baxendale* (preserved by s54 Sale of Goods Act 1979). In other words he must prove that Saul knew of circumstances which would indicate to a reasonable man that the type of loss suffered was not unlikely to occur if delivery was late. Although the exact formulation of this rule is impossible, the 'not unlikely' test of probability seems as good as any other and synonymous with most in *The Heron II* (1969). We are told that Saul knew that Blue wanted the generator for use in the event of a power cut, this clearly puts him on notice that there would be a loss to Blue if his works had to stop production when the electricity was cut off.

Nonetheless there is more to recovering damages than coming within the rules in *Hadley* v *Baxendale*. In particular, in this case, it is necessary to prove that Blue acted reasonably to mitigate his loss (*British Westinghouse* v *Underground Railway* (1912)). His problem is proving that will be to show that it was reasonable to allow his business to suffer losses during the winter, rather than purchasing a generator elsewhere. By the time the winter came it would have been clear that Saul was not likely to deliver, therefore at that stage the delay in delivery would have amounted to a repudiatory breach. Therefore Blue should have taken reasonable steps to minimise his loss. The duty to mitigate does not require the victim of a breach to do anything unreasonable and the effect of this is that Blue would not be expected to buy a substitute generator if it would be unduly expensive. But the evidence we have is that generators were available at about the same price that he had agreed with Saul. Therefore, unless special circumstances can be proved which made it impractical for Blue to buy a substitute, he did not take reasonable steps to mitigate his loss and he will not be able to recover damages for lost production.

ii) For resale

Much of the discussion relating to the first generator is relevant to the claim as regards the second. Again the evidence suggests that no damages will be recoverable under s51 Sale of Goods Act 1979, because there was no loss of capital profit. The recoverability of damages under the second head of *Hadley* v *Baxendale* will be governed by the same principles stated above, namely did Saul have knowledge of fact which would indicate to a reasonable man that this type of loss was not unlikely and, if so, did Blue act reasonably to mitigate his loss?

There can be no doubt about Saul's knowledge of the fact that Blue wanted the generator for resale. But the two questions mentioned merge into one when considering whether it was foreseeable that Blue would suffer a loss of profit if Saul did not deliver. Unless there are special circumstances of which we have not been informed, it looks as though Blue could have bought a substitute generator in order to fulfil the sub-sale. The difficulty, though, is that he may not have been able to buy one of the same specifications from anyone other than Saul. If he could have bought a substitute of those specifications, then he should have done so and can claim no damages for the loss of expected profit. If, on the other hand, such a generator could only be bought from Saul, then the recoverability of lost profit rests solely on whether Saul knew that the resale was likely to be subject to the specifications of one of his generators.

The second head of *Hadley* v *Baxendale* does not require the contract breaker to have precise knowledge of all the facts of a sub-sale in order for him to be liable for loss of profit on the sub-sale. All that is required is that he knows of circumstances which would indicate to a reasonable man that a loss of the type concerned was not unlikely. Therefore one must ask whether Saul's knowledge of the fact of resale made it foreseeable that a sub-sale to precise specifications was not unlikely. There is insufficient evidence to be able to give any definite advice on this matter, but it seems that the fact of resale by a businessman would indicate to a reasonable man that the resale would be a formal contract where specifications would be stipulated. Therefore, in the absence of further evidence, it can be stated that Saul's degree of knowledge of the likely consequences of his breach extended to knowledge of resale of the specific thing sold to Blue. Then the only question would be whether the loss suffered was of a type which was foreseeable as not unlikely. In *Victoria Laundry* v *Newman Industries* (1949) (and see also *Parsons* v *Uttley Ingham* (1978)) the Court of Appeal drew a distinction between normal profit and abnormal profit for the purpose of defining what is foreseeable as likely to occur naturally as the result of a breach which halts a business. The same sort of division must be drawn when considering what type of loss is foreseeable in this case. The type of loss which is foreseeable where a sub-sale is lost is a loss of normal profit. The profit to Blue of this lost sub-sale is claimed to be almost the price at which Blue bought the generator in the first place. Unless such a large profit margin is usual (or, at least, not unusual) when such generators are resold, Blue will not be able to recover £4,000. He will, however, be able to recover the amount of profit which is usual in such cases.

iii) Advice

Blue is advised that he will not be able to recover damages for non-delivery under s51 Sale of Goods Act 1979. But he will be able to recover damages under s54 if he can prove that it was reasonable not to buy substitute generators and that the losses are of a type foreseeable as being not unlikely to result from the breach by Saul. His prospects of recover as regards the first generator are slim. His prospects as regards the second generator are better, but he will be able to recover at most the normal amount of profit from such a sub-sale.

13 REMEDIES OF THE BUYER, I

13.1 Introduction

A buyer has a number of remedies to compel the seller to fulfil his duties, the main one being to repudiate the contract and reject the goods.

This is a remedy which will apply primarily where the seller's breach has 'gone to the root of the contract' and is of fundamental importance. Thus, a breach of one of the terms implied by SGA or where the seller's act is a breach of an innominate term or frustrates the whole purpose of the contract are all situations where the remedy will apply.

Additionally, the buyer will also have a power of rejection if he is expressly permitted to do so under the terms of the contract; or where he is given such a right according to implied terms; or implied by trade customs; or implied because of previous dealings between the parties.

13.2 Key points

It is important that the student understands the following:

a) *Time and method of rejecting the goods*

   The goods cannot be rejected after the point of acceptance. What amounts to acceptance on the part of the buyer is discussed in (c) below. Acts which indicate rejection are potentially limitless, there is no formal definition of rejection as such. Whatever form the act of rejection takes it must be unambiguous and a direct indication to the seller of the buyer's refusal to accept the goods.

b) *Effects of rejection by the buyer*

   Section 36 SGA provides:

   'Unless otherwise agreed, where the goods are delivered to the buyer and he refuses to accept them, having the right to do so, he is not bound to return them to the seller but it is sufficient if he intimates to the seller that he refuses to accept them.'

Note therefore that the rejection must be proper, that is, must be exercised in circumstances when it is correct for the buyer to repudiate the contract in refuse to accept the goods.

c) *Instalment contracts*

If the contract in question is severable, then one defective instalment (or more) may give a buyer the right to reject the goods, but each case depends on its individual circumstances and it is possible no right exists for the buyer to reject in such cases. In particular, the courts will take into account the proportionate importance of the breach to the contract overall and the degree of probability that the defect(s) will be repeated. If the whole contract is non-severable, despite the fact that the goods are being delivered in instalments then the buyer may generally reject all the goods on the basis of a breach of contract by the seller in any one or more instalment.

d) *Loss of the right to reject*

It has already been stated that the right to reject is now lost only because of acceptance by the buyer. It used to be the case that once property in the goods had passed to the buyer he no longer had the right to reject, but the Misrepresentation Act 1967 amended the old Sale of Goods Act 1893 and right to reject is now unaffected by passing of property to the buyer.

Obviously, it is of crucial importance to define the point of acceptance.

SGA provides in ss34 and 35(1) some guidelines, which are too lengthy and complex to quote in full here. Briefly, s34 requires that if goods not previously examined are delivered the buyer must be allowed reasonable time and opportunity to examine the goods before he can be deemed to have accepted. Section 35(1) provides, essentially, that the moment a buyer indicates he is accepting or does some act 'inconsistent with the ownership of the seller', or allows a reasonable amount of time to elapse while still retaining the goods, then all these can be construed as acts of acceptance. There was prior to 1967 some conflict between the two sections since a buyer might sometimes do some act inconsistent with the seller's continuing ownership (which was acceptance under s35(1)) while still not having had reasonable opportunity to examine the goods (which, according to s34, would not yet be acceptance). The Misrepresentation Act 1967 amended the wording of the old SGA slightly so that s35(1) is now to be read in the light of s34 and, to a large extent, the inconsistency is therefore now resolved. Sections 34 and 35(1) are still, however, subject to minor ambiguities and there is a very great deal of case law on the subject. The student should refer to the textbook for fuller details.

13.3 Analysis of questions

While there are an assortment of questions on buyer's remedies which include court actions (damages, specific performance) (see chapter 14), there is remarkably little on the buyer's right to reject. Occasionally, where a question deals with the implied terms as to quality of goods especially ss13-15; the buyer's option to reject the goods if they do not conform to standard is mentioned but this rarely forms a major part of the answer. Most recently in Q2 of the 1992 paper the buyer's right to reject formed a substantial part (but not the whole) of the answer. This question and solution has already been quoted in chapter 8. The question quoted below, contains other elements of sale of goods law (which should be familiar ground to the student by now!) but it is, perhaps the only question to require treatment of the buyer's right to refuse to accept the goods at any length.

13.4 Question

Yellow Motors Ltd who carry on business as car dealers, seek your advice as to their legal position concerning:

i) a Renault which, on 3 January 1985 its owner, Green, instructed them to obtain offers for, but was instead sold by them to Jones; and

ii) a Ford which they bought from Thompson Ltd another car dealer, and subsequently delivered on approval to Clark.

You make the following notes:

i) As to the Renault

Value of car about £6,000. January 5: Green's death mentioned in local paper. January 13: car sold to Jones at York cattle market. Sale was on a Sunday. Time 4.30 pm. Receipt signed by Jones. Liability for any breach of Sale of Goods Act 1979 excluded. Car sold for £4,500. Gearbox irreparable.

ii) As to the Ford

Purchase price £7,000. Terms were 'as she lies'. Steering defective. January 30: car delivered to Clark on approval for seven days. Price £7,200. February 3: car sold by Clark to Grant. Car involved in accident due to steering. March 5: car found in scrap metal yard. Clark insolvent. Price of £7,200 not yet paid.

University of London LLB Examination
(for External Students) Commercial Law June 1985 Q2

Skeleton solution

- First car - liability to Green - conversion.
- First car - liability to Jones; s12 SGA; nemo dat rule; exceptions; s2(1) Factors Act; ss21, 22 SGA; s14 SGA remedies.
- Second car - rights against Thompson; s14 SGA; exclusion clause; UCTA.
- Second car - rights against Clark; sale or return; passing of property; s14 SGA remedies.

Suggested solution

a) *The Renault*

i) Liability to Green

The Renault was given to fellow Motors Ltd for the purpose of obtaining offers for it. There was no authority to sell. Therefore the sale to Jones was a conversion of the car which leaves Yellow Motors Ltd liable in conversion to the true owner Green (The alternative remedy of redelivery in s3 Torts (Interference with Goods) Act 1977 is not available because Yellow Motors Ltd are not in possession). In fact Green has died therefore any action would have to be taken by his executors (or administrators if he died intestate). The normal measure of damages for conversion is the value of the injured party's interest at the time of conversion (*Chinery* v *Viall* (1860)), which will be the market price at the time of conversion (*Rhodes* v *Moules* (1895)). Since the price obtained by Yellow Motors Ltd appears not to reflect that value, the amount of damages will be £6,000 not £4,500.

ii) Liability to Jones

The sale of the car to Jones was not made as agents for Green but as principals. Therefore there was privity of contract between Yellow Motors Ltd and Jones. There were two breaches of contract by Yellow Motors Ltd. The implied conditions in s12(1) and s14(2) Sale of Goods Act 1979 were breached. The facts given indicate a breach of s14(3) as well, but this is not really any different to the breach of s14(2).

As regards s12(1), there is an implied condition that the seller of goods has the right to sell at the time property is to pass under the contract. The sale here was of specific goods (s61(1) Sale of Goods Act 1979 (SGA)), therefore, in the absence of evidence to the contrary, it is to be assumed that property was to pass at the time the contract was made (s18 r1 SGA 1979). Yellow Motors Ltd breached s12(1) in two ways. Firstly, they were not given authority to sell, merely to obtain offers. Secondly, and as a consequence of their lack of authority, they did not pass good title from Green to Jones.

A limitation on the quality of possession of a bailee is the same as a limitation on the authority of an agent. Yellow Motors Ltd were instructed to obtain offers, this limits their right to possession in that they were not entitled to do anything with the car other than obtain offer. The sale to Jones was, clearly, more than the obtaining of an offer, therefore this was outside the rights of Yellow Motors Ltd. This expression limitation of the right to possession meant that there was no right to sell and, therefore that s12(1) was breached.

There is authority that s12(1) can be breached even if the seller passes property and good title to the buyer (*Niblett* v *Confectioners Materials* (1921)). This does not detract from the fundamental rule that a failure to pass good title is always a breach of s12(1) (*Rowland* v *Divall* (1923)). In this case, because Yellow Motors Ltd did not have title when they made the sale to Jones, so they could only pass good title by virtue of an exception to the rule nemo dat quod non habet. The Sale of Goods Act 1979 contains several exceptions to the rule (ss21-25 and s48(2) SGA 1979 and also s2(1) Factors Act 1889), the only relevant exceptions to this case are those in s2(1) Factors Act 1889 and ss21 and 22 of the 1979 Act.

By virtue of s2(1) Factors Act 1889 a mercantile agent in possession of goods with the consent of the owner can pass good title to a bona fide buyer without notice provided the sale was within the normal course of his business as a mercantile agents. Section 1 of the 1889 Act defines mercantile agent as someone whose customary course of business is to sell, buy, or consign goods for sale or raise money on their security. We are not told whether Yellow Motors Ltd normally act as agents for owners of cars, but that does not matter.

If they were in possession in order to consider offers for the disposition of Green's car, they will be treated as mercantile agents.

The 1889 Act requires that the mercantile agent has possession with consent of the owner. In this case Green died before the sale. Did his consent to Yellow Motors Ltd's possession of his car cease on his death? By virtue of s2(2) Factors Act 1889 consent is deemed to continue until the buyer from the mercantile agent has notice that it has been withdrawn. The burden of proving lack of notice will lie on the person claiming the protection of the Factors Act. This point was made in *Heap* v *Motorists' Advisory Agency* (1923), in the context of a claim by the buyer that he was entitled to retain possession against the original owner. There is no reason to think that it does not apply where any other party alleges that s2(1) gave a buyer title. The test for notice is objective and the mere mention of death in a local paper would not amount to notice (*Evans* v *Trueman* (1830)). Therefore Yellow Motors Ltd were in possession as mercantile agents with consent.

There are two points which seem to prevent the application of s2(1) here. Firstly, the circumstances of the sale may indicate the lack of authority to sell. In *Janesich* v *Attenborough* (1910) it was held that the charging of an abnormally low price in very suspicious circumstances would be enough to put a reasonable man on notice. That seems to apply to the facts of this case. Secondly, the sale by the mercantile agent must be in the ordinary course of business of a mercantile agent. This requires that the sale must be within normal business hours, at a proper place of business and in all respects in a manner which would not indicate to a reasonable buyer that there was anything wrong (*Oppenheimer* v *Attenborough* (1908)). The sale of a car in a cattle market on a Sunday would indicate to a reasonable man that there was something wrong. So, it is submitted, Jones did not obtain good title by virtue of the Factors Act 1889.

Section 21 Sale of Goods Act 1979 allows a non-owner to pass good title if the true owner is precluded by his conduct from denying the seller's right to sell. This is sometimes described as an estoppel, but in fact contains two principles. The first is that if the owner of goods appoints an agent to sell, he cannot deny the agent's right to sell. The second is the estoppel point, if a representation is made to a third party that the possessor of goods is owner or has the right to sell then the representor-owner will be estopped from denying the right of the seller to sell. The reason why the agency point is not one of estoppel is that merely by giving an agent possession the owner does not make a representation that the possessor has the right to sell (*Eastern Distributors* v *Goldring* (1957)). There can be no doubt that s21 does not apply to pass good title to Jones in this case. Green gave Yellow Motors Ltd possession, there was no actual authority to sell, therefore s21 cannot apply. The doctrine of apparent authority in agency cannot be applied because it relies on representations being made by the true owner, and again, the law does not regard the mere giving of possession to be a representation that the possessor has authority to sell.

Section 22 Sale of Goods Act 1979 acts to pass good title to a bona fide purchaser without notice who buys goods in market overt. A market is market overt if it is an open legally constituted market. The section only applies if the goods sold are of a type normally sold in the market concerned and the sale takes place in the hours of daylight. No doubt York cattle market is market overt for the purposes of the sale of cattle (Pease and Chitty's *Law of Markets and Fairs*, but it cannot be market overt for the sale of motor cars. Therefore s22 cannot give Jones good title.

For these reasons it is submitted that Jones has a right of action against Yellow Motors Ltd for breach of s12(1) Sale of Goods Act 1979. That action will not be defeated because the exclusion clause is void by virtue of s6(1) Unfair Contract Terms Act 1977. Section 12(1) Sale of Goods Act 1979 is a condition, not a warranty. Therefore, theoretically, Jones has a choice of remedies. He may terminate the contract, by rejecting the car, and sue for damages; or he may accept the car and sue for damages to compensate him for any loss he has sustained. There is a third option available when s12 is broken, which is to sue for recovery of the purchase price on the ground that the consideration for its payment has wholly failed (*Rowland* v *Divall* (1923)).

In fact the remedies open to Jones may be more limited. As has been shown above, Jones does not have title to the car, it still belongs to Green (or rather his estate). Therefore Jones is liable in conversion to Green. He would avoid an action in conversion if he rejected the car back to Yellow Motors Ltd. Indeed if Green's executors were to sue Jones and obtain an award of damages these would have to be refunded to Jones. Furthermore if Jones were sued he could join Yellow Motors Ltd as a third party, which may leave Yellow Motors Ltd liable in costs. The result of this is that Jones will be most likely to reject the car and sue for damages, or for refund of the price paid. He would not be obliged to pay anything for use of the car prior to rejecting it (*Rowland* v *Divall* (1923)).

It has already been mentioned that Yellow Motors Ltd breached s14(2) SGA (as well as s12) and possibly s14(3) as well.

Both s14(2) and s14(3) imply conditions into sale contracts. Therefore the breaches by Yellow Motors Ltd give rise to a choice of remedies for Jones. He could accept the goods and sue for damages, or he could reject the goods, terminating the contract, and sue for damages including the recovery of the price. For reasons given above it is unlikely that Jones would accept the car voluntarily. It appears that he has accepted the car, though, by virtue of s35 Sale of Goods Act 1979. Section 34 of the Act gives the buyer a reasonable time in which to examine the goods to see whether they are of the necessary quality. Once this reasonable time has run out the buyer is deemed to have accepted, whether he has bothered to undertake an examination or not. The sale took place on 13 January 1985. It must be assumed that advice is being given on 6 June 1985.

This delay of nearly five months is far longer than would be required for examination of the car. Therefore the right to reject has been lost and Jones' only remedy for the breaches of s14 will be damages. The measure of damages for defects is set out in s53(3) of the 1979 Act and is the difference in value between the goods as they were when delivered as they would have been with a proper gearbox. This measure can only be assessed accurately by referring to a great deal of expert evidence. To save time and money the normal assessment of this measure of damages is with reference to the cost of repair. In *Minster Trust* v *Traps Tractors* (1954) Devlin J in the High Court held that where it is difficult to assess the s53(3) measure then the actual cost of repair by a reasonable repairer would be taken to be the measure of damages.

b) *The Ford*

i) Rights against Thompson

The problem with apply s14(2) here is that the sale was made 'as she lies'. So, in this case, we must consider whether the term 'as she lies' means that Thompson Ltd were never under an obligation to deliver a car of merchantable quality or whether they were under that obligation but were not liable in damages if they failed to perform it. The question is important because s6(3) Unfair Contract Terms Act 1977 prevents the exclusion of liability for breach of s14 Sale of Goods Act 1979, but does not prevent you excluding the term which s14 implies. In other words we must ask whether the term 'as she lies' means that no term is implied that the car should be of merchantable quality or whether it just aims to prevent damages being recovered once the implied term is broken. The 1977 Act could be rendered useless if it were possible to avoid it by drafting exclusion clauses so that they prevent terms being implied in the first place, and for this reason alone all exclusion clauses in sale contracts must be construed as limiting secondary obligations only, not primary obligations. Therefore the effect of the term 'as she lies' is to attempt to prevent the buyers, Yellow Motors Ltd, from recovering damages if the car turned out not to be merchantable (see Yates, *Exclusion Clauses in Contracts*; Coote, *Exception Clauses*).

A clause which attempts to prevent the injured party recovering for breach of s14(2) Sale of Goods Act 1979 must be reasonable where the buyer is not a consumer (s6(3) Unfair Contract Terms Act 1977). The test of reasonableness is contained in s11 and Schedule 2 Unfair Contract Terms Act. Section 11 lays down a very general statement of principal leaving reasonableness to be judged from case to case by the trial judge. Section 11 gives five examples of factors which must be looked for in sale contracts. None of the factors mentioned are applicable in this case. Therefore the question of reasonableness simply boils down to whether the term was fair and reasonable in the circumstances. It is submitted that there is only one argument which could prevent the clause from protecting the sellers. That is when a car is sold 'as she lies' this could be construed to mean that no extra description is made of the car than that it is what is seen by the buyer. In other words it could be argued that the term limits the contractual description but is not intended to oust the effect of s14(2). Although the *contra proferentem* rule must be applied where there is clear ambiguity in the clause, the House of Lords has recently made it clear that it should not be applied to create ambiguities which do not really exist (*Photo Production* v *Securicor* (1980); *George Mitchell (Chesterhall) Ltd* v *Finney Lock Seeds Ltd* (1983)). It is submitted that to restrict the term 'as she lies' to matters of description would be to create an imaginary ambiguity. For that reason the clause does not cover the breach of s14(2), the buyer had the chance to inspect the car before buying and simply took the commercial risk that it was defective. That being the case, there is no remedy against Thompson Ltd for breach of s14(2).

ii) Rights against Clark

The contract with Clark was one whereby Clark had an option to purchase for seven days from 30 January. This is normally called a 'sale or return' contract, though strictly speaking it is not a contract of sale (as defined by s2(1) SGA 1979) because there was no agreement that Clark would buy, merely that he had an option to buy if he wished. Such an agreement crystallises into a sale when the 'buyer' evinces the intention to exercise his option to purchase. There are three ways in which this can be done, set out in s18 r4 Sale of Goods Act 1979. The relevant one here is the doing of an act adopting the transaction (s18 r4(a) SGA 1979). When Clark sold the car to Grant he made it impossible for himself to return the car to Yellow Motors Ltd and that means he had adopted the transaction.

At the time of this sale Yellow Motors Ltd became entitled to the purchase price of £7,200. The fact that the price has not yet been paid is of importance, but its importance can only be understood after Clark's rights against Yellow Motors Ltd have been considered.

The sale to Clark was in the course of Yellow Motors Ltd's business, therefore the condition in s14(2) Sale of Goods Act 1979 was implied into the contract. The facts given show that the car crashed because of its defective steering. This is clear evidence that s14(2) was breached. As has already been stated, s14(2) implies a condition not a warranty therefore, prima facie, Clark had alternative remedies of rejection plus damages or acceptance plus damages. The right to reject will be lost if the goods supplied under the contract have been accepted by the buyer. The rules on acceptance are laid down by s35 of the 1979 Act. The relevant principle here is that goods are accepted if the buyer does an act inconsistent with the ownership of the seller. This is an unfortunate worded provision, since the seller, by definition, no longer has ownership once the sale has been executed in the majority of cases (the 'Romalpa' clauses are an exception). The meaning of this part of s35 is clear, though. It is aimed at preventing a buyer from rejecting goods if he has dealt with them in such a way that indicates that he treats himself as owner. Devlin J explained in *Kwei Tek Chao* v *British Traders and Shippers* (1954) that on rejection of the goods all rights in the goods revest in the seller. The effect of this is that the sale passes a conditional property to the buyer, with the seller retaining a reversionary property right.

If the buyer acts inconsistently with this residual right then he must be treating himself as the owner. An act inconsistent with the seller's reversionary right is one which takes the possibility of redelivery to the seller out of the hands of the buyer. As with s18 r4, discussed above, there is an alternative way to look at this matter. Not only can it be said that an act inconsistent with the ownership of the seller is an act whereby the buyer gives over control to a third party, this can also be put in terms of the buyer treating himself as having the only right to possession. If he sells to a sub-buyer, therefore, he treats himself as having not only the right to sell his right to possession during the examination period (s34 SGA 1979), but also as having the right to sell the right to possession after the examination period has elapsed. Again, which of these interpretations is correct, matters not, the effect of each is the same (An interesting point arises if the buyer sells to a sub-buyer but does not deliver to him. There is no authority on whether this is an act inconsistent with the seller's ownership. On the first argument advanced in the test it would not be, on the second it would). The effect in this case is that the sale and delivery to Grant was an act inconsistent with Yellow Motors Ltd's continued ownership and so Clark cannot now claim to be entitled to repudiate the contract for breach, he must settle for damages only.

The question of quantum of damages gives rise to further problems. There are two rules applicable (*Hadley* v *Baxendale* (1854)): the first is that the buyer may always recover the direct and natural loss (s53(2) SGA 1979; first rule in *Hadley* v *Baxendale*), the second is that he may recover additional loss if a reasonable man in the seller's position could foresee it as being not unlikely (second rule in *Hadley* v *Baxendale*, and see *Victoria Laundry* v *Newman Industries* (1949)). The first rule leads to an assessment of damages under s53(3) Sale of Goods Act 1979, mentioned above, which means in practice that Clark would be able to recover the cost of repairing the defective steering (*Minster Trust* v *Traps Tractors* (1954)). The second rule is difficult to advise on because we do not know whether Yellow Motors Ltd knew that Clark was going to sell the car and leave himself open to a claim in damages by a sub-buyer. That the sub-buyer, Grant may recover from Clark is clear; his action being for breach of s14(2) Sale of Goods Act 1979. His damages will cover not just the loss of the car, but also any physical injury he suffered as a result of the crash. There is insufficient evidence on which to advise Yellow Motors Ltd whether they will be liable to reimburse Clark any sum he has to pay in damages. The test is as mentioned above: did Yellow Motors Ltd know of facts when would indicate to a reasonable seller that such a loss was not unlikely?

Any damages payable to Clark for breach of s14(2) may be set-off by Clark against the purchase price (s53(1)(b) SGA 1979).

14 REMEDIES OF THE BUYER, II

14.1 Introduction

In the preceding chapter, one of the buyer's major rights, that of refusing to accept the goods, was dealt with. In this chapter the remedies are primarily those of damages awarded on different grounds. Which head the buyer chooses to sue under will obviously depend on the circumstances of the case; but frequently the actual measure of damages will be the same.

14.2 Key points

It is important that the student understands the following:

a) *Rescission for innocent misrepresentation*

Since the Misrepresentation Act 1967 the old rule that rescission was not available for innocent misrepresentation has been abolished. Also by virtue of s1(a) it is irrelevant whether the representation became a term of the contract or not.

b) *Damages for non-delivery*

Section 51 governs this form of damages for breach of contract. It lays down a rule which is the counterpart of the seller's right to sue for damages under s50, for non-acceptance of the goods. The measure of damages, as in s50, is the estimated loss naturally and directly resulting, in the ordinary course of events, from the breach of contract - in other words the basic common law rule in *Hadley* v *Baxendale*.

Section 51, like s50, also uses the 'available market' test. The award of damages of the difference between the market price at the time they ought to have been delivered and the contract price should put the buyer in the position he would have been had the goods been delivered.

There are certain instances, however, when the 'available market' rule is displaced. These include cases where there is no available market, or where the second rule in *Hadley* v *Baxendale* applies and the buyer may be entitled to special damages.

c) *Damages for breach of condition or warranty*

Section 53 SGA covers cases where the seller has committed a breach of condition or warranty. This includes cases where the buyer delivers the goods, but their condition amounts to a breach, or where the late delivery is in itself a breach of warranty.

Where the breach is a defect of the goods then s53(3) specifically applies which dictates that the measure of damages will be the difference between the value of the goods, as delivered, and the value they would have had, had the condition or warranty been fulfilled.

If the breach consists in late delivery of the goods, the usual measure of damages is the difference in value between when they *should* have been delivered and actual delivery. However, there are some variations in this rule, especially if the buyer is purchasing for his own use, in which case the damages will include not only the difference in value, but also the cost of hiring a replacement for the delay period, or inconvenience caused by doing without the goods.

d) *Damages in tort*

If a buyer has an immediate right to possession of the goods, it is, in theory possible to sue in tort for interference with goods. Since the measure of damages (assessed according to the ordinary common law rules as to tortious damages) cannot be greater than if suing for breach of contract; recourse is rarely had to an action for tort.

e) *Damages for misrepresentation*

Such a remedy would obviously only apply if there has been an actionable misrepresentation.

The courts will usually award damages under s2(1) or 2(2) if it is felt that rescission is inappropriate.

f) *Specific performance*

This remedy is provided for by s52 SGA. Among the conditions laid down by s52 is that the goods must be 'specific or ascertained' within the meaning of SGA. As in common law, specific performance is a discretionary remedy and s5(3) provides that the courts may apply 'such terms and conditions ... as seems just to the court'.

14.3 Analysis of questions

Where questions on buyers' rights to damages have occurred, then they tend to crop up in tandem with their counterparts in the field of sellers' remedies. Question 3 in the 1987 London University paper is a good example of this. See also chapter 36 for the 1993 paper; Q5 includes certain aspects of the buyer's right to sue for non-delivery and Q6, part (b) is concerned to a large extent with measure of damages.

The question in the preceding chapter has, among other subject matter, a certain brief reference to the buyer's right to damages. The question quoted below is fairly typical of its kind, and although it includes a reference to hire purchase the consumer credit content of the answer would actually be minimal.

14.4 Question

a) Discuss the concept of 'available market' in ss50 and 51 of the Sale of Goods Act 1979.

b) In March 1978 Jerrybuilders Ltd, a manufacturer of machinery, entered into two contracts with Hopeful Ltd, a carpet manufacturer, each contract being for the sale to Hopeful Ltd of an identical carpet weaving machine, warranted to produce 100 feet of carpet per hour, one machine to be delivered on 1 August and the other on 1 September 1983. The machines were priced at £30,000 each; and each contract provided that the price was to be payable by 30 monthly instalments commencing on delivery, and that the property in the goods was to pass on completion of the payments. The first machine was delivered and installed, but after it had been working for a fortnight, it was clear that by reason of its design the machine could only produce 50 feet of carpet per hour. Hopeful Ltd therefore rejected the second machine on 30 August 1983.

   By August 1983 the market price of comparable machines warranted to produce 100 feet per hour had fallen to £20,000 and a machine warranted to produce 50 feet per hour would fetch only £15,000. The delay in production caused by Jerrybuilder Ltd's breach of contract led Hopeful Ltd to lose a valued customer; and it also deprived Hopeful Ltd of an estimated net profit (before depreciation) of £1,000 during the month of August 1979.

   Advise Hopeful Ltd.

   Would it make any difference to your advice if the contracts between Jerrybuilder Ltd and Hopeful Ltd were of hire-purchase instead of sale?

University of London LLB Examination
(for External Students) Commercial Law June 1984 Q4

Skeleton solution

a) • Sections 50 and 51 SGA: concept of 'available market' common to both sections; relevant case law.

b) • Conditions, warranties implied by SGA, especially fitness for purpose.

   • Right of rejection by buyer loss of that right.

   • Damages for just machine under s53; damages for second machine for non-delivery.

   • Hire purchase alternative.

Suggested solution

a) Under s50(2) of the Sale of Goods Act 1979 the sellers' remedy for a breach of contract by the buyer is damages, the measure of which is the estimated loss directly and naturally resulting in the ordinary course of events, from the buyer's breach. Under s50(3) where there is an available market for the goods in question the measure of damage is prima facie to be ascertained by the difference between the contract price and the market or current price at the time or times when the goods ought to have been accepted or, if no time was fixed for acceptance, then at the time of refusal to accept.

Section 51 is the exact counterpart of s50 and provides that where the seller wrongfully neglects or refuses to deliver goods to the buyer, the buyer may maintain an action against the seller for damages for non-delivery. The measure of damages is as in s50, the estimated loss directly and naturally resulting from the breach but where there is an available market, damages are to be ascertained by the difference between the contract price and the market or current price of the goods at the time they ought to have been delivered.

It can be seen from these two sections that the concept of an 'available market' is very important to the remedy of damages for the seller or buyer for where there is an available market it is to be urged to assess damages.

The term 'available market' has not been defined by the Act but has been considered in a number of cases. In *Dunkirk Colliery* v *Lever* (1878) James LJ considered that an available market was a fair market where the sellers could have found a purchaser. This case was decided when the marketplace was the hub of commerce but in modern times this is not necessarily the case and more recent decisions have come to different conclusions about an 'available market'. Upjohn J in the case of *Thompson (WL)* v *Robinson (Gunmakers) Ltd* (1955) had to consider a case dealing with the sale of a new car which would only be sold at a fixed price. He indicated that the word 'market' had no particular legal significance and that in his view there was an available market if the conditions in the trade were such that vehicles could be freely sold. Jenkins LJ in the latter case of *Charter* v *Sullivan* (1957) criticised Upjohn J and said that the phrase 'market' involved the economic market where price was fixed by the law of supply and demand. In other words the term would not apply to a situation where the price was fixed.

If Jenkins LJ is correct the injured party will have to prove what his loss is by the test of what is naturally and directly resulting from the breach and not seek to rely on any reference to a fixed price.

b) The two contracts entered into with Jerrybuilders are contracts for the sale of goods and as such they will be governed by the Sale of Goods Act 1979. Both contracts contain a term that the machine in question will produce 100 feet of carpet per hour. The contracts will also include the terms implied by s14 of the Act that the machines should be fit for their purpose and be of merchantable quality.

The terms implied by the Act are conditions, a breach of which will allow the buyer to repudiate the contract and sue for damages. The term as to the capacity of the machines may be a condition or a warranty depending upon the importance the parties attach to it. It is not conclusive that the parties expressed the clause in terms of a warranty but this may be indicative of the parties' intention: s11 of the Act; and *Harling* v *Eddy* (1951).

Hopeful Ltd are carpet manufacturers and presumably were greatly interested in the 'warranted' capacity of the machines and in view of this it is likely that the courts would consider that the term was a condition. In any event s14(3) of the Act implies a term that where the seller sells good in the course of a business and the buyer expressly or by implication makes known to the seller any particular purpose for which the goods are being bought, there is an implied condition that the goods will be reasonably fit for that purpose unless the buyer does not rely or it is unreasonable for him to rely, on the seller's skill or judgment. It may be arguable that as Hopeful Ltd made it known that they required a machine producing 100 feet of carpet per hour, the sale of one producing only 50 feet per hour is not supplying goods 'reasonably fit for that purpose'.

It is likely that the supply of the first machine is a breach of condition allowing Hopeful Ltd to repudiate the contract and sue for damages. However, they have not rejected the first machine and presumably have carried on using it. If this is the case they will have lost their right to reject the machine and their only remedy will be to sue for damages: s11 of the Act. In the case of the second machine, this was rejected before delivery, presumably on the basis of an anticipatory breach and Hopeful Ltd will also be able to sue for damages.

Hopeful Ltd will be liable to pay £30,000 for the first machine but nothing for the second as this was legitimately rejected. Damages on the first machine will be assessed under s53 of the Act which provides that the prima facie loss is the difference between the value of the goods at the time of delivery and the value they would have had if they fulfilled the warranty. This is effect means that the prima facie measure will be £20,000 less £15,000, that is £5,000, but in practice higher damages are often awarded as in *Jackson* v *Watson* (1909) and *Mason* v *Burningham* (1949). In other words if the loss suffered by Hopeful Ltd is more than that amount they should be able to recover it, such as the loss of profit they have suffered although it will be difficult to assess damages for the loss of the valued customer.

Damages in relation to the second machine will be awarded under s51 of the Act for non-delivery. The prima facie award is to be ascertained by the difference between the contract price and the market price of the machine which in this case would give a negative answer. The effect of this is that only nominal damages could be awarded unless a greater loss could be proved.

If the contract was one of hire purchase and not one of sale the Sale of Goods Act 1979 would not apply, but similar provisions relating to Hire Purchase contracts appear in the Supply of Goods (Implied Terms) Act 1973 and in ordinary contract law and the position would remain the same.

15 CONSUMER PROTECTION

15.1 Introduction

In the days when the original Sale of Goods Act was drafted in 1893, it was assumed that the most typical transaction was between merchants, where the parties were of roughly equal status and bargaining power. The concept of a consumer - a private individual buying for his own use was hardly known. Today, much more attention is paid to the rights of the consumer buyer and he is given special treatment in a number of ways.

Already, the Unfair Contract Terms Act has been referred to on a number of occasions, which gives special consideration to the problems of consumer purchasers in a number of its sections.

In this chapter, just such another important statute: the Consumer Protection Act 1987, will be dealt with; at this stage only Part I is strictly relevant. The Act introduces a system of strict liability for defective products.

There is also mention in this chapter of some other legislation which has special relevance to consumers sales contracts and also a brief note on manufacturers' guarantees. It should be born in mind that the actual enforcement of this miscellaneous legislation has also been improved. It has always been the case that an orthodox court action, with the associated expense and other problems, has always been a strong deterrent to an ordinary individual trying to assert his rights. In 1973 the County Court Rules were amended to permit claims for less than £1,000 to be dealt with by a Registrar, usually using arbitration. Indeed if the amount involved is less than £500 the Registrar has the power to order arbitration even in the face of one party's refusal.

15.2 Key points

It is important that the student should understand the following:

a) *The Consumer Protection Act and product liability*

The key provision of the Act is s2(1) which provides:

'Subject to the following provisions of this part, where any damage is caused wholly or partly by a defect in a product, every person to whom subs(2) applies shall be liable for the damage.'

The relevant parts of the Act then go on to make it clear that any or all of the following are potentially liable: the producer of goods; those who sell goods under their own brand or trade mark, which, though produced by another are sold as the produce of that person; importers and various others.

Though the Act purports to impose strict liability there are a number of potential defences set out in s4; including that the goods were not supplied by way of business or with a view to profit and an important defence in s4(1)(e) that the state of scientific or technical knowledge at the time was such that one could not reasonably expect the producer of the goods to have discovered the defect.

For a more detailed account of the operation of the Act the student should consult a textbook; the terminology in particular is rigidly defined in Part I of the Act.

The overall effect of the Act is that the rights of a person injured by a defective product now encompass the old common law, not only in contractual liability, but also in the field of tortious liability. Additionally, however, the Act, in imposing strict liability on producers etc removes many of the difficulties that would previously have faced a person bringing an action at law. This is especially true of the difficulties in proving negligence under the old principles of *Donoghue* v *Stevenson* (1932) and the limitations placed under these rules on the amount of damages that might be recovered and the heads under which compensation might be awarded.

b) *Miscellaneous consumer protection statutes*

There are a number of statutes in force which, wholly or partly, seek to protect the consumer. It should not be forgotten, of course, that the terms implied into Sale of Goods Act especially as to quality of the goods, are in themselves an effort to ensure that in purchasing goods, consumers are provided with safe products which are 'fit for their purpose'.

Much of the consumer legislation of the 1960s and 1970s is now incorporated into Part II of the Consumer Protection Act 1987. There are, additionally, statutes which control the quality and composition of food and drugs. Another consumer protection measure is the Trade Descriptions Act 1968. This creates a series of offences, punishable by criminal sanctions, if a false trade description is applied. Most notable of all, of course, is the Fair Trading Act 1973 which set up the office of Fair Trading and the post of Director General of Fair Trading. Essentially the function of the Director General's office is to keep a watching brief for any developments likely to injure the interests of consumers. Additionally the Director General may have functions under other legislation, as for example, administering the licensing system under the Consumer Credit Act 1974.

c) *Manufacturers' guarantees*

This is a generic term for the sort of written statement, sometimes called a warranty, which promise to make good any defect in the product, by replacement, repair or refund, within a stated time; which some manufacturers provide with their product. The goods most likely to carry these 'guarantees' are household appliances and cars.

The exact legal status of such promises is unclear. Certainly they provide, on some occasions, a useful addition to the consumer's existing statutory rights. At one time their wording caused criticism in some instances, because they took away more than they offered. Since the Unfair Contract Terms Act, however, this is no longer possible.

15.3 Analysis of questions

Consumer protection legislation has not figured largely in past papers. While, obviously one would not expect to find references to the Act prior to 1987, there *were* Consumer Protection Acts, and Consumer Safety Acts before that date, but no question required any treatment of such legislation; possibly because issues raised were largely questions of tort rather than contract. The first question quoted below also requires, as the student will see, some discussion of sale of goods law, including the topic of exclusion clauses. Indeed, on balance the topic of Consumer Protection Act would appear to be only about one quarter of the overall subject content. The second question is similarly a mixture of topics, with consumer protection only a minor part of the answer. Nevertheless, it is typical of its type.

15.4 Questions

Question 1

Taff, a Welshman, moves from Wales to England but wishes to remain able to watch television programmes broadcast in Wales in the Welsh language. He says this to Saylor, a television retailer, who tells Taff that he thinks that Taff lives close enough to Wales to be able to pick up a decent picture so long as he has a good television set and a good aerial. On his advice, Taff buys an expensive television set manufactured by Nipco in Japan, and imported and sold to Saylor by Implimt (although a cheaper set would have been just as adequate). He pays a sum which includes an amount for Saylor's arranging for Jobba, a television engineer, to fit an (expensive) aerial at Taff's house. The contract, signed by Taff, states that 'the buyer accepts the goods on the basis that all liability is excluded'. After the goods are installed, Taff invites his friend Paddy to watch the news in Welsh. As the reception is poor, Paddy adjusts the controls, then is electrocuted as the result of a defect in one of the circuits. Advise Taff and Paddy.

University of London LLB Examination
(for External Students) Commercial Law June 1988 Q5

Skeleton solution

- Taff: SGA; merchantability/fitness for purpose; exclusion clauses; UCTA; remedies.
- Paddy: action in negligence; Consumer Protection Act 1987.

Suggested solution

Both Taff and Paddy must be advised, but their rights are different, so they must be advised separately.

a) *Taff*

Taff bought the television from Saylor for a price which included an element for supply and installation of an aerial. He only made one contract, however, comprising the purchase of both television and aerial. The contract is governed by the Sale of Goods Act 1979 because in essence it is a contract of sale regardless that part of the price was for work by Jobba.

There are two possible breaches of the sale contract by Saylor. They are of the condition implied by s14(2) of the 1979 Act and of the condition implied by s14(3).

Section 14(2) implies a condition in all sales made by the seller in the course of business that the goods he supplies will be of merchantable quality. By s14(6) all circumstances must be taken into account, but the test of merchantability is that goods are merchantable if they are reasonably fit for the purpose or purposes for which goods of their type are commonly bought. There appear to have been two problems with the set supplied. Firstly the reception was not good and secondly it electrocuted Paddy.

The poor reception does not of itself render the television unfit for its normal purpose or purposes because it does not indicate that it would not give a good picture in a better reception area. The Court of Appeal in *Aswan Engineering Establishment Co* v *Lupdine Ltd* (1987) recently made clear that the condition implied by s14(2) is concerned with the general fitness of the goods for normal use and not with their fitness or otherwise for the buyer's intended use. Merchantability is, therefore, a general and not a specific concept, so even where, as here, the buyer has made very clear what he wants the goods for they will only be unmerchantable if they are unfit for any of their normal uses.

That Paddy was electrocuted when he tried to adjust the set is, however, clear evidence of unmerchantability. It is irrelevant that Saylor may not have inspected the set and simply relied on Nipco to manufacture safe sets. But, Saylor sold it and he is strictly liable for breach of condition if he sells goods which are unsafe because unsafe electrical goods are undoubtedly unfit for their normal purpose or purposes.

Taff made clear his intended use in that he said that he needed to be able to receive pictures from Welsh television. He was assured by Saylor that the set and aerial would allow him to receive the desired pictures and Taff relied on Saylor. Where a buyer makes clear his intended use for the goods and reasonably relies on the seller to supply goods suitable for that use there is a condition implied into the sale contract that the goods supplied will be fit for that use (s14(3) Sale of Goods Act 1979). The set and aerial did not succeed in allowing Taff to receive the quality of picture he wanted. It would therefore appear that the fitness for purpose condition has been breached. One matter on which there are insufficient facts, however, is whether an adequate picture could have been obtained had the set been adjusted. If it could then there would have been no breach in relation to the poor reception.

There was, however, a breach of the condition implied by s14(3) in that Taff made known that he wished to be able to use the set safely and this was not possible. He did not expressly state that the set had to be safe, but whenever goods are bought for one purpose (in this case to be viewed) the buyer makes known that he intends to use them for that purpose (*Priest* v *Last* (1903)). In other words the dangerous state of the television set amounted not only to it being unmerchantable but also to it being unfit for Taff's particular purpose.

Taff's remedy for breach of condition is to reject the goods and/or claim damages. From the facts given it seems that he has not lost the right to reject the goods because he has only used them once. There is a question, however, whether he may reject both the television and the aerial because there seems to be nothing wrong with the aerial. The breaches in relation to the television were breaches of condition and at common law such a breach gives the buyer the right to treat the whole contract as discharged (*Bunge Corp* v *Tradax SA* (1981)). But the contract is not discharged simply because there is a breach of condition by the seller, it is necessary for the buyer to accept the breach as discharging the contract (*Johnson* v *Agnew* (1980)). Taff may do this in words or by conduct but the easiest way is simply to write to Saylor and say that the goods are rejected and the contract discharged by virtue of the breaches which have occurred. He will then be entitled to his money back, but there is no evidence that he has suffered any other loss.

The contract signed by Taff contains a clause that he 'accepts the goods on the basis that all liability is excluded.' Because the breaches here are of the conditions implied by ss14(2) and 14(3) of the Sale of Goods Act 1979, any clause purporting to exclude Saylor's liability for those breaches is subject to s6 of the Unfair Contract Terms Act 1977. Because: (a) Taff did not buy the goods in the course of a business; (b) he did not hold himself out as buying in the course of a business; (c) Saylor sold in the course of a business; and (d) the goods are of a type ordinarily supplied for private use, so Taff dealt as consumer (s12 Unfair Contracts Act 1977) and s6(2) of the 1977 Act renders the exclusion clause void. It is not open to Saylor to argue that the effect of the clause is to prevent any conditions from being implied by the 1979 Act, because its wording says that 'all liability is excluded', it does not say that there is no liability in the first place.

Taff has no claim against Saylor, Implimt or Nipco under the Consumer Protection Act 1987 because he did not suffer any loss other than perhaps damage to the television and that it not a loss for which the 1987 Act allows a remedy (s5(2) Consumer Protection (CP) Act 1987).

b) *Paddy*

Paddy was not privy to the contract of sale between Taff and Saylor. Therefore he has no right to sue for breach of the conditions implied by the Sale of Goods Act 1979. Also it is far from clear whether Nipco was negligent in the manufacture of the set. It is obvious that a manufacturer owes a duty of care towards users of its products (*Donoghue* v *Stevenson* (1932)), but from the facts given it is not possible to say whether there has been a breach. In any event there may be a question whether English or Japanese law would be applicable to the question whether Paddy has an action against Nipco. Paddy does, however, have a right of action against Implimt and possibly against Saylor under the Consumer Protection Act 1987.

By s2(2)(c) of the 1987 Act an importer into the EEC of defective goods is liable for damage caused by the defect. Implimt imported the television into the EEC. The set was defective in that its safety was not such as persons generally are entitled to expect (s3(1) CP Act 1987). Paddy has the right to sue for the damage done to him because he has suffered personal injuries (s5(1) CP Act 1987). Because he suffered personal injuries the 'minimus loss' rule in s5(4) does not apply, that rule is applicable to claims for property damage only.

Further, we are not told whether Paddy has any way of ascertaining who imported the television. If he makes a request for that information to Saylor within a reasonable time of the electrocution and within a reasonable time of receiving the request Saylor fails to identify the importer, Paddy may hold Saylor liable for his injuries (s2(3) CP Act 1987).

Question 2

Manfred manufactures *Manmot* motorcycles, into which he puts gearboxes imported from Luigi's factory in Italy. Delbert is an authorised dealer in Manfred's motorcycles. Arthur enters Delbert's premises and orders a *Manmot* from him as a Christmas present for his son Simon. Simon takes his girlfriend Gertrude out for a ride but, due to the cold weather, finds it difficult to change gears, as a result of which he crashes, injuring himself and Gertrude. The motorcycle is taken to Delbert's garage. Delbert repairs it, replacing the engine with an engine of his own, and sells it to Gertrude's brother Tom. Advise the parties.

University of London LLB Examination
(for External Students) Commercial Law June 1992 Q6

Skeleton solution

- Rights of the consumer under Sale of Goods Act 1979.
- Effects of doctrine of privity.
- Ways to circumvent doctrine of privity:
  - using Consumer Protection Act 1987;
  - to sue for negligence.
- To whom does motorcycle belong?
  - passing of title under ss17-18 Sale of Goods Act 1979;

- mercantile agency;
- ordinary agency;
- sale by unpaid seller;
- sale by a seller in possession;
- estoppel.

Suggested solution

In respect of defective goods the consumer has certain inalienable rights under the Sale of Goods Act 1979 (SGA). These include particularly, s14(2) and (3) as to merchantability and fitness for purpose. The main problems are that, firstly, these rights are available to the consumer only against the manufacturer, if he is also the seller of the product in question direct to the consumer. In this case Manfred manufactures the *Manmot* motorcycle but imports the gearboxes from Luigi in Italy, and it is apparently the gearbox that causes Simon's accident. The other problem is that because of the rules as to privity of contract, it is not possible in common law for a non-contracting party, such as a member of the consumer's family (like Simon) or friend (like Gertrude), to sue the original seller, unless the buyer can be construed as being the agent for the injured party. In this case because the motorcycle is clearly stated to be required by Arthur as a Christmas present for Simon, the agent-principal situation clearly cannot apply.

Two ways of circumventing the limitations of the rule of privity of contract are: to proceed to sue for breach of statutory duty under the Consumer Protection Act 1987 (CPA); or to proceed under the law of negligence.

It should be noted with regard to the CPA that the primary objective of the legislation is to ensure through criminal sanctions that insofar as is possible safety requirements are complied with and accidents avoided. Thus it is an offence to supply, offer or agree to supply or possess for supply any goods which fail to comply with the general safety requirements of s10(1) of the CPA. (Note that s10(7) of the Act defines consumer goods and excludes, inter alia, motor vehicles. Whether *Manmot* motorcycles would qualify as consumer goods is therefore open to question.) Liability is strict (s2 CPA) with no need to prove negligence or fault, and is imposed primarily on the 'producer' of the product. Where two or more people are jointly responsible their liability is both joint and several: s2(5). It is doubtful, however, whether anyone would go so far as proceeding separately against Luigi. Liability does extend to suppliers such as Delbert, but usually only where either a person puts his own personal brand on the product, or who imports the goods from outside the EEC, or who cannot for whatever reason identify his source of goods. None of this would seem to apply to Delbert and any action Arthur and/or Simon and Gertrude take would therefore be against Manfred (and possibly Luigi).

A product is defective under s3 of the CPA if the safety of the product 'is not such as persons generally are entitled to expect'. This is largely a question of fact in each case. Part I of the CPA limits damage giving rise to liability to death and personal injury, loss of property in excess of £275, but not damage to the goods themselves (s5). Thus Simon and Gertrude's injuries would qualify for redress under the Act, but damage to the motorcycle itself would not.

Although the CPA is primarily concerned with criminal sanctions (and this means, of course, that the producer(s) and possibly the supplier in the circumstances outlined above, may face criminal prosecution for breach of the act and, if convicted, punishment by fines), it also makes provision for civil liability. It should be noted firstly that in the context of product definition, Part I of the Act covers all goods, not just consumer goods. Part I is concerned with civil liability. Part II, as already noted, defines consumer goods narrowly in a way which may exclude motorcycles, and it is this part which is concerned with criminal sanctions.

In order to establish liability under Part I it is necessary to establish not only that the goods were unsafe, but that they were supplied 'in the course of a business' (s4); that the defect existed at the time of supply (s4); that the damage was caused by the defect (s3); and that there was no contributory negligence s6(4). Most of this seems, self evidently, to apply, but the last two requirements are worth considering briefly and overlap to some extent. We are told that Simon finds it difficult to change gears 'because of the cold'. Obviously, if this implies that the gears are in no way faulty, but freak weather is to blame, it would act as a defence. Similarly, if there is contributory negligence on Simon's part, while it will not destroy his right of action, any damages may be substantially reduced (Law Reform (Contributory Negligence) Act 1943).

Similarly, note that by virtue of s4 CPA it would be a defence for Luigi to establish that the fault lay not in the gearbox but in the overall design of the product; for example that the cycle's design made it difficult to change gear, not that the gearbox was faulty.

So, to sum up thus far, Simon and Gertrude might have a right to claim under Part I of the CPA, but this in no way affects their right to bring a claim in tort. To succeed in a negligence action the plaintiff must successfully establish that:

- the defendant was under a duty of care to him;
- that there has been a breach of that duty;
- that as a result the plaintiff has suffered damage which is not too remote.

The leading case on the subject is *Donoghue* v *Stevenson* (1932), a case too well known to require further comment. Certainly to proceed in negligence gives fairly wide scope to claimants, the plaintiff might be anyone foreseeably injured by the product and the defect might not be in the goods, but in the packaging or instructions. However, one point to note is that for an action to be successful there must be no opportunity for any intermediate examination of the goods. It will be recalled that in *Donoghue* v *Stevenson* the bottle was opaque, precluding any reasonable opportunity to examine the contents. In *Evans* v *Triplex Glass Co Ltd* (1936), where a car windscreen suddenly shattered one year after purchase, it was held that the manufacturers were not liable as there had been ample opportunity to examine the windscreen in the interval. This raises the question of whether, had Simon examined or test-ridden the product, he would have realised the motorcycle had a potential defect. Finally, remember, even if a duty of care exists, Simon must establish not only that Luigi/Manfred/Delbert or whoever he chooses to sue failed to take reasonable care, but also the damage that occurred was not too remote. All in all it would seem easier to proceed with an action under the CPA.

As to the next part of the question, there are two distinct problems. Is the motorcycle now safe? And, secondly, does Delbert have the right to sell it - ie, can he convey title to Tom? There is of course the normal rule of 'caveat emptor' and since Tom is Gertrude's brother, he, more than anyone, should be aware that the motorcycle is not perhaps safe. Certainly by virtue of s14(3) SGA, where a seller in the course of a business sells goods which the buyer has expressly or impliedly said are for a particular purpose then there is an implied term that the goods should be 'fit for purpose'. But this is an adjustable standard as cases like *Bartlett* v *Sidney Marcus Ltd* (1965) show. Also s14(2) and (6) requires that the goods be of merchantable quality, unless either any defect is brought to the buyer's notice, or he examines the goods before buying. However, note that goods may have minor defects and still be of merchantable quality (*Millars of Falkirk* v *Turpie* (1976)).

However, there is no suggestion that Tom has been injured (yet!), or that the motorcycle is in any way unsafe despite its previous history. But if it should prove unsafe, because Tom is the direct consumer and because Delbert has virtually rebuilt the motorcycle , inserting his own engine, Tom may have the additional option, not open to Simon and Gertrude (for reasons as set out above), of proceeding under the SGA if the motorcycle should prove unsafe - as well as suing in common law for negligence, or proceeding under the CPA.

The final problem which needs sorting out is the ownership of the motorcycle. We are not told whether Arthur ever pays for the *Manmot* motorcycle he buys from Delbert. If he has done, of course the issue will be simplified considerably. If he did not pay, has title passed? Section 17 of SGA provides that title passes 'when the parties intend it to pass' and s18 is largely concerned with ascertaining that intention. For reasons of convenience delivery and the taking of physical possession are often equated with passing of title, though the parties may of course specifically stipulate otherwise. Or, alternatively, some act of unequivocal appropriation, such as Arthur's handing the keys/documents to the motorcycle to Simon, will indicate title has passed. So, even if Arthur has not paid, title may have passed to him from Delbert; he will of course still have to pay, but it will simplify Delbert's position vis-à-vis his sale to Tom.

There seem to be three distinct possibilities:

- Delbert is acting as Arthur's agent and Arthur is the true owner of the motorcycle;
- Delbert is an unpaid seller and sells as a seller in possession;
- Having handed the motorcycle to Delbert, Arthur is estopped from repudiating the sale.

Space precludes spending too much time on the various possibilities. The basic rule may be summed up as 'nemo dat quod non habet' - no-one can give better title than he himself possesses. Obviously, if title has for some reason not yet passed from Delbert to Arthur, this problem will not arise. Otherwise we can look at Part III of SGA which is concerned with the exceptions to the nemo dat rule; that is circumstances in which a non-owner may confer title. There are perhaps a dozen or more of these exceptions, the ones most likely to apply are listed above. Section 62 SGA specifically preserves the rules of agency - it is not clear whether in fact Arthur does return the motorcycle to Delbert with instructions to sell it. 'Ordinary' agency should be distinguished from sale by a mercantile agent under the Factors Act 1889 (s21(2) of SGA). The main requirements, that a mercantile agent must as a customary course of business sell the goods concerned (s26 SGA), and must be in possession of the goods with the consent of the owner (s2 Factors Act), appear to be satisfied, though the rule that the purchaser took in good faith and unaware of any lack of authority to sell might be more difficult to establish as Tom is Gertrude's brother and presumably fully aware of all the facts. If Delbert knew the motorcycle was not intended for sale and Tom was aware of this as well, the rules as to mercantile agency would not apply (*Stadium Finance Ltd* v *Robbins* (1962)). The Factors Act 1889, s8 and s24 SGA give rise to a very similar situation with regard to a seller who, having sold the goods, for whatever reason, remains in possession of them. Much the same rules apply as to mercantile agents. Section 38 SGA provides that an unpaid seller has certain statutory rights, even if title has passed, including a right of resale (*RV Ward Ltd* v *Bignall* (1967)). And, finally, s21(1) provides that if an owner of goods by his conduct implies that the seller has the right to sell, then good title will pass to the buyer and the owner will be estopped from denying the seller's right to sell.

All of this, must of necessity be somewhat generalised, partly because it is not clear in whom title rests, Delbert or Arthur (or even Simon), and partly because if title does vest in Arthur, it is not apparent on what basis the motorcycle went back to the garage or what, if any, instructions Arthur gave to Delbert.

16 SUPPLY OF GOODS AND SERVICES ACT 1982

16.1 Introduction

While the Sale of Goods Act 1979 (and the Supply of Goods (Implied Terms) Act 1973) covered contracts for sale of goods and hire purchase agreements, there was, until this Act no similar provision in legislation for those contracts for the supply of services. Such contracts were covered by common law. Also, it will be recalled, certain types of goods were excluded from the main Sale of Goods Act.

To remedy these defects, the Act was passed embodying in Part I provisions as to the supply of goods (especially transfer of property in goods and hire purchase contracts) and in Part II the provisions as to supply of services.

The obligations imposed on the supplier as to quality of the goods or services, ie title, description, fitness and so on, are virtually identical to those contained in SGA itself. It should be remembered, however, that despite the apparent similarities the type of contract involved will have a different economic basis. In contracts for sale of goods within the meaning of SGA 1979, the essence of the contract is that property in goods alone is intended by the parties to pass. In contracts covered by the 1982 Act, property in goods may indeed pass, but this is ancillary to the main transaction. Thus, a contract for the installation of a fitted kitchen would come within the Act because this is basically a contract for skill and labour. Property in the kitchen units and other materials used would pass, but as an integral part of the more complex main contract.

16.2 Key points

It is important that the student understands the following:

a) *Implied conditions and warranties*

All contracts within the scope of the Act will have implied into them the conditions and warranties as provided in ss2-5 of the Act.

These include: s2 - title

s3 - correspondence with description

s4 - merchantable quality

s5 - conditions as to samples.

The provisions and their effect are markedly similar to ss12,13, 14 and 15 of SGA 1979 and the student should remind himself of the relevant parts of the 1979 Sale of Goods Act.

b) *Hire purchase*

Prior to the 1982 Act simple hire or leasing agreements were outside the scope of the statutory terms which applied to hire purchase and conditional sale agreements.

Sections 6-10 of the Act extends the basic statutory provisions to cover this type of agreement.

c) *Exclusion clauses*

The basic rule is confirmed in ss11 and 16 of the Act.

Subject to the express provision of the parties the UCTA 1977 will apply.

Bear in mind that the UCTA only applies to consumer contracts; otherwise in non-consumer contracts exclusion or limitation clauses are permitted in so far as they are reasonable.

16.3 Analysis of questions

Past papers from University of London have contained only one question (below) which has required any necessity to discuss the Supply of Goods and Services Act 1982. Perhaps the fact that the 1982 Act's provisions mirror those of the SGA 1979 and Supply of Goods (Implied Terms) Act 1973 accounts for the paucity of questions. That part of the question quoted below was in fact linked with an essay-type question on agency. Since the question as it stood was fairly lengthy, only part (b) has been quoted here and students should bear this in mind. The agency and consumer credit aspects of the question may be referred to in more detail in Parts 2 and 3 respectively.

16.4 Question

Importer Ltd advertised in a trade journal a new type of 'Japanese Easiuse Lathe' as available for immediate delivery for a cash price of £17,999. The advertisement is read by Eager, who is about to set up a machine tool business, Eager Ltd. On telephoning Importer Ltd, Eager is assured that the lathe can be operated by an unskilled worker and invited to inspect one at the current local trade exhibition. Upon inspection, Eager is carried away with enthusiasm and immediately signs an agreement to take the goods on hp from Importer Ltd, paying a deposit of £3,000. The next day, Eager is advised by his bank manager that it would be more advantageous to lease the lathe. Accordingly, Eager returns to the trade stand and arrangements are made to replace the hire purchase agreement with a lease of the lathe from Crocodile Finance Ltd. The lease recites that the goods will be sold by Importer Ltd to Crocodile Finance Ltd; that in no circumstances is Importer Ltd to be treated as the agent of Crocodile Finance Ltd; and that Eager has not relied upon any representations by Importer Ltd as to the state of the goods or their performance.

Within a week of installation, Eager has discovered that Easiuse lathes are not of Japanese manufacture, can only be operated by skilled workers and that the one installed is materially different from the one he inspected on the trade stand. Upon complaint, Eager is mistakenly assured by Importer Ltd that the lathe has a ten-year manufacturer's guarantee. Finding Importer Ltd insolvent, advise Eager on both the following assumptions as to his signature on agreements:

1) Eager signed solely as agent for Eager Ltd; and

2) Eager signed in such a way that both he and Eager Ltd were co-parties.

(NB: Assume that all advertisements and documentation comply with the Consumer Credit Act 1974.)

University of London LLB Examination
(for External Students) Commercial Law June 1986 Q4(b)

Skeleton solution

- Lease not governed by CCA 1974 (see Part 2).
- Agency - actual authority/apparent authority?
- Sale by description s8 SGSA 1982.
- Section 9 SGSA 1982 on hire contracts.
- Hire purchase agreement between E and E Ltd as co-parties - regulated consumer credit agreement (see Part 2).

Suggested solution

1) *Eager signed solely as agent*

The initial HP contract was rescinded by agreement and no liability can arise under it (*Morris* v *Baron & Co* (1918)). The subsequent lease is not regulated by the Consumer Credit Act (CCA) 1974 because the hirer, Eager Ltd (E Ltd) is a limited company and not an individual (s189(1) CCA). E Ltd must be advised in relation to four matters, which are: (i) the effect of the lathe not being of Japanese manufacture; (ii) the effect of it being operable only by skilled operators; (iii) the effect of the one installed being different to the one shown to E; and (iv) the effect of Importer Ltd (I Ltd) saying that there was a ten-year manufacturer's guarantee. In advising E Ltd on these matters it is necessary to consider whether I Ltd was agent for CF Ltd.

E Ltd through its agent, Eager, signed a contract disclaiming that I Ltd was in any respect the agent of Crocodile Finance Ltd (CF Ltd). Such a disclaimer could be looked at in two ways: it may be that it is exactly what it claims to be, namely an agreement between E Ltd and CF Ltd that CF Ltd is not responsible for the acts of I Ltd; or it may be an exclusion clause whereby CF Ltd is attempting to avoid responsibility for the acts of its agent by claiming that in fact I Ltd is not an agent. Whether there is agency between CF Ltd, as principal, and I Ltd, as agent, is to be determined by investigating the relationship between them and also the relationship between CF Ltd and E Ltd, the third party. The relationship between CF Ltd and I Ltd will determine whether there is actual authority, that between CF Ltd and I Ltd will determine whether there is apparent authority. The disclaimer clause clearly rebutes apparent authority - there is no representation by CF Ltd to E Ltd that I Ltd is CF Ltd's agent, in fact there is a representation to the opposite effect. So the only question is whether there is actual authority. We are not told whether CF Ltd and I Ltd have made any sort of agency contract, so it will be assumed that the disclaimer represents the true position, that there is no agency between CF Ltd and I Ltd. On this basis the first of the two possible constructions of the clause mentioned above is submitted to be the correct one.

When I Ltd said the lathe was a 'Japanese Easiuse Ltd' this cannot be taken to be a description of the goods by CF Ltd. But, we are not told of the terms of the lease agreement signed by E and it would seem to be highly unlikely that no description of the goods was made. On the assumption that a description was contained within the contract so CF Ltd will be in breach of the condition implied into the hire contract by s8 of the Supply of Goods and Services Act 1982 if that description was not met. If the lathe was described as a 'Japanese Easiuse Lathe' then we must ask whether 'Japanese' was part of the description. Section 8 of the 1982 Act is the equivalent of s13 of the Sale of Goods Act 1979 in sale contracts and must be interpreted in the same way as s13; therefore we must ask whether 'Japanese' was a substantial ingredient of the identity of the goods hired (*Couchman* v *Hill* (1947); *Reardon Smith* v *Hansen-Tangen* (1976)). The origin of manufacture of goods often will not be part of their description because the origin will not matter to the hirer, but if it is the case that a Japanese Easiuse Lathe is different in kind to any other nationality of Easiuse Lathe, then the origin will be part of the description. Again we so not have sufficient information to be able to advise clearly on this.

Because CF Ltd are not responsible for representations made by I Ltd, so the statement by I Ltd that the lathe could be operated by unskilled workers would be of no effect. So, the question is whether the need for skilled operators is something which makes the lathe unmerchantable. Section 9 of the 1982 Act implies into hire contracts similar implied terms to those in s14(2) and 14(3) of the Sale of Good Act 1979, although the arrangement of subsections is different. On the evidence we have it does not appear that the lathe was not reasonably fit for the purpose or purposes for which goods of that kind are commonly supplied (s9(9) Supply of Goods and Services Act 1982), and therefore there would be no breach of s9.

That the machine delivered is different to that on the trade stand will not give E Ltd a remedy unless the hiring from CF Ltd can be seen to relate to the model displayed. In the absence of agency between CF Ltd and I Ltd there is no statement by CF Ltd that the lathe supplied should be similar to that on display, so there was no breach of s10 of the 1982 Act, the equivalent section to s15 of the 1979 Act. The point here is that there was no hiring by sample, the hiring was of the lathe actually supplied.

The assurance given by I Ltd that there was a ten-year manufacturer's guarantee does not affect CF Ltd because I Ltd was not CF Ltd's agent when making the statement and, in any event, it was made after the contract was concluded and so cannot affect matters (*Roscorla* v *Thomas* (1842)).

2) *Eager and Eager Ltd co-parties*

If the HP agreement was signed by E and E Ltd as co-parties, then it was a regulated consumer credit agreement, being a fixed-sum (s10(1)(b) CCA), restricted use (s11(1)(a) CCA), debtor-creditor-supplier (s12(a) CCA) agreement for credit not exceeding £15,000 (s8(2) CCA). The arrangements which were made to replace the HP agreement with a lease will be a rescission of the contract by agreement. The 1974 Act does not specifically set out the means by which such a rescission should be effected, but rescission by agreement is allowed at law and the Act does not purport to take that away (*Morris* v *Baron & Co* (1918)).

The lease is a regulated consumer hire agreement (s15(2) CCA) because E and E Ltd together count as an individual (s189(1) CCA). The 1974 Act will only regulate it if it is capable of lasting for more than three months (s15(1)(b) CCA) and does not require the hirer (E Ltd and E) to make payments exceeding £15,000 (s15(1)(c) CCA). We are not told that these two criteria have been met, but we are not told of any time limit on the hiring, so it will be assumed that it can run for more than three months and the advice of E's bank manager that it would be more economical to hire it than to pay the £17,999 cash price indicates that total payments required may well be no more than £15,000. If, in fact, the agreement is not regulated, then the common law applies as stated above, so the rest of this advice will proceed on the assumption that it is regulated.

The rescission of the HP agreement and its replacement with a regulated consumer hire agreement does not bring the case within those categories of multiple agreements within s18 of the 1974 Act. That section would only apply if both agreement exist side by side (s18(1) CCA), and does not apply where one agreement is rescinded and another made in its place. Consumer hire agreements are not classified under ss10-13 of the Act and this has the effect that s56 does not apply to them, therefore there is no statutory agency between CF Ltd and I Ltd. This, again, means that I Ltd were not the agent's of CF Ltd when negotiating the lease. Therefore the position is no different where E signs both on his own account and as agent for E Ltd from where he signs solely as agent.

PART 2

CONSUMER CREDIT

17 INTRODUCTION AND FORMATION OF THE CONTRACT

17.1 Introduction

The concept of consumer credit is an easy one to grasp. Essentially it covers the provision of finance for the acquisition of either goods or services. The main body of law on the subject is now contained in the Consumer Credit Act 1974 (CCA) which, it should be noted, did not come fully into force until 19 May 1985. This Act now regulates most consumer credit transactions, but it should be noted that other legislation may have relevance. It particular the Sale of Goods Act 1979 applies to conditional sales and credit sales and the Supply of Goods (Implied Terms) Act 1973 implies terms as to quality and title into all hire purchase contracts. It should also be remembered that, quite apart from the specific formalities required by CCA, the ordinary common law rules of contract will be applicable except where superceded. Thus, matters such as fraud, mistake, duress or illegality will apply as much to consumer credit contracts as to any other.

The 1974 CCA sets up a licensing system administered by the Director General of Fair Trading, and agreements made contrary to the licensing system are unenforceable. The Act also seeks to protect potential customers at the preliminary stages and so there are strict rules as to advertising and canvassing. For more details, the student should consult a textbook on the topic.

17.2 Key points

It is important that the student understands the following:

a) *Definitions*

There are many terms used in CCA which are defined to a lesser or greater degree in the Act itself. Most definitions are in s189 of the Act and, moreover, Schedule 2 of the Act contains some examples showing more explicitly what the new terminology means. Terms defined include the major forms of agreement: consumer credit; consumer hire; credit sale; conditional sale and hire purchase agreements being the main ones.

It is important to remember that the policy of the Act is to cover *consumer* credit agreements only. It does not apply where the purpose of the contract is to provide credit to commercial organisations. To this end the concept of a 'regulated' agreement is introduced by the Act (defined in s8) and this covers agreements which are not 'exempt' agreements as specified by s16 CCA. It is to regulated agreements only, that the Act applies. Essentially a regulated agreement is one when credit facilities are made available to a consumer.

Sometimes defining agreements in one particular way is inadequate, because agreements may have two or more than two functions at once. Such agreements are known as multiple agreements. It is clear that such agreements must be studied carefully and each separate stage identified to consider whether it comes within the category of regulated agreement and is hence within the confines of the Act. For example, a customer who goes into a shop and agrees to take a video recorder on hire purchase for £400 and also buys £50 worth of video films, makes two separate transactions and, while the first hire purchase contract is regulated, the second purchase of films is not.

To complicate matters further, the Act introduces the concept of principal agreement and 'linked' transactions. A linked transaction is one which is ancillary to the main consumer credit agreement, for example, a contract of insurance taken out at the behest of the creditor, for any major purchase such as a car. Section 19 CCA lists three main types of linked agreements; if a transaction comes into these (or other) categories it will be covered by the Act.

For various reasons, the parties may wish to modify or vary a regulated agreement so as to take into account new circumstances. Section 82(2) of the Act provides that the effect of such variation is to rescind the original agreement and replace it with the new. The new agreement is known as a 'modifying' agreement.

All regulated agreements must be further classified in accordance with ss10-13 of the Act. These sections deal with three pairs of definitions:

i) running account credit and fixed sum credit;

ii) restricted use credit and unrestricted use credit; and

iii) debtor-creditor-supplier credit and debtor-creditor credit.

Every contract therefore has three possible classifications, for example, hire purchase agreements could be described as fix sum, restricted use, or debtor-creditor-supplier agreements.

Space precludes a more detailed account of the statutory terminology and associated definitions; but the student should make sure that he is thoroughly familiar with this aspect of consumer credit law.

b) *Making the contract*

When a person acquires goods under a credit agreement he will normally negotiate with the dealer, the dealer will then supply the goods, and the creditor will supply the finance. An alternative possibility is that the dealer will sell the goods to the finance house, which in turn leases them out to the customer in a contract of hire purchase. This latter is a form of bailment and the ordinary common law rules as to bailment apply, but in fact the duties of the parties, within the context of the CCA are more specific than the ordinary law of bailment allows for.

Section 56(2) of the Act provides also that the negotiator, that is the dealer, shall be deemed to conduct negotiations in the capacity of agent of the creditor, that is the finance house, as well as in his own right. This has important implications in so far as the debtor's rights are concerned, especially with regard to misrepresentation. Effectively he has a right of action against both the dealer and the finance company in the event of any misrepresentation being made to him. Note that s56(3) makes void any clause purporting to exclude liability on the part of the creditor for statements made by the negotiator.

It has already been noted in the introduction that the ordinary common law as to contract will apply where not specifically excluded or inconsistent with the Act.

c) *Formalities*

While the ordinary common law rules as to contract are not basically altered by the Act, it does provide certain additional safeguards for the consumer.

One of the main protective measures of the Act is the requirement that the debtor receives certain written information to inform him of his rights and as to the potential effect of what he has signed. The basic provisions are contained in ss60-65 of CCA and are closely modelled on earlier hire purchase legislation. The rules about the form of the contract are very simple in principle, but extremely detailed.

In essence the buyer must be made aware of:

i) the rights and duties conferred on him by the agreement;

ii) the amount and rate of the total charge for credit;

iii) the protection and remedies available to him under the CCA;

iv) any other matters as laid down in governmental regulations.

The rules as to signature of documents and the provision of copies should be read thoroughly by the student.

d) *Withdrawal*

Section 57 of the Act deals with this. Effectively since it will apply in cases where an offer has been made, but not yet accepted it adds little to the common law rules of revocation. Section 57(4) provides that withdrawal has the same effect as cancellation (see below)

e) *Cancellation*

Sections 67-73 cover the cancellation of completed agreements. In this context, the Act does depart from standard common law rules, because normally revocation is no longer possible once acceptance has taken place. The Act is designed to give protection to the debtor in the form of a 'cooling-off period'.

Section 67 lays down conditions which must apply for a regulated agreement to be cancellable under the Act. They include requirements that oral representations must have been made in the pre-contractual negotiations, that those must be made direct to the debtor *in his presence*, by the negotiator and that the unexecuted agreement was signed by the debtor at premises other than those on which the creditor/negotiator normally carried on business.

The statute is thus designed to protect particularly those persons who may be visited in their own home by door to door salesmen who negotiate the contract and get it signed at the debtor's house or some similar place. The Act provides a fixed time for cancellation and lays down detailed rules as to the form cancellation must take and its effect; including the effect on linked transactions. Again, though the concept is straightforward, the rules are detailed and cannot be listed here. The student should make sure he is familiar with them.

f) *Variation*

Note the recent case of *Lombard Tricity Finance* v *Paton* [1989] 1 All ER 918 in which occurs a statement of the circumstances under which variation of terms may occur.

17.3 Analysis of questions

The topic of consumer credit in its most general form has cropped up a number of times in University of London past papers. In particular, definitions of different terms used in the Act have caught the examiners' eyes on several occasions. In truth, there is so much detailed and specific terminology, that this proves a constant favourite, without the examiners needing to repeat themselves too much. It is also possible to see, looking at past papers that it is quite common to set a question that needs some preliminary definitions and then requires the student to go on to something else - debtors' duties seems to be a strong possibility.

Formation and cancellation of the contract has occurred regularly, for example in 1989 (Q7) and 1991 (Q8). It is also quite frequently the case that aspects of consumer credit are combined with some aspect of sale of goods - see, for example, Q5 in the 1985 paper. The first question quoted below is unusual because it requires a direct comparison between hire purchase and sale of goods contracts.

The other two questions below are fairly typical of their kind and it should be noted that they overlap to some degree with other questions quoted later. See also question 3 in chapter 35, and Q7 of the 1993 paper in chapter 36.

17.4 Questions

Question 1

'A hire-purchase contract is really just a particular form of sale contract.'

To what extent is this true?

University of London LLB Examination
(for External Students) Commercial Law June 1992 Q3

Skeleton solution

- Definition of HP contract.
- Similarities to sale of goods contracts.
- Implied obligations under ss13-15 Sale of Goods Act 1979 common to both.
- Similar provisions as to exclusion clauses and Unfair Contract Terms Act 1977.
- Provisions of Consumer Credit Act 1974.
- Additional protection for consumers buying on hire purchase which consumers in sale of goods contracts do not have.

Suggested solution

A hire purchase contract is one which grants the debtor the option to purchase the goods if the terms of the agreement are complied with by him. But the debtor is not bound to exercise the option to purchase and consequently is not someone who agrees to buy goods (s61 Sale of Goods Act 1979 (SGA)), and so the transaction does not fall within the scope of the SGA. If approached from a realistic point of view, however, it may be seen that a consumer is entering into a hire purchase contract with a view to buying the goods. Probably one of the earliest cases to define a hire-purchase contract, (though it was not called that at the time) was *Helby* v *Matthews* (1895), where the House of Lords decided that the hirer of a piano had not 'agreed to buy' and therefore the contract did not fall within the ambit of the (then current) SGA. But from a commonsense point of view, sale of goods contracts and hire purchase contracts are so similar that they may in many ways be treated in the same manner. A hire purchase contract has much more in common, for example, with sale of goods, than with a contract for hire of goods which is a contract for bailment of goods in return for a rental, and where the hirer obtains only possession not ownership. The Supply of Goods and Services Act 1982 s6, in defining contracts for hire, specifically excludes hire purchase contracts. Since the passing of the Supply of Goods (Implied Terms) Act 1973, it has been common policy to assimilate the two types of contract.

For example, the implied obligations under s13-15 SGA as to correspondence with description, merchantable quality, fitness for purpose and correspondence with sample are incorporated into HP contracts by virtue of the Consumer Credit Act 1974 (CCA) Schedule 4, para 35 and ss8-10 of the Supply of Goods (Implied Terms) Act 1973. The working of these terms is not exactly the same as in the SGA, but to all intents and purposes the effect is the same as the implied terms in SGA. Thus, there is (s8(1)(a) of 1973 Act) an implied term as to title, s9(1) implies a condition as to correspondence with description, s10 contains provisions implying merchantable quality and fitness for purpose and s11 incorporates a term relating to sale by sample. There is no reason to suppose that these assorted sections will ever be construed separately or differently from their counterparts in SGA. It is interesting to note as well that much the same implied terms are also incorporated into HP contracts by virtue of common law (*Warman* v *Southern Counties Car Finance Corporation Ltd* (1949)), so that the debtor is really protected twice over.

One difference is that the doctrine of acceptance does not apply to hire purchase contracts in which the debtor deals as consumer, though there is a rule that prevents rejection once the contract has been affirmed after a breach. In effect the right to reject goods for breach of contract is treated in the same way as the right to rescind. The leading case on this topic is *Farnworth Finance Facilities* v *Attryde* (1970) in which it was held that where a motor bike, acquired on HP, proved to be faulty, the right to reject it could only be lost if the contract had been affirmed by the debtor. Not only does such affirmation require a decision by the debtor to go on with the contract, once the defects have become apparent, it also requires the debtor to have full knowledge of all defects. It used to be thought that if the goods persistently remained unfit, even after affirmation, then the debtor's right of rejection was resurrected. It is clear after *UCB Leasing* v *Holtom* (1987) that this is not so. Sale of goods contracts are governed by the rule that the right to reject will only be lost after acceptance by the buyer (ss34-35 SGA). While similar to affirmation, because of the different natures of hire purchase contracts as compared to sale of goods agreements, the two doctrines of affirmation and acceptance are quite distinct and separate.

Similar provisions apply to sale of goods and HP where exclusion clauses are concerned. The Unfair Contract Terms Act 1977 (UCTA) applies equally to both. In particular s6(1) provides that liability for breach of the implied undertakings as to title implied into sale of goods contracts by s12 SGA and into HP contracts by s8 of Supply of Goods (Implied Terms) Act cannot be excluded or restricted. This is so whether or not the parties deal 'as consumer'. Similarly, those terms as to description, quality and fitness and correspondence with sample implied by ss13-15 SGA and ss9-11 Supply of Goods Act cannot be excluded against any party dealing 'as a consumer'. Where neither party deals 'as consumer', the 'reasonableness' test (s11, Sched 2 UCTA) applies. The UCTA clearly equates sale of goods and hire purchase contracts, because s7 covers exclusion clauses in contracts *other than* those two - contracts for exchange, pledge, hire, etc are treated differently.

Thus far, it may be seen that with certain minimal differences, the two types of contract are indeed so similar that hire purchase contracts may be considered simply as another form of sale contract. There is, however, one important aspect we have not yet looked at, and that is the fact that under the provisions of the CCA the consumer who enters into an HP contract is given a great deal of additional protection which simply does not apply to a consumer entering a sale of goods contract. It is true that by its very nature the CCA limits the protection it offers to consumers only; in fact, comparatively few HP contracts are made by parties other than a business and a consumer. Most hire purchase contracts are entered into by consumers and therefore most contracts have this protection.

It is not possible to spend a great deal of time examining all the protection offered to a consumer by the CCA. Suffice to say it ranges from regulations which may be made by the Secretary of State (for example, as to form and content of advertisements); to a licensing system for those offering credit; to the fact that there exists a system of judicial control whereby 'unfair and extortionate bargains' may be challenged. Probably the three most important areas of protection offered to a consumer are:

- control over the exact form of the contract;
- rights of withdrawal/cancellation;
- power to have extortionate bargains reviewed.

We shall examine each of these briefly.

Contracts of sale of goods need to be in no particular form. While it is true that many firms now use the stereotyped 'standard form' contract, this is not required by the SGA. Hire purchase contracts entered into by a consumer, on the other hand, being 'regulated agreements' under the CCA, are subject to stringent rules, not so much as to the actual formation of the contract, but as to the documents the debtor must receive. Sections 60-65 of CCA regulate the final documentary form of the contract, the information which must be given to the debtor, the copies of documents he must receive and the timing of those documents. If an agreement is not in the prescribed form then it is improperly executed and cannot be enforced by the creditor without a court order.

Once made, as is always the case in contractual law, a sale of goods contract cannot be revoked or (usually) rescinded. The parties do not have the liberty to change their minds. A party to a regulated agreement under the CCA, most unusually, however, has a right of withdrawal (s57(3)) or cancellation (ss67-73). These rights are, of course, subject to a number of conditions, but they stem primarily from the need to protect consumers who may have been approached at their homes and subjected to pressures from, for example, door-to-door salesmen. At common law a party cannot unilaterally withdraw from a contract just because he feels like it: this 'cooling-off' period is unique to the CCA.

The power to have extortionate credit bargains reviewed by the courts (ss137-140 CCA) is in fact only a part of the wide protection offered to debtors by virtue of the power of the courts to step in to protect the weaker party if need be. Time orders (ie rescheduling of payments) (s129(2)(a)), amendment of agreement orders (ss127(5) and 129(2)(a)) and declarations (s142(1)), as well as the courts' powers to amend or cancel an 'extortionate' agreement, are all part of the protection offered by the CCA to the consumer debtor.

Thus it may be seen that while a hire purchase contract is, in many ways, similar to a sale of goods contract, having many of the same features, the fact is that, at least where the debtor is a consumer, he has far more protection legally than any ordinary purchaser.

Question 2

Campbell telephoned Holt Ltd, an electrical retailer, to inquire about obtaining a new electric mixer, record player and automatic washing machine. The same day, Holt Ltd sent a salesman, Starkie, to give a home demonstration. Campbell was satisfied with the models of mixer and washer demonstrated, agreed upon part-exchange prices for his own mixer and washer, and there and then signed hire purchase proposal forms in respect of these deals. Starkie gave Campbell copies of these forms, loaded Campbell's old mixer, record player and washer into his van, and persuaded Campbell to come with him, saying that he had a range of other models of record-player in his garage where he stored them for Holt Ltd. At Starkie's house, Campbell chose a record-player, agreed a part-exchange price for his old one, and signed a hire purchase proposal form to this effect in Starkie's van whence they had gone to hold their discussion out of the rain.

All three proposals were the next day accepted by Holt Ltd, which immediately posted copies to Campbell. That same day Campbell was declared redundant, and decided to withdraw from the deals. Accordingly, Campbell pushed a note through Starkie's door which explained his predicament and concluded:

'I am very sorry but I will not be able to make any payments. When should I return the mixer and washer?'

In consequence, Holt Ltd never delivered the new record-player, but instead sent Campbell a letter drawing his attention to the provisions of each of the hire purchase documents that the return of goods at the hirer's option could only be made at the premises of Holt Ltd and at the expense of the hirer plus payment of a cancellation fee of 20 per cent of the hire purchase price.

Campbell has now discovered that Holt Ltd has sold the part-exchange record player, and broken up the part-exchange mixer for scrap. He has made no payments, and two weeks later he put the new washer in an outhouse, from where it was stolen.

Advise Campbell.

University of London LLB Examination
(for External Students) Commercial Law June 1984 Q5

Skeleton solution

- Regulated agreement within meaning of CCA 1974?
- Definition of type of agreement.
- Offer and acceptance, revocation under common law.
- Cancellation rights: ss67, 68, 69; effects of cancellation.
- Rights of debtor to be informed of rights.

Suggested solution

This question relates solely to hire purchase law as governed by the Consumer Credit Act 1974.

The first question that must be answered is whether or not these transactions between Campbell and Holt Ltd are covered by the Consumer Credit Act 1974, which, inter alia, governs 'regulated' hire purchase agreements.

A 'regulated' agreement is defined under s8 of the Act as being a personal, non-exempt consumer credit agreement. It is clear in this case that the agreement is a 'personal' one because Campbell is clearly an 'individual' within s8(1) of the Act. It is not clear whether the agreement is non-exempt or a consumer credit agreement I have not been supplied with such information as the total credit or even the total price of the goods, nor the rates of interest.

There is no problem with regard to the fact that goods were given in part-exchange because the word 'deposit' is defined in s189 of the Act to include for this event.

Assuming that the agreements are covered by the Act they will be construed as fixed sum, restricted use, debtor-creditor-supplier transactions by virtue of ss10, 11, 12 of the Act.

Whether the agreements are covered by the Act or not, it is necessary to find out if the agreements were validly entered into. There needs to be an offer and an acceptance before there is a binding contract and that applies here as well as in other areas of contract. It is clear that by signing the forms Campbell has made an offer which was accepted by Holt Ltd. To be effective the acceptance must be communicated by the offeror but in most instances there is a clause in the agreement that states that the need for communication is waived, if this is present here the agreement will be binding at the time of acceptance. If such a clause is not present here the acceptance will be effective at the time of posting if that is a proper means of communication, if it is not, the acceptance will not be valid until the agreements arrive. In the unlikely event that the agreement is not valid until it arrives, there is no valid contract because Campbell's pushing a note through Starkie's door would amount to a revocation: *Financings Ltd* v *Stimson* (1962) (as Starkie would presumably be an agent for the receipt of a revocation. If the agreements are covered by the Act, Starkie would be an agent for the purpose under s56 of the Act) and s57 of the Act.

It is most likely that the agreements were concluded and thus it is necessary to consider whether they complied with the provision of the Consumer Credit Act 1974. I am not informed whether the agreements were in a state that all of their terms were readily legible and if they were not, this would be contrary to s61 of the Act.

Section 62 of the Act provides that if an unexpected agreement is presented personally to the debtor for signature but on the occasion when he signs it the document does not become an executed agreement, a copy of it and of any other document referred in it, must be then and there delivered to him. It appears that this was done in the case of the mixer and washing machine but not in the case of the record player. By s64 of the Act in the case of a cancellable agreement, a notice in the prescribed form indicating the right of the debtor to cancel the agreement, how and when the right is exercisable and the name and address of a person to whom the cancellation may be given should be included in every copy given to the debtor and must also be sent by post to the debtor within seven days following the making of the agreement. An agreement is cancellable if s67 of the Act is complied with, that is the antecedent negotiations included oral representations, those representations were made by a negotiator, in the presence of the debtor and were not signed at the negotiator's or creditor's premises.

In this case the agreements for the washing machine and mixer were signed in Campbell's premises and if oral representations were made by Starkie (which is very likely) these agreements were cancellable and a cancellation notice should have appeared with the copy of the agreement. The agreement for the record player was signed in Starkie's van which could not be defined as 'business premises' and again if oral representations were made by Starkie this agreement was cancellable and any copies of it should have contained a cancellation notice.

I am not informed as to whether ss60-64 of the Act were complied with but if they were not the agreement would not be enforceable save with a court order, s65 of the Act.

Assuming that the agreements were cancellable it is necessary to consider whether Campbell did cancel in accordance with s68 of the Act. To accord with that section, it is necessary that he serves a notice of cancellation between his signing the agreement and the end of the fifth day following the day on which he received the notice of cancellation under s64 of the Act. By virtue of s189 his notice of cancellation should apparently be in writing in order to be effective. Campbell sent a notice of cancellation in writing well within the statutory period and this will have effectively terminated the agreement.

The provision in the hire purchase documents purporting to say that he should pay a 20 per cent cancellation fee is void as being 'inconsistent with a provision for the protection of the debtor ... contained in (the) Act', by virtue of s56(3).

The effect of the cancellation is to terminate the agreements so that they are treated as never having been entered into s69(4). Any sum of money paid by Campbell is returnable as are the goods he provided in part-exchange. The goods should be returned 'substantially as good as when they were delivered to the negotiator' or Campbell shall be entitled to recover a sum equal to the 'part-exchange allowance' s73(2). The 'part-exchange allowance' is defined in s73(7)(b) to 'be the sum agreed as such in the antecedent negotiations or, if no such agreement was arrived at, such sum as it would have been reasonable to allow in respect of the part-exchange goods if no notice of cancellation had been served.

With regard to the washing machine supplied under the agreement, Campbell is by virtue of s72(4) under a duty to *restore* it to the supplier. The word 'restore' in this context means, hold the goods ready for collection and not to actually deliver them. Until they are collected a debtor is under a duty to take reasonable care of the goods for 21 days following the cancellation (s72) and it would appear that by putting the washer in the outhouse he is in breach of this duty and thus liable to Holts Ltd for the loss suffered: s72(11).

Question 3

Advise Horatio, who enters into agreement with the Finance-U Co to acquire the following goods, supplied by Denden plc:

a) A new refrigerator, hire purchase price of £300. Denden has a shortage of official agreement forms, so the basic terms are typed on a piece of paper with a note stating that the transaction is 'on Finance-U Co's usual terms'. A photocopy of the document is handed to Horatio. Two days later, before the refrigerator is delivered, Horatio telephones the manager of Denden's saying that he does not want the refrigerator after all. The manager does nothing, assuming that Finance-U Co will have already signed the agreement, although in fact this is not done until the following day.

b) A motor mower, hire purchase price £480. The agreement (top copy and an attached carbon copy) is sent by Finance-U Co to Horatio's home to look at. Two days later, Horatio takes it to Denden's premises, where he signs it and leaves both copies. After Horatio has paid £200, Finance-U Co hears that his lawn does not appear to have been cut recently and writes to demand information about the use and whereabouts of the mower. Horatio has been ill and fails to answer the letter or to pay the next two instalments. The mower is kept under a lean-to, where it occasionally gets wet and begins to rust. One night it is damaged by a falling tree in a freak hurricane. The following day, an employee of Finance-U Co calls on Horatio (who is out) and takes the mower away with him.

University of London LLB Examination
(for External Students) Commercial Law June 1990 Q8

Skeleton solution

a)
- Hire purchase generally - new goods - implied terms.
- Debtor-Creditor-Supplier/Debtor-Creditor agreements.
- Requirements/formalities for HP agreements.
- Cancellation.
- Relationship between Debtor/Creditor and Debtor/Supplier.

b)
- HP generally - secondhand goods.
- Formalities.
- Part payment. Possession and ownership differentiated.
- Protected goods.
- Re-possession - entry into premises - termination.

Suggested solution

In this question we are asked to advise Horatio (H) who has entered into two separate agreements with the Finance-U Co to acquire goods which are supplied by Denden Plc. Both agreements appear to be hire purchase agreements and therefore their formation and the obligations of the respective parties under them are regulated by Part V of the Consumer Credit Act 1974.

a) Under the first agreement H has entered into a hire purchase agreement to purchase a new refrigerator at a price of £300, the goods to be supplied by Denden Plc and the finance under the hire purchase to be provided by Finance-U Co. Certain agreements are exempt from the provisions of the CCA 1974 - most notably the 50 called 'small' agreements for restricted use credit (ie those regulated hire purchase agreements which do not require the hirer to make payments exceeding £50: s17(1)). We are given no information about the payments to be made by H; but it would appear that this agreement exceeds the £50 upper limit and the agreement is therefore not exempt under s17(1).

It is important at this stage to classify the agreements that H has entered into in order that one can fully advise him in respect of his rights and responsibilities thereunder. The 'agreement' in respect of the refrigerator appears to fall within the classification of a Debtor-Creditor-Supplier agreement. In essence this means that either the creditor is also the supplier of the goods or services or has an existing or contemplated business connection with the supplier. The other kind of agreement (that has not been entered into by H) recognised by the CCA ss12 and 13 is a debtor-creditor agreement where the creditor merely supplies the debtor with the needed credit facilities but the creditor is not also the supplier and has no business connection or contemplated business connection with the supplier.

As already stated, this arrangement appears to be a hire purchase agreement; such an agreement is defined by s189 CCA 1974, as being:

'an agreement, other than a conditional sale agreement under which goods are bailed in return for periodical payments by the bailee and the property in the goods will pass to the bailee if the terms of the agreement are complied with and the bailee exercises an option to purchase the goods'.

Often the retailer may choose to provide the finance for the agreement, but in the alternative a tripartite arrangement may be formed when the retailer sells the goods to a finance house and the finance house lets the goods out to the consumer on hire purchase terms. This has the net result that the finance house has in effect, made a secured loan to the debtor.

The questions here are whether or not the hire purchase agreement has been made in accordance with the appropriate regulations and formalities and secondly, whether H has any rights of cancellation when (two days after visiting the shop) he decides he does not want the fridge after all.

From the facts given, the agreement appears to be a 'regulated' agreement under s189 of the CCA 1974 and therefore must comply with the requirements of the Act in relation to disclosure of information, form and content, signature, copies and notices of cancellation rights. Section 60 of the CCA required detailed regulations to be made about the specified information to be included in the prescribed manner in documents for the making of 'regulated' agreements. The regulations made under s60 are known as the Consumer Credit (Agreements) Regulations 1983 and they provide that the agreement must be clearly legible and state the following information.

a) The amount of the credit or credit limit

b) The total charge for credit

c) Amounts and timings of repayment

d) The Annual Percentage Rate (APR)

e) Details of any security provided by the debtor

Additionally, the implied terms and conditions contained in the SGA 1979 ss12-15 are substantially repeated in relation to hire purchase contracts in the Supply of Goods (Implied Terms) Act 1973 (as amended) so that the hirer is in essentially the same position as regards title description, quality, fitness and sales by samples.

In most respects the apparent 'hire purchase' agreement entered into by H does not comply with the statutory requirements; in sequence these are as follows: Section 61(1)(a) CCA requires the agreement to be signed by the debtor or hirer personally and it must also be signed by or on behalf of the owner or creditor. Improper signatures means the agreement is improperly executed. Indeed the Consumer Credit (Agreements) Regulations 1983 prescribe a standard format for such signature boxes and additionally, if the agreement is cancellable, they cover a 'notice to cancel' box.

Sections 62 and 63 of the CCA contain detailed provisions in relation to copies of agreements to be provided to consumers. The debtor should receive at least one (and usually two copies) of the agreement and any other documents referred to in it; no details are given about whether or not the 'agreement' is cancellable, so one must assume it is bearing in mind H's actions. Breach of any requirements as to copies renders the agreement improperly executed (ss61-63). This agreement appears to be unexecuted at the time H was in the shop, we are not told if he signed it but can assume he did not. The agreement consists only of 'the basic terms', presumably repayments, price, APR etc and a note stating that the agreement is on Finance-U Co's usual terms.

H is given no notice of his cancellation rights under the special provisions thereon contained in s61(1)(a) to ensure the debtor is informed about his right to cancel. If the agreement is cancellable all the relevant copies under ss62 and 63 must be sent/given and contain a notice in the prescribed form setting out the rights of cancellation. A cancellable agreement is improperly executed if the requirements as to cancellation notices are not met; these requirements under the Consumer Credit (Cancellation Notices and Copies of Documents) Regulations 1983 require a notice of cancellation rights to indicate:

i) The right of the debtor to cancel

ii) How and when to cancel

iii) The name and address of a person to whom notice of cancellation may be given.

In conclusion then, this appears to be an attempt to make a regulated hire purchase agreement which fails for several reasons. Most notably, neither the debtor or creditor appear to have signed the agreement or the copies, secondly, the requirements of copies for what appears to be an unexecuted agreement (2nd copy within 7 days of the agreement being executed). Assuming the agreement to be cancellable no notice in the prescribed form about cancellation rights is contained in the agreement or sent to H. Lastly, the agreement is signed ex post facto to H's purported cancellation over the telephone by Finance-U Co (the creditor).

The agreement is in breach of the CCA in all these respects and therefore is improperly executed; the effect of an improperly executed agreement is that it can only be enforceable by an order of the court s65(1) CCA 1974. The court will look at culpability and the loss to the parties; in this case it appears to be Denden and Finance-U Co who are at fault and who fail to comply with the formalities. Accordingly, H will have effectively cancelled the agreement and it will not be enforced by the courts against him. Notice of cancellation is served by the telephone call under s69 CCA where the debtor or hirer can serve notice 'however expressed' on the agent of the debtor or hirer - no special or mandatory form of notice is required. There is no question of repayment of monies or liens as the fridge has not been delivered and no monies havc been paid.

b) In this case, we are again presented with a CCA regulated hire purchase agreement in respect of a secondhand lawn mower. However, the circumstances of the making of the agreement are very different and the questions of ownership, title and re-possession need to be settled.

In simple legal terms a hire purchase agreement is a bailment of goods (ie a delivery of possession of goods) plus the grant of an option to purchase. To be afforded the protection of the CCA such agreements should comply with the formalities that they be in writing, signed by both parties, contain all the agreed terms and that the correct copies and notices of provisions are completed. There appears to be some attempt here to infer that the agreement may be a 'cancellable' agreement because we are given few details about its exact nature but we are told that the agreement (top and carbon copies) are sent by Finance-U Co to H's home for him to peruse, and two days later he signs them at Denden's premises.

Whilst it is possible with some certainty to regard Denden Plc as the agent (and negotiator) for the creditor (ie Finance-U Co) it is almost impossible, bearing in mind the limited information about the formation of the agreement provided, to determine whether the agreement is cancellable under the four requirements necessary under s67 CCA 1974. We are not told whether any oral representations are made by the supplier or creditor, so under the fourth provision of s67 CCA it would appear that the agreement is prima facie not a cancellable one and the fact that H signs at Denden's premises is in this respect immaterial. He has had time to peruse the agreements and raise any queries and does not appear to be pressurised at the time of signing by his unfamiliar surroundings or sales techniques.

The problem then concerns the respective rights, duties and responsibilities of the parties (debtor-creditor and supplier) following the making of a valid agreement.

Horatio has paid £200 of the total hire purchase price of £480, this means the goods have not yet passed into his ownership (they will not do so until all instalments have been paid and the option to purchase exercised). However, the goods are protected goods under s90(1) CCA 1974. Section 90 states that goods are 'protected goods' at any time when:

a) The debtor is in breach of a regulated hire purchase or conditional sales agreement relating to goods; and

b) The debtor has paid to the creditor one-third or more of the total price of the goods; and

c) The property of the goods remains in the creditor.

Section 90(1)

This section is designed to protect the debtor against unscrupulous 'snatch-back' by the creditor and the debtor is afforded three-fold protection by the CCA so that before 'snatch-back' can occur notice must be given, any entry onto debtor's premises is restricted and the goods in any event may be 'protected'.

Under a hire purchase agreement the parties have certain rights, duties and obligations. The implied condition on the part of the creditor/credit broker is that the hirer will 'enjoy quiet possession of the goods': s8 Supply of Goods (Implied Terms) Act 1973. However, there is a corresponding implied obligation on the bailee of goods to use reasonable care in looking after the goods, the debtor will be liable in damages if he chooses not to exercise his option to purchase or the contract is determined for non-payment etc. If the goods are damaged during the currency of the agreement the onus is on the debtor to show he has taken reasonable care of them (*Joseph Travers & Sons* v *Cooper* (1915)). The debtor may be liable in damages for the loss caused to the creditor.

As already mentioned the lawn mower is 'protected' under s90 CCA as more than half the hire purchase price has been paid. Contravention of s90 means that the agreement is terminated, the debtor is released from all liability, the debtor is entitled to recover from the creditor all sums paid by the debtor under the agreement (s91 CCA 1974). Section 90 does not apply where the debtor has himself terminated the agreement or if the debtor agrees to the re-possession at the time.

It can be argued that by non-payment of two instalments H is in breach of the agreement and has thus terminated it, entitling Finance-V Co's representative to re-possess. However, his illness may have led to this as an oversight and additionally, he has not overtly repudiated the agreement, by for example, writing to the creditor or credit broker. In *Financings Ltd* v *Baldock* (1963) the Court of Appeal stated that mere failure to pay two instalments does not amount to repudiation to entitle the creditor to re-possess. The creditor in this case could only claim the arrears and damages for non-payment of the arrears.

The creditor or owner is not entitled to terminate the contract or re-possess the goods unless written notice has been shown of the termination (usually at least seven days default notice) ss87 and 92(1) CCA. 'The creditor is not entitled to enter any premises' to take possession of goods the subject of a regulated hire purchase agreement 'without a court order' and the debtor cannot recover possession of protected goods without a court order: s90(2).

The hurricane that damages the lawn mower is described as a freak. A lean-to may not be the safest place to keep the lawn mower - but the agreement has not been terminated by default (only two instalments not paid) or by notice. The goods are protected and Finance-U Co's representative gets no consent from H for re-possession at the time of his illegal entry onto H's premises. Thus the re-possession is illegal and H can treat the agreement as terminated and reclaim all £200 paid thereunder. He must make the goods available for collection but has no duty to delivery them himself to the creditor.

18 THE CREDITOR'S OBLIGATIONS

18.1 Introduction

The creditor has a number of duties, some by virtue of common law, some implied by statute, the most important Acts being the Sale of Goods Act 1979 and the Supply of Goods (Implied Terms) Act 1973 and of course the Consumer Credit Act itself imposes certain obligations on the creditor.

18.2 Key points

a) *Information*

The creditor is required, under the Consumer Credit (Prescribed Periods for Giving Information) Regulations 1983, to provide the debtor with information about the agreement he has entered into. In particular details should be given as to the amount already paid; how much is due, immediately; and how much remains to be paid in the future. Information as to the debtor's general rights should be contained in a regulated agreement and the Act provides that the debtor is entitled to a copy of that agreement initially and further information on (written) request. Additionally, should the creditor wish to take certain actions on breach the CCA s76 makes provision for the serving of a default notice and dictates the information which must appear in such a notice.

b) *Misrepresentations*

Most consumer credit transactions are entered into either as a result of the debtor visiting the dealer's shop or place of business, or as a result of door to door salesmen representing the dealer visiting the debtor's home to negotiate the transaction. In either case the debtor seldom has any contact directly with the creditor; the finance house. Section 56 of CCA 1974 creates a statutory agency, necessary because in common law the dealer will not always be the agent of the creditor.

By virtue of s56 the debtor is thereby protected against misrepresentations which may have been made in the course of the normal pre-contractual negotiations. The purpose of s56 is to make the creditor liable for statements made either by: (i) himself; (ii) a shop or garage which sells to the creditor goods, which are then let on hire purchase, or conditional sale, or credit sale to the debtor; or (iii) a supplier who sells goods to the debtor under a contract financed by a debtor-creditor-supplier agreement.

Section 56 does not impose any direct liability on the dealer when he acts as negotiator for the creditor, but he can be made personally liable. For such a situation to apply the relationship between dealer and debtor falls within the rule of *Hedley Byrne & Co Ltd* v *Heller & Partners Ltd* [1964] AC 465 then the dealer may be liable for the tort of negligent misstatement. In the vast majority of cases, though, this is unlikely.

c) *Implied terms as to title, quality description and sample*

Both conditional sales and credit sales are sales of goods and therefore the usual implied terms of SGA 1979 will apply. (See chapters 4 and 5). Hire purchase contracts are not sales of goods and therefore not governed by SGA but similar implied terms are contained in the Supply of Goods (Implied Terms) Act 1973 which have a virtually identical effect. (See chapter 16).

It should be noted, however, that the doctrine of acceptance as incorporated into SGA does not apply to certain conditional sales or to either regulated or unregulated hire purchase contracts. Essentially, the main difference is that the right to reject goods for breach of contract is treated in the same way as the right to rescind for misrepresentation. The right to reject will only be lost when the debtor has positively affirmed the contract. The leading case on this is *Farnworth Finance Facilities Ltd* v *Attryde* [1970] 2 All ER 774 but there is in general a lack of reported case law and the rules of rejection are still developing.

18.3 Analysis of questions

As noted earlier, in chapter 17, the questions on consumer credit, overlap with one another as to their subject matter. While the first two questions quoted below are, in part, concerned with formation of the contract and its subsequent cancellability, they are equally concerned to test the student's knowledge of the statutory requirements of the creditor to give information. They are, therefore, equally relevant to either chapter 17 or chapter 18. The third question is more unusual and requires the student to deal with HP contracts and implied terms and conditions therein, analogous to those relating to title, merchantable quality, etc contained in the SGA 1979. Questions of ownership and title need to be resolved, as does the matter of the purported lien and finally the fact that there is a reference to exclusion clauses and UCTA make this a wide-ranging question.

18.4 Questions

Question 1

Dick is a salesman, employed by the Audacious Encyclopaedia Publishing plc. He called on Ena and persuaded her and her husband Fred to sign an agreement for the purchase of an encyclopaedia by 30 monthly instalments. They paid a deposit of £25 and Dick handed over the first monthly instalment of the encyclopaedia at the same time. The agreement was signed on behalf of the company on 28 April 1987. Dick intended to call on Ena on 2 June to collect the first monthly instalment, but he was ill and delayed his visit until 9 June. Ena informs him that she wrote to the company on 2 May cancelling the agreement. She handed over the first part of the encyclopaedia and demanded the return of her £25. Dick said that he would have to consult his company. He then discovers that Ena's letter had never been received and that the first part of the encyclopaedia had been damaged, apparently by a child.

Discuss.

University of London LLB Examination
(for External Students) Commercial Law June 1988 Q8

Skeleton solution

- Regulation by CCA 1974.
- Formation of contract - copies.
- Cancellability - withdrawal - 'cooling-off'.
- Duty of care re goods.
- Recovery of deposit.
- Joint debtors - effect?

Suggested solution

We are not told whether the agreement signed by Ena and Fred was a conditional sale or a credit sale, but nothing revolves around this. It is clear, however, that it is not hire purchase because we are told that it was an agreement for the purchase of the encyclopaedia and hire purchase is not a contract of sale (*Helby* v *Matthews* (1895)).

A second matter on which we do not have information is the total price of the encyclopaedia. This is relevant in that the Consumer Credit Act 1974 will not regulate a conditional sale or credit sale where the amount of credit provided is in excess of £15,000 (s82 Consumer Credit Act (CCA) 1974). It is inconceivable that encyclopaedia will cost more than £15,000, so it can safely be assumed that the agreement was regulated. Whether it is conditional sale or credit sale it is classified by the Act as fixed sum, restricted use and debtor-creditor-supplier credit (ss10(1)(b), 11(1)(a) and 12(a) CCA 1974 respectively).

Ena and Fred are joint debtors in that they both signed the agreement. The Act treats them as separate debtors in that everything which ought to be done by a creditor towards a debtor must be done towards both debtors where there are two (s185(1)(a) CCA 1974).

When they were visited by Dick, Ena and Fred signed a document following persuasion by Dick. Any statement made by Dick amounted to antecedent negotiations and things he said in the course of those negotiations he said as agent of Audacious Encyclopaedia Publishing plc (s56 CCA 1974). At the time they signed it it had not been signed by Audacious Encyclopaedia Publishing plc and was therefore unexecuted after Ena and

Fred signed it. Because (a) the agreement was signed otherwise than at the business premises of Dick or Audacious Encyclopaedia Publishing plc; (b) oral representation were made by Dick during the course of antecedent negotiations; and (c) Audacious Encyclopaedia Publishing plc had not already signed it, so the agreement was cancellable by Ena and/or Fred (s67 CCA 1974).

Ena and Fred were entitled to receive a copy of the unexecuted agreement there and then when they signed it (s62(1) CCA 1974). As has been noted above, as joint debtors they are entitled to each receive a copy of any document which must be given by the creditor. We are not told whether any copy was given to them at the time. If none was given, the agreement was improperly executed and could not be enforced by Audacious Encyclopaedia Publishing plc without that company first obtaining a court order (s65(1) CCA 1974). In addition, because the agreement was cancellable, notices of cancellation rights should have been served at the same time as the copies of the agreement itself (s64(1)(a) CCA 1974).

The agreement was counter-signed by Audacious Encyclopaedia Publishing plc on 28 April 1987. But that signature would not itself conclude the contract because Ena and Fred had made an offer by their signatures and acceptance must be communicated to the offeror (*Powell* v *Lee* (1908)). If the postal acceptance rule applies to consumer credit agreements, the contract would be made as soon as the credit (Audacious Encyclopaedia Publishing plc) posts copies of the counter-signed (executed) agreement to Ena and Fred (*Adams* v *Lindsell* (1818)). If the postal acceptance rule does not apply the contract would only be made when the copies were received. In any event, Audacious Encyclopaedia Publishing plc was under an obligation to send copies of the executed agreement along with separate notices of cancellation rights (s64(1)(a) CCA 1974) to Ena and Fred by post (s63(3) CCA 1974) within the seven days following the making of the agreement (s63(2) CCA 1974). This is understood to mean within the seven days following the making of the contract. In a case such as this where the contract could only be made by the posting or receipt of the copies of the executed agreement, the creditor complies with its obligations by posting the copies, it does not have to post copies in order to accept the offer and then post further copies in order to comply with s63(2).

All of this has three effects on the facts given. Firstly, if no copies were sent or received no contract was ever made. Secondly, if copies were posted and received the agreement was cancellable until the end of the fifth day following the receipt of the copies of the executed agreement. Thirdly, if there was any failure to serve the proper copies or notices of cancellable rights, Audacious Encyclopaedia Publishing plc can only enforce the agreement by court order (s165(1) CCA 1974).

Ena's letter of cancellation which was posted on 2 May 1987 but not received was effective either to withdraw the offer made by her and her husband or to cancel the agreement. It would be a withdrawal of the offer if the contract had not been concluded by 2 May (s57 CCA 1974), and it would be a cancellation if the contract had been made (s69 CCA 1974). Therefore, whether or not Audacious Encyclopaedia Publishing plc gave Ena and Fred the correct copies and notices, the conditional or credit sale agreement is no longer in existence. It is irrelevant that Ena's letter did not arrive because a document sent by post is properly served whether or not it arrives (s176(3) CCA 1974). Further, it is irrelevant that only Ena wrote to withdraw/cancel because it is clear from the circumstances that she was acting on behalf of both herself and Fred and by s185(1)(b) her letter of withdrawal or cancellation has effect as though both she and Fred had written. Finally, the form of words used by Ena in her letter is irrelevant provided she made it clear she was backing out of the agreement (see s57(2) CCA 1974 for withdrawal and s69(1) for cancellation).

On withdrawal or cancellation Ena and Fred became under a duty to take reasonable care of the one part of the encyclopaedia which they had received (s72(4) CCA 1974). That duty is also deemed to have existed in the period prior to withdrawal/cancellation (s72(3) CCA 1974). The duty to take reasonable care terminated after 21 days because Ena and Fred received no written demand for the return of the encyclopaedia (s72(8) CCA 1974). After that 21-day period expired Ena and Fred were still under a duty of care towards Audacious Encyclopaedia Publishing plc's goods, but the standard of care was lower, being a duty to refrain from doing deliberate damage. Dick only collected the damaged part on 9 June which was 38 days after withdrawal/cancellation and it does not appear from the facts whether the damage was done before or after the 21-day period from withdrawal/cancellation expired. Indeed, we are also unable to say whether the damage was caused by a failure of Ena and Fred to exercise care. Any action Audacious Encyclopaedia Publishing plc may have for the damage is actionable as a breach of statutory duty (s72(11) CCA 1974). The 1974 Act does not state whether an action for breach of this statutory duty may be maintained where the creditor has not complied with the formalities rules, though there seems no reason why it should not be possible.

In addition to Ena and Fred being obliged to take care of the goods following cancellation, they have the right to recover the £25 deposit (s70(1)(a) CCA 1974). The deposit is repayable by the person to whom it was paid (s70(3) CCA 1974), which is Dick. Nevertheless, because Dick received it for the use of Audacious Encyclopaedia Publishing plc and appears to have received it within his actual authority as the company's agent, Ena and Fred may sue Audacious Encyclopaedia Publishing plc for its recovery as money had and received (*Branwhite* v *Worcester Works Finance Ltd* (1969)). Ena and Fred had a lien for the £25 over the part of the encyclopaedia which they had received (s70(2) CCA 1974), but have now lost that lien because they have handed it back.

Question 2

Aziz and Nasrul, who speaks very little English, are newly-weds who have just arrived in England. They visit the premises of Elekute plc to buy an electric kettle for £20. Jeevus, the salesman, who earns commission on all sales over £150, invites them to buy a new microwave oven for £180. Aziz says that they are short of money. Jeevus says that, if they buy the microwave, he will let them have the kettle free. To persuade them, he says that they can take them both away and try them at home. He fills a form on behalf of Elekute to enable them to buy the microwave on hire purchase from Kwikfilch Ltd, a company which finances hire purchase sales arranged by Elekute. He gives them the form to take away and read at home.

When they are at home, Aziz fills in the form and signs it but tells Nasrul that they will wait a few days before making a final decision. One week after their visit to the shop, and while Aziz is at work, Jeevus calls on Nasrul and asks her for the form back. She gives it to him. After Jeevus leaves, Nasrul's sister Ayesha tries to make a cup of tea with the kettle but it explodes, scalding her and causing a fire in the kitchen. When he returns home, Aziz puts the kettle and the microwave in the back garden and tells Nasrul that they will have nothing more to do with Elekute.

Advise Elekute.

University of London LLB Examination
(for External Students) Commercial Law June 1991 Q8

Skeleton solution

- Regulated agreement within meaning of CCA 1974?
- Rules of common law especially offer/acceptance.
- Rights of debtor to be informed of rights; copies of agreement, signature.
- Cancellation rights ss67-69.
- Misrepresentations by negotiator? Negotiator as agent for finance house.
- Supply of Goods (Implied Terms) Act as to merchantability and fitness for purpose of goods.
- Duty of care of debtor/hirer to goods during either contractual period or after cancellation.

Suggested solution

This question relates solely to hire purchase law, as governed by the Consumer Credit Act 1974 (CCA).

The first question that must be answered is whether the transactions in question (between Elekute (E) and Aziz and Nasrul (A and N), and similarly between Kwikfilch (K) and A and N are indeed completed contracts at all?

Section 8 of CCA governs all 'regulated' hire purchase agreements. A 'regulated' agreement is one defined under the Act as being a personal non-exempt consumer credit agreement. Certainly A and N are 'individuals' within s8(1) of the CCA. It is not clear from the wording of the question which of two categories the 'contract' may fall into. When a person acquires goods on credit he will normally negotiate with the dealer, the dealer will supply the goods, and the creditor will supply the finance. Alternatively the dealer may sell the goods to the finance house, which in turn leases them out to the consumer in a form of hire purchase known as bailment. Section 56(2) of CCA provides that the negotiator, that is the dealer, shall be deemed to conduct negotiations in a dual capacity, that is as agent of the creditor as well as in his own right.

Whether the agreements are covered by the CCA or not it is first necessary to decide whether any contract has been validly entered into. The ordinary common law rules are not basically altered by the CCA, it merely provides certain additional safeguards for the consumer. Is there offer and acceptance here? A and N take away the form, Aziz signs and fills it in and Nasrul hands it over to Jeevus. Even though Aziz has remarked to Nasrul that they will 'wait a few days to think it over' a week has apparently gone by ... more than their agreed few days. There would appear to be offer and acceptance and it seems likely that agreements were concluded. While still on the topic of ordinary contractual rules however, it may be worth pointing out that in view of the fact that A and N are said to speak very little English and have recently arrived in England, the thought occurs that, firstly, the necessary intention to create a legal relationship may not exist and secondly, in view of Jeevus' undoubted pressurising of the pair, their apparent agreement may be a product of undue influence. In either case this would have repercussions as to the validity of the contract.

However, because the CCA makes special provisions to protect consumers, it may not be necessary for A and N to prove that the contract is vitiated at common law. A number of alternatives spring to mind within the CCA.

Sections 60-65 of CCA contain a number of detailed provisions as to the form of the contract. Essentially the buyer must be made aware of:

i) the rights and duties conferred on him by the agreement;

ii) the amount and rate of the total charge for credit;

iii) the protection and remedies available to him under the CCA;

iv) any other matters which government regulations may from time to time lay down.

There are particularly detailed rules as to signature of documents and the provision of copies. While we are not told what precise form the document from E takes, we do know that A and N 'speak little English' and there is no indication that Jeevus has gone through the form with them, he simply tells them to take it away and read it at home. There is no mention at all of copies, and no indication whether copies of the agreement are to be forwarded to A and N within the relevant period. Thus we need to know not only that the form contains all the necessary information required by the CCA but that A and N understood it. If ss60-64 are not complied with there will not be an enforceable agreement, save with a court order (s65) which, in the circumstances is most unlikely to be granted.

The CCA gives added protection to consumers in the form of cancellation rights, ss67-73 cover the cancellation of completed agreements giving what is effectively a 'cooling-off period'. Section 67 lays down criteria that must be satisfied for an agreement to be cancellable. These include the requirement that oral representations must have been made in the pre-contractual negotiations, they must have been made directly to the debtor, in his physical presence, and the agreement must have been signed at premises other than those where the dealer/creditor carried on business. While the question is not specific as to whether oral representations were made by Jeevus, it seems most likely that in his enthusiasm to earn commission he would have made various claims for both microwave oven and kettle. All the other requirements of s67 are fulfilled and this would therefore appear to be a cancellable contract. Section 68 lays down the procedure for cancellation; it seems that apart from the physical act of putting the electrical goods in the back garden and saying they would have nothing more to do with E, A does nothing positive to take steps to cancel. It seems very likely that he has not received any notification of his rights of cancellation in any case and as stated earlier, for this reason the enforcement of the 'contract' is likely to present difficulties. If there is a valid contract, it seems that Aziz has not taken the necessary steps to cancel under s68 and the contract has not been brought formally to an end.

In the circumstances given, a further matter arises: the question of the deficiencies in the goods themselves. The implied terms and conditions contained in Sale of Goods Act 1979 especially in ss12-15, are substantially duplicated in relation to HP contracts in the Supply of Goods (Implied Terms) Act 1973 (as amended). The explosion of the kettle would indicate that in particular the requirements as to merchantability and fitness for purpose have not been fulfilled. It has already been noted that by virtue of s56 CCA, A and N are protected against any misrepresentation uttered by Jeevus in the course of the pre-contract negotiations. Of course, if there is no valid agreement, then liability will be tortious rather than contractual. In any event since the person injured is Ayesha, Nasrul's sister, the normal doctrine of privity of contract may prevent her seeking a contractual remedy herself. Although Ayesha was not privy to the contract between E and A/N she may have a right to sue under the Consumer Protection Act 1987. By s2(2) of that Act, an importer into the EC of defective goods is liable for damage caused by the defect. Because Ayesha suffered personal injuries the minimum loss rule as incorporated in s5(4) does not apply. This is, of course, provided Elekute are the importers. Since we are required to advise only E, it need not be taken further - though if Ayesha can trace the importers she will have a right of action against them.

We are told that Aziz puts not only the offending kettle, but also the microwave oven 'in the back garden'. It is clear that his intention is to have no further dealings with E, though it is not clear, as already pointed out, whether he is aware of his rights of cancellation or has taken any steps to cancel. In the case of a cancellable contract, which has been cancelled, Aziz would be under a duty to restore the goods to the supplier. By s72(4) CCA, the word restore has been defined as meaning holding the goods ready for collection rather than actively setting out to deliver them back. In any HP contract, the hirer has a duty of care towards the goods (*Joseph Travers & Sons* v *Cooper* (1915)), that is, a duty the breach of which will be negligence. The kettle may be beyond redemption, but to put the microwave in the garden, exposed to weather and a risk of theft, would appear to be negligence on the part of Aziz.

To conclude, three main questions require to be answered:

i) is there, under the ordinary rules of common law, a valid contract?

ii) does it come within the CCA, having been properly executed and all the detailed requirements of that Act complied with? and

iii) if it is a regulated contract within the CCA has Aziz taken steps to cancel?

It is only when the answers to these basic questions are given that it would be possible to advise E, both as to their liability for the defective kettle and as to their position with regard to either enforcement of the contract, or recovery of the goods.

Question 3

Delbert, a used car dealer in London, advertises for sale a 1966 Ford Consul, which he describes as being 'in as perfect condition as the day she was made'. Unknown to Delbert, the car was recently in a serious accident while on hire purchase from Finco Ltd to Roger. Roger had sold it to Delbert after repairing it.

Delbert tells Hiram that the car has only had one owner, so Hiram agrees to take it on hire purchase, which Delbert arranges with Finco Ltd.

The agreement between Finco and Hiram states that: 'This contract is made solely between the two parties hereto, no other person having authority to act in any way on behalf of any of the parties. The hirer takes the car as he finds it on inspection, which he agrees to make to satisfy himself of its condition. No liability of any sort is accepted by the creditor for its condition.'

The car regularly breaks down and Hiram incurs a great deal of expenditure having it repaired at Xerxes' garage. Since Finco's office is in Newcastle, Hiram calls in at Delbert's showrooms to inform him that, so far as he is concerned, the deal is off and he wants his money back; the car, he says, is at Xerxes' garage, where Xerxes is keeping it until his bills have been paid.

Advise Hiram.

University of London LLB Examination
(for External Students) Commercial Law June 1990 Q7

Skeleton solution

- HP generally - ownership, title and the implied conditions in the HP contract.
- DCS regulated agreements, the credit-broker as agent of the creditor, rights and duties of creditors and debtors inter se.
- Passing of title under HP agreements that have not been completed, private sales.
- Exclusion clauses UCTA, documents of title.
- Remedies, liens, misrepresentation.

Suggested solution

We are asked to advise Hiram (H). Delbert (D) is a used car dealer, presumably he has some knowledge and expertise that he applies when purchasing secondhand vehicles for re-sale to his clients. Additionally, in his trade he will have some knowledge of the proof of ownership and documents of title that are necessary to trade in secondhand vehicles. It is reasonable to assume that, with experience of this kind of motor vehicle sales, he will make (or should have made) some enquiries as to whether or not the vehicle was changed or encumbered in any way when he purchased the 1966 Ford Consul he is advertising, from Robert (R).

D has advertised the 1966 Ford Consul as being 'in perfect condition as the day she was made'; it seems unlikely that he will believe in the truth of this claim if (as is usual) he has inspected a vehicle which is 24 years old and has recently been in what we are told was a 'serious accident'. It seems unlikely (though possible) that the vehicle has had only 'one owner' as claimed by D to induce Hiram (H) to purchase the vehicle; the vehicle is 24 years old, but we know that R had it on hire-purchase from the same finance company that D acts as credit broker for, namely Finco Ltd. No finance company will agree to Hire Purchase over 24 years; so R could logically not have been the only owner. In other words D it appears, made two serious misrepresentations about the condition of the vehicle in written form when he advertises, knowing or suspecting his statement in this respect to be grossly misleading at least; and secondly, when he makes oral representations that the Ford has had only one owner.

Additionally, if he has made the usual enquiries and examined the log-book and title documents, he will not only know that his statements are untrue; but will probably have some inkling or direct knowledge that the vehicle was under HP from Finco to R.

We are confronted here by two separate hire purchase agreements in relation to the same vehicle; two agreements made at different times and to different 'owners' of the Ford, but both with the same creditor, Finco Ltd. In the present case D appears to have acted as a 'credit broker' by introducing H to Finco and arranging HP terms for H's purchase from D of the car. In this respect the arrangement would be a debtor-creditor-supplier agreement with A, Finco and D fulfilling respective roles. Moreover, the agreement will almost certainly be a 'regulated' agreement under the terms of the CCA 1974 s13 (for the present purposes we can assume that D and Finco are 'connected' and have a 'pre-existing arrangement' as to the hire purchase D arranges). We are not told the amount of the hire purchase or the repayment periods or amounts, but we can assume that the upper limit of the total hire purchase does not exceed £15,000 and that s8 (regulated agreements) CCA 1974 applies.

Some general points about the nature of both hire purchase agreements can be made at this point to enable us to fully explore the questions of ownership title and lien that arise subsequent to D selling the Ford to R.

The essential nature of a hire purchase contract as regulated by the CCA 1974 has been described as being a 'bailment' of the goods (ie a delivery of possession of goods plus the grant of an option to purchase the goods (Sir Gordon Borrie - Commercial Law 6th Edn). The working of the modern hire purchase contract was described in graphic terms by Lord Denning in *Bridge* v *Campbell Discount Co Ltd* (1962).

'It is in effect, though not in law, a mortgage of goods ... the finance house has become the owner of goods who lets them out on hire. So it buys the goods from the dealer and lets them out on hire to the appellant (bailee).'

A hire purchase contract is not a sale of goods because under hire purchase the customer is never bound to buy and only becomes the owner when all the instalments are paid and he has exercised the option to purchase (generally speaking).

Hire purchase contracts confer advantages on both parties: the bailee gets possession of the goods and the period of hire to pay for them with the option to own them at the end of the period, the bailer 'sells' the goods and receives interest on the hire purchase price. However, HP contracts also incur liabilities (and duties) and penalties for the breach of these.

The main duties of the bailee include to pay the instalments, to take reasonable care of the goods and not to relinquish possession to any third party, the principal obligations of the creditor include the implied terms as to fitness, title, quality etc (Supply of Goods (Implied Terms) Act 1973).

Before advising H, it is necessary to look at the chain of events that resulted in his taking the car on hire purchase from Finco after being introduced to them by D who is in effect a credit broker for Finco. The original HP agreement between R and Finco meant that Finco is the original creditor and R the original debtor. R damages and repairs the car and sells it (presumably for cash) to D. D acquires the documents of title, but Finco would not appear therein. R is in breach of his duty to Finco not to relinquish possession of the hire vehicle; he has at that stage no rights of ownership and no rights of disposal. We are not told if R has continued to pay instalments after selling to D or if he has discharged his debt to Finco. We can assume he has done neither of these. In any event R appears to be in breach of his duty to take reasonable care of the goods and has damaged them in an accident and resorted to re-pairing them himself. The debtor is not liable for fair wear and tear but the onus is on him during the currency of the agreement if the goods are damaged, to show that he has taken reasonable care of them: *Joseph Travers & Sons* v *Cooper* (1915).

Hiram takes the car following the misrepresentations by D about its condition, ownership and his (D's) title to sell to H. D also introduces H to Finco and Finco enter a second HP agreement with H (the first being with R) for the hire of the Ford. Finco already own the vehicle and are creditors to R. H signs an HP agreement which includes an exclusion clause.

As a purchaser from R, D could possibly have got good title to the vehicle if he knew nothing of the HP agreement between R and Finco. However, the fact that D is a secondhand car dealer denies him the 'special protection' afforded to a 'private purchaser' (someone who does not carry on a business as a dealer in motor vehicles or of providing finance for hire purchase transactions in motor vehicles) under Part III Hire Purchase Act 1964. Section 27 HPA 1964 Pt III provides where the bailee of a motor vehicle 'disposes' of it to a private purchaser who takes it in good faith and without notice of the hire purchase agreement 'such disposition' has effect as if the creditor's title to the vehicle had been vested in the debtor' immediately before that disposition.

There is a wealth of case law on the subject of goods sold on hire purchase being 'disposed' of during the currency of the agreement by the bailee; it would appear that by his breaches R has terminated his agreement with Finco and the latter are entitled to recover possession of the vehicle and to sue R for damages to their property through his negligence: *Ballett* v *Mingay* (1943). D appears to be the agent of Finco as he seems to have a 'pre-arranged' finance agreement to recommend customers to them (ie D is a credit broker under the CCA 1974).

D's misrepresentations are subject to the Misrepresentation Act 1967 s3 (which governs exclusion clauses excluding liability for misrepresentation), in that they induce H to purchase the car and appear to substantially influence his decision. As D's principal, Finco appears to be liable for these misrepresentations; when H sought HP from them they would have checked their records and seen that they already owned the Ford and that an HP agreement already existed in R's favour. D has 'special' skill and knowledge upon which H appears to rely - albeit that caveat emptor and the SGA implied conditions as to merchantable quality apply - these are displaced by D's skill and knowledge, his misrepresentations and the fact that the defects do not appear to have been evident on a 'reasonable' inspection by H prior to purchase.

The exclusion clause inserted by Finco appears to be invalid, as they know or should reasonably know, that R has an HP agreement on the Ford which they own already and in any event it does not appear to satisfy the 'reasonableness' tests set out in the UCTA 1977 (ss6 and 11). Additionally, they may be denied protection under HPA 1964 Part III because they provide finance for the purchase of vehicles and may be a 'dealer' thereunder.

Hiram appears to be within his rights to terminate the agreement by giving notice to the credit broker (D) as he has done; in *Financings Ltd* v *Stimson* (1962) Lord Denning expressed the view that the dealer was agent of the finance company for the purposes of receiving notice of the customer's revocation of his offer; so that communication by the customer to the dealer of his desire to withdraw his offer is equivalent to communication to the finance company; ss57, 69 and 102 CCA 1974. Under the principle that the principal is liable for any statements made by the agent during any 'antecedent negotiations' (including any representations made by the negotiator to the debtor (s56(4) CCA)), Finco will be liable to H for D's misrepresentations.

The lien purportedly exercised by Xerxes over the car for repairs may well be valid as, during the currency of an HP agreement, the hirer has the implied authority to deliver the goods to a third party for repair provided the act is reasonably incidental to his use of the goods. So in *Green* v *All Motors Ltd* (1917) it was decided that a lien to secure repairing charges was effective against the owner.

Thus, H should confirm the cancellation of the agreement in writing to Finco at their offices, he can then pursue the question of damages for breach of implied conditions as to title (s12) and merchantable quality and fitness for purpose (s14) Sale of Goods Act 1979 against Finco as they have allowed D to act as their agent and are liable for his and their own misrepresentations. The exclusion clause will almost certainly be regarded as 'unreasonable' (UCTA) and unenforceable. Xerxes will be able to exercise his lien over the goods for repairs.

19 DEFAULT BY DEBTOR

19.1 Introduction

As with any other contract, both parties are bound to the agreement. The main duties of the debtor are in regard to his duty to pay, which is fundamental to the contract, but he does not always have to pay at precisely the times stated in the contract. In hire purchase contracts or conditional sales agreements the debtor will have a duty of care toward the goods because, in this type of contract he is regarded as a bailee of the goods. The 1974 Act does not impose the duty, but it is almost always an express term of the contract; and in any case, the common law imposes a duty to take reasonable care.

It is usually of academic interest only to the creditor unless the contract is, for some reason, repudiated and the creditor needs to take back the goods.

In credit sales, no such duty exists because the goods belong to the debtor from the beginning.

Certain rights and obligations as to payment should be looked at more closely.

19.2 Key points

It is important that the student understands the following:

a) *The duty to pay*

At common law the duty to pay on time is an innominate term. That is, it is only by assessing the effect on the creditor if there is no payment, that one can see whether such breach goes to the root of the contract. If it does, the creditor will be entitled to treat the contract as discharged. Late payment is unlikely to be treated as of critical importance, unless the debtor shows by his conduct that he is unwilling to be bound further by the contract and unlikely to make any further payment at all.

b) *Damages for late or non-payment*

If the debtor's breach is repudiatory and the creditor repossesses the goods, the debtor will have to compensate the creditor not just for outstanding instalments, but also for loss of future benefits from the contract. A repudiatory breach is as noted in (a) above, one which is so serious, it indicates the debtor is unwilling to go on with the contract.

If the debtor's breach is non-repudiatory the creditor may choose not to repossess. If he does, however, his only entitlement will be those instalments due to date of repossession.

Interest is recoverable only on instalments paid late, if the contract expressly so provides. There is no automatic common law or statutory right to interest on late instalments.

It should be noted that the recent case of *Lombard North Central plc* v *Butterworth* [1987] 1 All ER 267 has meant that if the creditors makes time 'of the essence', by expressly using that or a similar phrase in the contract, punctual payment becomes obligatory and any failure to pay on time will effectively become a repudiatory breach.

c) *Default notices*

Section 87(1) of CCA 1974 specifies circumstances in which the creditor may wish to terminate, or sue for damages, (or missing instalments) or repossess the goods; the section provides that a default notice must then be served.

The form of the notice is dictated by the Consumer Credit (Enforcement, Default and Termination Notices) Regulations 1983: s88(1). In particular, among the information required to be given the default notice must specify the breach and indicate what, if it is capable of remedy, must be done to remedy it.

There is also a form of notice, issued under s76, which is a notification by the creditor that, although the debtor is not in breach, some event specified in the contract has occurred and the creditor therefore intends to repossess. These have been called non-default notices.

d) *Repossession*

If there is an express terms in the contract allowing repossession for any breach (or even in circumstances where there is no breach) then the breach need not be repudiatory. Otherwise, as already seen, the breach must be so serious as to indicate that the debtor is unwilling to go on with the contract.

Goods will be protected by s90(1) if more than one third of the total price has been paid, and such protected goods cannot be repossessed without a court order. However, if the debtor has himself terminated the contract, protection of goods will not occur (s90(5)). The debtor may waive his protection, or the need for a court order.

If the debtor has sold the goods to a third party or otherwise handed them on to a third party; the effects of the 'nemo dat' rule must be remembered. Of particular importance is the status of a private purchaser who buys a motor vehicle under Part III of Hire Purchase Act 1964 (see chapter 10). When repossession does take place the debtor is given some protection by s92 CCA which dictates that a creditor may not enter a debtor's premises in order to repossess.

e) *Acceleration clauses*

Contracts quite frequently contain a clause to the effect that on breach by the debtor the whole of the outstanding price becomes payable. These are known as acceleration clauses. Should a creditor wish to enforce such a clause he must serve a default notice (s87(1)(b)).

Acceleration clauses present few problems in the context of conditional and credit sales, because the debtor is bound to pay the full price anyway. But the essence of hire purchase contracts is that the debtor promises only to hire the goods, he will usually have an option whether or not to buy at a late stage in the contract. What he does not do, is to promise at the start of the contract, to pay for ownership of the goods. If an acceleration clause is included in most hire purchase contracts, it will effectively convert the contract into one of sale of goods, because it demands the debtor buys the goods.

f) *Minimum payment clauses*

It is common to find, in consumer credit contracts, a clause requiring some payment to be made should the debtor terminate the agreement.

The main reason is clear, the creditor wishes to ensure that should the goods have to be repossessed, any depreciation is paid for by the debtor.

Whether such a clause is valid will depend on whether it falls foul of the rule as to penalties.

Lack of space means that this complex common law doctrine cannot be examined here - and it should be noted that the penalty rule is equally applicable to acceleration clauses (above) - therefore the student should consult a textbook and make sure he is thoroughly acquainted with the subject.

19.3 Analysis of questions

While questions on consumer credit generally have been fairly common in University of London's past papers, the topics covered in this section have not featured very much as subject matter. However see Q7 1993 (chapter 36) which is, in part, concerned with default by debtor.

The question quoted below whilst superficially straightforward, actually covers some fairly tricky aspects: such as the apparent authority of a clerk to accept payment and the responsibility of a company for a crime committed by one of its employees. For further details on termination, see also chapter 20.

19.4 Question

Last summer, Andrea went on a spending spree and signed in respect of the following items three conditional sale agreements with Foxy Finance Ltd, each of which complied with all legal formalities: a television for £785, including a £50 charge for aerial erection; a video recorder for £690; and a second-hand moped for £300. So far, Andrea has paid under the three agreements respectively £270, £240 and £90. Having just been made redundant, Andrea has not made any payments in respect of the instalments due last month. She has just received a notice informing her that, as all three accounts are in arrears, Foxy Finance Ltd have instructed ET Repossessions Ltd to repossess all three items. Besides asking you to advise generally, Andrea in particular asks the following questions:

a) as to the television, whether she must honour a term of the agreement allowing Foxy Finance Ltd entry to her flat at any reasonable time of day to collect their goods;

b) as to the video recorder, whether she should accept the return of the last £20 instalment in respect of which Foxy Finance Ltd claim that the clerk to whom she made payment had no authority to accept it;

c) as to the moped, whether she can safely continue to park it overnight under her carport; and

d) in respect of a telephone threat, purportedly on behalf of Foxy Finance Ltd, that if the company does not recover either the arrears or the goods, she will never get credit again and her neighbours will inevitably learn of her financial embarrassment.

University of London LLB Examination
(for External Students) Commercial Law June 1986 Q5

Skeleton solution

- Types of agreement in each case.
- Arrears - repudiatory breach?
- Termination rights.
- Protected goods.
- Entry to flat - s92(1).
- Clerk as agent; nothing in CCA - common law as to agency?
- Duty of care to goods/bailment.
- Harassment s40(1) AJA 1970.
- Liability for criminal acts.

Suggested solution

General advice

The three conditional sale agreements are regulated consumer credit agreements being fixed sum (s10(1)(b) Consumer Credit Act (CCA) 1974), restricted use (s11(1)(a) CCA 1974), debtor-creditor-supplier (s12(a) CCA 1974) agreements for an amount of credit not exceeding £15,000 (s8(2) CCA 1974). Andrea (A) is the debtor, Foxy Finance Ltd (FF) is both the creditor and the supplier. Although there are three separate contracts, they are treated together for certain purposes of the Consumer Credit Act 1974, but not for all purposes.

A is in arrears under all three agreements, but it appears that she has only failed to make one payment under each, therefore her breaches are non-repudiatory (*Financings Ltd* v *Baldock* (1963)), unless FF inserted a clause making time of payment 'of the essence' (*Lombard North Central plc* v *Butterworth* (1987)), in which case even to be only slightly in arrears will be a repudiatory breach. This means that FF will only be allowed to repossess if there is an express term in each contract allowing repossession for any breach, and on repossession the only damages to which FF will be entitled will be the recovery of instalments which ought to have been paid up to the time of repossession (*Financings Ltd* v *Baldock* (1963)). A's position is that she may terminate the agreements under the power given by s99, or she may apply to the court for extra time to pay.

Termination under s99 would not be the best option for her because as with any contractual release (*British Russian Gazette and Trade Outlook Ltd* v *Associated Newspapers Ltd* (1933)) she would have to buy her way out of the contract. Section 100 requires a sum to be paid to make up to half of the total price (s100(1) CCA 1974), or the actual loss of the creditor if less (s100(3) CCA 1974), before A will be released. We are not given enough information to be able to say exactly how much would be payable for each item, but even if no sum is payable A would lose the goods and would not be able to recover payments which she has made.

On service of a default notice (which has been received in this case (a s87 default notice has been served)) the debtor (A) is entitled to ask the court for more time to pay, by way of a time order (s129(1)(a) CCA 1974). The court does not have to give such an order but if minded to grant one A could be given more time to pay (s129(2)(a) CCA 1974). One problem with such a course of action is that it requires A to institute proceedings, which could prove expensive even if she is successful in her application. An alternative course is to attempt to have the goods protected.

Goods supplied under a regulated conditional sale agreement are protected goods if one third of the total price has been paid, the debtor is in breach and the property in the goods remains in the creditor (s90(1) CCA 1974). Once goods are protected they cannot be recovered by the creditor without a court order (s90(1) CCA 1974, the consequences of wrongful repossession are set out in s91) and A could apply for a time order when FF goes to court to ask for a repossession order (s129(1)(b) CCA 1974). As regards the television the amount which would have to be paid before it is protected is the £50 installation charge and one third of the remainder of the total price (s90(2) CCA 1974), in other words £50 + (£735 ÷ 3) = £295. As regards the video recorder the relevant figure is £695 ÷ by 3 = £230, and for the moped, £300 ÷ by 3 = £100 (s90(1) CCA 1974). This would required A to make additional payments of £25 for the television and £10 for the moped, no further payment would be required for the video because £240 has already been paid, in other words the video recorder is already protected.

It is appreciated that A may have problems keeping up with the payments for all three items, but in order to secure her position she is allowed to appropriate any payment that she can afford to any of the three contracts (s81(1) CCA 1974). In other words, it does not matter whether she can afford to pay the instalments on all three items at the moment, she can buy time by making the payments required to protect the television and the moped and then asking the court for a time order which, if granted, would allow her to pay in smaller instalments, or over a greater length of time. It must be added that she is not automatically entitled to a time order and one will not be granted if there is no reasonable prospect of her being able to maintain the re-structured payments (s129(1) CCA 1974).

Andrea's questions

a) *The television*

The term of the conditional sale agreement allowing FF entry to her flat at any reasonable time is unenforceable. Section 92(1) of the 1974 Act provides that entry of the debtor's premises in order to repossess goods covered by a regulated conditional sale agreement may be made on order of the court only. Any contract term which is inconsistent with a provision in the Act to the protection of the debtor is void (s173(1) CCA 1974). Section 173(3) allows the debtor to consent to repossession even without a court order, but only if the consent is given at the time of attempted repossession; a prior consent, as in this case, would not be effective.

b) *The video recorder*

It is not entirely clear from the question how a payment came to be made which the finance company says was accepted without authority. It will be assumed that the clerk was an employee of FF at the time the payment was made. There is no provision in the Consumer Credit Act 1974 making anyone the agent of the creditor to receive payments (Goode, *Consumer Credit Legislation*). At common law a clerk in the employment of a finance company would have apparent, if not actual, authority to accept a payment from a debtor (within the rules in *Freeman and Lockyer* v *Buckhurst Park Properties (Mangal) Ltd* (1964) and *Armagas* v *Mundogas, The Ocean Frost* (1986)). The apparent authority would be general ostensible authority arising from the position to which the clerk has been appointed. Further, a clerk would have usual authority within the principle in *Watteau* v *Fenwick* (1893), but the true rule in that case is so unclear that it is best to rely on apparent authority only. A could, however, elect to accept the £20 refund, but this would leave her having to make a payment to ensure that the video recorder is protected. The size of that payment would only be £10, so it may be best for her to accept the £20 back and then pay £10 towards the video and use the other £10 as a payment towards one of the other items; it seems most sensible to apply that other £10 towards the moped because that is all that it will take to make it protected and all A would then have to do is find money for the television.

c) *The moped*

A debtor under a conditional sale agreement owes a duty of care to the owner of the goods by virtue of his, or in this case her, position as a contractual bailee. There is no provision in the 1974 Act covering the duty of care owed by a debtor, otherwise than on cancellation (s72 CCA 1974). The position at common law is that A is obliged to take reasonable care of the moped, in other words she owes a negligence duty of care (*Joseph Travers & Sons Ltd* v *Cooper* (1915)). This is so even if a time order has been made: see s129(4) CCA 1974. Whether it is reasonable in all the circumstances to park the moped under the car port is a question the answer to which depends on facts which we are not given. The effective loss to FF from any damage to or theft of the moped will be nil while she is still paying for it, it is only if FF are to repossess it that they may be prejudiced by any loss or damage.

d) *The threat*

If the threat was made by one of FF's employees, then two questions arise. Firstly what offence has been committed and secondly is FF responsible for it?

The first question is the easier of the two. Section 40(1)(a) of the Administration of Justice Act 1970 makes it an offence for someone to harass a debtor with threats which are calculated to alarm, distress or humiliate him. There is a defence if the creditor can prove that the pressure which was applied was reasonable, but that burden could not possibly be satisfied on the facts of this case (s40(3) Administration of Justice Act 1970). It is possible that the behaviour of FF's employee could amount to blackmail (s15 Theft Act 1968), but that is such a serious offence that it would be hard to prove it without strong evidence. The offence under the 1970 Act is more suitable in this case.

FF is a limited company and the criminal liability of a company depends upon the wrongdoer being part of the directing mind of the company (*Tesco Supermarkets Ltd* v *Nattrass* (1971)). This, in effect, means that unless the person who harassed A was a director or acted with the permission of the directors, then FF will not be responsible for it. In any event, liability under s40 is criminal only, it does not affect the enforceability of the conditional sale contract; in particular it is not a matter which can make the contracts extortionate credit bargains unless it was committed prior to the making of the credit contracts (s137 CCA 1974).

20 TERMINATION

20.1 Introduction

After the expiry of the withdrawal or cancellation period, both parties will of course be bound to the agreement, as in the case of any other contract. There are, however, two main exceptions to this. First, there is a right to pay off a credit agreement early. This right cannot be excluded by the creditors. The second exception is where the debtor wishes to escape a contract, usually of course, because he finds he cannot afford to continue. This is a much more restricted right; of necessity it must be restricted to those transactions where the creditor retains ownership of the goods. Consequently it does not apply to credit sales at all.

20.2 Key points

It is important that the student understands the following:

a) *Early settlement*

A debtor under any regulated consumer credit agreement, is by virtue of s94 CCA given the right to settle early.

The creditor has no ground of complaint because he gets repaid. He will not get all of the total, however, because there will be a rebate on the overall credit charge for early settlement.

The Consumer Credit (Rebate on Early Settlement) Regulations 1983 provide for the allowance of a rebate and dictate how this rebate is to be calculated. The regulations cover not only cases where the debtor is paying early for his own reasons, but also situations where the creditor is claiming early repayment by reason of the debtor's default.

b) *Creditor terminating*

It has already been noted in chapter 19 that the creditor has a right to terminate early if either the debtor commits a repudiatory breach, or if the agreement contains a clause expressly allowing termination in certain circumstances.

The procedure for such termination, especially the service of the default notice, and the form of the notice under the 1983 regulations have already been discussed in that chapter.

c) *Debtor terminating*

The difference between early settlement (see (a) above) and debtor's termination is that early settlement involves the debtor in settling all of his outstanding debts in full (subject to any rebate) while termination will allow him to conclude the contract without completing his obligations under it.

The right to terminate early often arises in cases where the debtor can no longer afford the transaction and is limited to hire purchase and conditional sales. Section 99 CCA dictates the circumstances under which a debtor may terminate. Section 100 CCA provides that on termination, although in addition to the return of the goods, the debtor may have to pay a sum of money to the creditor; the maximum he can be made to pay is the amount by which the aggregate of payments made falls short of half the total price. In other words, if the debtor has already paid half or more of the total price he may terminate without having to pay anything.

In fact, it is not always necessary to pay the full sum to make up half the total price. In at least three exceptional cases a lesser sum will be payable by the debtor. Such exceptions include: (i) transactions where the contract is silent on the question of payment of any sum on termination (s100(1)); (ii) transactions which do provide for payment of some sum, but the sum specified is less than the statutory figure (s100(1)); and (iii) where the court is satisfied that a sum less than the amount specified in s100(1) would be equal to the loss sustained by the creditor (s100(3)).

Once the debtor has terminated the agreement he is no longer entitled to retain the goods, unlike early settlement where he has paid in full and will, naturally, retain the goods. Should the debtor fail to deliver up the goods when required to do so, he will commit an act of conversion, for which the creditor has a choice of remedies.

20.3 Analysis of questions

For some reason, in those questions on consumer credit transactions, although cancellation and withdrawal crops up quite regularly, early settlement and termination does not.

In the previous chapter, the question quoted required a minimal reference to the possibility of termination under s99, but generally it was not a major topic of discussion, nor did rights of termination need detailed attention.

Similarly in University of London's 1983 paper, Question 5, the right to terminate came briefly under scrutiny in part b(i); but this right formed only a fractional part of the overall answer.

While the questions below require some attention to be paid to early settlement in particular, they are primarily questions, like so many others, on cancellation and withdrawal. These topics should already be familiar ground!

20.4 Questions

Question 1

Herbert and Winifred are an elderly couple. Winifred is visited at their home by Swifteye, a representative of Condoor Ltd, who interests her in one of Condoor's conservatories. She calls in Herbert from the garden and explains the terms to him. He signs a proposal form from Finco Ltd under which Finco lets the conservatory to Herbert on Herbert's paying a deposit of £400; after Herbert's payment of 24 monthly instalments of £50, property in the conservatory will pass to him. Herbert is also asked to pay £50 premium to Condoor Ltd for a maintenance agreement.

Swifteye also interests Herbert's and Winifred's son Denys in a conservatory and fills in another proposal for him. Denys is reluctant to enter into the agreement, so Swifteye leaves the form with him, telling him that, if he changes his mind, he can call into Condoor's office to sign it. The following day, Denys calls into Condoor's office where Swifteye tells him that, if he signs, he can have the conservatory for a deposit of £400 and twelve monthly payments of £90. He also asks him to take out a maintenance agreement.

Herbert and Denys telephone you to enquire what formalities are required by law for the above transactions, what are the consequences of non-compliance with them, to what extent they will be liable and how, if at all, they may get out of the agreements.

Advise Herbert and Denys.

University of London LLB Examination
(for External Students) Commercial Law June 1989 Q7

Skeleton solution

- Transactions within CCA 1974?
- Form of contract prescribed by regulations.
- Agreement with Herbert - is it cancellable? Withdrawal?
- Agreement with Denys - cancellable - withdrawal.
- Extortionate credit bargains especially as applied to Herbert.
- Termination/early settlement of contracts.

Suggested solution

Both these transactions fail within the Consumer Credit Act 1974. They are agreements between individuals (the debtors) and the creditor (Finco Ltd) whereby the creditor provides credit not exceeding £15,000. They are therefore regulated by the Act, and as such, are required to comply with certain formalities. The relevant provisions are contained in ss60-65 of the Act and fall into two parts, relating to the form of the contract and to the need to provide the debtor with copies.

The form of the contract is prescribed by regulations (Consumer Credit (Agreements) Regulations 1983). These regulations require that the document must contain all the terms of the agreement other than the implied terms; it must give all the relevant information as to how the agreement operates (Schedule 1); and the document must be legible. The agreement must be signed by the prospective debtor after all the relevant information has been inserted. This relevant information includes the cash price of the goods, the total amount payable, the amounts and times of repayments and the APR.

It must also include the names of the parties. These items of information may be written on the document. The rest of the contract must be in type-script.

If an agreement is not in the required form, or if it is not legible, or if the debtor signs the form before all the details have been filled in the agreement will be improperly executed (s61(1) CCA). This means that it cannot be enforced by the creditor without a court order (s65(1) CCA).

Sections 62 and 63 CCA lay down requirements as to copies of documents which must be given to the debtor. The debtor must be given a copy of the agreement as soon as he signs it. If the debtor's signature is, in effect, an offer and the form has to be sent to the finance company for it to accept that offer, the debtor must also be given or sent a copy of the executed agreement within seven days of the execution. If, however, the agreement is executed upon the debtor signing it, because the finance company has already signed its part of the contract or because it signs immediately after the debtor, the debtor will be given only the one copy of the agreement.

If, however, the agreement is cancellable, each copy of the agreement must contain notice of the debtor's rights of cancellation. If the agreement is executed when the debtor signs, he must be sent a separate notice of his cancellation rights within seven days. All second notices of cancellation must be sent by post.

If the necessary copies of the agreement are not given or sent to the debtor, the agreement will be improperly executed and can only be enforced by a court order. Such an order is called an enforcement order and will not be made unless the creditor gives the debtor the correct copy of the agreement before proceedings are instituted. Unless the debtor receives the second notice of his rights of cancellation the cancellation period remains open indefinitely.

Finally, as Swifteye is apparently negotiating a credit transaction, he must be licensed to do so, as must Finco Ltd. In the absence of such a licence, the agreement may only be enforced by order of the Director General of Fair Trading. He will make such an order only if he believes that the debtor has not been prejudiced by the fact that no licence had been obtained.

Herbert:

In advising Herbert, it has to be discovered whether or not the agreement is cancellable. For cancellation, s67 CCA lays down a number of conditions which must be satisfied. There must be oral representations made by a negotiator or someone acting on his behalf, in the debtor's physical presence and the agreement must be signed by the debtor at a place other than the place of business of the creditor or someone connected with the creditor. In the problem, the negotiator, Swifteye, discussed the terms of the agreement with Winifred whilst Herbert was in the garden. Winifred then explained these terms to Herbert. If Swifteye made no comment whatsoever but kept absolutely quiet in Herbert's presence, the agreement will not be cancellable. If, however, Swifteye made some statement to Herbert, if only to introduce himself and to say who he was representing, Herbert will have the right to cancel.

If the agreement is cancellable, Herbert may exercise his right of cancellation within five days of the day following his receipt of the second notice of cancellation. He must do so in writing to the creditor or to anyone involved with the creditor in the transaction, such as Condoor Ltd or Swifteye. The effect of cancellation is to rescind the agreement and any linked transaction. A linked transaction is defined by s19 CCA as including a transaction entered into at the suggestion of the creditor or his representative for a purpose relating to the principal agreement. In Herbert's case, the maintenance agreement for the conservatory would be a linked transaction and this would be cancelled along with the main, credit, transaction. Herbert would recover all the money he had paid and would not be liable under the agreement he had signed.

If the agreement was not cancellable, Herbert would still have the right to withdraw at any time before his offer (made by signing the proposal form) was accepted. This right is contained in s57 CCA. Herbert must give notice of revocation to the offeree (Finco) or to a negotiator of the transaction (Swifteye). Withdrawal of the offer will also prevent the maintenance agreement coming into effect and Herbert is entitled to the recovery of any money he has paid under the finance agreement or any associated transaction. In other words, if Herbert withdraws the effects will be the same as if he had had the right to cancel and had done so.

If Herbert has no right to cancel and if he is too late to withdraw, because Finco has already accepted the offer, his rights to get out of the agreement will be the same as Denys's which we will deal with shortly. It may, however, be possible for Herbert to argue that the agreement is an extortionate credit bargain. These are agreements which require grossly exorbitant payments or which otherwise contravene the principles of fair dealing. In deciding whether the agreement is extortionate, the court will look at such matters as the rate of interest charged and the age, health and experience of the debtor. We are told that Herbert is elderly and that they are paying more for the conservatory than Denys. Herbert merely has to allege that the bargain is extortionate and the burden will then be placed on Finco to prove that it is not. If the court finds that the agreement is extortionate it has the power to re-write the terms of the contract, by reducing Herbert's obligations or in any other way making it a fairer transaction.

Denys:

Denys is not in as strong a position as Herbert. He has called in Condoor's officer to sign the agreement and therefore there is no question of him having any right to cancel. If the agreement is executed when Denys signs he will also have no right to withdraw. If, however, Deny's signature is merely an offer, he will have the same rights to withdraw as Herbert. There is no question here of the contract with Denys being an extortionate credit bargain.

If Denys cannot withdraw from his undertaking, he will be able to get out of the agreement by early settlement or by terminating the contract. These rights will also be available to Herbert if none of the rights discussed above apply to him.

The debtor under any regulated consumer credit agreement will be entitled to settle early. This means that the debtor pays all the money he owes before the contract date. He should write to the creditor to discover how much is owing and then give notice in writing to the creditor and settle the indebtedness (s94 CCA). Because the debtor is settling early, he is entitled to a rebate on the interest which is payable. The method of calculating this interest is called the Rule of 78 and is contained in the Consumer Credit (Rebate on Early Settlement) Regulations 1983.

Denys may also terminate the agreement at any time before the final instalment falls due to be paid. This right is available only to debtors under a hire-purchase or conditional sale agreement. The right to terminate is given in s99 CCA and it will be exercised by notice to the creditor.

If the debtor does terminate, he must pay all instalments outstanding; bring the amount paid up to half the total hire-purchase or conditional sale price, unless the agreement or the court specifies that a smaller amount should be paid; allow the creditor to reposses the goods; and pay damages for any failure to take reasonable care of the goods. The effect of termination is to end the contract. The debtor will be under no further liability to pay any instalments under the contract.

If he has signed the agreement and has no right to revoke his offer, these are the only ways in which Denys can get out of the contract of his own volition. He could, of course, default in making the monthly payments and leave it to Finco to owe him. If he did this he could find himself liable to pay damages in breach of contract.

Question 2

On 1 October 1991, Henry enters into a written agreement at Ian's shop to purchase a *Seedy* compact disc player from Ian for £720, the price to be paid in 18 monthly instalments of £40. On 1 May 1992, only the first instalment has been paid. Ian demands immediate payment of the arrears or return of the player. Henry tells Ian that he could keep up the instalments but not if he has to pay off the arrears straight away as well.

Ian has a friend Jon who wishes to buy a second-hand *Seedy* player. Ian tells Henry that he will release him from his contract if he returns the *Seedy* and enters a replacement contract to buy a *Hifly* hi-fi system for £1,080 payable in 18 monthly instalments of £60. Ian delivers the *Hifly* to Henry's house and, since he does not have any new agreement forms with him, he and Henry agree to use the form for the original *Seedy* contract and to make appropriate changes on it. Ian then sells the *Seedy* to Jon for £600.

As the *Hifly's* amplifier is not working properly, Henry gets a friend of his to replace some of the Japanese parts with German ones. However, he notices little improvement. As one of his children accidentally scratches it, he decides that he is better off without it anyway and on 1 June decides not to continue with the agreement.

Advisé Henry.

University of London LLB Examination
(for External Students) Commercial Law June 1992 Q8

Skeleton solution

- Consumer Credit Act 1974.
- Regulated agreements.

- Non payment, repudiation and termination.
- Re-possession.
- Cancellation.
- Formalities.
- Loss of right to cancel.
- Duty to keep goods safe.

Suggested solution

The Consumer Credit Act 1974 (CCA) controls the working of contracts under which individuals are given credit. One of the most common types of such contracts is the credit sale agreement under which the customer agrees to pay the purchase price (or part of it) in instalments. The main feature is that property in the goods passes immediately to the buyer in a credit sale, even though the purchase price has not been paid in full.

The agreement will be a 'regulated agreement' within the meaning of the CCA. One assumes, for convenience, that the agreement made on 1 October 1991 was in every way in accord with the requirements of the Act as to formalities.

The most important duty of a debtor under a regulated agreement is to repay. This is a fundamental duty, but the obligation to pay is not always interpreted too literally when it comes to times of payment, provided payment *is* made. Mere failure to pay does not entitle the creditor to repossess unless the breach is very serious, or unless the agreement stipulates that 'time of payment is of the essence' (*Lombard North Central plc* v *Butterworth* (1987)). It is not known whether Ian so stipulated in the agreement, but no mention is made of a 'time of the essence clause'. Is Henry's failure to pay to be judged a 'serious' breach? Considering he has paid only one of the first seven payments and has not built up any sort of record of steady, regular repayments, it might be argued that this is sufficiently serious to warrant Ian's demanding repossession, and for him to treat the contract as discharged. The main question is whether Henry has shown that he is unwilling to continue the contract - is his conduct repudiatory? This is largely a question of fact in each case. Certainly failure to pay one or more instalments has been held in the past to be not so serious as to indicate the debtor was repudiating the contract, (*Financings* v *Baldock* (1963)), but a lot depends on just how badly in arrears the debtor actually is (*Overstone* v *Shipway* (1962) and *Yeoman Credit* v *Waragowski* (1961)). Here Henry is heavily in arrears, but his remark to Ian that 'he could keep up the payments' is not indicative of a man who wishes to end the contract.

But nowadays this is largely academic, because most agreements usually contain a provision allowing the creditor to terminate and repossess upon *any* breach by the debtor. If there is no such clause, then wrongful repossession by the creditor will be conversion, because it would wrongfully interfere with the debtor's right to possession. In the case of a credit sale, it will also be a breach of contract, specifically of s12(2)(b) of SGA 1979 which implies a warranty as to title and quiet enjoyment.

In any event, before the creditor may terminate and repossess under the agreement, a s87 default notice must be served on the debtor in the form and manner dictated by s88..

But in addition to the two questions which must be asked - namely, is there a clause in the contract which Henry signed allowing for termination and repossession upon any breach?; and secondly, if not, is Henry's conduct so serious or so repudiatory as to amount to breach? - there is a third important question that needs to be considered. That is whether in the light of Henry's *new* arrangement with Ian, one could say that they have entered into a mutual variation of the contract and that this is not really true termination and repossession as much as the substitution of one contract for another. Such an arrangement would be governed by common law, not statute.

On balance, however, it would seem that whether because there is a clause permitting it in the contract, or whether because Henry's failure to pay can be considered serious enough to warrant it, the contract is at an end and Ian is justified in repossessing the goods. In theory Henry has not - at least from the information available - terminated the contract. Indeed, he says 'he could keep up' - indicating his desire to continue. Nevertheless, he has apparently handed back the *Seedy* CD, thereby waiving his rights and obviating any need for Ian to obtain a court order for repossession (*UDT* v *Ennis* (1968)). It is important, however, that the debtor be fully aware of his statutory rights and protection before he can be said to have truly waived any rights and consented to repossession (*Mercantile Credit* v *Cross* (1965)).

Assuming that either repossession can be said to be justified or if not that Henry has consented to Ian's action, what of the second contract between them? The Act lays down complex rules as to formalities which must be complied with before the contract can be said to be properly executed and valid. We are told that, because of a lack of new agreement forms, Henry and Ian simply use the old form from the previous agreement and amend it. Sections 60–65 of the CCA make a number of detailed rules, perhaps the most important of which in the present context are the requirement that the agreement be legible and contain all the relevant terms, and that copies be supplied to the debtor within a stated time. It is not clear whether, because of all the alterations, the contract is comprehensible, nor is it clear whether all the terms of the new contract are contained in the written version. Certainly no further copy, informing him of his rights of cancellation etc, seems to have been delivered to Henry within the statutory time limit. Such an agreement, if it does not comply with all statutory requirements, will be unenforceable unless the court grants an enforcement order: s65.

Sections 67-73 of CCA provides for certain regulated agreements to be cancelled. Two problems occur here. Is the second agreement between Henry and Ian within this group, and secondly is Henry's conduct in deciding not to continue with the contract on 1 June 1992 capable of being construed as cancellation?

Section 67 lays down the conditions which must be complied with before an agreement can be considered cancellable. These include, most importantly in the present case, the requirement that the agreement must be signed at a place other than the business premises of the creditor (the agreement is signed at Henry's home), and that the antecedent negotiations must have included oral representations made by the creditor or his agent (the Act makes no rule that these should take any particular form, so that Ian's preliminary assurances to Henry will probably qualify).

So, if the agreement is cancellable, has it been cancelled? We are told that the whole business of substituting one agreement for another, repossessing the *Seedy* and delivering the *Hifly*, takes place between 1 May and 1 June, but we are not told any exact dates. The 'cooling off period', or time for cancellation, starts when the debtor signs the agreement and ends on the fifth day following the day when he receives his notice of cancellation rights: s64(1)(b). If that notice is not sent, or never received, cancellation remains possible almost indefinitely. We do not know when, if at all, Henry receives his notice giving him details of, inter alia, cancellation rights. If Henry does decide to cancel and is still in time to do so, he must cancel in writing (s69 and s189 CCA) and restore the goods to the creditor s72.

But what of his conduct in getting a friend to replace certain parts of the CD with units of some other manufacture? The first thing to note is that if the goods are purchased on a credit sale agreement, title passes to Henry straightaway and although he still has to pay for them the goods are his and he may do what he wishes with them. In a credit sale, ss34-35 SGA provide that once a buyer has accepted the goods, then his right to reject will be lost. Obviously tinkering with the CD and substituting parts of a different origin can be taken to be decisive acceptance of the goods by Henry, and it seems doubtful whether he can then say he is rejecting the goods by exercising his right of cancellation.

There is, in any regulated agreement, a duty of care towards the goods in question. In credit sale contracts this extends throughout the cooling-off period up to and including 21 days from the date of cancellation. 'Normal' fair wear and tear is excluded, but even if the scratch by the children, perhaps part of normal household usage were excluded, the act of Henry in asking a friend, apparently unqualified, to insert parts of a foreign manufacture into the CD would seem closer to a breach of his duty to take reasonable care of the goods: s72.

So, to sum up as to Henry's position. With regard to the first agreement, Ian's repossession will be legitimate if either the agreement contains an express clause permitting it, or the failure to pay is such that it amounts to repudiation of the contract on Henry's part, or thirdly if Henry can be said to have waived his rights on repossession. Otherwise the repossession of the goods and subsequent sale to Jon, will be wrongful and amount to conversion.

As the whole situation has been caused by Henry's failure to pay more than one instalment however, and since he has had use of the *Speedy* CD for about seven months, it is doubtful whether he would be entitled to anything other than nominal damages by way of redress. Though the courts do have power to amend agreements (s136 CCA) they will not do so if there is no prospect of the payments being made. Henry is unlikely therefore to get the first Agreement reinstated.

As to the second Agreement Henry may have a right of cancellation. If so he must give notice in writing and restore the goods *undamaged* (s72(4) CCA). He is not actually under a duty to deliver the goods physically to Ian, but simply to keep them safe for collection (s72(5) CCA). But since while he is in possession of the goods he has a duty to take reasonable care of them, he is not only in breach of his duty as bailee of goods at common law (s72(11) CCA) but also in breach of his statutory duty. This duty ceases 21 days after written notice of cancellation, but of course all the harm has been done before 1 June, when Henry decides not to go ahead with the contract. It is not clear whether the *Hifly* CD is not working properly, or whether this is simply Henry's opinion. Of course, in any contract for sale of goods (credit sale) there are implied terms as to fitness for purpose and merchantability. But Henry's proper course of action would be to return the goods as faulty, not get a friend to repair it, or simply decide not to pay. A debtor cannot simply stop paying and abandon the contract. He should continue to pay and claim compensation for the loss incurred through the faulty goods. Where a debtor is sued for failing to pay, and he argues in his defence that the goods did not work properly he will have a counterclaim. But it is a counterclaim only, Henry cannot simply abandon the need to pay altogether. He may make a separate claim for repairs and for loss of use, which he may off-set against his continuing obligations under the contract. If he decides to cancel and restore the goods, he may have to pay compensation for harm caused to the CD.

21 JUDICIAL CONTROL

21.1 Introduction

The courts' intervention may take several forms. Primarily, of course their major interest is to protect the debtor and preserve his rights.

In certain circumstances if a regulated agreement is 'improperly executed' it will only be enforceable by order of a court. Similarly, in cases where a debtor is temporarily in financial difficulties, but does not want to abandon the agreement he may apply to the court for more time to make his payments to the creditor. And finally the courts have the power to re-open consumer credit transactions which are suspected of being extortionate in some way.

These aspects of judicial control will be examined in a little more detail below.

21.2 Key points

It is important that the student understands the following:

a) *Enforcement orders*

Not all the court orders for which a creditor may apply are, strictly speaking, enforcement orders. Enforcement orders are defined statutorily in s189(1) CCA as being available for improperly executed agreements or securities only. However, as used in the wider more colloquial sense, enforcement orders are likely to be requested by the creditor on at least three occasions. These are:

i) the creditor may claim sums which the debtor has not paid, which is, obviously a form of enforcement of the agreement;

ii) the creditor may claim for damages which are due because the agreement has been breached and here again it is likely to be a form of enforcement. Essentially, what the creditor is relying on are the terms of the agreement;

iii) a claim for possession of the goods by the creditor is effectively a claim to have the terms of the agreement enforced. It should be remembered from the preceding chapter that where the goods are protected the creditor will need a court order in any case. Thus, where goods are protected and the buyer wishes to repossess by reason of improper execution of the agreement by the debtor, he will in fact need two court orders, one for repossession of protected goods and one for enforcement.

Application for an enforcement order is made by virtue of whichever section of CCA requires the creditor to obtain such an order.

Section 127 determines how the courts should approach such applications. The county court has jurisdiction to determine any action which is take to enforce a regulated agreement a security or a linked transaction, even if the amount in dispute is greater than the county court's usual limit of £5,000. The form of application is laid down in County Court Rules O13 r1(2) and requires the creditor to state for what purpose he is applying for an enforcement order and what section of the CCA allows him to do so.

The courts powers are extensive and varied but space precludes their being dealt with fully here. The student should refer to a textbook for full details.

b) *Time orders*

Section 129 CCA allows the debtor in certain circumstances to ask the courts for more time to complete the contract. A debtor may not apply for a time order unless the creditor has applied for an enforcement order, or has served a default notice, or has applied for repossession of the goods.

The debtor cannot simply apply to the courts on his own initiative for an extension of time. The court has power under s129(2)(a) to reschedule payments to a point at which they virtually re-write the contract. There is provision in s130 permitting the court to make a time order without hearing evidence of means, if the parties consent. Normally, however, s129(2)(a) requires the court to make a full investigation of the debtor's (and any surety's) means before making any order. The orders which the court makes, can if it so decrees be made in a suspended or conditional form. Any action by a debtor is not covered by s141 and so an application for a time order may be heard in either the County Court or the High Court, depending whether the amount involved is in excess of £5,000.

c) *Extortionate credit bargains*

When it is considered that the CCA repealed the Moneylenders Acts of 1900 and 1927 and incorporated many of their provisions it is, perhaps, not surprising that ss137-140 of CCA allow control of all extortionate credit transactions, whether regulated under the Act or not.

The courts' jurisdiction is extremely wide. The debtor or surety may apply if: (i) the creditor is taking any action against either of them or; (ii) by an independent action; or (iii) in any other proceedings (say a civil action for debt against the creditor by other creditors, or bankruptcy proceedings) where the amount payable under a seemingly extortionate agreement is relevant.

An application concerning a transaction which is regulated will go to the county court regardless of how much money is involved. In the case of non-regulated agreements the choice of court will depend on whether more or less than £5,000 is involved.

The powers of the court are comprehensively laid down in s139(2) CCA and the student should study this section carefully. Courts have powers, ranging from the right to set the contract aside completely, to the power to alter contracts to an extent that they have effectively re-written the terms.

21.3 Analysis of questions

Judicial control, in the form of time orders, has made one or two appearances in past papers. In chapter 19, for example, we see a time order mentioned as just one, of a list of possibilities open to a debtor.

For some time there was little relevant case law on the question and then in 1986 two important cases occurred as to the question of extortionate bargains, so it was, perhaps, not surprising to find the question quoted below in the University of London's 1987 paper.

The question deals also with other ways in which a court might seek to give relief to the debtor, including more time to pay, and so seems particularly appropriate to this chapter.

21.4 Question

a) Assess the scope and significance of the 'extortionate credit bargain' provisions of the Consumer Credit Act 1974.

b) Dizzy was a 25-year-old single parent whose sole source of income was her business as a double glazing consultant. Requiring a car for the purposes of her business, she approached Claude, a car dealer, who persuaded her that her best course of action was to purchase a new Osram car with a loan from Dastardly Finance Ltd. A proposal was submitted to Dastardly, whose agency search against her was clear, apart from two recent credit rejections. Accordingly, Dastardly agreed to make Dizzy a personal loan for the purchase of a new Osram car and to advance her £5,500 for 12 months at 35 per cent APR. As a result of Dizzy's subsequent default, Dastardly have instituted proceedings for the recovery of the sum outstanding plus interest.

   Advise Dizzy on the basis of the following facts: at the time the loan was made to Dizzy, rates of interest charged by Dastardly's competitors ranged between 27 per cent and 33 per cent for newer used cars, but only about 25 per cent for new cars; but since then rates have fallen steadily and are currently some 10 per cent points lower.

University of London LLB Examination
(for External Students) Commercial Law June 1987 Q8

Skeleton solution

a)
- Sections 137-140 CCA as to extortionate credit agreements.
- Two general tests as laid down in s138: criteria.

- Undue influence.
- Relevant case law.

b)
- Repudiatory/non-repudiatory breach?
- Time orders.
- Extortionate bargain.
- Means/background of Dizzy to be taken into account each time.

Suggested solution

a) Extortionate credit bargains

Sections 137-140 of the Consumer Credit Act 1974 provide machinery for the re-opening of credit agreements which the court considers to be extortionate. Unlike the vast majority of the Act, these provisions apply to non-regulated agreements as well as regulated ones. The power given to the court is supplementary to its equitable jurisdiction in the fields of undue influence and penalties.

The basic rule is laid down in s137, and s138 defines when a credit agreement is extortionate. There are two general tests for whether an agreement is extortionate, namely (a) if it requires the debtor to make payments which are grossly exorbitant; and (b) if it otherwise grossly contravenes ordinary principles of fair dealing.

Neither test is defined precisely, but s138 mentions many factors which should be taken into account. These is authority that s138 is exhaustive of the relevant matters (*Davies* v *Directloans Ltd* (1986)).

The first test covers such things as extremely high rates of interest and excessive payments required under such things as maintenance contracts which are linked transactions.

The court tends to shy away from defining what is a proper rate of interest for a creditor to charge because there are so many factors which might justify a high rate in one case but not in another. In *Davies* v *Directloans Ltd* (1986) the judge looked in particular at two matters in deciding that the rate of interest charged was not exorbitant. First, he made a comparison between the rate charged to the debtors in that case and the rates charged by other creditors for the type of loan in question, and on finding that the rate was not far higher than the normal market rate refused to say that it was excessive. Second, he analysed the amountof risk which the creditor undertook, holding that because there seemed to be a good risk of default so it was justifiable to charge more interest.

Previous legislation had a rate of interest (48 per cent per annum) below which it was presumed that the rate of interest charged was acceptable, but above which the creditor had to justify its charge. The 1974 Act does not adopt such an approach, and the analysis of the judge in *Davies* v *Directloans Ltd* (1986) shows that there is no such cut-off figure. Any level of interest which is challenged as exorbitant must be proved not to be by the creditor (s171(7) Consumer Credit Act (CCA) 1974), and it is artificial to add an additional hurdle by saying that the burden of proof can be easily discharged up to a certain rate, but not when the interest charged is above that rate.

The second sort of extortionate credit bargain arises where the agreement otherwise grossly contravenes ordinary principles of fair dealing. This covers cases of undue influence (*Coldunell Ltd* v *Gallon* (1986)) and also cases which fall short of the strict requirements of the undue influence doctrine but in which the judge feels that the debtor needs protection. Failure to explain the legal effect of the contract and the degree of pressure under which the debtor made the contract (s138(3)(b) CCA 1974) may both be taken into account, even if the pressure is not directly caused by the creditor. For example, a debtor who is pushed by other creditors for payment may wish to borrow in order to pay them; if the creditor knows this he may feel that he can take a charge over the debtor's or another's property unnecessarily or otherwise manipulate the agreement to his benefit and the court would have power to step in, although it is unlikely to do so unless the creditor acted unfairly.

The importance of the extortionate credit bargain provisions can only be seen by realising that they are part of a wide range of powers given to the court to give relief to the debtor. Their importance in protection of the debtor, therefore, is somewhat limited because in many cases other protection is equally efficacious. As regards third parties, however, like sureties, little other effective protection exists, so ss137-140 will have a greater part to play.

b) Dizzy

We are not told the extent to which Dizzy is in default, but it will be assumed that whether her breach was serious or minor Dastardly Finance Ltd had the right to terminate the contract, because that right is a common ingredient of credit agreements.

If she has committed a non-repudiatory failure to pay she will be liable at common law only for outstanding instalments at the time Dastardly Finance Ltd terminated the contract (*Financings Ltd* v *Baldock* (1963)). If, though, her breach was repudiatory she would be liable to repay not just the principal sum but also the interest, although Dastardly Finance Ltd would have to give a rebate for early receipt of the money (*Yeoman Credit Ltd* v *Waragowski* (1961)). In either event Dizzy would be faced with having to pay immediately when it seems that she can only really afford to pay over a period of time. This may require her to sell the car in order to raise the money to pay and that is a course which she will want to avoid if at all possible.

In such cases the debtor is entitled to ask the court to give her more time to pay (s129 CCA 1974). She need not take separate proceedings for this purpose, but can ask for that relief when Dastardly Finance Ltd takes her to court (s139 CCA 1974). The court may re-schedule payments to allow smaller instalments to be paid (s129(2)(a) CCA 1974) or to allow the instalments to be paid at greater intervals than agreed in the loan contract (s129(2)(b) CCA 1974). Because the contract is of loan and is not a sale or other supply of the car from Dastardly Finance Ltd to Dizzy, so there is no scope for it to be re-possessed by Dastardly Finance Ltd, but this does not prevent the court making a time order.

In addition, the court may feel able to re-open the loan agreement on the basis that it is an extortionate credit bargain. There does not appear to have been any sharp practice by Dastardly Finance Ltd or by Claude, but the rate of interest charged is clearly very high. Section 138 of the 1974 Act sets out those factors which the court will take into account in deciding whether the rate charged is 'grossly exorbitant', although the use of the adjective 'grossly' does not add anything and the court is simply concerned to see whether, bearing in mind the matters in s138, the rate is excessive (*Davies* v *Directloans Ltd* (1986)).

The rates of interest in the market at the time ranged from 27 per cent to 33 per cent for used cars but was only 25 per cent for new cars; the car bought by Dizzy was new therefore she was charged 10 per cent over the standard rate. Dastardly Finance Ltd will have to prove that there was justification for it charging such a high rate. Although the company did not know it, it seems that such a rate may have been a fair reflection of the risk it was undertaking because Dizzy had been rejected twice before. The Act does not specifically say that only the degree of risk known to the creditor is relevant although it requires the degree of risk 'accepted' by him to be investigated (s138(2)(a) CCA 1974) and, it is submitted, a creditor cannot be said to accept a risk which he does not know about.

Furthermore, only the rate of interest prevailing at the time the agreement was made is strictly relevant although knowledge or understanding that the rate is likely to fall may be considered relevant (s138(2)(c) CCA 1974). If, therefore, it appeared that market rates were likely to fall in the year of the loan then there will be a strong argument for this rate of interest being exorbitant.

It is not possible to give any clearer advice than that Dizzy will have a strong argument for the rate of interest to be re-assessed and/or the schedule of payments to be altered.

22 CREDIT CARDS

22.1 Introduction

Credit cards involve the provision of credit in two ways. Firstly, when the debtor is provided with the card he is given a general credit facility which he may use to draw money directly. Secondly, when he uses the card to buy goods or services he is given credit to the value of those goods or services. It should be noted, incidentally, that the use of a credit card as a cheque card does not involve the provision of credit (provided of course it is not used to guarantee more than the mandatory £50 or £250 according to type of card). Should a credit card be used as a means of identification to secure credit of more than £50 (or £250) then that will be a normal consumer credit transaction. Several different acts have relevance here. Where a debtor buys goods using a card the Sale of Goods Act 1979 applies and similarly the purchase of services will be affected by the Supply of Goods (Implied Terms) Act 1973. The primary act is, however, the Consumer Credit Act 1974.

22.2 Key points

It is important that the student understands the following.

a) *The agreement*

If a credit card is used to obtain money and there are only two parties, the agreement is for a fixed sum (s10(1)(b)), unrestricted use (s11(2)) debtor-creditor (s13(c)) credit. Use of a credit card to obtain goods or services involves a fixed sum (s10(1)(b)), restricted use (s11(1)(b)), debtor-creditor-supplier (s12(b)) credit. In addition to these classifications, credit cards also fall within the ambit of s14 because they are credit tokens. Section 14(3) provides that whenever a debtor uses his credit card, he is provided with credit. Section 10(3)(a) provides that primarily it is the credit limit which governs whether the agreement is regulated within the meaning of the act, rather than each individual provision of cash. However, the use of a credit card to obtain money, goods or services does not fall within the Consumer Credit Act if the amount involved is less than £50.

In calculating the credit limit it is important to remember that interest charges are not, in themselves credit.

Repayment figures are not (since 1978) statutorily fixed and the obligations of the debtor depend on the contractual terms agreed.

Default by a credit card holder is treated in the same way as default by any other debtor and the creditor has the same rights and obligations with regard to default notices, termination and so on.

b) *The goods*

It has already been stated that the debtor who buys goods using a credit card has the usual protection afforded by SGA 1979.

The contract of sale is a linked transaction s19(1)(b) CCA; and is with the supplier only.

However, s75(1) of CCA provides that in cases involving misrepresentation or breach and where the item of goods is of between £100-£30,000 in value, the debtor will have a joint right of action against both supplier and creditor.

c) *Loss and misuse of cards*

Note first, that the debtor is not precluded from an action against the creditor under s75(1) (above) merely because he has misused his card and exceeded his credit limit when making the purchase which is the subject of his action.

Credit cards remain the property of the creditor at all times, though the debtor has a duty to take reasonable care of the card. Provided he acts reasonably he is protected from having to reimburse the creditor for misuse by a third party. This is not an absolute protection, however, as by s84(1) he may be required to pay the first £50 of loss, following misuse of the card. Once he has notified the creditor, orally and in writing, of the loss or theft of the card he will normally have no further liability, unless, as has already been noted, he acted unreasonably and this prompted the loss or theft.

22.3 Analysis of questions

Questions which concern credit cards are comparatively rare. Only one question in the University of London's past papers deals with the topic at any length; and is quoted below. The question is also unusual because it is in essay form. Although part (b) at first looks like a problem it requires, in reality an essay requiring a discussion of the CCA 1974 terminology, in particular those aspects applicable to credit cards.

It should be noted that the subject matter is not confined to credit cards, but it forms a major part of the answer.

22.4 Question

a) Explain the concept of 'credit' in the Consumer Credit Act 1974.

b) The Midshires Bank plc (the Bank) set up an associate, Midcard plc, to issue credit cards to customers of the Bank for use in obtaining: (i) cash on credit from Midcard plc, to be paid by branches of the Bank acting as agent for Midcard plc; and (ii) goods from retailers who have agreed to honour credit cards issued by Midcard plc.

The credit limit is £40. In pursuance of this arrangement, Midcard plc issue a credit card to Eager, a customer of the Bank.

Analyse the categories of legal relationships arising under the Consumer Credit Act 1974 in connection with the use of this credit card by Eager.

University of London LLB Examination
(for External Students) Commercial Law June 1987 Q7

Skeleton solution

a)
- Section 9 CCA 1974.
- Use of interest on loan.

b)
- Credit card has two credit functions.
- Multiple agreements.
- Running account credit.
- Relationship between Midshires Bank and Midcard.
- Debtor-creditor-supplier agreements.
- Restricted use card.
- Liability for misrepresentation.

Suggested solution

a) *'Credit'*

Section 9 of the Consumer Credit Act 1974 defines credit as including a cash loan and any other form of 'financial accommodation'. Unfortunately, 'financial accommodation' is not defined.

The essence of credit agreements is that one person (the debtor) is provided with money by another (the creditor) and is under an obligation to repay that money, or is supplied with goods which he does not have to pay for until some time after delivery. The provision of money covers straightforward things like cash loans, but also covers overdrafts and credit or charge cards whereby the debtor buys goods from a shop (the supplier) which is paid by the creditor who is, in turn, repaid by the debtor.

The provision of goods by creditor to debtor occurs where there is a credit sale or a conditional sale. Such agreements are sales of goods and are regulated by the Sale of Goods Act 1979, save that in some circumstances the doctrine of acceptance does not apply to conditional sales (s14(1) Supply of Goods (Implied Terms) Act 1973). Section 9(3) of the 1974 Act expressly includes hire purchase agreements within the definition of credit agreements. This recognises the reality that hire purchase agreements are sales in disguise even though they are, in form and legal effect, arrangements for the hire of goods over a set period of time coupled with an option to buy (*Helby* v *Matthews* (1895)).

Professor Goode states that the essence of credit is 'debt deferment' but also states that a debt must be deferred for a significant length of time before it counts as credit (*The Consumer Credit Act, A Students' Guide*). The reason for this is that there may be many ordinary sales of goods where the buyer agrees to pay a day or two, or maybe a week after delivery. It is inconceivable that the complex formalities provisions of the 1974 Act should have to be complied with in all such situations.

In many cases the difference between simply allowing a little time to pay and providing credit is that interest is charged where credit is provided. This is not a requirement of the Consumer Credit Act, but in practice those who allow more than a few days to pay do so for reward.

b) *The Midshires Bank plc*

The issue of a credit card like the one in this case gives rise to a multiple agreement (s18(1)(b) Consumer Credit Act (CCA) 1974). The card serves two purposes, namely as a facility to obtain cash advances and as a facility to obtain goods. Multiple agreements fall to be regulated by the Act in different ways according to which facility is being used at any one time. Credit cards are credit tokens within s14.

i) Provision of cash

The credit card provided by Midcard plc can be used to obtain money from branches of the Midshires Bank plc. When it is so used there is a cash loan from Midcard plc to Eager. There are three parties involved, the Midshires Bank plc, Midcard plc and Eager.

The Midshires Bank plc set up Midcard plc as an associate and by virtue of s184 of the Act they are associate companies. This has various effects under the Act in relation to licensing (Part III CCA 1974) and responsibility for the imposition of improper pressure on the debtor (ss137-140 CCA 1974) but nothing of particular significance to credit cards.

When Midcard plc issued Eager with the credit card it provided him with a facility for obtaining cash loans. The loans were made by Midcard plc itself, even though the money was paid by the Midshires Bank plc, because the bank acted as Midcard plc's agent when paying over money. The contract under which the credit card was given to Eager is classified under the Act as a contract for running account credit (s10(1)(a) CCA 1974). When the card is used for cash advances the credit provided is unrestricted use (s11(2) CCA 1974), debtor-creditor (s13(c) CCA 1974) credit. It is unrestricted use because Eager actually gets cash which he can use as he wishes, and it is debtor-creditor because there are only two parties involved and there is no supply of goods to Eager. Because the credit limit is under £50 the agreement is a small agreement (s17 CCA 1974), but this does not mean it is not regulated and therefore does not affect the legal relationship between Midcard plc and Eager.

The advance of money by the Midshires Bank plc to Eager does not involve any specific relationship between the bank and the debtor, save that the bank is the agent of Midcard plc and will be liable to Eager for its defaults just like any other agent.

ii) The provision of goods

When the card is used by Eager to buy goods there are, again, three parties involved, namely Midcard plc, Eager and the shop.

The relationship between Midcard plc and Eager is similar to that in part (i) above, but there are two significant differences. Firstly, the agreement is debtor-creditor-supplier because the use of the card to obtain goods from the shop is permissible by virtue of pre-existing arrangements between the shop (the supplier) and Midcard plc (the creditor) (s12(b) CCA 1974). Secondly, the card provides Eager with restricted use credit (s11(1)(b) CCA 1974) because he does not actually get his hands on cash, merely on goods for which Midcard plc pays the shop and Eager repays Midcard plc. Midcard plc is not, however, responsible to Eager for any breach of contract or misrepresentation by the shop because such liability only arises where the value of goods supplied is between £100 and £30,000 and the credit limit here is below the lower of those figures (s75 CCA 1974).

When Eager uses the card to obtain goods there is a sale to him by the shop. That sale is regulated by the Sale of Goods Act 1979 and is not a credit sale or conditional sale. It is a cash sale, the cash price being supplied to the shop by Midcard plc which acts as Eager's agent for the purpose. The shop is responsible for any breach of or misrepresentation in the sale contract and cannot escape that responsibility by arguing that Eager should look to Midcard plc for recompense.

Between the shop and Midcard plc the Act has little application. Their arrangements are a matter of commercial rather than consumer credit.

PART 3

AGENCY

23 INTRODUCTION

23.1 Introduction

Agency is a legal concept which occurs where one person (the principal) authorises another (the agent) to act on his behalf; either generally, or for some specific purpose. The nature of the act to be done by the agent is usually to do with the negotiation of contracts on behalf of the principal. It is important to stress the mutual nature of the agreement - an agent will not become one merely by virtue of nomination by the principal, he must consent to act. The acts of an agent will affect the legal rights and liabilities of the principal.

It is important to distinguish agency from other relationships which may look similar such as master and servant, professional adviser and client, estate agents and so on. The fact that these relationships does not however preclude that of agency, hence, for example, in a professional adviser/client relationship the adviser may then go on to act as agent in the orthodox way.

Unlike the two preceding parts of this WorkBook there is no statutory code which regulates the dealings of principals and agents. Much of the law on the subject originates from common law rules; though, of course certain statutes do have relevance.

23.2 Key points

It is important that the student understands the following.

a) *Creation of agency*

There are four main ways in which agency may be created:

i) *express creation:* the simplest form, often the result of a contract negotiated specifically for the purpose;

ii) *creation by estoppel:* in such cases where a person represents that another is acting as his agent he will subsequently be estopped from denying the existence of agency;

iii) *creation by ratification*: even where the initial act was unauthorised a principal may acquire rights and subject himself to liabilities by retrospectively approving the act of agency;

iv) *by certain statutory provisions:* for example the CCA 1974 which in debtor-creditor-supplier contracts sets up a form of statutory agency whereby the supplier is regarded as the agent of the creditor.

All the methods listed above are modes of creating agency; there is a conscious act or a statutory provision to bring the agency relationship into being. It should be noted that it is also possible for agency to be implied:

- by the conduct of the parties; or
- by operation of law (for example an agency of necessity).

The whole subject will be dealt with in more detail in chapter 24.

23.3 Analysis of questions

Obviously, any question on the matters raised above must of necessity expect an extremely brief answer. Consequently, questions on introductory matters have tended to be linked with some other topic; often for example the question may also cover creation of authority which is the subject of chapter 24. The first question quoted below is one of the very few, which confines itself entirely to introductory matters. The second question, while appearing to be extremely generalised, could quite legitimately be situated in the far more limited field of chapters 26-27 on personal liability of an agent.

23.4 Questions

Question 1

'No word is more commonly and constantly abused than the word "agent".' (*Kennedy* v *De Trafford* [1897] AC 180 at p188 - per Lord Herschell).

Discuss this statement and consider the definitions of of an 'agent' which have been suggested.

University of London LLB Examination
(for External Students) Commercial Law June 1985 Q1

Skeleton solution

- Introduction to the question - analyse question and what it requires.
- Examples of agency relationships.
- Definitions - textbooks - articles - case law.
- Nature of agency, legal status of agent.
- Misuses of word 'agent' - reasons for misuse.
- Conclusion.

Suggested solution

The words of Lord Herschell were spoken in a case where the plaintiff tried to establish that the defendant was liable for breach of a fiduciary duty, by relying on the defendant's description of himself as an agent. The case has been cited as authority that it is not possible to admit agency because whether one person is another's agent is a question of law and only matters of fact can be admitted (Treitel, *The Law of Contract*). The important principle, then, is that agency is a legal concept which should be used like other legal concepts, as a term of art and not indiscriminately. The question whether the word 'agent' is commonly abused can only be answered by considering the many instances when it is used to describe a relationship which is not a true agency. Therefore to consider whether the word is commonly abused it is necessary to see what it means in law, and the extent to which it is used to mean other things. It is not possible to discuss all the definitions of agency which have been attempted by writers and judges, so only the most authoritative will be examined. It may be helpful, however, to consider some of the different circumstances in which agency can arise in order to show why it is easy for confusion to arise.

The most common type of relationship in which agency is said to arise is the case of employer-employee, where the employee has to undertake certain tasks or make certain contracts on behalf of his employer. But agency can arise equally in more informal circumstances, for example when a child goes to a shop to buy goods for his parents. Likewise agency can arise between the parents themselves. A common example for students would be where one flatmate pays a communal bill on behalf of all. These cases all concern agency arising from agreement of the agent to act for the principal. It is also possible for an agency to arise even without agreement, for example where there is an agency of necessity (*Great Northern Railway* v *Swaffield* (1874)). The variety of possible agencies is incalculable, yet attempts have been made to find one definition to cover all cases.

Fridman has suggested, albeit tentatively, that agency is 'the relationship that exists between two persons when one, called the agent, is considered in law to represent the other, called the principal, in such a way as to be able to affect the principal's legal position in respect of strangers to the relationship by the making of contracts or the disposition of property (*Fridman's Law of Agency*). This definition is the result of Professor Fridman's examination of many definitions from other writers which he considered were either too narrow or too broad. He openly admits that it is not possible to define agency other than by considering its consequences. In other words he looks backwards from the result of decided cases where one person's acts bound another in order to try to establish the principle being applied by the courts. This definition has the benefit of stating what the consequences of agency are, but does not help us to discover when the relationship of agency will arise. Other definitions have attempted this latter task.

The standard textbooks on the law of contract all contain chapters on agency and it is interesting to note that the definitions of agency given are concerned primarily with agencies which arise under contract - in other words by agreement. So, Cheshire and

Fifoot talk of agency being 'a comprehensive word which is used to describe the relationship that arises where one man is appointed to act as the representative of another' (Cheshire, Fifoot and Furmston's *Law of Contract*). Similarly Treitel talks of agency being 'a relationship which arises when one person, called the principal, authorises another, called the agent, to act on his behalf and that other agrees to do so', and Anson defines an agent as one who 'may represent or act on behalf of another, with that other's authority, for the purpose of bringing him into legal relations with a third party' (Anson's *Law of Contract*). The differences between these three definitions may be matters of semantics, but it is submitted that there is a discernible difference of emphasis nonetheless. Cheshire and Fifoot when talking of 'appointment' put emphasis on agency being a position to which someone may be elevated.

Treitel, on the other hand does not see agency as a distinct office, but considers it to be merely a clothing of one person with authority whether formally or informally and Anson is also concerned with the fact of clothing someone with authority without that person having to occupy a specific position of office. Each of these three definitions is adequate as far as it goes, but none can be said to be comprehensive.

Other writers have tried to be comprehensive in their definitions. For example, Dowrick examined the consequences of agency and felt that the only comprehensive definition would be one which stressed that agency arises by operation of law and not necessarily by agreement or a conscious decision of the principal to authorise the agent (Dowrick, 'The Relationship of Principal and Agency' (1954) 17 MLR 24, 26). This theme was also employed by Reynolds who argued that it is vital to differentiate between cases where agency arises by agreement and cases where agency arises in the absence of agreement (Reynolds, 'Agency, Theory and Practice' (1978) 94 LQR 224). Although Reynolds did not attempt a comprehensive definition of agency, his criticism of the normal contractual approach shows that any definition must take into account the fact that agency does not arise by operation of law, whether the operation of the law is in giving legal effect to the agreement of the parties or in imposing agency because of the circumstances of a particular case ((1978) 94 LQR 224, 227-8).

The final definition which will be considered here is that contained in the leading textbook on agency. Bowstead lays emphasis on consent as being the essence of agency, saying: 'agency is the relationship which exists between two persons, one of whom expressly or impliedly consents that the other should represent him or act on his behalf, and the other of whom similarly consents to represent the former or so to act (*Bowstead on Agency*; and see *Garnac Grain* v *Faure and Fairclough* (1968)). This introduces a different conceptual approach to those discussed so far. It does not restrict agency to cases of contract and it attempts to cover such matters as agency of necessity by an explanation of implied consent on the part of the principal and agent. This approach, therefore, is the only one in the major textbooks which makes it clear that the essence of agency is that it arises by operation of law. In order to explain how the law operates it does, however, rely on contractual ideas, especially when saying that both parties must consent, but that such consent may be implied rather than expressed.

Therefore, we can see that there is a modicum of agreement about what agency is, and therefore what an agent is. But differences of emphasis arise in attempting to explain how agency itself arises.

In order to understand how the word agent can be abused it is necessary to go beyond definition, however, and consider if there is some aspect of a true agency which does not arise in cases where there is an agency but nevertheless one person has altered the legal position of another. It can be seen from decided cases that an agent may affect the position of his principal in three ways. Firstly he may make a contract professing to be an agent and within the scope of the authority which the principal has vested in him. For example, if someone is employed to work as a salesman for a company, the person with whom he makes contracts of sale is not contractually bound to the salesman, he is bound to the salesman's employer (*Maddick* v *Marshall* (1864)). In this first case, therefore, the agent affects his principal's legal relations with a third party but then drops out of the picture. The second case is where the agent makes a contract which he has been expressly authorised to make, but deals with the third party as principal not as agent. For example, if the salesman sells secondhand cars from his home on behalf of the employer, but the third party buyer does not know he is an agent - he sees the salesman as the owner. In this case the principal's interest in the car is transferred to the buyer and the buyer may sue the principal for damages if something goes wrong, but the agent and third party have made a contract where the third party, objectively, has contracted with the agent alone; therefore the agent is also liable on the contract (*Humble* v *Hunter* (1848)).

It must be added, though, that the third party will be obliged to elect whether to sue the agent or the principal once he discovers the fact of agency (*Scarf* v *Jardine* (1882)). Nevertheless, this second type of case is one where the agent does not drop out of the transaction once the contract is made - both principal and agent are considered to be under a degree of liability to the third party. The third case is where the agent professes to be acting as an agent, but in fact exceeds his authority. It is only in exceptional circumstances that the principal will be bound by the act of the agent, and, therefore, the agent may well be personally liable without the principal being liable (see Fridman). For example, if the seller of a secondhand car professes to sell it for Mr X where in fact he has rented it from Mr X and has no right to sell. In such a case it is tempting to say that the contract must be void since no one may sell without being the owner or having the permission of the owner to sell. But, of course, the true position is not that the contract is void, but that the agent has warranted his authority, and is liable for the breach of this promise (*Collen* v *Wright* (1857)). These different situations show that the essence of agency is that the agent may affect the legal position of the principal provided he acts within the scope of his authority, but he may also be liable personally. Outside these three situations a person may be described as an agent, but he will not be an agent. It is only within these three cases that true agency arises.

The most common abuse of the term agent is in the field of the buying and selling of real property, where the figure of the 'estate agent' appears (the rest of this essay discusses points made in the article by Reynolds cited above). An estate agent is not normally employed to make a contract or other disposition of property, but is employed simply to effect introductions and arrange for surveys and the like. The difficulty arises because there is clear authority that an estate agent may be in a fiduciary position to his client (*Regier* v *Campbell-Stuart* (1939)). It is tempting to say that this arises because of agency, but in reality it does not, it arises because of the position of trust in which the estate agent is placed. A relatively new example of this type of abuse of the term agent arises in attempts to get around the doctrine of privity of contract, particularly when it is attempted to give a stranger to a contract the benefit of an exclusion clause. In *The Eurymedon* (1975) the contract between the carrier and the owner of the goods carried stated that stevedores would be employed as agents so that they could rely on limitations of liability if they damaged the goods. That seems to be an acceptable use of the term agent, but problems arise when considering the way in which the stevedores were employed. They made a contract not directly with the owners of the goods, but with the carrier, who was said to be the agent of the owners for the purpose of the making of this contract, but in fact all the carriers did was pass on an offer, they did not fall within any of the three true cases of agency (see Reynolds (1978) 94 LQR 224, 229-230). See also *Preston* v *Markheath* (1988) as to creation of agency in the context of estate agents.

A second category of cases has shown that sometimes parties wish to create a fictitious agency in order to give one of them a degree of security in a sale. These are the 'Romalpa' cases (originating with *Aluminium Industries* v *Romalpa Aluminum* (1976)). It is widespread for a seller who wishes to have security to include a term in his contract of sale that he retains ownership in the goods sold and that if they are sold on by the buyer the sale is as agent of the original seller. The whole area of Romalpa clauses is complicated by the fact that sellers attempt to impose legal doctrines into circumstances for which they are not suitable, in order to attempt to gain priority over other creditors if the buyers are insolvent. It is, of course, quite fictitious to say that the true nature of the agreement between buyers and sellers in such cases is that the sellers shall remain owners and the buyers be merely bailees who sell on as agents. The sellers never expect to demand return of the goods, therefore there is no true bailment (see generally *Coggs* v *Bernard* (1703)). The consequence of this is that sales of the goods supplied by the buyers to third parties are not in reality sales as agents, they are sales as principals.

It can be seen, therefore, that any definition of agency which includes the cases where the 'agent' is like an estate agent - a mere conduit pipe - or like a 'Romalpa' buyer - a fictitious agent - will fail to do justice to the useful legal concept of agency. The indiscriminate use of the term agent to describe someone who in some way acts on behalf of another likewise leads to confusion in definition of the central concept of agency. It is by no means easy to agree with Lord Hershell that no word is more commonly or constantly abused, but if his language is understood to be a call for more precise definition of agency then it can be said with some confidence that he was correct.

Question 2

'Any agency situation looks like a simple triangular arrangement but it is not simple. It is a combination of three distinguishable but interconnected two-party relationships: between principal and third party, principal and agent, and agent and third party.' To what extent is this an accurate or useful analysis?

University of London LLB Examination
(for External Students) Commercial Law June 1991 Q1

Skeleton solution

- A general picture of agency, the roles of principal, agent and third party.
- Agent will normally 'drop out'.
- Cases where he does not; personal liability.

Suggested solution

The idea of agency is that a relationship will exist between a principal and an agent, whereby the agent, if he is acting within his authority, may bind the principal in a contract with a third party. To this extent the wording of the question is a reasonably accurate description of the agency situation. But it is over simplified.

By the very nature of agency the agent is acting merely as a go-between and thus the general rule evolved that an agent could derive no benefit (or detriment) from the principal's contract with the third party. In normal circumstances he could neither sue nor be sued on that contract. This rule was seen to be a matter of commercial necessity, because if an agent were to be deemed automatically liable on the contract there would be no need for the agent - principal relationship; nor indeed would many people agree to become agents, knowing they could at any time be liable on a contract they had supposedly negotiated for someone else.

Thus the important and overriding principle in all agency situations is that the contract entered into is the contract as between the principal and the third party. The agent 'drops out' of the transaction and does not become a party to it: *Montgomerie* v *UK Mutual SS Association* (1891).

However the agent does not always drop out; in certain circumstances he may become personally liable on the contract and in such cases, the first relationship noted in the question, that between principal and third party, never comes into existence. It may be, of course that the principal will intervene to take over the contract, in the agent's place, in which case the agent's personal liability will cease, but in most cases of personal liability of the agent there are, so to speak, only two (or possibly even one) sides of the 'triangle' present.

Firstly, it should be noted that for reasons of his own a person will sometimes purport to be dealing for a 'principal' who is completely fictitious and non-existent. If a person is really principal and agent all rolled into one he will not be an agent as such even if he describes himself as one (*Schmalz* v *Avery* (1851); see also *Kelner* v *Baxter* (1866) and s9(2) of European Communities Act 1972). In such circumstances an 'agent' will be held personally liable on the contract because there is no principal; here there is only one relationship - as between the so-called 'agent' and the third party. Of course the 'agent' may subsequently find himself a principal, perhaps by a process of ratification, in which case the normal machinery of agency, with its three-cornered set of relationships, would swing into existence.

If an agent makes a contract under seal in his own name, it has been held that he will be personally liable on it, even though he describes himself in the document as agent (*Hancock* v *Hodgson* (1827)). A further example of an agent being personally liable was where an agent acted on behalf of a foreign principal; there was previously a presumption to this effect. In *Teheran-Europe* v *ST Belton Tractors Ltd* (1968) this presumption was held to apply no longer. In certain circumstances the agent may simply accept personal responsibility, either expressly or impliedly where there is a custom in a particular trade or industry to that effect (*The Swan* (1968); *Hutchinson* v *Tatham* (1873)). In such cases both principal and agent will be jointly and severally liable.

Perhaps the most important instance of agent's personal liability, however, is in connection with the doctrine of the undisclosed principal. An agent must be held liable here, because the third party is unaware of the agent-principal relationship. It may well be that the agent's liability will end when the existence (and identity) of the principal is revealed and the principal intervenes, but in some cases the principal cannot intervene and the agent's liability continues. In *Humble* v *Hunter* (1848) the agent, in negotiating for an undisclosed principal, described himself as 'owner of the ship'. When the principal, the true owner of the ship, sought to intervene to enforce the charterparty contract, it was held that he could not do so, as his existence was impliedly denied by the agent describing himself as 'owner of the ship'. The agent remained personally liable. (See also *UK Mutual SS Assurance* v *Nevin* (1887)).

It can thus be seen that there are many instances where the agent will be liable personally on the contract and the principal-third party relationship will never come into existence. It should be remembered also that even in circumstances where an agent is not personally liable, he may be liable to the third party for a breach of warranty of authority. If he acts outside his authority then the third party may sue. This right was first clearly established in *Collen* v *Wright* (1857). The measure of damages here is such as will put the third party in the same position as he would have been in had the agent had full authority. Thus, if the contract fails for some other reason, or is successful regardless of the agent's lack of authority, there will be no damages payable because no loss will result to the third party which is specifically attributable to the agent's acting without due authority. Note, from *Yonge* v *Toynbee* (1910), that an agent may be liable even if he acts in complete good faith.

Thus there are three ways in which an agent may affect the position of his principal. Firstly he may make a contract professing to be an agent and with full authority from his principal. In such cases the agent effects his principal's relationship with the third party and then drops out - the normal agency situation. Secondly an agent may make a contract which he has authority to make, but deals with the third party as principal not agent. As in cases like *Humble* v *Hunter* (above) the third party has contracted objectively with the agent alone, therefore both agent and principal will be liable. The agent does not drop out of the transaction once the contract is made; both agent and principal will be considered to be under a degree of liability to the third party. It is true however that once the fact of agency is discovered the third party must elect to sue either the principal or the agent; he cannot sue both (*Scarf* v *Jardine* (1882)). Finally where the agent exceeds his authority the agent may well be liable without the principal incurring any obligations at all towards the third party.

24 CREATION OF AUTHORITY

24.1 Introduction

Methods of creation have already been discussed, briefly in the previous chapter. As well as being classified as either express or implied modes of creation of agency have other possible classifications as well. For example, express creation can also be described as creation by agreement, or creation by contract; although this latter may be misleading as a contract as such is not always necessary.

Allied to the subject of methods of creation of agency is the question of the extent of the agency created by each particular method. There is some confusion here between the terminology used in different reference books; some of the terms overlap.

Probably the most straightforward approach is to list agents' authority as follows.

a) Actual authority: that authority given to an agent created by agreement. The scope of actual authority will be determined by studying the actual agreement, which may contain express or implied authority.

b) Apparent authority: that authority an agent has when created by estoppel.

c) Usual authority: this can cover either of the first two and can be actual or apparent. If a person is appointed to an agency which carries standard powers and duties he will have usual actual authority. Or, the principal may represent to a third party that the agent holds a particular office that carries standard powers, in which case the third party presumes the agent to have usual apparent powers.

As has already been noted here, the student reading several different authorities may come across slightly differing terminology and there is, in any event, a considerable blurring and merging at the edges of the definitions so that they overlap to some degree.

24.2 Key points

It is important that the student understands the following.

a) *Creation by agreement*

It is possible to create agency not only by express agreement, but by implied agreement. No contract, as such, is necessary to create agency by agreement, but there very often will be a contract. The form that the creation of agency takes bears a strong resemblance to the making of contracts, so that just as one can have highly formalised contracts made by deed, or a simply oral contract, or even a contract implied by conduct, so, in just the same manner one can have agency created in any of these ways.

Where agency is created by agreement the agent possesses actual authority. If the contract is specific, the extent of an agent's powers may be discovered by studying the terms of the contract by which the agency was created. If the creation of agency is by implied contract, the extent of the agent's actual authority may be ascertained by applying normal constructional rules as to implied terms to the contract of agency.

This mode of creation and the three that follow are treated only in the most superficial way and the student should read further on the subject. In particular the relevant case law should be studied carefully.

b) *Creation by estoppel*

In order for agency by estoppel to exist, the following conditions must exist:

i) there must be a representation that authority as agent exists, either directly or from a course of dealing;

ii) the representation must be one of fact and not law;

iii) the representation must be to the effect that the agent is authorised to act as agent, not some other representation as to capacity;

iv) the representation must be made by the principal himself;

v) the representation must be made to a third party, not to the world at large;

vi) the third party must have actual knowledge of the representation and must have had no reasonable opportunity of discovering the truth (that the 'agent' was not 'authorised');

vii) the third party must have relied on the representation and entered into a contract with the agent.

(There are numerous leading cases here, that the student should be familiar with. See, for example, the recent case of *Charrington Fuel Oil Ltd* v *Parvant Co Ltd* (1988) The Times 28 December.)

When agency is created by estoppel it gives rise to 'apparent' or 'ostensible' authority. These terms are interchangeable.

c) *Creation by ratification*

The concept that a principal can adopt an act done on his behalf, thereby setting up a form of agency retrospectively, has already been noted in chapter 23. There are a number of conditions that must be satisfied before an unauthorised act of agency can be ratified:

i) the agent must have made the contract as agent in the first place;

ii) the principal must have capacity to do the act; he cannot ratify an illegal or ultra vires act;

iii) the principal must have been in existence at the time of the contract;

iv) the principal must ratify 'in time'. If time is 'of the essence' the principal must ratify within time stated, or otherwise within a reasonable time;

v) the act of ratification must be unequivocal; mere passive aquiescence is not sufficient.

The effect of ratification is simply to put all the parties concerned, principal, agent and third party into the same position in which they would have been had the agency existed at the time the contract was made.

d) *Creation by operation of law*

Two instances exist where agency comes into operation by the rules of common law. Agency of necessity has already been mentioned in chapter 23, the other is agency by reason of cohabitation. Both, nowadays have only limited application; though they do occasionally arise.

Agency of necessity will only apply if certain conditions are present:

i) it must be impossible to communicate with the owner of goods, or he must refuse deliberately, to give instructions;

ii) the agent of necessity must act in good faith and the interests of the owner;

iii) his act must be commercially necessary.

Agency of necessity applies only where goods have been entrusted to a bailee (usually for transportation) and the above conditions apply. Because of modern communications systems such emergencies rarely arise nowadays and agency of necessity is, correspondingly rarely found.

There used to be a rule that a wife was to be regarded as the agent of her husband when making contracts for necessaries, but changing social habits made this rule largely irrelevant and that form of agency was abolished by the Matrimonial Proceedings and Property Act 1970. There is still, however, a presumption in common law that where a man and woman cohabit, regardless of whether married or not, then agency may arise. This presumption is, however, of little practical importance.

24.3 Analysis of questions

As already noted in chapter 23 questions on agency overlap considerably. It is not at all uncommon to have wide-ranging questions that demand a good working knowledge of almost all the agency syllabus. Question 1 of the 1986 University of London paper, for example, which is quoted in chapter 27 requires inter alia an account of the main types of agency and the primary methods of creation. The first question quoted below might equally well apply in other sections, it has a certain generality about it that makes it similar, in particular, to the question in the preceding chapter. The second and third questions, while basically relatively straightforward questions as to agency and the forms it takes, relate also to aspects of agents' duties (especially as to bribes and secret profits). While at first sight these questions are remarkably similar, in fact the combination of topics and emphasis is quite different.

24.4 Questions

Question 1

'The definition of 'agent' is elusive because the word does not have one specific meaning.'

Discuss.

University of London LLB Examination
(for External Students) Commercial Law June 1989 Q1

Skeleton solution

- Modes of creation of agency.
- Powers of various types of agent.
- Relationship of term 'agent' to the person who uses it.
- Application to the question, specifically.

Suggested solution

An agent is a person who acts on behalf of another, the principal, in such a way as to be able to affect the principal's legal position in relation to strangers to the relationship by the making of contracts or the disposition of property. In other words, an agent is a person through whom the principal acts in entering binding legal relationships with third parties.

This definition implies that there is some element of consent by the principal to be represented by the agent and by the agent to act in this capacity. As the majority of agencies are created by agreement, this consent is usually present. In these circumstances, provided the parties comply with the terms of the agreement there is no difficulty in defining the function of the agent.

In some cases, however, one person may bind another in a contract with a third party even though the act is outside the scope of the authority which has been given or is undertaken without any authority at all. The principal is not intending to act at all and does not wish to enter a binding contract with the third party. Nevertheless he will be bound by the contract made on his behalf. The person who negotiates the contract is not an authorised agent at all. He merely has the ability in law to act as if he were. Such a person is also described as an agent.

The term 'agent', therefore, covers a number of different people. First it includes those who are authorised to act in a particular way and who do act within the scope of their instructions. These are agents in the full sense of the word. They may be appointed either expressly or by implied agreement as in *Biggar* v *Rock Life Insurance Co* (1902). They may even be given authority retrospectively by ratification as in *Bolton Partners* v *Lambert* (1889). In all these cases, however, the agent is given actual authority by the principal to act in a certain way and to bind the principal in contracts with third parties.

Even if the agent acts outside the terms of his express instructions, however, he may still be treated as acting within his actual authority. This will occur for example, when the principal's instructions are ambiguous or if they give the agent a discretion, as in *Comber* v *Anderson* (1808). In all these cases, the principal has instructed the agent to act, and the agent has acted, in a particular way. The principal intends to act through the agent in entering binding legal relationships with other people.

There are other cases, however, in which no such intention can be found. These are situations where the law considers that third parties who deal with someone who appears to have authority are entitled to treat that person as having such authority even though the principal who is bound by these acts had no intention of creating that person his agent for these purposes. There are two types of authority which may arise in these circumstances. These are usual authority and apparent authority.

Usual authority occurs where an agent is employed in a particular trade or business. Such a person will bind his principal by acts which agents of this type normally can do, even though the principal has instructed the agent not to make agreements of this kind. This occurred in *Watteau* v *Fenwick* (1893) where the owner of a public house (the principal) was bound by a contract made by the manager of the public house (the agent) with a third party, even though the manager had been told not to act in this way. The contract was one which such managers usually could make and the principal had to commit it even though he had not intended to be committed in this way and despite the fact that the agent had exceeded his express authority.

Apparent (or ostensible) authority is, in fact, no authority at all and yet contracts made within the scope of this authority will bind the person on whose behalf the act was apparently carried out. Apparent authority is based on estoppel. It was defined by Diplock LJ in *Freeman and Lockyer* v *Buckhurst Park Properties (Mangal) Ltd* (1964) (see also *United Bank of Kuwait* v *Hammond* (1988) as to ostensible authority of a solicitor) as being a legal relationship between the principal and the third party created by a representation made by the principal to the third party which is intended to be and is in fact acted upon. The representation is that the agent has the power to act in a particular way. When the agent does so act, the principal is estopped from denying the agent's authority and is bound by the contract which has been made even though the principal did not intend the agent to have any power.

For apparent authority to arise, therefore, there has to be a representation made by the principal to the third party. Such a representation may be by words or conduct (*Spiro* v *Lintern* (1973)) but it must come from the principal and not the agent (*Farquharson* v

King and Co (1902)). It must be made to the person who relied on it entering the contract. If these requirements are present, the principal will be bound even though he had no intention that the agent should act in this way or that such a contract would be made by the third party. The principal's liability is based on the fact that, by his representations, he is estopped from relying on the true state of affairs in attempting to avoid liability under a contract made in this way.

Finally, another type of authority which may bind a principal is authority created by operation of law. This will rise where there is a sudden unforeseen emergency which carries with it the risk of damage to the principal's goods or interests. If it is impossible to contact the principal, the person in possession of these goods may take all steps that are reasonably necessary to preserve the principal's interests and the principal will be bound by these acts even though he had not authorised them. As a general rule, authority of necessity will arise only where there is a pre-existing agency relationship between the principal and the person who acts to preserve the principal's interests. It may arise where the goods are in the possession of captains of ships, as was shown in the case of *Couturier* v *Hastie* (1856), or in the possession of other carriers, as in *GNR* v *Swaffield* (1874). The only case where a pre-existing agency is not necessary is where a person accepts a bill of exchange for the honour of the drawer.

The word 'agent' therefore covers a number of ideas, ranging from a person who is actually authorised to act in a particular way by the principal, to a person who binds the principal without the principal's knowledge or consent. This may arise because of the position in which the agent has been placed, or because of the principal's conduct in relation to the third party, or even because of the circumstances that have arisen.

What these types of agency have in common is that the agent has the power, whether by agreement or by operation of the law, to bind the principal in contract with a third party. The 'elusive' part of the definition relates to the ways in which an agent is created as such. The definition of an agent, however, is not so elusive. It is, as was said at the beginning, a person who acts on behalf of another in such a way as to be able to affect that other's legal position in relation to strangers to the relationship by the making of contracts or the disposition of property. This definition, given by Fridman (*Law of Agency*), defines the powers of all agents, however those agents were created.

Question 2

Peelsy plc, a drinks company, places advertisements as follows: 'We sell the widest range of wines, beers and drinks. Details available from our authorised outlets.' Peelsy has representatives at three outlets in Mykindatown: Alphonse and Bruno, who are both managers of shops carrying Peelsy's name; and Capone, the manager of a third shop, which Peelsy bought from Capone and which still trades under the name 'Capone's'. All three managers sign contracts on 1 January 1990 stipulating that they will be employed for a minimum of three years, though Capone's contract also provides that his employment will continue so long as 'Capone's' remains profitable. The contracts forbid the managers from selling products not supplied or ordered by the head office of Peelsy.

Advise Peelsy in the following cases:

a) Alphonse sells 20 cases of Vin Plonc to Theo, who only agrees to buy it on Alphonse's 'personal guarantee' that it will increase in value by 10 per cent in five months; it does not.

b) Ulrich runs a grocer's shop near Bruno's shop. He does not normally sell alcoholic drinks. In March, there is a shortage of cocoa, a product which Peelsy does not normally supply. Ulrich tells Bruno that, if he can obtain some cocoa through one of Peelsy's contacts, he will also buy 50 cases of wine and pay Bruno himself £100 for his help. He receives the cocoa and wine, for which he has not paid, and pays Bruno half of the £100 'on account'.

c) Vivien, Capone's former landlady, normally buys her drinks from another supplier, Squelch; but, in part settlement of Capone's unpaid rent, she orders 100 cans of soft drinks from Capone.

d) In June, Peelsy decides to sell the three shops to Squelch, who wishes to demolish them and to develop a wine superstore on the best of the three sites, the 'Capone's' site.

University of London LLB Examination
(for External Students) Commercial Law June 1990 Q4

Skeleton solution

- Definition agency generally.
- How agency arises - duties, obligations of the agent.
- Holding out as agent. Agency by estoppel. Duty of agent not to make secret profit, duty to account.

Suggested solution

Many commercial transactions in the field of commerce are conducted through agents who act as intermediaries and represent the interests of their principals in the conduct of the principal's business. The essential point to be borne in mind is that the relationship between agent and principal is essentially a binding contractual one which imposes upon both parties rights, duties and obligations. In this example, we are told that the trading relationship established between the drinks company (Peelsy Plc) and its agents Alphonse (A) Bruno (B) and Capone (C) is a fixed term contract for three years; although Capone has an additional element in that his agency is stated in the contract to 'continue so long as Capone's remains profitable'. The contracts given to A, B and C forbid them to sell products not 'supplied' or 'ordered' by their Peelsy head office. In all four parts of the question we are asked to advise the parent company (P).

a) A has agreed to sell 20 cases of Vin Plonc to T and has given a personal assurance that the wine will increase in value by 10 per cent over five months. This guarantee, it must be stressed, is a personal one; at no time does Peelsy appear to have incorporated this into their agency contract with A or other agents.

A is under a contractually binding agreement to sell Peelsy's products, presumably in return he is given his commission on sales, marketing support and the various other incentives available to commercial agents. What needs to be considered is the nature and extent of A's agency with Peelsy.

A has an express contract and can sell products supplied by or ordered from Peelsy. Assuming Vin Plonc falls into one or both of these categories, then A is authorised to sell the product. The general nature of a contractual agency is that the principal (P) invests the agent (A) with actual authority to act on behalf of P. When A has carried out his duties to the best of his abilities then he is entitled to his remuneration under the contract of agency, but must then leave the third party with whom he has contracted on his principal's behalf to assume that the contract was between P and the third party. The agent has actual 'express' authority to perform acts specifically referred to in the agency contract, and he (A) has 'usual' authority to bind his principal to any act done, or contract made by A if it is necessary for or reasonably incidental to carrying out the authority expressly given to A, or is of a type that someone in A's trade or profession usually does have authority to make (*Watteau* v *Fenwick* (1893)).

However, the agent is not entitled to exceed these 'express' and 'usual' authorities and bind the principal to contracts that the principal has not authorised or has no knowledge of. So whilst it may be usual or express that A does his best to promote 'Vin Plonc' to customers, the giving of a 'personal guarantee' that it will increase in value in a short time period is outside his express contractual agency and also exceeds his presumed or usual authority. The agent's implied duties (over and above his express contractual duties to his principal) are to act in good faith in pursuance of the principal's interest, a duty to account, to make full disclosure of all material facts and not to exceed his authority or make a secret profit (any such profit to be accounted for).

In the giving of a personal guarantee without making full disclosure to his principal, A has exceeded his authority. He does not appear to be acting in the interests of P and in the event that T decides to sue on the 'personal guarantee' P would be an undisclosed principal. Accordingly, P has the option to either ratify the guarantee (in which case he (A) would have had to have expressly named P at the time the contract with T was made (*Keighley, Maxsted & Co* v *Durant* (1901)) and P will have to unequivocally adopt all of A's actions after full disclosure thereof by A.

It seems unlikely that P will wish to ratify A's actions as they are to his detriment and A did not name P when the contract was made; accordingly, if T decides to sue, P and T are entitled to hold A personally liable on his personal guarantee (see *Mercantile Credit Co* v *Hamblin* (1965).

b) Clearly B, as agent of Peelsy is only expressly authorised under the contract he has signed, to sell goods 'ordered' or 'supplied' from Peelsy. Ulrich has requested B to obtain cocoa through one of P's contacts; so we do not know if the goods (ie the cocoa) are ordered directly from or supplied by P.

The agency of B would normally be limited to his express (ie 'actual' contractual) or implied (ie 'usual') authority. Peelsy appears to be a general vendor of drinks of all varieties and makes and has placed advertisements to this 'effect we sell the widest range of wines, beers and drinks, details available from our authorised outlets'. B is an authorised outlet for these purposes. We are told however, that despite the wide range of drinks sold by Peelsy through its authorised outlets, that the cocoa requested by U in March is not normally supplied by them.

Thus we can assume that B has exceeded his actual and usual authority on two counts; possibly even three and is therefore in breach of his agency contract with P. He has agreed to approach 'P's contacts' and obtain cocoa, usually outside P's trading sphere and he has received a secret profit (albeit only 1/2 the agreed amount) from U. Additionally, B appears to allow U to take wine without paying for it and this is a possible fourth breach of agency.

Taking all these facts together it is obvious that B is not acting in the interests of P, that he does not hesitate to breach his actual and usual agency authority, that he has not made full disclosure of his actions (by approaching P's contacts and obtaining cocoa to supply U) and that, most importantly, he has made a secret profit and has not observed his implied duty to account therefore to P.

These flagrant and repeated breaches of contract are fatal to B's agency contract with Peelsy. B is in breach of several contractual and implied duties of agency; not least amongst these the refusal to obey the lawful instructions of the principal and is therefore liable in damages to his principal (*Cohen* v *Kittell* (1889). Additionally, he has permitted a conflict of interest to develop between his personal interest and the duty of full disclosure to the principal. In this case the principal may set aside the transaction for wine and cocoa with U and claim any profit (£50) made by B. In *Boardman* v *Phipps* (1967), the Court of Appeal held that an agent who makes a secret profit is in breach of the duty of good faith to the principal and such secret profit must be accounted for and is recoverable at law by the principal (*Lucifero* v *Castel* (1887)).

Lastly, B appears to have breached the duty not to misuse confidential information acquired as a result of agency (*Robb* v *Green* (1895)) in using 'contacts' properly belonging to P. P can sue for breach of agency, require the handing over of the secret profit, seek damages against B for breach and possibly require B to pay personally for the wine and cocoa not paid for by U.

c) Capone has sold V some soft drinks which were presumably supplied to him by Peelsy head office. The problem C faces is whether he is using his agency contract to satisfy a personal debt; this appears to be the case. C has not made full disclosure and the 'set-off' he has allowed against his debt to his former landlady on the drinks could amount once again to the making of a secret profit.

This may not prove fatal to C's agency contract and he may be able to claim his remuneration (ie - commission) from Peelsy if he can repay the debt to Peelsy and can prove he has substantially performed his contract (*Rimmer* v *Knowles* (1874)).

However, a major duty of an agent is to keep proper accounts of all transactions entered into on his principal's behalf and to keep 'agency money' separate from his own. Roskill RJ said in *Aluminium Industrie Vaassen BV* v *Romalpa Aluminium* (1976):

'If an agent lawfully sells his principal's goods, he stands in a fiduciary relationship to his principal and remains accountable to his principal for those goods and their proceeds.'

If he does not keep 'agency money' and his own separate, there is a presumption the whole amount belongs to the principal. In any event it appears that C will have to account to Peelsy and at least repay the balance of the soft drinks sold to V.

d) This situation requires us to look at the agency - principal relationship from the principal's point of view. The mutual responsibilities of the agency contract are to a greater extent reciprocal; just as the principal can expect the agent to make full disclosure; so the agent can expect a reciprocal duty from the principal.

We have already been informed that Squelch is the rival of Capone's and by implication Squelch must be in competition with the three outlets who act as agents for Peelsy. The sell off by Peelsy to Squelch who intend to demolish all shops and construct a wine superstore on Capone's site amounts to a breach of the agency contract by Peelsy, the principal in this case.

Furthermore, the promises embodied in Capone's contract (originally bought out by Peelsy) that he can continue to trade under his own name and that the contract will continue so long as 'Capone's remains profitable', have also been broken as well as the original three year trading agreement in A, B and C's cases.

All things being equal, and treating P's breach as if none of the problems referred to above had occurred, then A, B and C are entitled to damages for breach of their contract. They are also entitled to an indemnity against P for any expenses and losses incurred as a result of their acting on their principal's behalf - so for example, purchase of leases, advertising, stock in trade etc, can all be claimed by A, B and C (see eg *Hitchins, Harrison, Woolston & Co* v *Jackson & Sons* (1943)).

Additionally, the agents are entitled to claim remuneration from the principal as by contract this has been expressly agreed; so their damages will consist of loss of remuneration and profits if the sell off goes ahead and the wine superstore is built (*John Meacock & Co* v *Abrahams* (1956)). This is a fixed term contract in the case of A and B; in C's case he may be able to claim what is known as 'continuing commission' as he had an agreement that his employment would continue 'so long as he continued to trade profitably'. As he appears to be so doing even the termination of the agency contract cannot prevent him claiming, as this kind of commission depends on the construction of the contract. (See *Wilson* v *Harper, Son & Co* (1908) where the agent's executors were entitled to receive commission after the death of the agent because the contract stated commission was payable 'as long as we do business'.

Finally, all three agents who are entitled to claim an indemnity or remuneration or both can exercise a lien against goods of the principal which are in their lawful possession as agents until their claims as agents are met; the lien will probably be a 'general' lien arising from the trade usage so it will be exercisable over stock in trade, equipment, etc.

Question 3

Albert appoints Boyce to manage his retail business 'under the name "Boycey's" for five years on a commission of five per cent of the agreed sales' in order to enable Boyce to accumulate sufficient capital to marry Albert's daughter Cassandra. Albert forbids Boyce to have any dealings with Albert's rival Del.

Del offers to sell Boyce fifty satellite television dishes for £50 each, it being agreed that, if Albert objects, Boyce will resell them as Del's agent and they will divide equally between themselves any profits made on resale. Boyce pays Del £2,500 for the dishes with Albert's money. He sells twenty of them in the business's shop for £100 each and keeps the £2,000 received in a bag in his briefcase.

Cassandra breaks off her engagement to Boyce and Albert dismisses him without having paid him any commission.

Albert then discovers that several of his customers are complaining that their dishes are defective and that they want their money back plus damages.

Advise Albert and Boyce.

University of London LLB Examination
(for External Students) Commercial Law June 1991 Q4

Skeleton solution

- Agency, forms of appointment.
- Types of agency.
- Payment by commission.
- Agency coupled with an interest; applicable here?
- Agent acting outside his authority.
- Liability of principal.
- Personal liability of agent.
- Agent's misconduct. Bribe or secret profit?
- Breach of condition as grounds for termination.
- Withholding of commission.

Suggested solution

Albert's (A) appointment of Boyce (B), to manage his retail business would appear to be creation of agency expressly and in this particular context it seems unlikely that such an agreement would not have been the result of a contract negotiated specifically for the purpose, though it is not essential that a contract be drawn up.

Where agency is created by agreement, the agent has actual authority. If the contract is specific, the extent of the agent's powers may be discovered by studying the terms of the contract by which the contract was created (*Hely-Hutchinson* v *Brayhead* (1968); *Biggar* v *Rock Life Insurance Co* (1902)) or the terms of the contract and thus the mode of appointment may be implied. Since we know that quite a few things are specifically incorporated into B's agreement with A - the duration of the contract, payment, terms of reference - it seems unlikely that any terms would have to be implied. However if need be, implied actual authority can be discovered by applying the normal rules as to implied terms in a contract (*Freeman & Lockyer* v *Buckhurst Park Properties* (1964); *Shirlaw* v *Southern Foundries* (1939) and other similar cases).

When an agent carries out a job that normally carries with it certain powers, then all the normal powers that go with that job will be given to the agent, unless the parties have expressly excluded them (see *Hely-Hutchinson* v *Brayhead* (above)). This is known as usual authority. It may be seen that in the agreement between A and B, A has specifically curtailed what may be seen as a normal business manager's powers to deal with whomsoever he wishes. This question of what constitutes usual powers arises most often in cases like this one where an agent is given specific instructions not to make certain contracts. This will give rise, should the agent in defiance of his instructions purport to make such a contract, to problems of apparent authority. We shall deal with this aspect later.

Thus, we know that B has been appointed expressly, probably by a contract drawn up specifically for the purpose: that as shop manager he will possess 'usual powers' save insofar as he is specifically forbidden to deal with Del (D). This is usual actual authority.

It seems convenient at this point to discuss the fact that B is appointed so that he can save money to be married to A's daughter, Cassandra. It is true that there is a strong presumption that domestic agreements between family members and close friends are not intended to be contractually binding, but this is in any event a rebuttable presumption and seems something of a red herring. This factor will have far more significance in the context of agent's remuneration, which we shall now move on to.

Agency agreements commonly provide for payment by commission. There is in fact no legal general duty to do so on the part of the principal; the agent will only be able to enforce an express or implied agreement if he has earned that commission. Here the agreement between A and B is express and clear, 5 per cent of all sales for five years. When an agent breaches his duties he cannot claim his commission unless either the employer waives the breach or the breach is unrelated to the earning of his commission (*Andrew* v *Ramsay* (1903), *Hippisley* v *Knee Bros* (1905)). When the contract comes to an end either naturally, or because of breach, the right to commission will of course normally cease.

Certain types of agency are held, however, to be irrevocable; they cannot be terminated. Power of attorney is the most common example, but also included are forms of agency where the agent is said to have authority coupled with an interest, that is, where the agent is given authority in order to secure some property right. A common situation is where the principal owes the agent money and appoints the agent to enable him, through the earning of either commission or salary, to be paid in full. In such cases the principal cannot deprive the agent of his security, cannot terminate the agent's authority (*Spooner* v *Sandilands* (1842)). Is the present situation, in which B is to be employed for five years at a 5 per cent commission in order to save enough to marry A's daughter, a similar situation? Does B have authority coupled with an interest? It seems most unlikely. A does not actually owe him any money, nor has he promised him any sort of payment for wedding his daughter. In any event, the marriage is called off. We are told that B in specific defiance of his instructions not to deal with Del does so. Two main questions arise from this: is A bound by these contracts, despite his instructions to the contrary, and secondly is B personally liable on the contracts? A third problem arises insofar as one needs to assess whether this breach of contract is sufficient to bring B's authority to a halt.

Firstly, it should be stated that in certain circumstances a principal may be liable, even though he has specifically instructed his agent to the contrary, on contracts the agent makes. Does that apply here? Where an agency is disclosed, whether the principal is named or not, any contract made with apparent authority will bind the principal. The fact that A has instructed B not to make a certain type of contract will have no effect on the third party's rights to sue the principal. Despite the fact that the business is to be run under the name 'Boycey's', which may at first sight give the impression that the fact of A's existence and B's agency is undisclosed; it is in fact apparent from the exact terms of B's and D's agreement that D is not only aware of A's existence, but also knows in all probability (though this is not absolutely certain) that B is in breach of his instructions. If D is unaware that B has been told specifically not to deal with him, B may be liable to D for breach of warranty of authority (see s*Collen* v *Wright* (1857)).

If an agent discloses the existence of his principal to the third party, under normal circumstances he then drops out and has no further liability. In certain circumstances he may undertake personal liability on the contract. It must be clear that he is doing so. Is this the case in the agreement between B and D? The main criterion is that it must be objectively apparent from the dealings between agent and third party that the agent intends to be personally liable (*Universal Steam Navigation Co* v *McKelvie* (1923)). Since B and D talk of the contract's alternative performance should A object, it seems clear that B is intending to be personally liable if need be. In such cases the third party will have a right of election; he may sue either the principal, or the agent, though not both: *Benton* v *Campbell-Parker* (1925). The question has sometimes been raised as to whether this also applies in cases of a disclosed principal (which is the situation here), but most of the standard textbooks appear to be of the opinion that the doctrine of election applies equally to disclosed and undisclosed agency situations.

But what about 'Boycey's' customers? B makes contracts with these, selling them satellite dishes, which are turning out to be defective. Are they aware of B's agency? It seems less likely. As shop manager, in a business that bears his name, they probably assume him to be the sole party. If they are aware of his agency then they presumably believe him to have usual authority. As stated earlier, in such cases the principal will be liable, even if like A he has specifically forbidden the agent's conduct.

Finally, what of B's misconduct? All agents owe a fiduciary duty to their employers, encompassing inter alia the duty not to make a secret profit. Is the £2,000 kept in a briefcase by B a secret profit? Though it is not certain (B could argue that he has simply been keeping it for A) it seems likely that the very fact of not paying it into the business in the normal way amounts to an illicit act. In the recent case of *Anangel Atlas Compania Naviera SA* v *Ishikawajima-Harima Heavy Industries* (1990), the court held that the main test of whether a payment amounted to a bribe or secret profit was whether it created a conflict of interests. The receipt of such a secret payment will bar an agent from receiving remuneration (see *Andrew* v *Ramsay* above). This would appear to be a secret profit rather than a bribe and A will therefore not have the remedies as against D that he would have had had the £2,000 been an outright bribe (*Mahesan* v *Malaysian Government Officers' Co-operative Housing* (1979)).

Breach of a condition by the agency, as in this case, amounting to misconduct, will not automatically bring the contract to an end. Like all contracts, the ordinary contractual rules will apply and it must be decided whether the breach is so crucial as to amount to sufficient grounds for termination. We do not know how B carries out his duties otherwise, nor what proportion of trade these 50 satellite dishes represent. If B is otherwise a good competent manager and the satellite dishes are a small part of the overall turnover, it may be that his 'misconduct' is so minimal as to preclude his dismissal. Similarly to dismiss without permitting B to earn his commission may be a wrongful act on A's part. If his other functions are performed effectively and this misconduct is a minimal act, it will have no effect on the rest of the business. Thus if turnover has been about £100,000 in a year, to deprive B of his 5 per cent commission because of a breach of condition costing £2,000 would be excessive and wrong. But if sales are very low, obviously proportionately the misconduct may be reckoned more serious. In the final analysis, the question of payment of commission (as opposed to an agreed salary or fixed fee) is a difficult and unresolved one anyway, and an agent who has committed a breach of his duties will obviously be in a very weak position; but ultimately each question needs to be resolved on its individual facts.

25 POWERS OF ATTORNEY

25.1 Introduction

A power of attorney is a formal mode of creating an agent, by deed, for certain purposes. Since 1971 all powers of attorney have been required to be signed and sealed and strict rules of construction apply to the document of appointment. A common reason for using power of attorney is if the principal (donor of the power) envisages being absent or physically infirm and wants someone, the agent (donee or attorney) to manage his affairs.

25.2 Key points

It is important that the student understands the following.

a) *Construction of powers of attorney*

   There are, basically, two rules here. Firstly, ambiguities in a power of attorney will be construed against the agent. In other words the courts will lean in favour of restricting the scope of an agent's authority, should there be any doubt on the matter.

   Secondly, no parol evidence is admissible as to the nature of the power, if it would alter the terms contained in the deed.

b) *Powers of Attorney Act 1971*

   Section 1 lays down the general rules as to the execution of a power of attorney. Certain further sections cover such aspects as proof of power of attorney (s3); revocation and subsequent personal liability of the agent (s5) and the powers of an agent (for example power of an agent to execute documents in his own name for the donor (s7)).

   Additionally the Enduring Powers of Attorney Act 1985 lays down certain rules where the donor is mentally incapable.

25.3 Analysis of questions

This is, perhaps not surprisingly, an area of agency law which has slipped through the net as far as University of London papers, at least, are concerned. It is a very specific area of law and there is not really enough material to set an entire question without venturing into some very obscure byways.

It is possible to envisage that it might be linked in tandem with some other topic; perhaps as suggested below.

25.4 Question

a) 'There is no rule of law that in a hire purchase transaction the dealer never is, or always is, acting as agent for the finance company or as agent for the customer.' *Mercantile Credit Ltd* v *Hamblin* [1965] 2 QB 242 at 269 per Pearson LJ.

   Discuss.

b) Discuss the proposition that a power of attorney is irrevocable.

Written by Editor

Skeleton solution

- Status of HP contract under consideration.
- C/L - no presumption as to agency but can be rebutted.
- 1974 CCA s56.
- Irrevocable power of attorney by statute.
- C/L rules.
- Effects of revocation.

Suggested solution

a) A hire purchase contract is one whereby goods are leased to a customer by a creditor and the customer has an option to buy them at the end of the period of hire (*Helby* v *Mathews* (1895)). A typical way in which such a transaction is entered into is that a customer sees goods in a shop which he cannot afford to pay for immediately, so the shopkeeper refers him to a finance house which buys the goods from the shopkeeper and then lets them under the HP contract to the customer. The position of the shopkeeper, the dealer, is that he is in a position to make representations and promises about the goods concerned and is also in a position to influence the HP contract. The customer may think that he is agreeing to buy the goods from the shop, but the reality is that he does not agree to buy, he merely has an option to buy which he may exercise at a later date and any purchase that he may make will be made from the finance company and not from the shop. Therefore the position of the shopkeeper is important - what is to happen, for example, if he misstates something during negotiations, will the finance company be responsible?

   The answer to that question depends on the status of the HP contract under consideration. If the customer is an individual (s189(1) Consumer Credit Act (CCA) 1974) and the amount of credit advanced does not exceed £15,000 (s8(2) CCA 1974), then the agreement will be a regulated consumer credit agreement and the position of the dealer will be as stated in the Consumer Credit Act 1974. If, on the other hand, either of the criteria mentioned is not met, then the agreement will not be regulated and the position of the dealer will be governed by the common law.

At common law it has been said that there is no presumption that the dealer is the agent of the finance company either when making representations or promises about the goods or when doing acts in connection with the HP agreement. In *Branwhite* v *Worcester Works Finance Ltd* (1969) the customer filled in a proposal form, the effect of which was to offer to take a car on HP from the finance company, but left blank the parts of the form relating to the cost of the car. These blanks were filled in by the dealer with a grossly inflated figure and the dealer sent the form to the finance company, which attempted to accept what appeared to be an offer by the customer to take the car at the high price. At first instance it was held that there was no contract because of the absence of consensus ad idem (Clerkenwell County Court, unreported). The House of Lords had to decide whether a payment of £130 which had been made to the dealer as a deposit could be recovered by the customer from the finance company; the customer argued that it had been paid to the dealer as the agent of the finance company and also that because it had been passed on to the finance company by the dealer as part payment under a contract which did not exist, so it was recoverable as money paid for a consideration which had wholly failed. This latter argument succeeded, but the former was rejected by the majority who approved the dictum from Pearson LJ in *Mercantile Credit Ltd* v *Hamblin* (1965) which is cited in the question.

The common law does not, however, say that the dealer is never the agent of the finance company, it merely says that there is no presumption that he is an agent. Therefore the facts in each case must be examined to see whether agency can be found. In *Financings Ltd* v *Stimson* (1962) the Court of Appeal held, by a majority (Pearson LJ dissenting), that the dealer was the agent of the finance company with authority to receive the revocation of an offer made by a customer. It cannot be said that misrepresentations or promises made by the dealer will necessarily be imputed to the finance company, but they may be if the circumstances are appropriate. This result is not as harsh as it may appear because in many cases the dealer will be personally liable for his misstatements on a collateral contract (*Andrews* v *Hopkinson* (1957)).

In cases regulated by the 1974 Act, the HP agreement is classified as a fixed sum (s10(1)(b) CCA 1974), restricted use (s11(1)(a) CCA), debtor-creditor-supplier (s12(a) CCA) agreement and there are statutory agency rules in s56. Section 56 lays down rules which are rather obtusely worded; the effect of them is that if the dealer is to sell the goods to the finance company which will then supply them to the customer on credit terms, then the dealer is a negotiator (s56(1)(b) CCA 1974) and the finance company is responsible for his representations made during negotiations with the customer (s56(2) CCA 1974). This statutory agency during negotiations cannot be ousted by agreement between customer (debtor in the terminology of the Act) and the finance company (creditor in the terminology of the Act) (s56(3)).

In addition to agency during negotiations, so that the finance company is directly responsible for misrepresentations, the dealer can be the creditor's agent at other times. The dealer is an agent to notice of rescission (s102(1) CCA 1974) and various statutory notices (for example, notice of withdrawal, s57(3)(a), and notice of cancellation, s69(6)(a) CCA), the overall effect of the Act being to make the dealer authorised to act on behalf of the finance company in all cases where the customer might reasonably expect him to be so authorised.

b) In some cases a power of attorney is irrevocable and in any event at common law a power of attorney would be revoked by the death or mental incapacity of the donor of the power.

Construction of the deed by which the power of attorney is granted is, both by common law and statute, strict. Therefore if some event is specified as bringing the power to an end, the happening of such an event is the signal for revocation of the power.

Section 4 of the Powers of Attorney Act 1971 creates certain cases in which an exception to the normal rule of common law, as noted above applies. This section applies only to powers of attorney which have been expressed by the donor to be irrevocable and have been given to the donee as security. It is clear from the wording of the section that death or mental incapacity will not revoke the power and the only way it can end will be with the consent of the donee.

Additionally, the Enduring Powers of Attorney Act 1985 (ss1 and 2) lays down circumstances in which a power of attorney can survive the mental incapacity of the donor. The main requirement under this act is that the power be an 'enduring power' within the meaning of the Act and properly executed according to its provisions.

Because of the possibility of revocation the Powers of Attorney Act 1971 (s5) makes provision for the protection of third parties who deal with an agent believing him to have power of attorney when it has in fact been revoked. Similarly some degree of statutory protection is needed for the donee of a power who acts without notice of the revocation, who might otherwise find himself personally liable.

26 CONTRACTS MADE BY AGENTS

26.1 Introduction

Provided the agent acts within his authority, as we have already seen, contracts that an agent negotiates and other acts of his will bind the principal. (Even if the original act was unauthorised the principal may assume liability by ratification.)

The general rule, that the principal will always be bound by the agent, is not entirely the full picture however, because sometimes both agent and principal will be jointly liable and sometimes the agent alone will be personally liable.

The rights and duties of the principal against third parties and toward them depend to a large extent on whether the principal is disclosed or not. This will be examined further below.

26.2 Key points

It is important that the student understands the following:

a) *The disclosed principal*

A disclosed principal is one whose existence is known to the third party at the time of making the contract.

He may be named, or the third party may be aware of his existence, but not his identity.

The basic distinction between the two is that if that principal is named, then only that person may intervene to take over liability; but if the principal is not named, in theory, several alternative principals could exist. In reality because of the rules relating to ratification there is usually only one true principal capable of existing. The general rule is that where the agent discloses the existence and (possibly identity) of his principal the agent is not liable on the contract and privity of contract exists between principal and third party.

Sometimes this is not true, either because the principal does not exist, or the agent has undertaken personal liability or the agent is deemed personally liable for policy reasons. For further details as to the rule of the disclosed principal together with the exceptions noted above, the student should consult one of the textbooks on the topic.

b) *The undisclosed principal*

An undisclosed principal is one of whose existence the third party was unaware at the time of making the contract and usually the third party has believed throughout that the agent was contracting on his own behalf. The rights of an undisclosed principal are limited in a number of ways to avoid prejudice to the third party who believed he was contracting with the agent possible. In general, however the undisclosed principal may have the right to intervene, to assume performance of the contract. It should be noted that the limitations on the rights of the undisclosed principal to intervene are designated for the protection of the third party. Therefore the principal can never use lack of disclosure as a defence, in the event of the third party wishing to sue him. The limitations placed on an undisclosed principal include the following.

Firstly, the principal, should he choose to assume liability must act strictly within the terms of the contract already negotiated between agent and third party.

Secondly, when it comes to the attention of the third party that there is an undisclosed principal in existence, he has a choice of action. He can enforce the contract against either the principal or the agent (but since he has negotiated only one contract) not both. The nature of such election by the third party is that it is an informed choice, freely made. Therefore such an option cannot usually be taken until the third party learns of the existence of the principal. Once the third party, having knowledge of the principal commits an unequivocal act showing his intention to proceed against one or the other, he cannot subsequently change his mind.

Thirdly, should the agent be able to show that he wished to deal with the agent personally and no one else, then the undisclosed principal may not be able to intervene.

There is considerable case law on the doctrine of the undisclosed principal, with which the student should make himself familiar.

c) *An agent acting outside his authority*

Any contract made outside the agent's authority will not bind the principal unless he chooses to ratify.

The third party is not unprotected, however, because the third party will be entitled to sue the agent personally. The third party's rights are as though the agency had never existed.

It should be noted, however, that in certain cases the agent will have warranted his authority to act. In such a case, even if the agent acts in good faith, even if he honestly believes the principal exists, or will eventually ratify; if he does not have the authority he professes he will be liable for breach of warranty of authority.

The damages recoverable are those which are the natural consequence of the breach of warranty. The aim is to put the third party in the position which he would have occupied if the agent had been authorised. Thus if the contract would have been unenforceable for some reason there is no additional loss to the third party by reason of the breach of warranty of authority and no damages will be awarded.

26.3 Analysis of questions

It has already been noted, that a favourite approach for examiners in the University of London paper is to ask long general questions requiring a good knowledge of almost all the agency syllabus. In the course of such questions, the problem of an agent's acting outside his authority and his power to bind the principal in contractual dealings, inevitably crops up; but not in much detail.

A rather different format is shown in Question 1 of the 1984 paper which requires a detailed knowledge of the area of law dealing with agent's personal liability. It is, as should be noted, an essay question which seems quite common among agency questions.

The first question quoted below, while not confined to agent's authority to contract is a useful example to look at. (The other issues it deals with have largely been covered already in chapters 23 and 24 or will be covered in chapters 28 and 29.) The second question is a difficult question which concentrates on a specific aspect of the law of agency and relates it to the general law, especially contractual law as to privity of contract. Q1 of the 1992 paper followed very similar lines and was also concerned with justification for the doctrine of the undisclosed principal.

26.4 Questions

Question 1

Brown was an amateur yachtsman and the owner of the Greenways Motel. On 2 January 1982, he left it in charge of Williams with instructions 'to manage it in his absence', and agreed to pay him a commission of half a per cent of the annual turnover. He also instructed Williams to sell his Rolls Royce for '£30,000 or near offer'. The next day, Brown set off on a 'round the world' race.

He has now returned and seeks your advice, saying:

'I find that Williams arranged for a new roof to be installed at a cost of £40,000 and the contractors are pressing me for payment. He bought large supplies of wine from Central Wine Stores, although I told him that he was in no circumstances to purchase wine from them as I had had a row with their managing director in December 1981. Williams ordered supplies of stationery from Universal Paper Ltd for the use of the motel guests, at a cost of £2,000 and their bill has not been paid. He sold my Rolls Royce to Henry for £29,000 after getting it overhauled first of all at a cost of £540. Henry gave him £200 to clinch the deal. Rolls Royce have gone up in value and I should like mine back. Williams sold my two caravans, which were in the motel car park, at a price of £2,000 each, as he wanted more space for the guests' cars. The motel was burnt down last night. I had not insured it, but I find that two days after I returned, Williams had insured it on my behalf for 12 months for £500,000.'

University of London LLB Examination
(for External Students) Commercial Law June 1983 Q2

Skeleton solution

- General vs specific agency.
- Acting outside authority, express prohibitions.
- Undisclosed principal.
- Ratification.
- Doctrine of apparent authority.
- Agent's personal liability.
- Principal's duty to indemnify (see also chapter 28).
- Fiduciary duties of agent: bribes (see also chapter 28).
- Termination (see also chapter 28).

Suggested solution

It is clear that Williams is a general agent, as opposed to a special agent. His authority is authority to conduct a series of transactions involving a continuity of service, rather than a particular act. Its management of the state involves many particular acts. Of course in relation to the Rolls Royce, Williams is a special agent - his agency just comprises one act - the sale of a car. He could possibly be categorised as a factor in relation to the Rolls Royce sale, but this would depend upon a finding that Brown appointed him in the course of business which would seem unlikely here. The importance of this distinction between a special and a general agent concerns the extent to which that agent can alter the position of his principal, but since both depend upon the terms of the contract creating the agency relationship, read in conjunction with what is usual or reasonably necessary, the practical effect of the distinction is likely to be small.

The effects of acting outside the authority conferred by the contract creating the agency relationship, are simply that the principal will not be bound to a third party, unless the principal adopts what has been done in excess of authority by ratifying it, and the agent will be liable to the principal for breach of contract, and the third part for breach of warranty of authority.

a) In relation to the roof Williams' power to affect the legal position of Brown depends upon the contract of authority. This may be express, or an implied authority. The express authority given depends upon what the word 'manage' connotes. Since that is to be read in connection with 'absence' and since there is no express duration to the agency, then it may well be that Williams has actual authority to commission a new roof, provided, of course, such was necessary for the continued running of the business and was consistent with good management. Alternatively such authority could be implied from the contract. This would be the case if commission of a new roof was necessarily incidental to running the business. The third type of actual authority, namely usual authority, is not relevant here - that is the authority which an agent in a particular trade would normally possess. Managing a business does not fit into any of the existing categories of usual authority, which tend to embrace those trades or professions where agents are inevitably employed.

So, Williams' authority in relation to the roof may be express or implied - if implied there is a deemed consent of Brown. Since there is no contrary instruction from Brown, his consent may readily be deemed - given the extended period of his absence and the difficulty which Williams would have in contacting him.

The effect of this is that the principal is bound by the contract even though he is an undisclosed principal. So long as the agent acts within the scope of his authority in contracting with the roof contractors, Brown can sue and be sued on the contract, even though he is an undisclosed principal. Thus, he will be obliged to pay the roof contractors.

b) Certainly, Williams' has neither express or implied authority to purchase wine from Central Wine Stores, given the contrary express stipulation by Brown. On that basis, Brown himself is not liable on the contract if Williams has not actually paid for the wine. No consent can be deemed to Brown because there is an express prohibition. If the wine has been bought and paid for out of the motel account, then Brown will be able to sue Williams for breach of contract - because here the agency was contractual. The measure of damage will be calculated in accordance with the general rules in *Hadley* v *Baxendale* (1854).

However Brown may be under a liability on the contract - he may be bound - which will prevent him pursuing any remedy against Williams - because the latter's authority may be extended by the doctrine of apparent authority, where the law operates to protect third parties who act on a reasonable inference that an agent was so authorised.

There is, obviously, already in existence, a principal/agent relationship although in this instance the authority to 'manage' conferred on Williams and limited by an express prohibition. The application of the doctrine of apparent authority extends that to apply to acts undertaken by the agent which the principal never agreed that he should undertake. As the Court of Appeal made clear in *Freeman and Lockyer* v *Buckhurst Park* (1964) there must be some sort of representation by Brown that the agent has his authority. It can be constituted by conduct, as was the case in *Lloyd* v *Grace, Smith and Co* (1912). The representation may be made to the public at large. In this case the representation could be constituted either by simply leaving the whole business in the hands of Williams or by not informing Central Wine that no purchases would be made from them, if the Motel previously dealt there, as would seem to be the case. Provided Central Wine have no notice of the agent's want of authority, then I would suggest that the doctrine of apparent authority could operate here. Particularly relevant is the fact that in so sense can the agent be said to be acting otherwise than in the interests of the Motel, because constructive knowledge that an agent is acting in his own interests will defeat the apparent authority. As noted above, it in no way depends upon a deemed consent, while implied authority *does* so depend.

c) With the stationery, since this is for the use of the Motel guests, it is likely that such an order will be covered if not by an express authority, at least impliedly - making Brown liable on the contract - creating a direct contractual relationship between Brown and Universal Paper. Clearly it would be difficult to say that the supply of paper would *necessarily* be incidental to Williams' agency but if paper had usually been supplied by Brown, then Williams' order would be within the authority to manage the Motel. Brown must pay the bill.

   On the other hand, if paper has never before been supplied, and if the nature of the Motel makes the supply of paper an unjustifiable luxury, with Williams, as it were, embarking on a frolic of his own, then Brown will not be liable on the contract and Williams will be liable personally to the third party, Universal Paper, who contracted on the basis of a warranty of authority. Brown can, of course, sue Williams on that basis for breach of the agency contract, although since Brown will not be bound by the contract his damages are likely to be nominal.

d) Firstly, Brown will be obliged to indemnify the agent for the £450 spent in overhauling the car. Here is an implied duty on the principal to indemnify the agent against expenses incurred in the performance of an undertaking. To make the principal so liable, however, Williams would have to show that he acted within his authority of *Bayliffe* v *Butterworth* (1847). Since the express authority given to Williams involved an element of latitude - 'or near offer' Williams' sale would appear to be authorised even though cars have increased in value. The £200 given to clinch the deal, however, would seem to be tantamount to a bribe. The principal, in such a case, clearly has an election whether to sue for the return of the bribe on the basis of a personal liability to account (*Lister* v *Stubbs* (1890)) or whether to sue the agent just for the profit made from accepting the bribe - there is little difference in the case. It is worth pointing out however, that on the authority of *Liste*r, there is no question of proprietary whim - the agent is simply treated as a debtor for the sum of £200 and accordingly under a personal duty to account - he is not to be treated as a constructive trustee.

e) There is no doubt that Williams has no express authority to sell Brown's caravans. The only possibility that such may be authorised would lie in Williams establishing that such a sale is necessary for managing the business. Presumably, if guests cannot park their motor vehicles then business would suffer, although in this case an extension of the business would seem to be involved, rather than mere management of it. Unless some event has occurred to reduce parking space, extending parking space is more like an improvement or extension of the business, which it would be difficult to accept as being implied into the given contractual authority. On this basis, Brown can sue Williams for breach of the contract of agency, with substantial damages being the value of the caravans - namely the loss to Brown flowing directly from the breach.

f) Agency may be terminated simply by the expiry of the allotted period. Since the restrictions is to manage it until Brown's return, on his return the agency is determined. The effect of this is that the principal cannot be made liable for anything done by the agent, unless he ratifies it. In the absence of evidence of ratification here, we must ensure that Brown is not liable on the contract of insurance nor can he claim the benefit of it.

Question 2

'Agency is an entirely sensible exception to the general doctrine of privity of contract, made necessary by good sense. Commerce could not function well or conveniently without intermediaries. That does not, however, justify the limits to which the agency doctrine is pushed by the further, unwarrantable, doctrine of the undisclosed principal.'

Discuss.

University of London LLB Examination
(for External Students) Commercial Law June 1990 Q2

Skeleton solution

- Origins of principle of agency and undisclosed principal.
- Development of doctrine.
- Privity of contract generally.
- Statement of doctrine.
- Is the doctrine 'unwarrantable'?
- Why must the doctrine prevail?

Suggested solution

In the modern commercial law it is not always possible or expedient for the parties to a contract to meet personally or to contract in their personal or corporate capacity directly with one another. Agency in all its various and extended forms allows the proper functioning of contracts of this nature and if operated successfully can benefit all three parties; namely the principal, the agent and the person with whom the contract is made by the principal. It is possible, therefore, to see the logic in the proposition that 'agency is an entirely sensible exception' to the general doctrine of privity of contract, made necessary by 'good sense' and that 'commerce could not function without it' (ie Agency).

Some statement of the general principles of agency are relevant when exploring the proposition that the fact that agency is an exception to the general rules relating to privity of contract and that the doctrine of 'undisclosed' principal is 'unwarrantable' as an extension of the former fact. The general rule in agency is that a disclosed principal is not bound by any act of his agent which is outside the scope of the agent's implied or apparent authority: *Sorrell* v *Finch* (1977). This holds true unless the principal in fact authorised the agent to do the act or ratified it.

The doctrine of the undisclosed principal can be broadly stated thus; an undisclosed principal may sue or be sued on any contract made on his behalf, or in respect of money paid or received on his behalf, by his agent acting within the scope of his actual authority: *Thomson* v *Davenport* (1829). However, the rights of the undisclosed principal to sue, and his liability to be sued on a contract made by his agent may be excluded if inconsistent with the terms of the contract, express or implied. There was an attempt earlier this century to establish precedent for the fact that a contract is that of the undisclosed principal, just as in cases where the principal is disclosed, eg *Keighley Maxsted & Co* v *Durant* (1901). The reliability of such cases is now in some doubt and according to Barsted on Agency (p313) the doctrine of the undisclosed principal 'even as an exception to the general rules of the privity of contract is "unusual" ' since the tertius is not mentioned nor indeed contemplated by one of the parties, and furthermore takes liabilities as well as rights.

The doctrine of the undisclosed principal is best explained in the terms as being an essential commercial convenience but that the justice of the principal receiving (in some cases) a benefit without incurring a liability is disputable. It is important to distinguish situations where the principal is disclosed but not named from those where there is total non-disclosure of the existence of a principal; in the latter cases the third party would no doubt consider themselves to be contracting with the agent and have no knowledge of the principal. The understatement of the doctrine of the undisclosed principal is that the principal intervenes on the contract of the agent. See for example *Spurr* v *Cass* (1870) where S, a solicitor, practised in the name of S & G; C was also a solicitor, but acted as clerk to S. Held, that S, being the real principal, was entitled to sue alone upon a contract made in the name of the firm.

An example of a contract where the undisclosed principal intervened on the agent's contract and was subsequently sued can be taken from *Kinahan & Co Ltd* v *Parry* (1910) where A appointed B as manager of an hotel owned by A and the licence was taken out in the name of B. A told B to order spirits from a certain brewery only, but B disregarded this instruction and ordered whisky from C. Held: A was liable to C for the price of the whisky. Perhaps the most celebrated case in this respect was *Watteau* v *Fenwick* (1893) where it was held that the principal was liable to pay for cigars ordered by the licensee and manager of an hotel who carried on the business in his own name. The court held it was within the authority usually confided to the manager of an hotel to purchase cigars on credit, despite the fact the manager had been expressly forbidden so to do by the principal.

Grievances in law about the question of the undisclosed principal usually arise when the undisclosed principal succeeds in getting a third party to do something because he employs an agent and remains undisclosed himself. Thus, as for example, where a person bought some land which he knew the owner would not sell to him but was entitled to enforce the contract on the grounds that the contract was assignable, *Dyster* v *Randall and Sons* (1926) (a decision that has been much criticised subsequently).

The grounds why the doctrine of the undisclosed principal may be regarded as unwarrantable were adequately stated in *Watteau* v *Fenwick* by Wills J (at pp348-349). 'Once it is established that the defendant was the real principal the ordinary doctrine as to agent and principal applies - that the principal is liable for all the acts of the agent which are not within the authority usually confided to an agent of that character ... Otherwise in every case of undisclosed principal ... the secret limitation of authority would prevail and defeat the action of the person dealing with the agent and then discovering that he was an agent and had a principal.

To conclude the doctrine of undisclosed principal is a necessary if dubious extension of the doctrine of privity of contract because otherwise there would be no way of limiting the extent of the latter doctrine. So many factors (for example the degree of knowledge of the third party, the legal/illegal intention of the agent, the capacity of the agent etc) could otherwise prevail and create even greater problems - the undisclosed principal in this respect represents the 'lesser of two evils'.

27 TORTS COMMITTED BY AN AGENT

27.1 Introduction

The law on this topic overlaps to a considerable degree with the common law rules as to the vicarious liability of an employer for his employees' torts. However, not all agents are employees, some may fall into other categories, for example, independent contractor.

Perhaps the closest analogy is that of an employee who does the job he is paid to do, but does it negligently or commits other torts. Thus, an agent who acts within his actual authority in negotiating a contract, but commits a tort while doing so, will be the liability of his principal. However, bear in mind that an agent, because of the doctrine of apparent liability can *appear* to be authorised to contract and to bind his principal, but in fact be outside his actual authority. So the analogy is not an exact one.

The approach taken by the courts is to ask how far apparent authority of an agent is relevant in the context of torts committed by him. This approach means, among other things that the courts distinguish between fraud and other torts. Where fraud is concerned, a principal is liable only where it is within an agent's actual or apparent authority to commit fraud. With non-fradulent torts the difference between agents as employees or as independent contractors is ignored; all are presumed to be employees and the usual rules as to vicarious liability for torts apply.

27.2 Key points

It is important that the student understands the following.

a) *Fraud*

The most likely possibility is that the agent will commit the tort of deceit. Whether or not the principal must share liability for such a tort is the subject of considerable litigation, with which the student should familarise himself.

At the moment the position would appear to be that the principal will be liable for the fraud of his agent where the transaction which the agent carried out tortiously was within the agent's actual or apparent authority.

b) *Other torts*

Where an agent commits a tort other than fraud the test is, as has already been noted, the same as for vicarious liability. In other words, was the agent acting in the course of his employment when he committed a tort.

While, obviously, it is of great importance to know whether the agent was acting within his actual or apparent authority this is not apparently the only test.

Unlike fraudulent torts, this is not an area of agency law where there has been much case law and so there has been little discussion of such questions. Certainly, if the agent is on what the courts call 'a frolic of his own', that will take him outside the normal course of his employment and the principal will not be liable.

27.3 Analysis of questions

With the exception of the question quoted below, the torts of an agent have not provided any substantial question. Even if, occasionally a general question as to agent/principal relationship requires mention of the possibility that a tort might be committed by the agent, it requires only the most superficial treatment.

Even the question below is not confined to agents' torts, but the other subject matter should already be familiar from chapters 23 and 24 or if not will be dealt with in chapter 28.

27.4 Question

'As a general rule, a principal is responsible for all acts of his agent within the authority of the agent, whether the responsibility is contractual or tortious.' (Halsbury)

Write a memorandum illustrating this general rule and showing the exceptions thereto.

University of London LLB Examination
(for External Students) Commercial Law June 1986 Q1

Skeleton solution

- Modes of creation of agency; actual or apparent authority; agency within those limits binds principal in contract.
- Agent acting outside his authority - agent's personal authority.
- Ratification; estoppel.
- Tortious liability; overlap with vicarious liability.
- Fraud, non-fraudulent torts.

Suggested solution

An agent is someone who has the power to affect the legal liabilities of his principal towards third parties (Fridman's *Law of Agency*). This definition excludes from the category of agent many who are often described as agents. Indeed, any 'agent' who does not have the power to make contracts on behalf of another is not a true agent (Reynolds, 'Agency, Theory and Practice' (1978) 94 LQR 224). The power of an agent to bind his principal depends on the scope of the agent's authority. There are three types of authority, actual, apparent (or ostensible) and usual.

Actual authority is the power expressly or impliedly conferred on the agent by the principal. The principal-agent relationship is usually created by agreement between the two parties and their agreement is to be construed as though it were a contract. This has the result that express terms and implied terms may be found; the express terms will dictate the express actual authority of the agent and the implied terms the implied actual authority. One common example of implied actual authority arises in cases where the agent is appointed to a position which usually carries with it a set of powers. In such a case those usual powers will be implied into the agency agreement as a matter of custom. In such cases it can be said that the agent has usual actual authority.

When the agency agreement has been construed and the actual authority of the agent discovered, then any contract made by the agent within that actual authority will bind his principal. It matters not whether the third party with whom the contract is made knows that the agent is agent or knows the true scope of the agent's authority. If the agent declares his agency and acts within the scope of his actual authority then the principal is bound by the contract made, and the agent is not personally liable on it (there are exceptions in certain limited cases, see Fridman). In cases, however, where the agent does not disclose the fact of his agency the third party has the option of holding the agent bound by the contract instead of the principal (*Clarkson, Booker Ltd* v *Adjel* (1964)). In such a case the agent is entitled to be indemnified by the principal for any liability which he incurs (*Bayliffe* v *Butterworth* (1847)), but the principal himself will not be able to enforce the contract, nor will he be personally liable on it (*Clarkson, Booker Ltd* v *Adjel* (1964)).

Apparent authority is the authority of the agent as it appears to the third party (*Hely-Hutchinson* v *Brayhead Ltd* (1968)). The principle behind apparent authority is one of estoppel - where the principal has represented the third party that someone is his agent, he is estopped from denying that agency if the third party acts in reliance on the representation (*Freeman and Lockyer* v *Buckhurst Park Properties (Mangal) Ltd* (1964); *Armagas* v *Mundogas, The Ocean Frost* (1986)). There are essentially three elements to the estoppel; firstly the principal must make a representation to the third party, secondly that representation must be that someone is his agent and thirdly the third party must rely on that representation.

The first element causes many problems. It is necessary that the principal makes a representation. There may be many cases where the only person with whom the third party communicates is the supposed agent himself, in such cases it is hard to see how the principal makes a representation, but in fact the representation can arise in two ways. Firstly it may be that the agent occupies a position which itself leads the third party to believe that he is authorised to make the contract under consideration (this was described as ostensible general authority by Lord Keith in *The Ocean Frost*). For example, if the third party negotiated with the managing director of a company and knows him to be the managing director, then the third party can rely on the representation made by holding the agent out as having all the usual powers that a managing director would normally have. The representation may be subtle, it may arise from a course of dealings where the third party is led to believe that the managing director is empowered as a managing director would normally be empowered, or it may arise from the agent managing director being allowed to use company notepaper which describes him as managing director. In such cases the third party is not dealing with the agent only, he is in reality dealing with the agent relying on a previous representation from thc company. The second way in which the principal may be making a representation in such cases arises where the third party has never dealt with the company before and the only person with whom he has any communication is the agent. If a man is appointed managing director he is authorised to call himself managing director. Because such a statement - 'I am the managing director' - is within his actual authority, so the company is making it, because the act of an agent within his authority is the act of the principal. So, there is a representation by the principal that the person is managing director and without anything more this will lead the third party reasonably to believe that the agent has all the authority which a managing director would normally have (*Freeman and Lockyer* v *Buckhurst Park Properties (Mangal) Ltd* (1964); *Hely-Hutchinson* v *Brayhead Ltd* (1968)).

Where apparent authority arises there may be actual authority. For example, if a man is appointed managing director of a company and no limits are put on his authority by the company, then a third party dealing with him may agree to a contract which the agent is actually authorised to make and also may be relying on some representation that he has that authority. It matters not in such cases whether one says the principal is bound because of actual or apparent authority, because the result is the same.

There is no scope for apparent authority unless the third party is led to believe that the agent is an agent (*Rama Corporation* v *Proved Tin and General Investments Ltd* (1952)). But, where such a representation is made by the principal, the agent binds the principal to contracts made within his apparent authority even where this is outside actual authority.

Usual authority may or may not exist as a separate category of authority. The case of *Watteau* v *Fenwick* (1893) holds that any contract made by an agent within the scope of the authority usually given to an agent of his type will bind the principal whether or not the principal has expressly instructed the agent not to make such contracts and whether or not the third party knows the agent to be an agent. If *Watteau* v *Fenwick* is correct, which is in doubt, it creates a potentially massive inroad into the principle that an agent must act within his actual or apparent authority in order contractually to bind his principal.

There are some cases where contracts made by an agent within his actual or apparent authority do not bind the principal. The first such case is not a true case of the agent acting within his authority at all. It arises where the third party has notice that the agent is acting outside the scope of his actual authority. Even where there is a representation that the agent is authorised to make the contract concerned, if the third party knows that he is not so authorised, the act of the agent will not bind the principal (*Armagas* v *Mundogas, The Ocean Frost* (1986)). Where the third party is guilty of bribery the contract made by the agent is voidable at the option of the principal (*Boston Deep Sea Fishing and Ice Co* v *Ansell* (1888)). Bribery, in this context, means the payment of a secret profit to the agent whether or not there is a corrupt motive behind the payment. It is not clear on the authorities as they stand at the moment whether it is necessary that the secret profit must be an inducement to enter into the contract in order for it to render that contract voidable. The better view is that the contract should only be voidable if it was induced by the secret profit, and that any payment made after the contract was completed should be a secret profit and recoverable by the principal from the agent, but should not have any effect on the contract which was properly made. It is arguable that in cases where a bribe has been paid the reason why the principal is able to avoid the contract is because it is not within the scope of the agent's authority to make a contract when he has been bribed, but such an explanation fails to take into account that the contract will be binding on the principal if not avoided.

Agency can arise by ratification, which is the subsequent adoption by the principal of a contract ostensibly made on his behalf at a time when the agent was not authorised to make it: *Keighley Maxsted & Co* v *Durant* (1900). In such a case the agent does not really act within the scope of his authority at all, because he has none, but the principal is, nonetheless, bound.

The liability of a principal for the torts of his agent overlaps with the rules of vicarious liability in tort generally, and have yet to be fully worked out by the courts. The key to unravelling the difficulty in this area is to appreciate that an agent is one who has authority to make contracts on behalf of his principal. Such a person may be a servant or an independent contractor. If he is a servant, then there is no problem in holding the principal liable for any tort committed within the course of employment. But the position in relation to independent contractors is that the employer is not vicariously liable except in very special and limited circumstances. In relation to agents the position is that a distinction is drawn between fraud and other torts.

In cases of fraud the position is that it must be asked whether the contract which the agent made fraudulently was one which was within his apparent authority. If it was, then the principal will be bound by the fraud in the same way that he is bound by the contract itself. The essence of this is that if the principal would be bound by the contract if made honestly, then he is bound by the contract if made fraudulently and is also liable for the fraud itself. This cannot be explained by saying that the principal is liable for the fraud because he benefits from the contract, because the rule applies even where the principal does not benefit from his agent's fraud (*Lloyd* v *Grace, Smith & Co* (1912)). However, if the agent acts outside his apparent authority and acts otherwise than for the benefit of his principal, the principal will not be liable for the fraud unless the third party can prove that the agent was actually authorised to act in that way, which he rarely will be. This position is the result of the analysis of the law in the most recent House of Lords' case, *The Ocean Frost* (1986), which involved a case of a fraudulent servant, but the principle was stated as a general rule applicable to agents who are independent contractors as well as those who are servants; a much cited dictum to the contrary by Denning LJ in *Navarro* v *Moregrand Ltd* (1951) was disapproved.

In cases involving torts other than fraud, *The Ocean Frost* does not really help. Lord Keith said that different considerations would apply and, indeed, he said that Denning LJ's dictum may have some validity in such cases. Denning LJ argued that a principal would be liable for all acts of his servant or agent within the course of employment whether or not within the scope of actual or apparent authority. This dictum equates the liability of a principal with that of an employer, and, presumably, means that the principal is not liable for the torts of an independent contractor who is his agent unless the tort was within the authority of the agent. In *Kooragang Investments Pty Ltd* v *Richardson and Wrench Ltd* (1982) the Privy Council held that the negligence of an agent would not bind the principal unless within the course of the agent's employment. In that case a negligent valuation of land was carried out be an employee of the defendants for the benefit not of the defendants but of another company. It was held that unless he was acting within the course of his employment he could not make the principal liable for his negligence. This case does not help us to find the rule in relation to independent contractors.

We have already seen that Denning LJ in the *Moregrand* case said that we must ask not whether the agent is acting within the scope of his authority but whether he was acting in the course of employment - was he doing the right thing in the wrong rather than doing the wrong thing entirely? It makes sense to say that the negligent misstatement of an agent should bind the principal if the end result is that the agent makes the contract which he is authorised to make and that, indeed, was the position in *Hedley Byrne* v *Heller and Partners* (1964), where an agent was negligent in representing the creditworthiness of a company. Denning LJ was equating all agents with servant whether the agent is in fact a servant or independent contractor. This means that one should assume that the agent is an employee, a servant, and ask whether the master is vicariously liable; in other words is the act which is done negligently one which is within the course of employment? If so, the principal is liable, if not then he is free from liability. Whether the agent is in reality a servant or independent contractor makes no difference because he will be presumed to be a servant. This rule can be justified if it is remembered that an agent is someone employed to make a contract with a third party; therefore the scope for the agent making the principal liable in tort is limited to torts committed when making the very contract which the agent is employed to make.

It cannot be pretended that the present state of the authorities in this area is entirely happy. Why a distinction should be drawn between fraud and other torts is not clear, in principle one would expect a principal to be liable for all torts committed within the scope of the agent's authority; whether the tort is fraud or anything else, but that is not the position.

28 OBLIGATIONS OF PRINCIPAL TO AGENT: AGENT TO PRINCIPAL

28.1 Introduction

The rights and duties of principal and agent are largely determined by the agreement they make.

However, two points should be noted in this context.

Firstly, not all agents are created by contract and the agreement may be informal. In such cases the agents 'rights' (for example to payment) may be difficult to enforce in a court of law.

Secondly, bear in mind that with regard to the agent's duties towards his principal, even an agent created in a non-contractual agreement, will have some duties by virtue of his fiduciary position. Therefore, while the principal may not be able to enforce a non-contractual agreement, the agent's position will be in some ways analagous to that of a trustee and he may owe duties by virtue of his fiduciary status, which a court will enforce.

It is also important to bear in mind that while the agent and principal owe duties to each other, those duties are not reciprocal; they are not carbon copies of each other.

By and large the law gives more protection to the principal, imposing more duties on the agent than is true in the reverse.

Finally, while the common law implies a number of rights and duties on each side into an agency relationship, it is of course always possible in an agency created by contract to include express terms which impose additional obligations. It is probably more difficult, however to exclude the standard rights and duties, especially if these encroach in some way on the rights of third parties.

28.2 Key points

It is important that the student understands the following.

a) *Obligations of principal to agent*

While, as has been noted, it is always open for the parties expressly to incorporate terms into a contract of agency imposing extra liabilities on the parties, the principal's main duties toward his agent are concerned with payment.

The principal must pay the agent the remuneration agreed on. If there is no payment specifically mentioned, there is an implicit agreement to pay a reasonable remuneration if the agent is employed in a capacity where it would be normal to expect payment. If any trade custom or usage applies this may be taken into account in assessing what constitutes a reasonable payment.

Agency agreements commonly provide for payment by commission, that is, a percentage of the profit on, or of the total value of the transaction which the agent is to negotiate. It would seem from the relevant case law that where payment by commission is agreed on, unless the parties expressly agree to the contrary (or a trade custom applies), the principal need not necessarily allow the agent to earn that commission. For example there is, apparently no legal reason why the principal, having engaged an agent on a commission basis to sell his house, should not then proceed to sell it directly to a third party without the intervention of the agent. However, as already stated, much does depend on the agreement between principal and agent; and the student should read further as to the overall position and related case law.

The agent has a right of indemnity which is quite separate from other rights of payment. This right will arise, firstly, if the agent spends money in the performance of his agency duties and, secondly, the agent may become liable in contract or tort to a third party (or even commit a criminal offence) in the course of his agency. In the first instance, the principal must repay all reasonable expenses incurred - here a great deal depends on the agreement between the two as to what constitutes reasonable expense. In the second case, the principal will be liable to indemnify the agent, provided always that the agent was acting within his actual authority. The agent will *not* be able to claim indemnity if he was in breach of his duties to the principal.

The agent can enforce his right to payment or indemnity in several ways. The most obvious possibility is to sue for damages for breach of contract, but if the agency was created in a non-contractual way, that option may not be open to the agent. To seek a way round this problem the agent might seek restitution (which does have several limitations) or exercise a lien over the principal's goods.

b) *Obligations of agent to principal*

The duties of an agent are many and in some cases may be increased by express terms in the agreement.

Primarily, they include the following.

i) To carry out instructions

If the agreement is non-contractual the situation is more difficult, but if there is a contract, disobedience (including complete inactivity) will be a breach of contract.

ii) To act with due care and skill

An agent is bound to exercise such skill as he possesses and act as he would in the conduct of his own affairs, but additionally he must exercise a degree of skill and diligence appropriate to the agency.

Of recent years, the common law rules have been enhanced by legislation like the Supply of Goods and Services Act 1982, where s13 provides that there is an implied term that the supplier (agent) will carry out the service with reasonable care and skill.

It should be noted that even a gratuitous agent owes a duty to act with care and skill reasonable in the circumstances.

Obviously however the extent to which the agent is paid, or even if he is paid at all, will determine what is 'reasonable'.

iii) Not to delegate

In general an agent cannot delegate his duties unless he is specifically authorised to do so.

It is, however, common, because of general practice in trade usage to allow an agent to delegate to sub-agents.

iv) Fiduciary duties

These really fall into three main categories:

- *duty not to have conflicting interests* - here no distinction is made between contractual or non-contractual agents. It is not necessary that any loss to the principal be proved. In certain cases, with the proper informed, consent of the principal the agent may be allowed to use his position to his own advantage as well as that of the principal;
- *an agent must not make a secret profit or take a bribe.* This duty overlaps with conflict of interests just discussed. As to the distinction between a secret profit and a bribe, the student should consult a textbook for further details but see in particular the recent case of *Logicrose Ltd* v *Southend United FC* [1989] 1 WLR 1256 as to the duties of an agent with regard to bribes and secret profits;
- *the duty to keep accounts.* Every agent should keep his principal's money separate from his own and keep correct accounts of his dealings undertaken as agent.

The remedies of the principal against an agent who fails as to one or more of the above duties will vary. Lack of space precludes the principal's rights against defaulting agents from being dealt with here, so the student should read further on the matter and look at related case law.

28.3 Analysis of questions

It has already been noted several times that examiners for the University of London seem to like the general far-ranging type of problem. The first question quoted below is one of the very few that requires detailed knowledge of a particular aspect of principals' or agents' duties. The second is general and typical of its type, and it includes a considerable number of topics relating to agents' duties.

The form of question one is more likely to see, appears to be a question like Question 2 of the 1984 paper (quoted in chapter 29) in which the question of bribes does arise but needs to be dealt with in the context of a much wider problem. On Question 3 of the 1985 paper in which, again, agent's duties to his principal, especially as to bribes or secret profits arises. As before this is part of a much wider question on agency topics. See also Q4 1993 (in chapter 36).

28.4 Questions

Question 1

The simple picture of agency which is often presented is one where the agent acts solely and absolutely in the interest of the principal. In reality, a commercial agent is one who is providing a service to the principal, doing so in the interest of himself as much as of the principal and whose rights and duties should be viewed in the light of that.

Discuss.

University of London LLB Examination
(for External Students) Commercial Law June 1988 Q2

Skeleton solution

- Nature of agency, contractual/non-contractual duties.
- Fiduciary duties arising by virtue of equity.
- Comparison of fiduciary duties with duty to obey instructions.
- Breach of fiduciary duties.

Suggested solution

An agent is someone whose acts affect the legal relations of another (the principal) with a third party. The legal relations affected are normally contractual relations, and the agent either makes or performs a contract on behalf of his principal.

There is no necessity for an agent to be appointed with any formality or to be paid for what he does, because the nature of his status as agent is factual - if he in fact has authority to make or perform the principal's contract then the way in which he and the principal have arranged matters between themselves is irrelevant. A great many agents act for others because they are paid to do so. Some are nothing more than employees, but others are freelance agents who act for different principles in relations with different third parties. Common examples are estate agents and factors. The rights and duties of all agents in relation to their principals are the same, however, whether they are full-time employees or independent contractors brought-in to do just one job.

The rights and duties of agent and principal to each other are a matter for their agreement. But it is impracticable to expect them to cover every aspect of their relationship, so the law will fill the gaps. The agent's duties are divided into two types: duties arising by agreement and fiduciary duties. The principal, however, owes only one type of duty, which is in relation to payment.

The agent's duties fall into two types because there are two aspects to his position as agent. Firstly he is obliged to carry out instructions, and this imposes duties of obedience and of care. Secondly he is obliged to act wholeheartedly for his principal, he should not allow himself to be put in a position where he faces a conflict of interests either because he is acting for someone else as well as his principal and that other's interests are not the same as the principal's, or because he is making a secret profit for himself.

The duty to obey instructions is fundamental to the very concept of agency in many cases. Clearly if someone is asked to do something on behalf of another, but is not contractually bound to do so (for example where he is not promised payment), he is under no enforceable duty to perform the task. But if he is promised payment or if he takes on the task he is asked to perform, he must do what he has been promised payment for and must act within reasonable care and skill. There is no question of these duties being unduly onerous or unfair because they are the same duties which arise in any case where someone is promised money in return for work or undertakes to do something for another; a duty of care may arise simply because the person takes it upon himself to act: *Chaudhry* v *Prabhakar* (1988).

The fiduciary duties, however, are very strict and, in some instances, can be seen to be unfair to the agent. These duties are to avoid a conflict of interests, not to make a secret profit and not to delegate unless delegation is expressly or impliedly allowed; often the three duties can overlap so that one act is a breach of two or more of them. There are some decided cases where the effect on the agent of the fiduciary duty was penal. For example, in *Industrial Development Consultants Ltd* v *Cooley* (1972) the defendant was managing director of a company (IDC) which wanted a particular contract with the Eastern Gas Board. The Board would not use IDC, so the defendant left his job, set up his own company and bid successfully for the contract. It was held in the Queen's Bench Division that the defendant had to account to his former employers for all profits made under the contract. Because he had found out about it in the course of his work with IDC, so he owed a duty to IDC to use that knowledge to their benefit only.

The result of this case is manifestly absurd because IDC could not possibly have obtained the contract with the Gas Board themselves. Perhaps it can be justified by saying that IDC would have continued to have the benefit of the defendant as their managing director had he not left to take the contract himself, but it is hard to see why this is relevant because his leaving was not a breach of contract. Had he given IDC notice of why he was leaving they could not have prevented him from doing so and the information he used was of no benefit to them.

The position is even harsher to the agent where he makes a secret profit while in employment. In *Andrews* v *Ramsey & Co* (1903) the receipt of a secret profit by an auctioneer disentitled him from claiming payment for his work. This loss of the right to payment will arise even if the work was done properly and the principal received the same benefit as he would have done had there been no breach of duty.

To avoid the harshness of these principles, the agent must disclose the conflict of interest or the secret profit to the principal and the principal must waive the breach of duty. Where there is such waiver the agent is treated as though he is not in breach and may retain any profit he has made. It is not easy to explain in general terms how this waiver arises because some of the authorities appear confusing. In *Harrods Ltd* v *Lemon* (1931) Harrods found themselves working for both vendor and purchaser of a house. They disclosed this to the vendor and she consented to them continuing to act for her. The Court of Appeal held that they were entitled to commission from her because she had waived the breach of duty when it had been disclosed. Because there had been full disclosure and the waiver was unambiguous, so Mrs Lemon had no cause for complaint.

By contrast in *Hippisley* v *Knee Bros* (1905) a commission was received by auctioneers from a printer who had printed advertisements, but the principal was charged the full price by the auctioneer for the advertisements. The Court of Appeal held that this did not prevent the auctioneers from recovering their commission in full from the principal. There had been no disclosure of the extra profit being made by the agents, but the contract made with the printer was held not to be part of the duties the auctioneer was appointed to carry out (viz the sale of the principal's property) and therefore was irrelevant to the right to recover profits. It is not easy to see why the contract made with the printers was irrelevant, because it concerned the principal's property and the principal had to pay the agents for the advertisements.

The position of the agent who makes an additional profit depends upon whether that profit was made in the performance of part of his duties as agent (*Hippisley* v *Knee* (1905)). But it is difficult to define exactly when it will be seen as part of that duty and when it will not. Of course the law must avoid agents acting dishonestly to the detriment of their principals, but it is hard to justify a rule which allows the principal to recover the agent's additional profit and/or deprive the agent of commission where the principal's position is not affected adversely. There seems no reason in principle why an agent should not be allowed to make whatever profit he can provided he also does what the principal asks him to do. A duty of disclosure must exist where the acts of the agent may adversely affect the principal, but to extend that duty in the way that cases like *Industrial Development Consultants Ltd* v *Cooley* (1972) extend it is hard to justify. The principal in such a case can protect himself by an express term in the contract appointing the agent that information must be used wholly for the benefit of the principal, but even then, if the principal could not get any benefit from the information there is no reason why the agent should not gain whatever benefit he can.

Freelance agents like commercial factors are employed from contract-to-contract and knowledge and experience which they pick up over their years in business are assets which they will use to the benefit of anyone who employs them. Dishonesty on the part of an agent, by failing to obtain the best deal possible for his principal in order to make additional profits for himself or another will always allow the principal a remedy because it would amount to a failure to exercise the requisite standard of skill and care.. There is, however, no justification for penalising commercial agents where they do their job properly and incidentally make money themselves.

Question 2

Pinto, an importer, leases premises in which he instals Ajax to handle the distribution of his goods in England.

Tamara asks Pinto to deliver 500 bales of cotton to her but Pinto tells her, 'You can buy your cotton from Ajax.' Tamara orders 500 bales from Ajax but, when she opens the bales, the cotton is discovered to be mouldy.

Pinto tries to persuade Teddy to buy 200 barrels of oil from him but Teddy says he cannot pay because he is owed money by Ajax. In the presence of Tim, Pinto says to Teddy, 'That's alright; Ajax works for me; if you take the 200 barrels, you can sort out the money when you collect them from him.' Teddy agrees to buy the oil.

Pinto tells Ajax that he has met Tim and never wants to do business with him. Knowing that Pinto imports Forekz beer, Tim orders 5,000 cans from Ajax, who delivers to Tim 5,000 cans which he has obtained from Sudgen, another importer. The beer turns out to be old and bad.

Advise Pinto.

University of London LLB Examination
(for External Students) Commercial Law June 1992 Q4

Skeleton solution

Tamara

- Creation by agreement/agency by estoppel; rule in *Hely-Hutchinson* v *Brayhead.*
- Mouldy cotton a breach of s14 (possibly s15) Sale of Goods Act 1979?
- Actual authority.
- Remedy against Pinto.
- Possible remedy against Ajax in certain cases.

Teddy

- Pinto's statement to Teddy.
- A guarantee or an indemnity.
- Significance of distinction?

Tim

- Ajax's misconduct.
- Does it affect Tim's rights/remedies?

- Pinto's rights against Ajax.

Suggested solution

We are told merely that Pinto 'instals' Ajax to handle distribution of his goods in England. What we are not told is how this 'installation' takes place, ie by formal contract, expressly, impliedly or other means? What makes it more confusing is that in each of three transactions different rules seem to apply. It is perhaps easiest to deal with each transaction separately.

Tamara's cotton

Agency can arise by estoppel where there is a representation made by the principal to the third party that the agent has authority to enter into certain acts on his behalf. But we also know that Pinto has 'installed' Ajax as his agent, hence there is already creation by agreement. Lord Wilberforce noted in *Hely-Hutchinson* v *Brayhead* (1968) that where there is agency created by agreement there is no need to investigate whether there was also a representation of authority made by the principal. There are two different forms of authority - actual authority (created by agreement) and apparent or ostensible authority (created by estoppel). Moreover it is not entirely clear whether Pinto has in fact made a representation. He remarks that 'You may buy your cotton from Ajax' but in fact does not say specifically that Ajax is his agent; nor, at least, from the minimal facts ascertainable from the question, does he necessarily imply it.

When Tamara discovers that the cotton is mouldy it will of course be a breach of the Sale of Goods Act 1979 (SGA), especially s14(2) as to merchantable quality, and if the cotton was bought on the basis of a sample, of s15. One assumes that the entire lot of 500 bales is affected. So, against whom does she have a right of action? In the normal way of things, once the contract is made the agent drops out and if there is a breach of contract then any subsequent dispute is between principal and third party. The only exceptions would be if the agent has not disclosed the fact of his principal's existence, or if he has made himself personally liable on the contract. It is assumed that Tamara is aware of the fact of Ajax's agency; though if this is not the case of course she does have the option of suing either Pinto or Ajax. As to the second possibility, it is nowhere implied that Ajax has made himself personally liable. In view of Pinto's appointment of Ajax it is presumed he possesses 'actual' authority, that is the power to do whatever is mentioned in the agreement, together with whatever is impliedly necessary to perform the agreement properly. If it is not clear what the agreement involves the courts will imply that provided the agent acts in good faith and reasonably then he will be within the bounds of his authority (*Ireland* v *Livingstone* (1872); *Shirlaw* v *Southern Foundries* (1939)). In the light of Lord Wilberforce's remarks in *Hely-Hutchinson* (above) it seems that, because Ajax possesses actual authority, it is not necessary to look further, to estoppel, for the source of his authority. Any redress Tamara seeks therefore must be from Pinto, the principal. This will be true, even if Ajax is guilty of some misconduct (eg this is not Pinto's cotton he has imported, but some cheap substitute). Though, of course, if an agent is guilty of misconduct, his principal may have a right of action against him.

Teddy's oil

Because of the fact that Ajax owes money to Teddy, and because Pinto effectively says to Teddy that he will make sure Teddy gets his money, it is necessary to ascertain first of all whether Pinto has effectively given a guarantee to Teddy, or possibly an indemnity.

A guarantee is an undertaking to answer for another's default, and requires the default of the principal debtor in order to render the guarantor liable to action. It is to be distinguished from a contract involving a primary obligation to the creditor, known as an indemnity. A good example is *Birkmyr* v *Darnell* (1704) in which A said to B, 'Supply goods to C and I will see you get paid.' But Pinto does not quite say this. When Teddy says he cannot buy oil because he cannot afford to until Ajax repays him, Pinto effectively implies that the money Ajax owes him can be deducted from the money Teddy owes him (Pinto) for the oil. Does Pinto's apparent assumption of the debt amount to either guarantee or indemnity? Professor Goode points out that it is not at all uncommon to find contracts of a hybrid nature which have characteristics of both guarantees and indemnities. The usual reason for wishing to categorise them specifically is that while the Statute of Frauds s4 applies to guarantees, it does not to indemnities. If, as seems to be the case here, there is nothing in writing and no written note or memorandum by way of evidence that Pinto ever made his promise, then should Pinto suddenly change his position and demand the full amount for the oil, Teddy's only chance is to claim Pinto's promise amounted to an indemnity. This, not being subject to the Statute of Frauds, may be enforced on a purely verbal basis. Difficulties of proof would not arise, because Pinto makes the comment in the presence of Tim, a third party. The application of principles applying here can be seen in *Mountstephen* v *Lakeman* (1871).

Tim's beer

An agent owes a duty of obedience to his principal and in appointing Ajax, Pinto gives him specific and explicit instructions not to do business with Tim. Two separate problems arise as to result of Ajax's misconduct - does Tim have a remedy for the bad beer against Pinto, or has the agent's misconduct rendered the agent liable instead of, or in addition to, his principal? The second problem relates to the extent to which his principal may have a remedy against Ajax for his misconduct. Where an agent is appointed to a job which carries standard duties and powers, the agent will be said to have 'usual' powers. This 'usual' authority has been examined by the courts in a number of cases. In *Daun* v *Simmins* (1879) the manager of a public house bought spirits from someone he was told he should not deal with. The third party was not allowed to enforce the contract against the principal because he was found to know about the restrictions placed on the agent.

In *Watteau* v *Fenwick* (1893) a hotel manager was told expressly not to buy cigars on credit. The principal was held liable on the contract, despite the restrictions placed on the agent, primarily it seems because the third party did not even realise the manager was an agent, let alone know the restrictions placed on his agency.

It seems that in cases where an agent is appointed to do a job which usually carries with it certain powers, the agent will bind the principal, provided he acts within this usual authority, whether or not the third party knows he is an agent. To decide whether Tim may sue Pinto for the breach of contract therefore, two factors will be important. First, is Ajax's job one that carries 'usual' authority, and secondly is Tim aware that Ajax is Pinto's agent, and that he (A) has been banned from ever dealing with him?

As to whether Pinto has a right of action against Ajax for his misconduct, it was established in *Christoforides* v *Terry* (1924) that a principal's remedies are threefold:

- there may be a claim for damages for breach of contract (the principal-agent relationship is a contractual one);
- the agent may be required to state an account, so that any profit the agent has improperly made may be recovered;
- any claim for remuneration or indemnity by the agent may be rejected.

We have already noted that Pinto is, in all probability, liable on the contract with Tim and that will no doubt be reflected in any award of damages in the first situation. It is not at all obvious that Ajax has made any secret profit, though the fact that he has obtained the beer from Sugden indicates that he probably has. If so, he will of course be personally liable to Sudgen. It is not known how Ajax is to be paid, ie by commission or salary? Certainly his act may preclude his claiming commission on this deal; if he receives a salary he may lose a part or all of it (*Andrew* v *Ramsay & Co* (1903)).

Note that by dealing with Sugden, Ajax may have set up a conflict of interests and be in breach of his fiduciary duty to Pinto. It used to be thought that where an agent takes a bribe (and it is not clear whether Ajax has actually done so from Sugden) the principal could recover both damages for breach of contract and the amount of the bribe. Since *Mahesan* v *Malaysian Government Officers' Co-operative Housing Society* (1979), however, it has become obvious that the principal must select one or the other.

29 TERMINATION OF AGENCY

29.1 Introduction

In those forms of agency which are not contractual, either party can withdraw at any time without legal liability.

If the agency was formed by contract the contract may end by any of the methods which would bring an ordinary contract to an end, such as frustration. Obviously discharge by mutual agreement is another possibility.

The principal's death, bankruptcy or mental disorder will bring the agency to a close whether or not these facts are known to the agent, as will the agent's death, bankruptcy or mental disorder if these facts make him unable to perform his duties. (But see Key point (b) following: as to irrevocability.)

Note that the principal may at any time revoke, or the agent renounce, the agency, even if the agency was created by deed.

29.2 Key points

a) *Method and effect of termination*

Termination may be provided for in the contract where, for example, the parties expressly cover the question of termination by mutual agreement, or termination on the happening of a particular event. It is also possible to set a particular time after which the agency will lapse or specify that the agency is to achieve a particular purpose after which the agency will come to an end.

Even if the parties do not expressly cater for these possibilities, trade usage or custom may in some cases imply provisions as to termination into the contract creating the agency.

Otherwise, as has already been noted, the ordinary common law rules as to termination will apply.

One problem which does occur from time to time, is whether a breach of condition by one party, especially the agent, will automatically bring the agency to an end. Certainly, because of the doctrine of apparent authority it will sometimes appear to a third party that an agent is authorised even though there has already been a breach of contract. The two rules are difficult to reconcile and the student should read further on the subject and look at relevant case law.

b) *Irrevocable agencies*

It has already been noted that a principal has power to revoke at will.

In chapter 25 the irrevocability of certain types of powers of attorney was described and obviously this type of agency is an exception to the general rule.

Added to this exception should be those types of special agency where the agent has an authority coupled with an interest. This will arise for example where the agent is given the agency as security: for example, where the principal owes the agent money and employs him as agent as a means of settling the debt.

Such forms of agency cannot be revoked at will.

29.3 Analysis of questions

There are, surprisingly, no questions that deal at length with termination in University of London past papers.

While only a minimal portion of the question quoted below deals with termination, all the other issues have already been dealt with in foregoing chapters.

29.4 Question

Warren carried on business as a builders' merchant. In April 1982, he was taken ill and placed Baker in charge as a managing agent under a contract, which stated (inter alia) that:

i) the appointment was to be irrevocable for three years;

ii) Baker was not to carry on a similar business himself before or after the termination of the agreement within five miles of the site of the business;

iii) Baker was not to buy any goods from Washtime Supplies Ltd; and

iv) Baker would be paid £2,000 a year salary and a commission of one per cent on the turnover of the business.

In April 1984, Warren was restored to health, and sold the business. He seeks your advice and states:

'I have discovered that Baker bought 200 baths from Washtime Supplies Ltd but did not pay for them. He sold 400 washbasins to Sunshine Developers Ltd and charged them a specially low price and obtained a commission from them for doing so. He sold a number of waterpipes to Delta Homes under a contract excluding liability for breach of any condition, statutory or otherwise, and the company are suing me because some of the waterpipes were made of cheap plastic and leaked. Baker bought 500,000 tiles from Everglaze Tiles Ltd which were much in excess of my requirements and I do not want to have to pay for them. Baker is pressing me for commission. Six months ago, he started up a business as a builders' merchant in the next road to my premises, and I have lost a lot of money as a result. Can any of the creditors set off against me any debts which Baker owes them?'

Advise Warren generally.

University of London LLB Examination
(for External Students) Commercial Law June 1984 Q2

Skeleton solution

- Type of agency, ie general or specific; express or implied.
- Principal's objections to third party.
- Agent's obligations to third party; agent's breach of warranty of authority?
- Agent's breach of contract - acceptance of a bribe?
- Termination/revocation.

Suggested solution

The contract that Warren entered into with Baker was a contract of agency whereby Baker was appointed as a general agent, that is an agent who has authority to act for his principal in all matters concerning a trade or business. This means in effect that Baker was given a wide authority to deal with Warren's business.

The agency is expressed to be irrevocable and this means that the agency cannot normally be terminated without both parties' consent: *Gansson* v *Morton* (1830).

Otherwise, since a time limit was expressed to terminate early it would be a breach of contract. However the rule in *Levy* v *Goldhill* (1917) will apply and agency can be terminated by the principal at instant notice, but it would be noted that this revocation will give rise to an action for damages for breach of contract. If Baker is an employee of Warren's he is entitled to a reasonable period of notice on revocation (*Martin-Baker Aircraft Co Ltd* v *Murison* (1956)). Even agencies expressed to be irrevocable can be terminated and the revocation need not take the same form as the contract, for example a written contract can be revoked by a verbal announcement, or by conduct as in Warren's case.

The terms of the agency agreement specifically stated that Baker was not to purchase any goods from Washtime Supplies Ltd. This term is a limitation on Baker's authority and as such it means that Baker had no authority to enter into the contract that he did. He acted in breach of the terms of his contract and whether Warren can terminate the contract of agency because of this breach will depend upon the importance of the breached term to the parties. In view of the fact that the contract is expressed to be irrevocable it is unlikely that the breach will terminate the contract and Warren's only action will be for damages.

Whether Warren is bound to pay for the 200 baths depends mainly on Washtime Supplies Ltd's knowledge. As Baker's authority is limited in this respect there is no actual authority for the contract and clearly Baker's act has not been ratified. However, if Washtime can prove that Baker had ostensible authority to buy the baths then

Warren will be bound. The three requirements of ostensible authority were stated by Slade J in *Rama Corporation Ltd* v *Proved Tin and General Investments Ltd* (1952) to be firstly a representation; secondly, a reliance on the representation; thirdly an alteration of position. By allowing Baker to manage his business he was making a representation but whether Washtime relied on the representation will depend on their knowledge. If they knew of the limitation, Warren would not be liable, but if they did not (as is likely) Warren would be liable for they altered their position by selling the baths. It could be argued that, as in *Midland Bank* v *Reckitt* (1933) Washtime should have inquired as to Baker's authority because he was doing an act outside the scope of his usual authority by purchasing so many baths, but this is unlikely.

With regard to the 400 washbasins that he sold at a specially low price, this does appear to be a serious breach of his contract of agency. In all contracts of agency an agent has a duty of fidelity. He must account for all payments received and is under a strict duty not to accept bribes. A bribe was defined by Slade J in *Industries and General Mortgage Co* v *Lewis* (1949) as a secret commission paid by a person to an agent with whom he is dealing, knowing that that person is acting as an agent and without disclosing the payment to the principal. If these conditions are present here then Baker will be liable to account for the bribe and interest on it from the time the payment was made, the contract with Sunshine Developers Ltd will be void at Warren's instance and probably more importantly, Warren will be able to terminate the contract of agency. The receipt of a bribe is a fundamental breach of the contract and even though it is expressed to be irrevocable it will be terminated at Warren's instance. If he has taken this course then he will not be liable to pay any commission.

The waterpipes that were sold to Dolton Homes were presumably sold with the authority of Warren because their sale would be in the scope of the agent's authority. There is sometimes a problem as to whether a third party can rely on an exclusion clause in a contract. This problem does not arise here because the contract was made on Warren's behalf and thus he can take the benefit of the exclusion clause. The contract does not appear to be in the form of a consumer sale but does appear to be on a standard form contract. The effect of this is that although Warren can exclude liability he can only do so as far as is fair and reasonable: Unfair Contracts Act 1977. Whether this exclusion clause is fair and reasonable will depend on many factors such as the price of the pipes, the strength of the bargaining positions of the parties and whether any inducements were offered to agree the term: Schedule 2 of the Act: *George Mitchell (Chesterhall)* v *Finney Lock Seeds* (1983).

The purchase of the tiles was presumably within the scope of Baker's actual authority unless he put some limitation on the quantity of goods to be purchased. Even if such a limitation was present Warren might be bound by Baker's ostensible authority if the three requirements of *Rama Corporation* are present and the question would turn on whether Everglaze Tiles Ltd should enquire into any limitation of authority. This is unlikely here and it is probable that Warren will have to pay for the tiles.

Baker set up a competitive business six months ago in breach of the express terms of his contract of agency. It also appears that he was in breach of his contract by setting up a business during the three year duration of the agency relationship. The term in the contract is a restraint of trade clause and as such it will be prima facie void unless proven to be reasonable. Here it is likely that the clause will be reasonable because there is an interest to protect, in that there are trade connections that Baker will have made. Warren should apply to the Court for an injunction to prevent Baker from carrying on the business.

The creditors would be able to set off debts by Baker which were incurred when he was acting as an agent but they will not be able to set off any debts owed by Baker since he started his new business for his change of address should put his creditors on notice.

PART 4

EXPORT SALES

30 SALE OF GOODS

30.1 Introduction

Where English law applies to a contract of international sale, then, obviously relevant legislation such as Sale of Goods Act 1979 and Supply of Goods and Services Act 1982 will apply.

International contracts for goods to be sold are often made on standard form contracts. The provisions relating to the sale of goods or supply of services may be expressly incorporated into the contract, or they may be implied by virtue of the statute.

In Part 1, the whole topic of sale of goods has already been dealt with and the following items should be read in conjunction with that chapter.

30.2 Key points

It is important that the student understands the following.

a) *Conditions and warranties*

Whenever there is a contract for sale of goods governed by English law, then the SGA 1979 applies.

That act classifies the respective obligations of the parties as conditions or warranties. An innominate term is neither a condition nor a warranty and while the Act does not expressly mention them the courts have ruled (for example in *The Hansa Nord* [1976] QB 44) that the argument that the Act excludes such terms is fallacious.

b) *Principal provisions of SGA 1979*

Those sections of SGA 1979, especially ss12-15 as to title and quality of goods, s30 as to quantity, ss34-35 as to acceptance and s29 as to delivery have already been discussed in the relevant chapters of Part 1. The student should not only re-read the appropriate parts of this Workbook, but should refer to more specialised textbooks for relevant case law, of which there is a considerable amount.

c) *The unpaid seller*

Sections 38 and 39 SGA 1979 cover the rights of the unpaid seller, in particular with the right of the unpaid seller to exercise a lien over goods, or stop in transit or even re-sell goods.

Obviously, since these are international contracts, stoppage in transit, in particular, may in reality be difficult to pursue for purely practical reasons; but the fact that the Act makes for such remedies remains unaltered, at least in theory.

d) *Exemption clauses*

The Unfair Contract Terms Act 1977 applies to contracts where one of the parties deals as a consumer.

However the Act is specifically stated not to apply to international supply contracts as defined in s2.

Therefore even if an exclusion clause is validly incorporated into the type of contract concerned, whether or not it is effective will be largely a question of construction. This has already been dealt with in chapter 7.

e) *The passing of property*

The question of when property passes is important as it is this that determines which of the parties will have liability for loss or damage to the goods.

Section 17(1) SGA 1979 provides:

'Where there is a contract for sale of specific or ascertained goods, the property in them is transferred to the buyer at such time as the parties intend it to be transferred.'

In cif contracts, the intention of the parties is that property will only pass when all the relevant documents are transferred. In the absence of a bill of lading, for example, it was considered that the delivery of goods at the shipper's request against letters of indemnity was effective to transfer property in cargo to the receiver, thereby discharging the shipper's liability for the cargo (see *Enichem* v *Ampelos* (1989) The Times 11 August). In fob contracts, property passes on shipment, the moment the goods go across the ship's rail.

Like all rules, there are exceptions and in any event these guidelines only apply to specific or ascertained goods.

Section 18 r2 further provides that if something needs to be done to specific goods to put them in a deliverable state, property will not pass until this has been done.

And again, s18 r3, says that where goods need to be weighed or measured to calculate the price, property will only pass after the weighing or measuring. Goods which are unascertained present problems. Section 16 SGA provides that property only passes when they become 'ascertained'. Section 16 is silent as to what might constitute ascertainment but s18 r5, says that if the goods are unconditionally appropriated to the contract this will be sufficient for property to pass.

The simplest form of appropriation might be delivery to the carrier for shipment. However it must be unconditional - merely labelling or creating the goods is not sufficient; the act must be an unequivocal sign of appropriation.

f) *Reservation of property*

All the rules in SGA 1979 as to passing of property are subject to an overriding right of the parties to indicate that they wish property to pass at some point other than that provided for by statute.

A seller can indicate that he is reserving a right of sale by one of the following methods:

i) when he takes a bill of lading from the carrier following shipment of the goods, by ensuring he or his order is designated as consignee;

ii) if he takes a bill of lading in the buyer's name and retains it;

iii) by sending a bill of lading, together with a bill of exchange drawn on the buyer for the price of the goods.

See *Mitsui & Co* v *Flota Mercante* (1989), on reservation of property until full payment.

g) *Romalpa clauses*

Like the methods mentioned in (f) above, this is a means whereby the seller indicates he does not wish property in the goods to pass in the manner and at the time provided for in SGA 1979. Instead he is reserving rights in the contract goods, usually until payment.

Where such a clause is utilised in a contract, the question as to whether or not it is effective to retain seller's title as security for the purchase price will depend on the circumstances of each case.

Where goods, in which title is retained, are sold to a third party, buying in good faith and without notice, from a party in possession of the goods, then a Romalpa clause may not be adequate to prevent that third party acquiring good title under s25 SGA 1979.

NB: It should be repeated that this account of the role of SGA in the field of export sales, is only at the most superficial level. It cannot be stressed too highly that the student should read further on the topic, especially as to related case law.

30.3 Analysis of questions

The question of the effect of Sale of Goods Act 1979 (and to a lesser extent Supply of Goods and Services Act 1982) and associated legislation on export sales is a topic which has cropped up on a number of occasions in University of London past papers. It is, for example, quite feasible that in a general question on export sales the possibility of cif and fob contracts encountering difficulties will be incorporated into any problem scenario. Those problems might include defects in the contract goods, risk, passing of property, acceptance and so on, all covered by provisions of SGA 1979. Therefore, this chapter and chapter 31 (following) overlap to a large extent.

The problems quoted below are good examples of the type of question referred to - the issues at stake are not confined to terms implied by SGA; but include topics raised in chapter 31, as well.

30.4 Questions

Question 1

Robinson Ltd, an exporter and importer of toys, entered into the following transactions:

i) A sale of 2,000 boxes of 'toy soldiers in French uniform' to Northern Supplies Ltd cif New York 'cash against documents'.

ii) A purchase of 4,000 'toy pistols' from Advanced Products Ltd fob Singapore for delivery at London.

iii) Sales of 2,500 Christmas tree lights to members of the public at £3 each through Robinson Ltd's mail order department.

Each contract excluded liability 'for (a) a breach of any implied terms as to fitness or merchantable quality; (b) negligence of the supplier; or (c) death or personal injury suffered by customers using the goods'.

Robinson Ltd consult you and state:

i) As to the toy soldiers

We tendered to the buyers a certificate of insurance, an invoice and a bill of lading. The buyers accepted them and paid us the price. They sold 1,000 cases of the goods to Palace Developments Ltd, who rejected them on the ground that the cases contained soldiers in German uniform. We are told that 500 other cases were damaged by fire while at sea. Northern Supplies Ltd are claiming back the whole of the purchase price from us.

ii) As to the toy pistols

We heard that the goods might have been damaged by rain at Singapore before they were loaded, but the sellers refused to allow us to inspect them until the vessel, which we had nominated to carry the goods, reached London. We did not insure the goods as we expected the sellers to do so. Forty five of the pistols were lost at sea in a storm. When the rest arrived, we discovered that 500 pistols were made of metal, and they could not be sold in this country because of various safety regulations.

iii) As to the Christmas tree lights

The electrical circuits on the tree were faulty. The lights bought by Mrs Smith caught fire, and her dining room furniture was destroyed. Another set was bought by Mrs Jones, and she died as a result of burns when they exploded. Mrs Jones' executor and Mrs Smith have made claims against us.

Advise Robinson Ltd.

University of London LLB Examination
(for External Students) Commercial Law June 1983 Q4

Skeleton solution

i)
- Cif, cash against documents sale.
- Property in goods passes when - who bears risk of damages in transit?
- Breach of condition?
- Exclusion clause - UCTA - reasonableness.
- Right of rejection.

ii)
- Fob contract, risk until shipment on seller - s32 does it alter position?
- Frustration.
- Right of rejection.

iii)
- Sections 14(2), 14(3) as to quality of goods - action in tort.
- Measure of damages.
- UCTA, s6 - does Mrs Smith deal as a consumer?

Suggested solution

i) On this cif, cash against documents sale, two issues arise - firstly whether property in the goods has passed so that Northern Supplies bear the risk of damages in transit, and secondly, whether Northern Supplies are prevented from rejecting the goods, thus losing their right to claim the price, if indeed they have such a right.

The sellers have fulfilled their obligations to the buyer in relation to the tender of the appropriate documents - invoice, certificate of insurance and the bill of lading, which is the document title to the goods. The prima facie presumption in the cif sale is that the buyer bears the risk from the passing of the goods over the rail but, of course, he is protected via insurance. But this depends usually on the price of the goods being paid when the documents are tendered, so that the right of the buyer to reject, at least the documents, is lost when they were taken up on exchange for payment. That coincides with an unconditional appropriation of the goods to the contract. The transfer of the bill of lading is prima facie evidence of an intention to pass property.

However, where the contract is cash against documents, the inference is that no property passes until the price has been paid - *Ginzberg* v *Barrow Haematite* (1966). That has occurred, so when the buyers accepted the documents and paid the price, property in the goods passed and it is an inference that the buyers bore the risk - s20(1) 1979 Act. As Lord Parker said in *Comptoir d'Achat et de Vente du Borrenbond Belges SA* v *Luis du Ridder Lda, The Julia* (1949) in a cif sale, property generally passes on shipment. So, Northern Supplies have no cause of action against the sellers for damage by fire at sea.

To claim the price, the buyers must terminate the contract. To do this, they must show either a repudiatory breach on the part of the sellers or a breach of condition. That will enable the buyers to reject (s11(4) allowing) and thereby treat the contract as discharged. In that event, the buyers have two options, either they can recover the price on the basis of total failure of consideration, or, instead of pursuing their restitutionary remedy, they may claim damages for non-delivery under s51(1). However, that is dependent upon either:

- the buyers rejecting *all* the goods; or
- the buyers rejecting part and keeping part, if the contract is severable.

In that instance they may claim part of the price related to what they reject.

Now there is not evidence that the contract is anything other than an entire contract with an individual delivery obligation, as in *Rosenthal* v *Esmail* (1965), so I propose to discount possibility (b). The right of the buyers to claim the price will depend on their ability to reject the 2,000 boxes.

Is there a breach of condition? There is a purported exclusion of liability under the statutorily implied conditions in s14(2) and s14(3). That there is a breach of s13, would seem to be difficult to argue. What is delivered to the buyers were still toy soldiers so that the descriptive words used to identify the goods would not seem to cover the uniform description. Such is not necessary to identify the goods (*Ashington Piggeries* (1972)) . There cannot be a breach of s14(2) - the defect, if any, is a descriptional defect, (possibly rendering the goods unfit for their normal purpose if that is considered to be resale) and is *not* a quality defect. Clearly the goods were merchantable within s14(6). Re s14(3), it could be argued that there was a breach. The sub-buyers did, after all reject, and it is almost certain that Northern would know that the buyer's purpose for which the goods had to be reasonably fit, was *resale*. If that is the case, then following Lord Guest in *Ashington Piggeries* (1972) actual communication need not be proved, provided Northern *knew*.

On the assumption that there was a sufficient breach of condition, the purported exclusion must be reasonable within Sch 2 of the 1977 UCTA s6. The term itself must be reasonable, to be tested in the light of the circumstances prevailing at the date of contracting. This applies even though the parties were not consumers because s6 has a wider operation than the rest of the Act - s6(3).

If there is a right to reject, it may well have been lost, under the doctrine of acceptance. If it is lost, then the condition sinks to the level of a warranty, and the only remedy the buyer can pursue is damages for breach of warranty under s53(1) - which, in this case, will be substantially less than damages under s51(1) because, in hypothesis, there will be no right to claim under s51(1) unless all the goods have been successfully rejected - damages under s53(1) will only be awarded in relation to half the boxes.

The question is whether the buyer has done an act inconsistent with the ownership of the seller, within s35. For the purposes of the mechanics of rejection, I am assuming that for the purposes of s26, the buyers, actually *can return the goods*, when they come to give notice of rejection. Of course, if they cannot, then the rule in *Lyons* v *May & Baker* (1923) bars rejection. This part of s35 is subjected to s34(1). Now these sections were drafted on the basis that it is the goods themselves which the buyer must have had a reasonable opportunity of examining so they sit uneasily with cif contracts - where acceptance of the documents and acceptance of the goods are separate acts. If the defects in the goods were apparent on the fact of the documents, then the right to reject will be lost - if the buyer accepted the documents when they indicated that some boxes contained soldiers in different uniforms, s35 would bar rejection. The buyer would have had a reasonable opportunity to examine for the purposes of s34(1) and *Hardy* v *Hillerns & Fowler* (1923) says that a resale is an act inconsistent with the ownership of the seller. On the other hand, if as is much more likely, the defect was not apparent on the fact of the documents, then the rule in *Hardy* cannot apply unless there is examination first, so the buyers would be able to reject and claim the price back.

ii) Risk issue

In an fob sale apart from the provisions of s32, risk, until shipment will be on the seller, and will pass to the buyer on shipment. If that applies then Robinson Ltd will have no remedy for the pistols lost at sea. Generally this will mean that in an fob contract, provided the seller fulfils his obligations, it will be the buyer's duty to insure. All that the seller has to do is to ensure that conforming goods are put over the rail of a ship nominated by the buyer in Singapore for delivery to London and to provide the buyer with documents enabling him to obtain possession. Insurance is the business of the buyer, because property in general, will pass as soon as the goods are placed on board (s18 r5(2)). Even if a contrary intention could be inferred, through the seller retaining a bill of lading, risk will pass to the buyer on shipment - *Stock* v *Inglis* (1884).

While this is the general position, it could be that s32(3) alters the obligation on Robinson Ltd. Although there is not enough information in the problem to reach a definite conclusion, under s32(3), the seller must give such notice to the buyer to enable him to insure (*Wimble* v *Rosenberg*

(1913) held that that applied to fob contracts, as a risk-deeming provision). However, the practical effect of that is limited by the fact that the Court of Appeal in *Wimble* held that the 'notice' requirement under s32(3) was satisfied if the buyer already had sufficient information at his disposal to insure. Considering that it is the buyer who nominates the ship, that will generally be complied with.

- Frustration

If the safety regulations were imposed after the contract was concluded it could amount to a frustrating event, on account of supervening illegality for the effects of which cf the 1943 Act.

- Rejection

The buyer has the right to reject goods if there is a breach of contract by the seller. The most likely possibility is comprised in s14(3). To establish a breach, the buyer would have to show that the particular purpose - resale - was communicated to the seller, although the observations of Lord Guest in *Ashington Piggeries* (1972) raise a presumption of communication if the sellers can be shown to have known of the purpose. However, generally, the suitability of goods for resale is up to the buyers - as the Court of Appeal made clear in *Teheran-Europe* v *Belton Tractors* (1968). If metal pistols could not be sold, on that basis, there would be no breach of s14(3). It will be difficult for the buyers to show that they relied on the skill and judgment of the seller with respect to the fitness of the goods for resale. However, the onus under s14(3) is on the seller to prove that there was no reliance by the buyer and as Lord Denning MR in Teheran-Europe said, reliance can be assumed until the contrary is proved.

As before, the purported existence of liability under s14(3) must be subjected to the requirement of reasonableness in Sch 2, even though the parties were not dealing as consumers.

iii) Mrs Smith can proceed against Robinson under s14(2) of the 1979 Act, s14(3) or sue in tort. Her contractual action will be aimed to recover damages for breach of warranty. The first limb of the rule in *Hadley* v *Baxendale* (1854) (in s53(2)) will present no difficulty - damage to her furniture as the result of defective electrical equipment, is, most probably, a direct and natural consequence.

This was the rule adopted by the trial judge in *Parsons* v *Uttley Ingham* (1978) and, to a certain extent, it conflicts with the formulation of the majority of the Court of Appeal, although, in this instance, there is unlikely to be any practical difference. The Court of Appeal were attempting to formulate a rule covering the recovery of consequential loss arising, after defective goods have been accepted, and stated that it sufficed that the sellers should appreciate the 'serious possibility' of physical damage, even if the severity of the loss could not reasonably have been envisaged. The trial judge had eschewed that technical approach and applied s53(2) - the first limb of the rule in *Hadley* - on the basis that the *exact* physical damage was the direct and natural consequence of the breach.

Now, assuming a breach and that the loss is not too remote, s6 of the 1977 UCTA renders any purported exclusion of ss13-15 void as against a consumer. The three requirements of 'dealing as a consumer' would have to be made out here - and Robinson Ltd would seem to be selling in the course of business, Mrs Smith was not buying in the course of business and the goods are probably those ordinarily supplied for private use. A void exclusion clause attracts penal consequences.

Alternatively, Mrs Smith could sue in tort although little would be gained by that step.

Mrs Jones' executor has exactly the same claim on the same basis and in a consumer contract, s2(1) of the 1977 Act ensures that any attempt to exclude liability for death or personal injury is *void*.

Question 2

Sandra ships from Buenos Aires 3,000 tons of corned beef aboard Oasis' ship the mv Sturmer, bound for Liverpool and Glasgow. Sandra receives from Oasis three bills of lading, each for an unspecified 1,000 tons. She contracts to sell 1,000 tons to Kelvin cif Liverpool and 1,000 tons each to Lynda and Miranda cif Glasgow. Sandra instructs Oasis to discharge 1,000 tons at Liverpool and 2,000 tons at Glasgow.

Sandra delivers one bill of lading to Kelvin's bank, under a letter of credit, in return for the bank's acceptance of a bill of exchange payable on 1 June. When Sandra presents the bill of exchange for payment on 1 June, the bank refuses to pay it. Sandra therefore instructs Oasis that the 1,000 tons to be discharged at Liverpool is not to be released to Kelvin but is to be held to Sandra's order. However, Kelvin agrees to resell the 1,000 tons for cash to Norma, to whom he delivers a bill of lading.

After the ship leaves Liverpool, Sandra delivers one bill of lading each to Lynda and Miranda on payment of cash. The following day the Sturmer collides with the ss Drongo and sinks. Ignorant of the collision, Lynda sells her part of the cargo to Miranda, to whom she endorses her bill of lading.

Advise the parties.

University of London LLB Examination
(for External Students) Commercial Law June 1991 Q7

Skeleton solution

- International sale contracts and Sale of Goods Act 1979.
- Unascertained goods.
- Passing of property; risk.
- CIF contracts.

- Bills of exchange; dishonour; duties of bank.
- Rights of the unpaid seller; insolvent buyers.
- Impossibility and frustration; SGA 1979 ss6 and 7.

Suggested solution

Where English law applies to a contract of international sale, then relevant legislation, in this case the Sale of Goods Act 1979 (SGA), will apply. We are not told in this instance whether English law does apply, but it seems very likely and the rubric on the examination paper confirms this, and we shall proceed on that assumption. While all the usual implied terms as to title, fitness and so on apply as provided for by ss12-15 SGA, these are not really at issue here. What is important is the question of the passing of title especially since the goods are unascertained, or would appear to be. There is nothing in the wording of the question to indicate that each separate 1,000 tons is in a separate hold of the ship or crated up separately. Indeed we are told in the second sentence that the bills of lading are each for an 'unspecified' 1,000 tons of corned beef.

The basic rule as to unascertained goods is laid down in s16 SGA which states: 'Where there is a contract for the sale of unascertained goods, no property in the goods will pass to the buyer unless and until the goods are ascertained.' Goods will be ascertained by their appropriation, or possibly by exhaustion. Also to be taken into account at this point is Rule 5 of s18 SGA which provides in part: 'where there is a contract for the sale of unascertained goods by description ... and goods are unconditionally appropriated ... either by the seller with the consent of the buyer, or the buyer with the assent of the seller, the property in the goods passes to the buyer ...'

Like all the rules of s18, Rule 5 is subject to any contrary intention evinced by the parties and this is important because cif contracts have their own rules as to the passing of property; title normally passes when the documents are handed over to the buyer. All the provisions in SGA 1979 as to the passing of property are subject to an overriding right of the parties to indicate that they wish property to pass at some point other than that provided for by statute; the provisions are guidelines only.

Property thus passes when the parties intend it to pass, and if no such clear intention can be found property passes according to the rules of s18 SGA 1979, the most important of which, Rule 5, has already been noted. Rule 5 mentions the point of 'appropriation' of the unascertained goods and because this is a series of cif contracts it is possible to say with some degree of certainty that appropriation occurs when the seller tenders the bill of lading for payment to the buyer or the buyer's agent (*Arnold Karlberg* v *Blythe* (1916)). There is no indication in the question that either Kelvin or Sandra had any other intention. A seller can indicate that he is reserving a right of sale by one of several methods (*Mitsui & Co* v *Flota Mercante* (1989)), but no such reservation of title would seem to apply in the contract as between Kelvin and Sandra. The prima facie presumption in a CIF sale is that when the seller tenders the appropriate documents, invoice, certificate of insurance and bill of lading to the buyer or buyer's agent this will be evidence of unconditional appropriation. If need be the bill of lading alone may be sufficient (see Carriage of Goods by Sea Act 1992) especially if supported by other circumstances. Clearly Kelvin's conduct in reselling the 1,000 tons to Norma indicates that he considers appropriation to have occurred.

The normal practice is that in cif contracts, a bank has a dual role when accepting documents: firstly it acts as agent for the buyer and secondly, it acts on its own account and is contractually liable to pay the seller on presentation of the correct documents. Acceptance of the bill of exchange will amount to payment, but the bank has refused to pay it. It is not clear whether this is on Kelvin's instructions, or because of some negligent act on the part of the bank. Certainly in issuing a bill of exchange in return for the bill of lading and then dishonouring it, it would appear that Sandra has not been paid. Moment of payment, and hence moment of appropriation, is the point at which the bill of exchange is honoured. It might be argued, assuming both the presentation date of the bill and its dishonouring on the instructions of Kelvin, that he is indicating his rejection of the goods. If, of course, the fault is entirely that of the bank Sandra will be able to obtain redress under s40 Bills of Exchange Act.

If Sandra's instruction to Oasis, on learning that the bill of exchange has been dishonoured, is taken as an indication that title has not yet passed and Sandra is reserving her property in the goods then problems arise as to Kelvin's purported resale to Norma. It is obviously an act incompatible with Sandra's rights as seller and indicates that Kelvin at least considers appropriation in the goods to have taken place and title in them to vest in him. He will be deemed to have accepted the goods under s35 SGA even if his dishonouring of the bill of exchange (assuming this to be Kelvin's act) means that no payment has been made.

The question of the passing of property will be of significance in assessing Sandra's rights and remedies. It is only after property has passed that the seller can maintain an action against the buyer for the purchase price of the goods. While the property remains in the seller, his action for the buyer's breach of contract can only lie in damages. This means that the seller must try to mitigate his loss by selling elsewhere, (if there is an available market). The measure of damages will be the difference between the contract price and the available market price, regardless of how much the seller has actually obtained on resale. If property has passed to the buyer however, the seller may argue that mitigation in the form of resale is no longer possible and may thus sue the buyer for the agreed price.

Apart from these rights, if the seller is unpaid he will be able to exercise the right of lien - stoppage in transit - even though property may have passed. The important thing here is to discover whether Sandra has retained physical possession, at least in a constructive form, in that the goods are still in the hands of the carrier. It would seem from Sandra's instructions to Oasis that she is effectively exercising this right of lien, (coupled with a right of resale, possibly - the carriers are told to await Sandra's instructions). This right of stoppage in transit would obviously, assuming the goods have not through some error been released to Kelvin, take priority over Kelvin's sale to Norma.

Because the price has fallen due and Sandra has not been paid Kelvin will, by virtue of s61(4) SGA 1979, be judged insolvent. Insolvency is not in itself repudiatary (*Ex parte Chalmers* (1873)), but obviously specific failure to pay as a deliberate act may be so.

To progress further, to the situation after the ship leaves Liverpool. Firstly we are told that Sandra delivers one bill of lading each to Lynda and Miranda on payment of cash. Under normal cif rules, and unless Sandra has in some way indicated her intention of reserving title, then property, and risk, will pass to the buyers.

The SGA makes some provision for impossibility and frustration, but in each case (ss6 and 7 respectively) the SGA applies only to specific goods. Since there are two separate orders of corned beef aboard the 'Sturmer', these goods are initially unascertained. In any event the sections will apply only before risk passes to the buyer. So, will the contract between Lynda and Miranda be for specific goods? We are told that Lynda sells her part of the corned beef to Miranda as against an endorsed bill of lading. When the two cargoes are joined together they become, presumably, ascertained by a process of exhaustion. In other words there is now only Miranda's corned beef on board the 'Sturmer' and presumably the goods are now ascertained or specific. But when does property pass? The basic rule according to s2(1) of the Carriage of Goods by Sea Act 1992 is that property passes on transfer of the bill, unless any contrary intention can be found. Transfer of the bill of lading is a symbolic delivery of the goods. Without further details of Lynda and Miranda's agreement it is difficult to be sure, but it would seem likely that delivery has been effected when the bill of lading is endorsed.

Section 6 SGA provides that, where there is a sale of specific goods and without the knowledge of the seller those goods have perished at the time the contract was made, then the contract is void. Section 7 provides that where there is an agreement to sell specific goods and subsequently the goods, without fault on the part of the buyer or seller, perish before the risk passes to the buyer, the contract is void. Self evidently therefore the exact sequence of events is important. We are told that Lynda is 'ignorant' of the collision - the clear implication being that the contract was made after the goods perished. This would bring Lynda and Miranda within s6, which deals with antecedent impossibility, rather then s7 which deals with subsequent impossibility.

So, to sum up, Sandra's redress may be against the bank, if there is negligence on its part, otherwise she must proceed against Kelvin. As already stated her exact rights will depend on exactly when property passed. Norma, Kelvin's purported customer, would similarly depend on this factor. By delivering a bill of lading as against cash, Norma would *appear* to have title to the goods. But two important qualifications must be borne in mind. Firstly property may never have passed to Kelvin himself and secondly whether or not this is so, as an unpaid seller Sandra has a lien and a right of stoppage in transit and ultimately a right of resale that will take priority. Norma may have to seek redress against Kelvin under ss51 and 53 SGA. Such steps might include suing for damages for non delivery of goods, or for breach of implied condition as to title (s12 SGA).

The contracts between Sandra and Lynda/Miranda seem to have been performed straightforwardly enough. Risk has passed to them as buyers. Since the subsequent contract between Lynda and Miranda is probably void, each must bear the loss of her individual cargo.

31 INTERNATIONAL SALE CONTRACTS

31.1 Introduction

International sales naturally involve the shipment of goods between countries. Over the years, international traders have evolved highly specific forms of contracts which reflect the fact that most of their business is transacted at great distance. The terminology, which is very specific, denotes the obligations which mercantile law implies into such contracts. Thus for example fob (meaning free on board) denotes that the seller places the goods on the agreed ship; the expense of getting them to the ship is the seller's - shipping at the expense of the buyer. Similarly 'ex ship' means that the seller must cause the goods to be taken from the ship by which they travelled and conveyed onward to the buyer, again at his expense.

Such descriptions as applied to contracts will also determine the point at which risk and property pass.

It is proposed in this chapter to deal primarily with fob and cif contracts since these are the most widely used but the list that follows gives some idea of other possible forms.

Fob free on board

Fas free alongside ship

For free on rail

Fot free on truck

Cif cost, insurance, freight

C & f cost and freight

In each case the description denotes the extent of the seller's liability and by implication the point at which property and hence risk pass to the buyer.

31.2 Key points

It is important that the student understands the following:

a) *Cif contracts*

The initials, as noted earlier, stand for cost, insurance, freight as these are the three main items of expenditure incurred by the seller in shipment of the goods. Therefore, if A purchases goods from B on cif terms, the price quoted by B will include all necessary expenditure involved in the shipment of those goods, ie the price of the goods themselves, the premium for insuring them in transit and the freight costs for their carriage by ship to their port of destination.

It should be noted that the terminology used by the parties should not be deemed conclusive. It is feasible for the parties to nominate a contract cif, but on examination of all the circumstances, for it to become apparent that this description is incorrect. Or the reverse may apply.

Property in the goods normally passes when the documents are handed over to the buyer and it was noted in chapter 30 (ante) how important the implied provisions of the Sale of Goods Act are in this context.

A cif contract normally provides for payment of cash in exchange for the documents, and the fact that the goods have not arrived when the documents state, does not normally excuse the buyer from making immediate payment. However, this in no way prejudices the buyer's right to reject the goods as defective once they do arrive.

For detailed information as to rights of rejection the student should consult a textbook, but it should be noted that rights of rejection under SGA 1979 have been briefly dealt with in chapter 1 of this WorkBook.

The seller's main duties can best be summarised as follows:

i) make out an invoice of goods sold;

ii) ship at the port of shipment goods answering the description in the contract;

iii) procure a contract for freighting the goods by ship to the destination referred to in the contract;

iv) arrange for insurance of the goods during shipment;

v) within a reasonable time send to the buyer the shipping documents concerned (ie invoice, bill of lading, policy of insurance etc).

However it should be noted that simply because the parties reallocate their risks the contract is not deprived of its cif description. The fundamental characteristics of a cif contract should remain unchanged, but it is quite possible for the parties to make minor changes in the sequence described above.

The obligations of buyer and seller in a cif contract are not only comprehensively described in many judicial decisions, but they may also be found in a document produced by the International Chamber of Commerce.

The terms listed in this document, are commonly referred to as Incoterms and they will apply if the parties expressly incorporate them into the contract, or use a standard form contract which, by trade usage is covered by the documents.

It is not proposed to quote the list of Incoterms; a student should already be familiar with them; but obviously they have the effect of ensuring uniformity and standardisation in cif contracts.

b) *Fob contracts*

As noted earlier the initials fob stand for free on board. The seller places the contract goods on the agreed vessel at the agreed port of shipment and all the costs of carriage are borne by the buyer. It is therefore not the seller who is the shipper, but the buyer, who receives the bill of lading directly through his agent.

This will obviously affect the passing of property and risk. Normally property in the goods passes to the buyer the moment the goods go on board. It is important to note, however that there are exceptions to this rule which are quite significant. For example, if the goods are loaded with a number of others of the same description, so that at point of loading they are unascertained; then property will only pass when something is done to render them ascertained in a deliverable state.

Since risk usually passes on shipment any damage occurring prior to shipment is the seller's responsibility. Once the goods are over the ship's rail the buyer assumes responsibility for any damage.

Note that some contracts are designated; 'fob - additional services'. Under such a contract the parties may re-allocate their obligations under the contract; in particular certain duties, normally those of the buyer, may be undertaken by the seller as the buyer's agent. It does not normally, however, make any difference to the passing of property in the goods.

Usually the fob seller's duties may be summarised as follows:

- make an invoice of goods sold;
- to ship at the port of shipment, goods of the description in the contract;
- to nominate a shipping date and notify buyer of that date;
- to tender to the buyer invoice and bill of lading.

Where the contract is fob - additional services and the seller acts as buyer's agent he will often undertake duties such as procuring appropriate insurance; but of course it will be at the buyer's expense.

Note that, as with cif contracts, the duties of the parties may be regulated by Incoterms.

For further details, both as to the working of cif and fob contracts and also as to the other specialised forms of contract listed in the introduction; the student should consult the appropriate textbook.

31.3 Analysis of questions

Questions on international sale contracts in University of London's past papers almost invariably couple together cif and fob contracts. The other, less usual variations such as fot or for have never yet formed the topic for a question, it does not of course follow that they never will!

Sometimes the topic will be linked with the question of financing; Q3 in the 1986 paper or Q6 in the 1989 paper (which is quoted in full in chapter 32, following) are good examples of this type of question. The first question quoted below is not an ideal question. It is so drafted as to be rather ambiguous and there is a marked lack of definite factual information so that a number of assumptions need to be made in answering it. But, apparently, the examiner intended it be a question on parties obligations in fob and cif contracts respectively and it would therefore seem to be a legitimate inclusion here. The second question deals with export trade and manufacturer's liabilities in a fairly straightforward way. Unusually the contract here is a c & f (cost and freight) rather than the more usual cif or fob. For other typical examples of questions on cif/fob contracts and aspects thereof, see Q7 of the 1992 paper and most recently, Q8 of 1993 (see chapter 36).

31.4 Questions

Question 1

Samuel ships 50,000 tons of oil from Texas to Southampton aboard the mv *Lenuf.*

He sells the 20,000 tons in No 1 Hold to Boomer fob US port, taking a bill of lading to his (Samuel's) own order, payment to be made by Boomer's bank cash against documents on arrival. After the vessel arrives, the bank pays on tender of the documents and the oil is pumped into Boomer's storage tanks. Boomer then discovers that the documents presented included a certificate and not a policy of insurance, that the total volume of oil in the hold and pumped into his tanks was only 18,000 tons, and that the oil is not of the quality agreed in the contract.

The master of the *Lenuf* also issues a bill of lading to Samuel for the 30,000 tons of oil stores in No 2 Hold. Samuel sells 25,000 tons of this to Cuthbert cif Southampton, payment to be under a letter of credit to be issued by Cuthbert's bank. The bank accepts a bill of exchange on Samuel's tender of documents which include a delivery order for the 25,000 tons. The remaining 5,000 tons are sold ex *Lenuf* to Dirk. Dirk informs Cuthbert that the oil he has bought is of inferior quality, so Cuthbert declines to take delivery of his 25,000 tons and instructs his bank not to pay Samuel.

University of London LLB Examination
(for External Students) Commercial Law June 1987 Q6

Skeleton solution

- Governed by English law.
- Fob - strict or 'additional services'?
- Obligations of parties under Fob contracts.
- Breach of s14(2) as to quality?

- Defects in bill of lading.
- Cif contracts.
- Duties of parties under cif, especially as to delivery and tender of documents.
- Ex ship contracts.

Suggested solution

a) *Boomer*

Boomer bought 20,000 tons of oil on fob terms. We are not told any details of the fob contract and, in particular, it is not known whether it was strict fob or fob and additional services. Since Samuel appears to have arranged for insurance, so it seems that it is probably a form of fob and additional services.

The goods sold were specific goods, being identified and agreed upon as the oil in Hold No 1 (s61(1) Sale of Goods Act (SGA) 1979). That there were only 18,000 tons there and not 20,000 is something which, prima facie, places Samuel in breach, because he described the specific goods as '20,000 tons'. This breach, accordingly, is of the condition implied by s13 of the Sale of Goods Act 1979.

There appears to have been a breach of the condition implied by s14(2) as well in that the oil was not of the quality agreed. This agreement could, of course, have made the requirement that the oil meet a particular quality an express condition of the contract, but it makes no difference to Boomer's position whether the failure to match that quality is seen as breach of an express or implied condition.

Boomer had the right to inspect the oil on arrival in order to see whether it matched the required description and quality (s34 SGA 1979). There appears to be little difficulty, on the limited facts given, in finding that Boomer may still reject the oil. Provided the bill of lading has been made over to Boomer, property has passed to him - it passed when the bill of lading was indorsed. But if he rejects the goods then he must also reject the bill of lading and on doing this property will revest in Samuel. The acceptance of the bill of lading by the bank will not estop Boomer from rejecting it when it is discovered that it does not properly state the quantity of goods, because its acceptance was not with knowledge of the deficiency.

It is the buyer's duty to arrange marine insurance of goods sold on fob terms, and if the seller takes out insurance he does so as agent of the buyer (*NV Handel My J Smits Import-Export* v *English Exporters Ltd* (1957)). We are not told whether the method of payment here required Samuel to present an insurance policy. It is unlikely that it did because there was no documentary credit as such, but merely payment against documents. Provided he took out insurance which in fact covered Boomer's marine risk then Samuel will not be in breach by tendering only a certificate of insurance.

Boomer may, in the alternative, choose to take action against the ship owner, whoever he may be. Whether such an action is open depends upon facts which are not given, but it would be open if the shipowner falsely represented on the bill of lading that there were 20,000 tons in Hold No 1, or if he falsely represented anything about the quality of the oil (s4 Carriage of Goods by Sea Act 1992). It is unlikely that he would have said anything about this second matter, but likely that the bill would have named the quantity.

b) *Cuthbert*

Cuthbert has bought a quantity of unascertained goods on cif terms to be paid for by documentary credit. The bank paid against a delivery order rather than the bill of lading which would normally be required. Whether this was a good tender by Samuel depends upon the terms of the credit, about which there is no information. It may be that because the sale is of a part of a bulk quantity so it can be inferred that a delivery order would be good tender under the cif contract, but this would have to be a delivery order issued by the ship otherwise Cuthbert would have no contractual right to demand delivery from the ship (*Comptoir d'Achat et de Vente du Borrenbond Belges SA* v *Luis du Ridder Lda, The Julia* (1949)). It cannot be said with any certainty whether the delivery order was a ship's delivery order or was a document emanating from Samuel himself.

On the assumption that the delivery order was not a valid document under the contract of sale it is highly unlikely to have been valid under the documentary credit either. The normal practice is that the bank has a dual role when accepting cif documents, firstly it acts as the agent of the buyer for the purpose of the cif contract and secondly it acts on its own account and is contractually liable to pay the seller on presentation of the correct documents. The acceptance of the bill of exchange by the bank amounted to payment under the credit. But it did not amount to acceptance of the cif documents by Cuthbert, because the bank acted outside its authority in accepting documents which did not comply with the cif contract and Samuel had notice of this want of authority.

Samuel's position, therefore, is that he has received payment from the bank but has not had the documents accepted by Cuthbert. Therefore Cuthbert is still entitled to reject the documents, provided he has not accepted them either expressly or by delaying in rejecting (*Biddell Bros* v *E Clemens Horst Co* (1912)). It appears that there may have been acquiescence here because Cuthbert has refused to accept the goods and they would only have been physically delivered after the documents had been accepted by the bank. If there has indeed been physical delivery of the oil to the port of destination (Southampton) and if Dirk was correct in saying that the oil was of poor quality then Cuthbert would be entitled to reject it for breach of the implied condition of merchantable quality. An attempted rejection prior to arrival would not be effective because the right to reject only crystallises on arrival (*Gill & Duffus SA* v *Berger & Co Inc* (1984)).

c) *Dirk*

Dirk's position can be stated quite simply, although we are not told whether he has received delivery of the oil or whether his stated complaint about quality is justified. A sale ex ship requires the seller to deliver the goods from the ship on arrival directly to the buyer who is the obliged to pay unless he can find a breach of condition in which case he may reject, like any other buyer who finds goods to be a breach of condition (*Yangtsze Insurance Association* v *Lukmanjee* (1918)). On the assumption that Dirk is right about the poor quality of the oil he would be entitled to reject the oil tendered and would not have to pay.

Question 2

Selim contracts to sell the following goods:

a) To Barbara, 500 tons Western White Wheat c & f Liverpool; the wheat is shipped from New York on 1 June; on 5 June, the carrying vessel sinks; on 6 June, Selim tenders the shipping documents to Barbara.

b) To Betty, 1,000 gallons Australian perfume ex ship *Mangel* at Liverpool; Betty fails to pay Selim for a previous cargo (of cork hats, which she has been unable to resell), so Selim orders the master of the *Mangel* to deliver the perfume to Thurstan, a friend of Selim's to whom Selim wishes to make a present of the perfume.

c) To Billy, 60 chainsaws. Billy contracts to resell them to Tom, and instructs Selim to deliver them to Tom. Six weeks after delivery of the chainsaws, two of Tom's customers complain to Tom that they have been injured because of defects in the chainsaws. Tom recalls all the chainsaws which he has sold, reimburses his customers for their losses and returns the whole consignment to Billy, from whom he claims repayment.

Advise Barbara, Betty and Billy.

University of London LLB Examination
(for External Students) Commercial Law June 1990 Q6

Skeleton solution

a) Definition of c & f, effects thereof, documents of title in relation thereto, frustration of contract by natural disaster.

b) Ex ship contracts - definitions thereof, implications of such contract, rights and duties of parties to c & f contract.

c) Defects in products. Consumer Protection Act - SGA 1979 s14(2) and (3).

Suggested solution

a) In this contract we are told that the wheat has been shipped from New York on 1st June and that four days later the ship sinks; two days subsequent to the sinking the seller (Selim) tenders the shipping documents to the buyer (Barbara). The contract has been made 'c & f'. This stands for 'cost and freight'; the basis of the agreement is that the seller has to arrange the carriage of the goods to the named foreign port of destination at his (ie the seller's) expense but not at his risk (which latter ceases when he places the goods on board ship at the place of shipment). In one aspect the 'c & f' contract differs from the Cif contract (namely the seller does not have to arrange marine insurance, but if he does then this must be paid for at his expense) in all other respects it is the same.

The essential element that is missing then in the contract between 'B' and 'S' is that of insurance, normally the proper division of responsibilities is resolved by Cif contracts (here the (i) stands for insurance). Sometimes a 'c & f' contract will contain words such as 'insurance to be effected by the buyer' and it has been held that these words are not merely declaratory but amount to a contractual obligation on the part of the buyer to take out the usual insurance policy (see *Reinhart Co* v *Joshua Hoyle & Sons Ltd* (1961)). So we are presented with a situation where the goods are placed on the ship and ostensibly where the seller has discharged his responsibilities. In the absence of express agreement to the matter of insurance it must be decided who bears the loss of the wheat and also whether or not the seller is lawfully entitled to tender documents of title after the loss of the goods in ocean transit and thus claim the purchase price of the goods.

It has been held that even though goods are lost in a cif contract the seller still has the lawful right to tender the documents of title and to claim the purchase price - even in one case where the seller 'knew' the goods were lost when he offered the documents (*Manbre Saccharine* v *Corn Products Co* (1919)). As already stated, the same principles apply in cif and c & f contracts and thus the tender of documents to claim the price is lawful. The buyer's usual remedy is a claim against the carrier either on the basis of the latter's negligence or because the buyer is an assignee of the bill of lading. There is one (albeit small) possibility of a claim by 'B' against 'S' here and that is that if, contrary to the terms of s32(3) of Sale of Goods Act 1979 the seller has failed to give adequate notice of the shipment of the goods to enable the buyer sufficient time to insure the goods, then the goods would travel, exceptionally at the seller's and not the buyer's risk - but this does not appear to be the case as Barbara's claim will be against the carriers.

b) This contract is expressed to be 'ex-ship' Mangel and is for 1,000 gallons of perfume. There appears to be some dispute about a previous contract for shipment by Selim to Betty of cork mats, and in respect of these Selim appears to be an 'unpaid seller'; Betty's excuse for not paying being related directly to her inability to resell goods delivered to her under a contract of sale.

The Judicial Committee of the Privy Council examined and defined the meaning of an 'ex-ship' contract as denoting 'that the seller has to cause delivery to be made to the buyer from a ship which has arrived at the port of delivery and has reached a place in which is usual for the delivery of goods of the kind in question.'

The clause is also contained and defined in the Incoterms that regulate such international shipping contracts. The nature of the obligations under the term 'ex ship' are that the seller has to pay the freight and the buyer is only bound to pay the purchase price if actual delivery of the goods is made at the stipulated port of delivery' thus if for example, the goods are lost in transit the buyer is not obliged to pay the price upon tender of the documents and can in certain cases claim the price he paid in advance.

Thus the property in the goods will only pass (unless otherwise agreed) when the goods are handed over to the buyer after arrival of the ship at the agreed port of destination.

The seller herein appears to have exercised his right of 'stoppage in transit in accordance with s45 Sale of Goods Act 1979'; under this section three conditions must be present before the right to stop in transit arises. Namely

1) The goods must be in transit and the goods are in transit when they have passed out of possession of the seller into possession of an independent carrier.
2) The seller must be an unpaid seller.
3) The buyer must be insolvent.

All three of these conditions appear to have been satisfied in particular the third one as under s61(4) SGA 1979 a person is 'deemed to be insolvent with the meaning of the Act if he has either ceased to pay his debts in the ordinary course of business or he cannot pay his debts as they become due ...'. The goods are in transit according to section 45(1) 'goods are deemed to be in transit from the time when they are delivered to a carrier ... for the purpose of transmission to the buyer ... until the buyer or his agent in that behalf, takes delivery of them from the carrier.

As delivery has not taken place this appears to be the valid exercise of the remedy of stoppage in transit by Selim which Betty will have no defence against.

c) Selim has contracted to sell 60 chainsaws to Billy who in turn has re-sold them to Tom; it appears that the goods have not been delivered to Billy who has instructed Selim to act on his behalf and deliver them on to Tom. When, six weeks later Tom's customers are injured by defects in the saws, Tom takes the prudent step of re-calling them and he also reimburses his customers and returns the goods to Billy from whom he bought them. We are concerned therefore with the duties of the seller and the retailer and possibly also the manufacturer (we do not know if Selim has manufactured the goods).

There are statutory duties imposed upon sellers under s14(2) and (3) Sale of Goods 1979 which are 'inalienable'; the seller is liable in this respect for 'merchantable quality' and 'fitness for purpose' without proof of lack of care on his part, in other words liability is strict. A common law expedient available to a seller who receives defective goods from a manufacturer and sells them on to the buyer is that of breach of implied warranty. If the buyer sues the seller fro breach of warranty of fitness for purpose then the seller may sue his manufacturer and in turn claim an indemnity (eg *Dodd* v *Wilson* (1946)).

Product liability is now covered by the Consumer Protection Act 1987 and the basic principles of protection for consumers are contained therein. These are that any person who suffers damage which is caused by a defective product, is entitled to sue the producer without being required to prove fault. Section 5(1) of the CPA defines damage as 'death or personal injury or any loss of damage to any property (including land)'.

It appears therefore, that Tom can return the goods to Bill and claim damages under SGA 1979 s14(2) and (3). Additionally, the two injured customers can claim against the manufacturer under CPA 1987 if they can prove their injuries resulted from the defects in the product. Billy will be entitled to recover the price paid for the products from the manufacturer and damages for loss of profit.

32 BILLS OF LADING

32.1 Introduction

A statutory definition of a bill of lading may be found in s1(4) of Factors Act 1889 which states:

'The expression document of title shall include any bill of lading, a dock warrant, warehouse keepers certificate and warrant or order for the delivery of the goods and any other documents used in the ordinary course of business as proof of possession or control of goods ...'

A bill of lading may be of several different types: it may be in complete form, containing all the clauses, or an abbreviated version - a 'short form bill' - containing only the more important clauses.

It may be a 'containerised bill' where the shipped goods are packed in containers or a 'combined transport bill' where the shipment requires not only carriage of the goods on board ship, but other modes of transport as well. 'Received for shipment' bills indicate that the goods have been received by the carrier and held under his control whereas a 'shipped' bill indicates that the goods have actually been placed on board ship.

Obviously, to some extent these classifications overlap. The law relating to bills of lading is contained in common law and also statute, especially the Carriage of Goods by Sea Act 1992.

32.2 Key points

It is important that the student understands the following:

a) *Common law*

At common law a bill of lading has three distinct functions:

i) document of title;

ii) receipt for the goods;

iii) evidence of contract of carriage between shipper and carrier.

In the first case the fact that a bill of lading is a document of title entitles the person in possession of it to take possession of the goods from the carrier. Transfer of a bill of lading therefore amounts to a symbolic delivery of the goods.

The mode of transfer depends on the way in which the consignee was designated: whether the bill was an 'order' bill or a 'bearer' bill.

The bill of lading will not only serve as a receipt to show that shipment has occurred, it will also contain a statement on the condition of the goods at time of shipment. If the bill of lading says the goods are in apparent good order then this is a 'clean' bill; if the carrier has any reservations then the bill would be 'claused'.

The third function of a bill of lading - to act as evidence of contract of carriage between shipper and carrier is largely self evident. (See the recent case of *Ngo Chew Hong* v *Scindia* (1988) for further comments as to a bill of lading's status as evidence of contractual dealings between the parties.)

b) *Statutes: the Bills of Lading Act 1855 and Carriage of Goods by Sea Act 1992*

The Bills of Lading Act 1855 was originally passed to remedy a defect in the law whereby the buyer in an international sales contract would be unable to sue the carrier for loss or damage to the goods. Because of the doctrine of privity of contract, the buyer had no contract with the carrier, only with the seller of the goods. By virtue of the Act, regardless of the doctrine of privity the buyer had, provided the requirements of the Act were met, a right to sue the carrier/shipper in respect of breach of contract. One major shortcoming of the Act was in contracts where goods were carried in bulk. Although initially it was intended to reform the Act only in this respect, it became apparent that major changes were necessary and in 1992 the Carriage of Goods by Sea Act repealed the Bills of Lading Act 1855 and replaced it. The COGSA is a wider reaching act than its predecessor, covering not only bills of lading but also sea waybills and other similar documents. Much of the law remains the same: to that extent the COGSA is a consolidating act, but one major change is of great importance. The COGSA divorces rights of suit from passing of property. This has the practical effect that pledgees and others such as banks, who take a bill of lading by way of security, will be able to sue on the contract; no longer will such parties have to rely on the fiction of an 'implied contract'. However, it should be noted that the provision (under s1 of the 1855 Act) that once the Act had operated in favour of a consignee/indorsee of a bill of lading, the original shipper was no longer entitled to sue on the bill of lading remains unchanged (s2(5) COGSA) insofar as it relates to bills of lading. However, if a sea waybill is involved the shipper's rights remain operative (s2(5) COGSA).

c) *Indemnities*

At common law it is perfectly possible for a carrier to insert into a bill of lading, a clause relieving him or even exempting him completely from liability for statements made in the bill. Provided such an exemption clause covers the statement in question, it may serve as evidence that any damage was not caused by the carrier but occurred before shipment. Indemnity clauses are not linked only to physical defects, but may be used to indicate a carrier's reservations about, for example, the buyer's rights to possession.

Whether or not the courts will apply such indemnity clauses depends largely on the circumstances of each case.

d) *Contract of carriage*

The shipper/seller and the carrier are quite free to negotiate any terms they wish as to shipment of the goods. The bill of lading is not the entire contract of carriage because the terms of the agreement are not to be found only in the bill; they may for example have been agreed orally beforehand, or be implied by trade usage. However the bill is useful evidence as to the existence of the terms of the contract of carriage negotiated by the parties.

Under common law there is an implied rule that if the bill conflict with any prior agreement, the bill will be superceded by any clear rights, agreements or obligations expressly negotiated by the parties.

Problems may arise, however, when the bill is transferred to a third party with no knowledge of the terms of any agreement between shipper and carrier. The basic rule is straightforward enough, the bill of lading becomes, so far as the third party is concerned, the sole contract of carriage. However, in some cases the bill of lading may refer to the agreement between shipper and carrier and specifically states that this will apply to any third party transferee of the bill.

Space precludes dealing with problems of incorporation of such agreements at this point, but the student should read further on the matter; indeed on bills of lading generally, along with associated case law.

32.3 Analysis of questions

Bills of lading as such, have never, on their own formed the subject matter of a question.

It is more usual to see them in a general problem, usually concerning cif and/or fob contracts; and since they normally form only a minimal part of the answer they do not need to be treated in very great detail.

It has already been noted that the topic cropped up (very briefly) in Q6 of the 1987 paper (see chapter 31).

The question quoted below is another of the same type, concerning a number of issues in the export sales field. There is, perhaps, fractionally more required on the topic of bills of lading.

32.4 Question

Steven agrees to sell to Tinks 100 boxes containing 50 copies each of the book *Seditious Voices* to be shipped on or before 1 May 1989, c.i.f. Basra, payment to be by letter of credit 'on tender of documents to Barcoutts Bank'. Steven then contracts to obtain an import licence for Tinks. The books are put on board m.v. *Rushmoor* on 30

April but a fire breaks out of the vessel on the following day and some of the boxes containing the books are wetted while the fire is being extinguished. The boxes are therefore unloaded and the books repacked in 50 boxes, each containing 100 books. They are reloaded on 2 May. The master of the *Rushmoor* signs a bill of lading for '50 x 100 *Seditious Voices* shipped by 1 May 1989'.

Tinks sends a copy of the sale contract to Barcoutts, instructing it to pay on tender of the correct documents. Tinks then hears of the events connected with the fire and telephones Barcoutts to ensure that the bill of lading is for 100 boxes of 50 books each, since boxes of 50 books each are more easily sold to sub-buyers. When Steven presents the documents, Barcoutts therefore rejects them. Steven takes the bill of lading back to the owner of the *Rushmoor*, who agrees to have the books repacked on the voyage and issues a fresh bill of lading for 100 boxes of 50 books each, which Steven then presents to Barcoutts. However, Tinks has heard that Steven has been unable to obtain an import licence, so instructs Barcoutts not to pay under the credit.

Advise the parties.

University of London LLB Examination
(for External Students) Commercial Law June 1989 Q6

Skeleton solution

- Cif contracts - rights + duties of parties.
- Application of SGA 1979 to cif.
- Bills of lading - accuracy - right to reject documents.
- Terms of contract - innominate terms - breach.
- Right to reject goods.

Suggested solution

Steven has sold the books to Tinks on a cif basis. This means that the obligation of shipping the good and all the costs involved in their shipment, will be borne by the seller, this expenditure being included in the amount paid by the buyer. Cif means Cost, Insurance and Freight. These are the main items of expenditure met by the seller. Cif contracts are essentially contracts for the sale of goods, so the Sale of Goods Act 1979 (SGA) will apply to the transaction.

Under s17 SGA, property in specific or unascertained goods passes when the parties intend it to pass. If no such intention can be discovered, property passes according to the Rules in s18 of the Act. By s20, whoever has property in the goods also bears the risk of those goods being accidentally damaged or destroyed. A cif contract, however, is a contract for the sale of documents and property in the goods represented in the documents will pass when the seller tenders the bill of lading to the buyer or to the buyer's agent, in this case, Barcoutts Bank (*Arnold Karlberg* v *Blythe* (1916)). When the fire breaks out on the m.v. Rushmoor, therefore, the goods are still at the risk of the seller, Steven.

The fire and its consequences, however, appear not to have harmed the books. The problem arises in relation to the way in which the books are packed. The contract requires them to be delivered in 100 boxes of 50 books each. After the fire, they are re-packed in 50 boxes, each containing 100 books. The way in which the goods are packed could be argued to be outside the scope of s13 SGA in that they are not necessary to identify the nature of the goods (*Ashington Piggeries* v *Christopher Hill* (1972)), nor do they state or identify an essential part of the description of the goods (*Reardon Smith* v *Hansen-Tangen* (1976)). The way in which the books are packed, however, is an express term of the contract which the seller has broken. If the buyer had stressed the importance of this term when the negotiations for the contract were being undertaken, it will be a condition. If, however, it is not possible to categorise the term in this way, it will be treated as an innominate term and the court will 'wait and see' the effects of its breach. On the facts of the problem it would appear that the effects could be serious for the buyer. In either case, therefore, if the books are delivered incorrectly packed it would appear that Tinks could reject them for breach of the express term.

The date on which the goods are to be shipped under a cif contract is part of the description and therefore falls within s13 SGA. It is therefore an implied condition that the goods will be shipped by the agreed date and if they are not, the buyer will be entitled to treat the contract as repudiated and claim damages for any loss suffered as a consequence. By shipping the books after the date required by the contract, Steven is in breach of an implied condition.

Tinks, the buyer, has two rights of rejection. He may reject the documents or he may reject the goods. The documents tendered to Barcoutts do not comply with the contract. This is breach of the doctrine of strict compliance as stated in *Equitable Trust Co of New York* v *Dawson Partners* (1926). Barcoutts, therefore, is entitled to reject the documents in the form in which they were originally submitted. When the document is re-written to comply with the contract, Barcoutts, as Tink's agent, may accept it. There is no duty to do so. See also *Proctor & Gamble Philippine Manufacturing Co* v *Kurt A Becher GmbH* (1988) for details as to misdated bills of lading.

If Barcoutts does accept the new documents Tinks may have a further remedy if the wrong date of shipment is still shown. If, when the goods arrive, it is clear that the date must have been inaccurate, Tinks can sue Steven for loss of the right to reject the documents (*Kwei Tek Chao* v *British Traders* (1954)). The measure of damages will be the loss arising directly and naturally from the breach, s51 SGA. If there is an available market for the books, the measure of damages will prima facie be the difference between the contract price and the market price of the goods at the time of delivery. In *Sharpe* v *Nosawa* (1917) it was held that in a cif contract, the time of delivery is the time of tender of the documents. Tinks will also be able to claim damages on this basis if Barcoutts accepts the revised bill of lading but, when the books arrive, it is discovered that they have not been repacked as required under the contract. Tinks has the right to examine the goods on arrival (s34 SGA).

Steven is also in breach of his undertaking to obtain an import licence for Tinks. From the wording of the question, it appears that this promise is not part of the original contract of sale. Under a cif contract, the seller's obligation is to help the buyer obtain such a licence. If Stevens has not helped, then he will be in breach of the original contract. If there is no breach of the contract for the sale of the books, Tinks will have to pay for them and bring a separate action against Steven for breach of the separate contract to obtain an import licence.

If the promise to obtain an import licence is part of the contract, then this imposes an absolute duty on Steven. His failure to obtain such a licence, therefore, will constitute a breach of the main contract and Tinks could treat the contract as repudiated.

33 METHODS OF FINANCING: BILLS OF EXCHANGE

33.1 Introduction

A bill of exchange is defined in s3(1) of Bills of Exchange Act 1882 as follows: 'A bill of exchange is an unconditional order, in writing, addressed by one person, to another, signed by the person giving it, requiring the person to whom it is addressed to pay, on demand, or at a fixed or determinable future time; a sum, certain in money, or to the order of a specified person, or to bearer.'

Any instrument which does not in detail comply with these conditions is not a valid bill of exchange. On reading through s3(1) most of the terminology is self explicit and it is not proposed to go into further detail in this chapter.

Needless to say, the student should ensure that he understands each part of the definition and is aware of relevant case law.

Most of the law on the subject is incorporated in the Bills of Exchange Act.

33.2 Key points

It is important that the student understands the following.

a) *Holders of the bill*

According to s2 BEA a holder is a payee, bearer or indorsee in possession of a bill. While it is easy to decide that someone is in possession of a bill it is less easy to define the *capacity* in which they hold the bill.

There are three main categories:

i) holder in due course;

ii) holder for value; and

iii) mere holder.

While it is not proposed to examine these categories in detail (suffice to say the student should already have done so!) it is important to point out that the category into which the holder falls will directly affect his rights to payment and will decide whether or not any defences can be raised against payment being made.

b) *Negotiation*

Bills fall into two main categories: order bills and bearer bills. The way in which the payee is designated will determine whether or not the bill is negotiable.

Section 8(1) states: 'When a bill contains words prohibiting transfer or indicating an intention that it should not be transferable ... it is not negotiable.'

If it is negotiable, the bill may be transferred by the holder to a transferee; the most common method being by negotiation and/or delivery.

For more details, especially as to forms of indorsement the student should refer to the appropriate text.

c) *Dishonour*

When a bill is duly presented for acceptance or payment it may be dishonoured, either by non-acceptance or non-payment. The law of the place where the bill is dishonoured will be the relevant one (see *G & H Montage* v *Irvani* (1989)).

Where any bill is dishonoured s48 BEA provides that notice of dishonour should be supplied to the drawer and to each indorser; within a reasonable time.

Where a bill has been dishonoured the holder of the bill has two choices. He can have recourse against prior parties and the drawer, the measure of damages being as prescribed in s57 or he can proceed to summary jurisdiction in which case the amount of damages will be the same.

33.3 Analysis of questions

There has, to date, been *no* question in past papers from University of London on this topic.

The question quoted below is a suggestion of the sort of approach an examiner might take were a question on bills of exchange to appear at some future date. It will be noted however that there is probably insufficient material to support a whole question.

33.4 Question

Once a bill of exchange has been drawn up, discuss the circumstances in which presentment for acceptance must be made.

Written by Editor

Skeleton solution

- Bills of exchange normally presented for acceptance/payment together.
- Section 39 BEA, certain types need to be presented for acceptance separately.
- Mode of presentation.
- Failure to comply with BEA.

Suggested solution

At some time after the bill has been drawn up, it will be sent to the drawee for acceptance. With the exception of certain limited situations as listed below, which require a bill to be presented for acceptance in advance of payment, most bills are not presented for acceptance until time for it to be presented for payment.

Acceptance and payment may thus take place virtually simultaneously.

The drawee will signify his acceptance of the bill by writing on and/or signing the bill.

A bill which must be presented for acceptance will be either one payable a certain number of days after sight, or at a place which is not the drawee's ordinary place of business. See the Bills of Exchange Act 1882, s39(1): 'Where a bill is payable after sight, presentment is necessary in order to fix the maturity of the instrument' and s39(2); 'Where a bill expressly stipulates that it shall be presented for acceptance, or where it is drawn payable elsewhere than at the residence or place of business of the drawee, it must be presented for acceptance, before it can be presented for payment.'

Where a holder is in possession of a bill which must be presented for acceptance separately and in advance of payment and does not comply with s39 by obtaining acceptance, the drawer and prior parties will be discharged as to their duties as to the holder if the bill is subsequently dishonoured (s40(2) BEA).

A holder of such a bill must present it within a reasonable time s40(1) and what is reasonable will depend on trade usage s40(3) BEA.

The rules as to presentment for acceptance are to be found in s41(1) and provided the holder has acted in accordance with those rules then if the bill is not accepted, the holder is entitled to treat the bill as dishonoured s42(1) BEA.

It is sometimes found that the drawee will accept, but impose conditions. Should the holder agree to such a 'qualified acceptance' he effectively agrees to vary the effect of the bill as originally drawn. He will to all intents and purposes be waiving his rights to treat the bill as dishonoured. The holder of a bill, provided he complies with the requirements of the Act in presentment is entitled to a 'general acceptance' ie unqualified by any conditions or reservations.

In the event that the drawee dishonours the bill, either by failing to accept it, or offering only conditional acceptance, the holder has immediate rights and need not wait until the bill is subsequently dishonoured by non-payment (s43(2) BEA).

It is important to note however that in order to secure such rights s48 of the Act requires the holder of a bill which has not been accepted to give notice of dishonour by non-acceptance to the drawer and prior parties. Failure to do this will discharge them from liability and lose the holder his rights under s43(2).

34 METHODS OF FINANCING: DOCUMENTARY CREDITS

34.1 Introduction

The documentary credit system is intended to give both buyer and seller a degree of protection which they would not otherwise have, given the fact that they will usually be separated by great distances; and since they are in different countries different currencies would apply.

The seller will primarily want to be sure that, having shipped the goods, he is paid for them. The buyer will want to ensure that, if he pays, the seller will comply with his requirements (because of transit problems it may be some time before he can actually check the goods for himself).

The buyer will open a credit facility, usually through a bank in his own country in favour of the seller. This offers the seller an assurance that payment will be made, provided the seller can in return prove that he has performed his side of the contract.

Payment under the credit facility will not, however be made, unless and until, the necessary documentation (evidencing contractual performance by the seller) has been presented to the bank. Often this is done by the seller instructing his own bank to act as his agent and present the documentation to the buyer's bank.

The sort of documents likely to be involved will vary; the buyer himself may if he wishes dictate documentation requirements, but the list is likely to include a combination of any or all of these: bill of lading, invoice, insurance policy, and/or bill of exchange.

34.2 Key points

It is important that the student understands the following.

a) *Uniform Customs and Practice (UCP)*

   The Uniform Customs and Practice for documentary credits is a set of rules issued by the International Chamber of Commerce and intended to regulate the operation of the system of documentary credits.

It should be noted that, under English law the use of UCP is not mandatory and will only apply where expressly incorporated into the credit arrangements by the parties. The student should familiarise himself with the subjects covered by UCP rules.

b) *The parties*

The rules here are long and complex and space precludes their being dealt with in anything but the simplest manner.

Briefly the parties may be listed as:

i) The applicant for credit - usually the buyer by whom the contract price is owed.

ii) The issuing bank - the buyer's own bank opens credit, probably having received some form of collateral from the buyer.

When the credit facility is open it will notify the seller, along with instructions as to how the seller must act to obtain payment.

iii) The correspondent bank - usually the seller's bank.

May act in an advisory or confirmatory capacity and its powers will vary accordingly.

In particular if selected as issuing bank to act as a correspondent confirmer bank its function will include that of actually making payment against the correct documents.

iv) The beneficiary - the seller.

Provided he presents the proper documents he will be entitled to payment regardless of any disputes that have arisen over the contract of sale.

c) *Varieties of credit*

Again the student should ensure that he reads further on the subject. In particular the following varieties of credit should be familiar ground to him:

i) back to back credit;

ii) packing credit;

iii) revolving credit;

iv) negotiation credits; and

v) transferable credits.

In many cases the name of the type of credit is indicative of the way it operates.

It should be noted that credits as such are non-assignable although the beneficiary may assign the proceeds of the credit provided the assignment is made according to the provisions of s136 of Law of Property Act 1925.

d) *The mandate*

The instructions given by the buyer or applicant for credit to his bank comprise the buyer's mandate.

The mandate must be clear and precise stating those documents against which the bank is to make payment to the seller or beneficiary (and sometimes listing those documents which if tendered will be unacceptable).

Where the mandate is ambiguous the common law allows the bank to interpret in the light of what is 'reasonable'.

Or, alternatively they may simply refer back to the buyer for further instruction. If, however, the bank proceed and pay, despite the ambiguity they will lose their right to be paid by the buyer if they have exceeded their mandate.

e) *Types of credit*

Credits may be either revocable/irrevocable and in the absence of any contrary indication the credit will be assumed to be revocable. The terminology is largely self explanatory because revocable credit can be amended or cancelled at any time, it obviously offers far less protection to the seller.

f) *Taking up the seller's documents*

The most likely documents to be required by the buyer to be presented by the seller have already been noted.

When the seller tenders those documents required, to the bank, it must examine all documents with reasonable care to ascertain, inter alia, that they are correct, consistent and the content is as required. The bank's liability is to take 'reasonable' care, they need not, for example, investigate a document's background if it is apparently in order and if a document appears to be the original (so marked) they need not set up tests to detect forgery. Obviously, however if the bank have any grounds for suspicion they must probe more deeply.

However, should a bank delay unnecessarily, it may be liable, at the very least to pay interest and any additional costs incurred by the delay: see *Co-operative Centrale Raifferson* v *Sumitomo Bank* (1988). Also, when the documents are correct and the bank refuse to pay or delays payment, it may find itself liable to the seller. If there is some deviation from the buyer's instructions, for example different documents presented, the rule of strict compliance operates. All terms of credit are construed strictly against the beneficiary.

Thus any deviation by the seller from the buyer's mandate, no matter how minor, may result in his losing the right to be paid.

34.3 Analysis of questions

Questions as to documentary credits have cropped up several times in University of London's past papers and are usually fairly straightforward.

There are at least two questions which link the topic with sale of goods in the context of export sales. Look for example at Q3 on the 1986 paper and Q6 in 1988 which are, all in all, really quite similar.

The first question quoted below is unusual, because it is the only one which is not in problem form, but instead is in the form of a straightforward essay question. The second question is extremely wide and covers aspects of all of Part 4.

34.4 Questions

Question 1

Give a general account of the *legal* position where an international sale governed by English law is financed by a banker's irrevocable and confirmed documentary credit.

University of London LLB Examination
(for External Students) Commercial Law June 1983 Q1

Skeleton solution

- Parties to contract, obligations.
- Revocable/irrevocable credits.
- Additional security for seller provided by irrevocable credit.
- Buyers mandate.
- Doctrine of strict compliance.
- UCP rules.

Suggested solution

The legal position where an overseas sale is financed by an irrevocable and confirmed documentary credit reflects the fact that the system is designed to provide security for either party which the actual contract of sale itself can never do and to raise credit - a problem which arises primarily because no seller or buyer will wish to commit working capital to goods in transit. Essentially, a third party (in the form of two banks issuing corresponding banks) agrees to be the drawee of the seller's draft and promises to honour it provided that the seller discharges his duties under the contract of sale. It is important to note that the legal position under the documentary credit system and the seller's right to claim payment thereunder is not subject to the seller performing all his duties under the contract of sale.

Firstly, from the point of view of the seller his legal rights conferred by the confirmed and irrevocable credit presents him with the most acceptable way of financing the sale. Provided the documents are tendered in conformity by the seller, the corresponding bank guarantees that it will pay against them, and it cannot withdraw that guarantee, even if the buyer subsequently instructs that that be done. The credit is irrevocable. Whether a documentary credit is confirmed or unconfirmed depends upon the role assumed by the correspondent bank. The correspondent bank may only act to notify the seller about the opening of the credit by the issuing bank and if that is the position, then the credit is unconfirmed although it may be irrevocable on the part of the issuing banker. In that case the correspondent bank is essentially an agent.

However, often the seller will seek to bind the correspondent bank with an irrevocable guarantee and in that case the correspondent adds his own guarantee to that of the issuing banker and the credit is confirmed. Each bank's undertaking is as principal, although the issuing bank's role is analogous to that of a commission agent, authorised to conclude a contract with the seller but on his own account. In practice a correspondent bank will never confirm a revocable credit.

Seller/buyer:

Legal consequences ensuing from the credit begin when buyer and seller agree to insert into the contract of sale a documentary credit clause. The buyer is then under an obligation to have a documentary credit opened in favour of the seller. It is a condition precedent to the seller's duty to deliver the goods, but need not necessarily be such for *all* the seller's obligations under the contract - for the seller may be under a duty to perform some act prior to the buyer's duty to furnish the credit. If the documentary credit clause stipulates an irrevocable confirmed documentary credit then that is what the buyer must provide. If no stipulation is made then it has been suggested that the contract of sale is incomplete *Schijveschuurder and Others* v *Canon (Export) Ltd* (1952) on principle, however, it is difficult to see why the approach of *Bailache* in *Giddens* v *Anglo-African* (1923) - namely that a presumption that an irrevocable credit must be furnished, is not good law, because that, after all furnishes better security for the seller, a presumption only to be overridden by express words.

The buyer's duty to furnish the credit is absolute within the time stipulated. This duty is not negated by factors beyond the buyer's control. In *Lindsay* v *Cook* (1953) on inter-bank communication delay, entirely independent on the fault of the buyers, nevertheless entitled the seller to repudiate the contract of sale. As against that strict duty, however, it is always open to the seller to waive the breach where a buyer has either failed to open a credit in time, or has opened one which deviates in some way from that specified in the contract. This, of course, may constitute a *strict waiver* (cf, Lord Denning in *Alan* v *El Nasr* (1972) or a *variation* of the contract. Whether one or the other applies depends upon the circumstances of the case, but the majority of the Court of Appeal in *Alan* v *El Nasr* opined that the waiver doctrine would not apply in cases where the buyer had not detrimentally relied.

Lord Denning, on the other hand, thought that wiaver operated *independently* of consideration and *detriment.*

With respect to payment, the seller is under a duty to claim payment from either the issuing bank or the corresponding banks - depending upon the term of the credit, and only in the rare instance of default of the relevant bank will he be entitled to claim from the buyer. If the seller fails to present the documents to the relevant bank - preventing him from claiming payment, the buyer will be absolutely discharged from his payment obligation. From the buyer's point of view, however, merely opening the credit itself will not operate to discharge the buyer. This was confirmed by Lord Denning in *Alan* v *El Nasr* who said that ordinarily when the contract of sale stipulates for payment to be made by confirmed irrecoverable documentary credit, then when that is issued and accepted by the seller, it operates as a conditional payment of the price. It did not operate as an absolute discharge. This was the ratio of the decision in the *Maran Road Saw Mill* v *Austin Taylor* (1975) where it was held that the opening of a credit operated only as a conditional discharge so that if an issuing bank failed to perform its undertaking given in the irrevocable credit, the buyer's duty to pay the price revived. The unusual feature of *Maran Road* was that there the question of discharging the buyer from a payment obligation arose *after* the buyer had placed the issuing bank in funds. The argument rejected was essentially that the buyer had already performed by remitting the stipulated amount to the bank. However, because the buyer had to *pay* by credit and not just *provide a documentary credit*, since the sellers had not been paid, the buyer's obligation revived. This has been criticised on the basis that it constitutes, essentially, a buyer's guarantee of the issuing bank's solvency, but against that it could simply be argued that the irrevocable credit constituted a security furnished by the buyer, for the seller and if that security fails, the buyer ought to bear the resultant loss.

These considerations affect the relationship between the seller and the buyer. But the irrevocable and confirmed result brings into existence four more contractual relationships - those between the buyer and the issuing banks, the issuing bank and the correspondent bank, the issuing bank and the seller and the correspondent bank and the seller.

There is no privity of contract between the buyer and the correspondent bank. However, for any default of the correspondent bank causing the buyer loss, the buyer has a remedy against the issuing bank - liable for the acts/omissions of its agent.

Issuing bank/buyer:

The relationship between the buyer and issuing bank is simply that of banker and customer, formed by a unilateral contract in which the buyer submits an application which constitutes an offer, the issuing bank accepts by issuing the letter of credit. As we have seen, acceptance of such a letter of credit does not discharge the buyer. So if the bank dishonours the draft by not paying, the seller may have recourse to the buyer. In that case, the buyer may have to pay twice - one to the seller and once to the Mercantile issuing bank. However, the court may release the buyer from any obligation assumed by him towards the defaulting issuing bank as in *Sale Continuation* v *Austin Taylor* (1967) where Paull J released the buyer from his obligation to the bank. The case has been criticised on the ground that by accepting the documentary credit in the first place the banker has *partially performed* its duties under the contract with the buyer and therefore there is no total failure of consideration when the bill is subsequently dishonoured and on the basis Gutteridge suggests that the buyer be *obliged to perform*. However, as Ackner J pointed out in *Maran Road* the main object is payment of the seller and this type of credit is simply to provide the buyer with short-term credit.

It is therefore wrong to regard the bank's act of accepting the seller's bill as performance of the bank's duties to the buyer *in any way*, and so there is a total failure of consideration. On that basis, *Sale Continuation* is quite acceptable.

The issuing bank is protected by the UCP against the risks that attach with the engagement of a correspondent banker. Article 10 of the UCP protects the issuing bank against liability for delivery, and generally under Article 12 of the UCP, if the issuing bank utilises the services of a correspondent banker, he does so at the buyer's risk and, accordingly, he therefore assumes no liability if the correspondent banker does not carry out his instructions. This applies even if the issuing bank has taken the initiative and selected the correspondent. This has been criticised and quite justifiably - Article 12 amounts to a disclaimer by the issuing bank of liability for the acts of its agent - the correspondent bank. Such a disclaimer leaves the buyer with no remedy because he cannot claim against the correspondent banker because of lack of privity. This is unjust since the issuing bank will select the correspondent bank, and it has been suggested that the courts would avoid the result by adopting the doctrine of fundamental breach to limit Article 12.

Issuing bank/seller:

Now, as between the issuing bank and seller an irrevocable credit creates a legally binding contract. It can therefore be enforced by the *seller*. The added element of confirmation means that the correspondent banker is jointly and severally bound with the issuing bank towards the seller - the two banks are therefore under similar obligations.

Now, it has been said that the issuing bank/seller contract is established as soon as the documentary credit reaches the hands of the seller, but this analysis is difficult to accept because it is by no means easy to find consideration moving from the seller at that time. However, Greer J in *Dexters* v *Schenkers* (1923) said that there was full and ample consideration because until the seller has got a banker's credit, the seller is not bound to send the goods at all. This depends upon reasoning that the seller becomes bound to ship only when the credit reaches his hands. Alternatively, it could be argued that consideration is furnished by the seller, on the basis of the irrevocable credit, to *demand payment from the buyer*.

The substance of the contract is an undertaking by the issuing bank that payment will be made on presentation of the documents. It is given as *principal*, not as agent of the buyer - like the issuing bank/buyer contract, the issuing bank's contract with the seller is completely *independent. It cannot be modified by the terms of the main buyer/seller contract.* Now, the question of whether the seller is to look for payment to the issuing bank first, or the correspondent bank defends his terms of the credit. The correspondent bank, adding its own name to the 'guarantee' to that of the issuing bank, in a sense becomes *both principal* to the seller and *agent* to the issuing bank. By informing the seller of the opening of the credit he acts as agent of the issuing bank but by conforming the credit he assumes towards the seller the role of principal.

NB: The only exception to the rule that the issuing bank/seller cannot be qualified by the buyer/seller contract arises in the case of fraud involved in *United City Merchants* v *Royal Bank of Canada*, *The American Accord* (1983) where a bill of lading was fraudulently dated so as to be within the letter of credit period, although in that case, because the fraud could not be imputed to the sellers there was no justification for the bank rejecting the documents. The fraud exception is limited and will rarely be successfully relied upon by an issuing bank - mere discrepancies between descriptions of the goods in the documents, and the goods actually shipped, will not indicate fraud.

Finally, as has been noted, there is a contract between the correspondent bank and the seller, with the former adding its name to the payment undertaking as *principal.* It is not joint and several liability but independent undertakings, so if the terms of the correspondent banker's confirmation are more restricted than those of the original credit, then the correspondent bank's liability to the seller is correspondingly more limited.

Question 2

Gracechurch Supplies Ltd bought the following goods under separate contracts governed by English law:

i) from Simpson Ltd

20,000 microwaves cif London.

ii) from Hart Ltd

15,000 video records fob Singapore for delivery in Beirut, Lebanon.

iii) from Young Ltd

2,000 word processors cif London.

Each contract stated (inter alia) that

i) Payment was to be made by irrevocable letter of credit at South Eastern Bank on presentation of the shipping documents;

ii) shipment was to take place in January/February 1986; and

iii) liability 'for breach of any express or implied warranty was excluded'.

The directors of Gracechurch Supplies Ltd consult you and state:

1) *Ovens*

We opened the credit in favour of the sellers on January 3, 1986. The bank paid on presentation of the invoice, the marine insurance policy and a 'received for shipment' bill of lading. When the ovens reached us, we found that the hinges on the doors were faulty but could be put right at a minimal cost. We sold 2,000 of them to Rees Ltd on the same terms. They returned them to us one month later on discovering that fault. The packing cases in which the rest of the ovens were packed were stolen property.

2) *Video recorders*

The credit was opened on December 28, 1985. We contacted the sellers and said that we wanted to inspect the recorders before shipment, but they would not allow us to do so. The bank paid on presentation of the shipping documents. On the arrival of the vessel at Beirut she and all her cargo were a total loss by shell fire in the civil war. We find that the recorders were shipped on February 3, but we knew nothing of this until after the loss.

3) *Word processors*

The bank paid on presentation of the shipping documents including bills of lading showing shipment on February 28. We had instructed the bank not to pay because there were some newer models on the way. On arrival 700 of the word processors had keys in the Greek instead of the English alphabet and were useless for our purposes as we intended to sell them to our customers in England. We spent £30,000 in advertising the word processors and our goodwill has been damaged. The bills of lading were forged and shipment took place on March 1.

Advise the directors of Gracechurch Supplies Ltd in relation to all the matters stated above.

University of London LLB Examination
for (External Students) Commercial Law June 1986 Q3

Skeleton solution

- UCP.
- International supply contracts not governed by UCTA 1977.
- Cif contracts.
- Fob contracts.
- Documentary credits.
- Rights and liabilities of banks in export sales.
- Bills of lading.
- Faulty goods - Sale of Goods Act - export sales.
- Rights and remedies of parties.

Suggested solution

a) *Introduction*

We are told that the contracts are governed by English Law. It will be assumed, where relevant, that the documentary credits incorporated the current UCP (Uniform Customs and Practice for Documentary Credits 1983 Revision) because it is the standard practice of the banks to issue credits on these terms. One other issue can be dispensed with at this stage, namely that because the contracts are international supply contracts they are not subject to regulation by the Unfair Contract Terms Act 1977 (see s26). All discussion of the exclusion clause, therefore, will revolve around the common law only.

b) *The ovens*

The credit ought to have been opened a reasonable time before the beginning of the shipment period (*Sinason-Teicher Inter-American Grain Corporation* v *Oilcakes &*

Oilseeds Trading Co (1954)). The failure to do this was a breach of a condition in the sale contract. There is some authority for the proposition that this is breach of a condition precedent to the very formation of the sale contract (*Trans Trust SPRL* v *Danubian Trading Co Ltd* (1952)), but nothing revolves around that because it is clear from the facts given that the sellers, Simpson Ltd (S), did not attempt to discharge the contract for this breach but affirmed it by shipping the goods. This will prevent any remedy being available unless S can prove that a loss resulted from the credit being opened late; which on the facts given they will not be able to do.

The documents presented to the bank included a received for shipment bill of lading. Such a document is not good tender under the CIF contract because it does not assure the buyer that the goods have been loaded (*Diamond Alkali Export Corporation* v *Fl Bourgeois* (1921)). Under the UCP a received for shipment bill can sometimes be accepted by the bank (article 25) and at other times a received for shipment bill can be transformed into a shipped bill (article 26). In the absence of agreement to the contrary a CIF contract can only be performed by the presentation of a shipped bill and the credit contract is likely to be read in this light. In principle the credit contract is a separate thing from the sale contract which it finances and therefore it should be possible for the CIF contract to require one document and the credit contract another. But, in the context of a normal CIF contract, the credit and sale contracts will be read together. The position here, then, is that the bank accepted a received for shipment bill in breach of its mandate. This has two consequences, firstly the acceptance of documents by the bank is not acceptance by the buyer under the CIF contract and secondly the buyer is not obliged to reimburse the bank.

As regards the first point, the bank is the agent of the buyer to accept the CIF documents (*Donald H Scott & Co Ltd* v *Barclays Bank Ltd* (1923); *Panchaud Freres SA* v *Etablissements General Grain Co* (1970)), and all the circumstances are known to the seller; therefore if the seller tenders documents which are not in compliance with the requirements of the CIF contract and the bank accepts them then the seller knows that the bank is acting outside its authority. In such circumstances the buyer can ratify the wrongful act of his agent, the bank, and on ratification it is deemed that the acceptance of the documents was valid as from the beginning (*Bank Melli Iran* v *Barclays Bank DCO* (1951)). As regards the second point, once the buyer ratifies the acceptance of the documents by the bank he is obliged to reimburse the bank the amount of the credit (and the bank's fee), but has a right of action against the bank for any loss arising from the wrongful acceptance of the documents (the buyer has a contract with the issuing bank; any wrongful acts by the bank will amount to a breach of that contract. It is assumed that South Eastern Bank was the only bank involved and worked through one of its branches when accepting the documents). The manner of ratification is a matter for the buyer, but physical acceptance of the goods by the buyer will amount to ratification (*Panchaud Freres SA* v *Etablissement General Grain Co* (1970)).

Therefore, on the facts we are given, the bank acted outside its authority when accepting a received for shipment bill of lading, but that wrongful act has been ratified and no loss has resulted from the bank's breach. Acceptance of the documents does not preclude the buyer from rejecting the goods if a breach of condition in relation to the goods can be proved which was not apparent on the face of the documents (*Kwei Tek Chao* v *British Traders and Shippers* (1954) and *Panchaud Freres* (above)).

Three matters fall for discussion in relation to the goods. Firstly the effect of the hinges being faulty, secondly the effect of the sale of 2,000 to Rees and thirdly the effect of the packing cases being stolen goods.

Faults in goods which are sold as new goods render those goods unmerchantable provided the faults did not arise at a time when the goods were at the risk of the buyer (*Jackson* v *Rotax Motor and Cycle Co* (1910)). In a CIF sale risk passes as from shipment (*Kwei Tek Chao* v *British Traders and Shippers* (1954)), which means at the time the goods cross the ship's rail (*Mowbray, Robinson & Co* v *Rosser* (1922)), so if the hinges were damaged in transit then GS must look to the ship for compensation because there will be no right of action against the sellers. GS will have a contract with the ship either by virtue of the Bills of Lading Act 1855 or by virtue of the parallel rule in *Brandt* v *Liverpool, Brazil and River Plate Steam Navigation Co* (1924); an action will be available in negligence provided GS had property in the goods at the time damage occurred, *The Aliakmon* (1986). On the other hand, the occurrence of this damage prior to shipment will give GS a remedy for breach of s14(2) of the Sale of the Goods Act 1979 against S. The fact that the hinges could be put right at minimal cost does not prevent the ovens from being unmerchantable because they will not be reasonably fit for their normal purposes (*Jackson* v *Rotax Motor and Cycle Co* (1910)). Furthermore there will be a breach of s14(3) because the purchase of 2,000 ovens makes known to the seller that they are being bought for a resale and they are not reasonably fit for resale if they have damaged hinges.

The remedy for breach of s14(2) and 14(3) is rejection of the goods and damages. Rejection will not be available for those of the goods which have been accepted. In most sales the contract will be entire and the buyer will lose the right to reject if he sells on any of the goods supplied. But if the contract is severable, a partial acceptance will not preclude rejection of the rest. The main factor determining whether a sale contract is entire or severable is, usually, whether there is delivery in instalments with each instalment being paid for separately (*J Rosenthal & Sons Ltd* v *Esmail* (1965)). In cases like the present where delivery of all the goods occurs at the same time, then there is no clear rule about how one judges whether it is severable or entire. The presumption is that where goods are shipped all in one consignment, the contract is entire (*Ross T Smyth & Co Ltd* v *Bailey, Son & Co* (1940), though the House of Lords accepted that the presumption is weak); but we are told that the 2,000 which were sold to Rees Ltd (R) were sold on the same terms, which indicates that the original sale was severable (the *Rosenthal* case is distinguishable because it is always a matter of fact whether a contract is or is not severable and in that case it was the course of dealings between the parties which prevented the shipment under two bills of lading from rendering the contract severable). We are told that the bank accepted 'a' received for shipment bill of lading, which indicates that there was only one bill; a matter which would normally make a resale of part of the goods difficult, but we are not told of any problems in effecting the sub-sale.

The question now is whether the goods have been accepted by GS. There is a long line of authority which holds that a resale and delivery of goods by a buyer amounts to acceptance because it is an act inconsistent with the ownership of the original seller (*Hardy & Co (London) Ltd* v *Hillerns and Fowler* (1923); *Perkins* v *Bell* (1893); *Molling* v *Dean* (1901)). Therefore, when GS sold and delivered 2,000 ovens to Rees Ltd (R) that was acceptance of those 2,000. R rejected one month after delivery and in many domestic sales this would be too late, but in a CIF sale, which usually involves an international element, this would not be such a long time that the right to reject for the breach of s14(2) was lost (*Kwei Tek Chao* v *British Traders and Shippers* (1954)). So there was acceptance by GS of the 2,000 sold to R.

But, there is an added complication caused by the third issue outlined above; the fact that the packaging of the rest of the ovens was stolen. Packaging is part of the goods supplied (*Manbre Saccharine Co* v *Corn Products Co* (1919); *Wormell* v *RHM Agriculture (East) Ltd* (1986)) and if there is a defect in packaging this can be a breach of s14(2); it can also be the case that s12(1) can be breached. In the present case part of the goods delivered have turned out to be stolen which necessarily means that S did not have the right to sell them. The doctrine of acceptance does not arise where there is a breach of s12(1) arising from the sale of stolen goods (*Rowland* v *Divall* (1923)), therefore the 18,000 ovens and their packaging can be rejected. It has been stated above that this contract is severable and so the acceptance of 2,000 will not preclude rejection of the 18,000 remaining (s11(4) Sale of Goods Act 1979 would not prevent rejection because that only applies to non-severable contracts).

In addition to having the right to reject goods for breach of condition, damages can also be claimed. GS will be able to claim the difference between the value that 18,000 ovens would have had if delivered on time and in the proper condition, and the contract price - in other words they can claim their loss of bargain, if any. It will not, however, be possible to claim any substantial sum to cover losses arising from resale because we are told that the hinges could be repaired at minimal cost and the failure of GS to effect such repairs before delivery to R means that the rejection by R could have been avoided and, therefore, that they have not reasonably mitigated their loss (*The Solholt* (1983)).

The exclusion clause in the contract will not help S because it only attempted to exclude liability for breach of warranty and the breaches here were breaches of condition. The fact that in relation to the 2,000 sold on to R the breach of condition falls to be treated as breach of warranty does not affect this because it only falls to be treated as a breach of warranty, it is still a condition which is breached (*Wallis, Son & Wells* v *Pratt & Haynes* (1911)).

c) *The video recorders*

The opening of the credit on 28 December 1985 was not too late, but may have been too early. Documentary credits do not remain open indefinitely and if they are opened too early the seller can be prejudiced by expiration occurring before he has had time to present documents to the bank (*Trans Trust SPRL* v *Danubian Trading Co Ltd* (1952)). However, on the facts given it appears that Hart Ltd (H) had ample time to present documents and so nothing revolves around the date of opening of the credit.

In sales on fob terms risk passes to the buyer at the time of shipment (*Pyrene Co Ltd* v *Scindia Navigation Co Ltd* (1954)), therefore, prima facie, any damage done during the voyage was at GS's risk. But it may be possible to shift this loss onto H if it can be proved that inspection of the goods 'before shipment' would have led to GS rejecting them.

The contract provided for shipment January/February; this allowed H to ship at any time within that period on the vessel nominated by GS (*J & J Cunningham Ltd* v *RA Munro & Co Ltd* (1922)). There is nothing to indicate that the bank was acting wrongly in paying against the documents. The only thing which went wrong was that H refused to allow GS to inspect the goods before shipment. This matter is of importance in the FOB contract only and does not affect the operation of the credit contract (*Hamzeh Malas & Sons* v *British Imex Industries Ltd* (1958)).

Section 34(2) of the Sale of Goods Act 1979 provides that the seller must on request allow the buyer an opportunity to inspect the goods at the time that delivery is tendered. The time of tender of delivery in fob sales is the time of shipment (*Bragg* v *Villanova* (1923)). There is nothing to indicate that GS would have found anything wrong at that time so as to justify rejection, but the inspection of goods bought under an fob sale may be in order to discover matters necessary for the buyer to take out effective insurance (this is the buyer's job unless otherwise agreed and there is nothing in the facts given to indicate that the seller had agreed to take out insurance for the buyer). Therefore, on the assumption that GS were unable to take out effective insurance because they did not have sufficient information about the goods we must ask whether H are responsible for the loss resulting.

It has been held that section 32(3) of the 1979 Act applies to fob contracts, so that H should have given GS notice of all matters necessary to allow the goods to be insured during transit (*Wimble, Sons & Co* v *Rosenberg & Sons* (1913)). Failure to do this means that the goods are at the risk of the seller during transit (s32(3)). In cases where the seller fails to give the buyer the opportunity to inspect the goods to which he is entitled, section 32(3) puts the goods at seller's risk during transit because unless the buyers were in a position to insure the goods from their own knowledge then the obligation remained on the sellers to furnish this information. It is not clear on the authorities how this matter affects the performance of the sale contract. In the present case the goods have not been physically delivered to the buyers at the port of destination and it may be that failure to give GS the chance to inspect means that delivery to the ship will not be construed as delivery to GS. On the other hand it may be that delivery to the ship was still delivery to GS, but that GS can complain about any damage occurring between that time and physical delivery to them; if this is correct then GS can sue for damages for breach of s14(2). The better view is that there is no delivery to the buyer until the goods arrive and therefore that GS can sue for damages for non-delivery since the video recorders have been destroyed (s51 SGA 1979).

GS are entitled to recover the purchase price as money paid for a consideration which has totally failed (s54 SGA 1979) and also damages assessed under s51(3) of the 1979 Act to cover the difference between the available market value the goods would have had on arrival and the purchase price (being damages under the first rule in *Hadley* v *Baxendale* (1854)).

The exclusion clause fails to help H for the same reason that it failed to help S under the CIF sale discussed above.

d) *The word processors*

The sellers, Young Ltd (Y), committed a breach of condition by shipping the goods late (the breach is of a s13 SGA 1979 because a March shipment is of a different commercial description to a January/February shipment: *Bowes* v *Shand* (1877)). Unless the bank knew that Y were personally involved in a fraud, the payment against apparently correct documents was a good payment within the terms of their mandate (*United City Merchants (Investments) Ltd* v *Royal Bank of Canada* (1983); UCP Article 15, *Gian Singh & Co Ltd* v *Banque de L'Indochine* (1974)). Therefore in the absence of clear evidence of the bank's knowledge of fraud, GS are obliged to reimburse the bank (*United City Merchants* case (1983)). Furthermore, once an irrevocable credit has been opened the buyer is not entitled to instruct the bank not to pay (*Hamzeh Malas & Sons* v *British Imex Industries Ltd* (1958)). The position of the bank is that it is liable to the seller (the beneficiary under the credit) once the credit has been opened, even though there is no consideration given by the seller, and will be liable in damages for wrongfully withdrawing the credit (see Benjamin's Sale of Goods). The buyer is not allowed to force the bank to incur liability to a third party, so once the credit is opened the bank is entitled to pay on presentation of apparently conforming documents.

We have already seen that Y have committed one breach of condition by shipping the goods late. This entitles GS to reject all of them on arrival. 700 of the word processors may have been unmerchantable or not fit for the buyers' particular purpose, but even though the contract may have been severable GS were not obliged to accept the other 1,300 because all 2,000 were shipped late. GS, therefore, are entitled to reject all 2,000 word processors; on the evidence we have the time for rejection has not yet passed.

In addition to being able to reject the word processors, GS are also entitled to damages for non-delivery and will be able to recover in damages for other losses provided it can be proved that Y knew of circumstances which would reveal to a reasonable man that such losses were not likely (the second rule in *Hadley* v

Baxendale as interpreted in *Victoria Laundry (Windsor)* v *Newman Industries* (1949) and *The Heron II* (1969)). The £30,000 spent on advertising and the loss of goodwill are only recoverable, therefore, if Y knew that they were not unlikely to arise as a result of late shipment. It is unlikely that the full £30,000 will be recoverable because GS could have mitigated their loss by accepting the 1,300 which were late but merchantable, so that less than the full £30,000 was lost (*Payzu Ltd* v *Saunders* (1919)). Damage to goodwill is only rarely recoverable and not in the circumstances of this case (*GKN Centrax Gears Ltd* v *Matbro Ltd* (1976)).

The exclusion clause is of no effect for the same reason given in relation to the other contracts.

35 CONCLUSION

35.1 A final note

Now that we have systematically worked through all the topics, it may be useful to add a final note in conclusion.

It will have been noted that questions do not fit into neat categories, and the subject matter often spills over into several different areas at once; examples of such wide ranging questions have been quoted wherever possible.

In Commercial Law papers, however, there is a tendency for a certain type of question to recur from time to time, which virtually covers the whole syllabus. Because Commercial Law is governed to a large extent by statute, it is not at all unusual to find a question on the merits of codification (1988 and 1991), or the conflicting interests in commercial law (1990 and 1991) or the relative merits of a particular statute (1988).

Such questions are very difficult to answer. At first sight they may seem easy, but the scope is potentially vast, covering as it does the whole syllabus, and there is often little case law or even literature on the subject. A student needs considerable self-discipline, not only to work out the exact limits of his answer (and stick to those limits!) but also to work out exactly which bits of the syllabus might be relevant and ruthlessly discard the rest.

Below are five examples of such questions. Students are advised to be very sure of their material before attempting such questions.

35.2 Questions

Question 1

'The value of the Consumer Credit Act 1974 is diminished by the complexity and inconvenience of many of its provisions.'

Discuss.

University of London LLB Examination
(for External Students) Commercial Law June 1989 Q3

Skeleton solution

- Crowther Committee.

- Law before 1974, weaknesses.
- Consumer credit transactions.
- Value of CCA 1974.

Suggested solution

The Consumer Credit Act 1974 (CCA) was passed following the report of the Crowther Committee on Consumer Credit. Before 1974, the law relating to consumer credit was contained in a large number of statutes and decisions. It lacked cohesion and was inadequate to deal with such an important area of activity. The Crowther Committee identified a number of weaknesses in the existing law. For example, the regulation of credit transactions which existed depended on the agreement's form rather than its substance or function; there was no distinction made between commercial and consumer transactions; much of the law had developed an unnecessarily technical approach; and, finally, what protection there was for consumers in credit transactions was inadequate.

The Crowther Committee, therefore, recommended a wholesale revision of this area of the law. The existing legislation was too inadequate and complex to enable the defects to be remedied by mere amendments. The Committee suggested that a uniform code for all forms of consumer credit should be drawn up and that this code should include more protection for the consumer who enters such a transaction. There should also be established a system of licensing for people who, as part of their business, are involved in the credit industry. These recommendations, together with certain additional safeguards for the consumer, were adopted by the Government and were incorporated in the CCA.

The Act repeals most of the previous legislation relating to consumer credit in all its various forms and replaces it with a single, unified code which covers all form of consumer credit and consumer hire. It is here that the complexity of the legislation becomes inevitable. To draft a code which covers the various types of credit, ranging from hire-purchase, conditional sales and credit sales, to bank loans, credit card transactions, pawnbroking agreements and hire contracts, calls for the introduction of new concepts which have to be wide enough to deal with every aspect of credit and yet sufficiently precise to be justifiable. There is, therefore, inevitable complexity and a large amount of cross-referring in the CCA which, although inconvenient at times, is nonetheless important to establish a satisfactory, all-embracing code.

The Act controls consumer credit in a number of ways. It provides for the licensing of people who are involved in consumer credit, consumer hire or ancillary credit business. This last category covers credit brokers, credit reference agencies, debt collectors and debt counsellors and adjusters. The Act also establishes the framework for the regulation of the licensing system and imposes restrictions on the ways in which credit business is sought. In these ways, the credit industry is regulated by the legislation.

There is also control over the credit transactions themselves. There are rules which relate to the form and content of consumer credit and hire agreements and to the information and documents which debtors and hirers are entitled to receive. In fact, the

Act governs the credit agreement from its negotiation to its termination, and gives the debtor protection against unfair treatment by the creditor. It also restricts the creditor's right to repossess the goods. As a final protection to the debtor, the county court is given full power to control the enforcement of a credit agreement. In certain circumstances, the court may modify the agreement and re-schedule its terms if it is found to be extortionate.

These controls apply to all forms of consumer credit agreement, and the CCA gives a general definition of an agreement which will be regulated. This fixes the parameters within which the Act will operate and also defines the circumstances within which the general regulatory provisions apply. A regulated agreement is a consumer credit or hire agreement which is not exempt. This is stated in ss189(1), 8(3) and 15(2). A consumer credit agreement is defined by s8(1) and (2) as an agreement between an individual (the debtor) and any other person (the creditor) under which the creditor provides the debtor with credit not exceeding £15,000. A consumer hire agreement is defined by s15(1) as being an agreement between an individual (hirer) and any other person for the bailment of goods which is not a hire-purchase agreement, is capable of lasting for over three months and does not require the hirer to make payments exceeding £15,000.

Between them, a consumer credit and a consumer hire agreement cover every possible form of consumer credit transaction. The difficulties arise, however, in relation to ways in which these transactions are controlled because there are a large number of methods of giving credit. Each method has different consequences at law and so each has to be catered for in the CCA. For example, if the agreement is for the hire-purchase of goods, the transaction involves a finance company which transfers possession of goods to the debtor who undertakes to pay a fixed number of instalments and who may, on completion of the payments, exercise an option to buy the goods. Until this time, ownership of the goods remains in the finance company. Another form of consumer credit is the credit sale, whereby ownership in the goods is transferred immediately to the buyer and the price is payable over a period of time. Bank loans and overdrafts, whereby the creditor has no interest whatsoever in the goods supplied, may also come within the definition of a regulated agreement.

It is clear, therefore, that although the definition of a regulated agreement is adequate to encompass the many forms of credit available, in relation to the control of these various forms the Act has to give much greater detail and introduce a number of new concepts. It is these concepts which give rise to the suggestion that the CCA is complex. For example, the Act distinguishes between debtor-creditor-supplier and debtor-creditor arrangements. It also distinguishes between fixed sum and running account credit. It introduces the ideas of the linked transactions and multiple agreements and of restricted - and unrestricted - use credit. It is by using these novel concepts that the Act can provide regulation for all forms of consumer credit.

The draftsman of the Act realised that these innovations could cause difficulties and so introduced two novel devices to help people who deal with the legislation. The first of these devices occurs in the definition section (s189 CCA). As well as providing interpretation of the words used in the legislation, this section states all the other sections in which definitions are given. Secondly, Schedule 2 of the CCA gives examples of how the new concepts in the Act will be used. In this second schedule a series of facts are given and these facts are analysed in the context of the Act. An index of the terminology thus explained is included at the beginning of the Schedule. Thus an innovative approach is taken to an innovative piece of legislation.

The value of the CCA is that, for the first time, all the law relating to the greatest part of consumer credit and hire is contained in one statute (and, of course, in the regulations made under it). It is also valuable in that the debtor is given greater protection and a greater right to information than ever before. To achieve its purpose it was inevitable that the Act would be complicated. It is covering a wide range of activity but does so as precisely as possible. With hindsight it can be seen that some variation in the section ordering would have been useful but this is a point which could be made about many Acts of Parliament. As a complete code for consumer credit and hire transactions, the CCA is a valuable piece of legislation and this value is in no way diminished by 'the complexity and inconvenience of many of its provisions.'

Question 2

'Although the Law Commission has decided that a comprehensive code for the general law of contract is not a good idea, that does not mean that there might not be a good case of such a Code for Commercial Law.'

Discuss.

University of London LLB Examination
(for External Students) Commercial Law June 1988 Q1

Skeleton solution

- Introduction
- Definition as commercial law
- Arguments for/against codification
- Existing codes eg SGA; CCA
- Practical difficulties

Suggested solution

The decision of the Law Commission not to attempt a wholesale codification of contract law has not prevented it from recommending certain changes of great significance. Undoubtedly the greatest change it has influenced is the passing of the Unfair Contract Terms Act 1977, but even that only covers part of the law relating to exclusion clauses.

The first difficulty in any discussion of the codification of English commercial law is to seek a definition of commercial law. A simple definition would be that it is the law concerning sale and supply of goods. Although this may have seemed an appropriate definition some years ago the financing of sale and supply transactions now takes up a great deal of time in the courts and the law reviews. It is, therefore, not possible to codify the position of buyer and seller without also codifying the position of the financier. This has been done to a certain extent by the Consumer Credit Act 1974, although that Act does not deal with the position of creditor and debtor where the debtor is a limited company or a group of limited companies.

Much of English commercial law is codified in statutory form already. Of particular importance are the Sale of Goods Act 1979, the Consumer Credit Act 1974 and the Unfair Contract Terms Act 1977. But no attempt has been made to codify the whole of the law of the sale and supply of goods. The present position is that most of the obligations of seller and buyer are defined by statute and the ability of either to exclude liability for his breach is limited. Also the provision of credit to persons other than limited companies is very strictly regulated. What has not been done is to draw together the present statutes or to codify agency law or the provision of credit to limited companies.

In favour of codification it can be argued that the present difficult caselaw on such basic matters as the duty to perform obligations on time (*Charles Rickards Ltd* v *Oppenheim* (1950); *Lombard North Central plc* v *Butterworth* (1987)) and the interpretation of s30 of the 1979 Act (*Gill & Duffus SA* v *Berger & Co Inc* (1984); *Regent OHG Aisenstadt* v *Francesco of Jermyn Street* (1981)) create such problems for both student and practitioner that some simplification of principle is necessary. Also many matters which arise frequently in the cases are not dealt with adequately by the present statutes, and in some cases are not dealt with at all, like the right of a commercial buyer to sell goods before property has passed to him (*Clough Mill Ltd* v *Martin* (1984)).

Against codification it can be said that much of the litigation in sale cases revolves around questions on which there is legislation already, but which can never be fully answered by Act of Parliament alone. The clearest example of this is the duty of a seller who sells in the course of a business to supply goods which are of merchantable quality (*Aswan Engineering Establishment Co* v *Lupidine Ltd* (1987)). This duty was put into statutory form by s14(2) of the Sale of Goods Act 1893, but whether goods are of merchantable quality is a matter of fact as well as law and it is only be judicial decisions that a general idea of what is and what is not merchantable can be developed. Section 15(3) of the Supply of Goods (Implied Terms) Act 1973, which has been re-enacted as s14(6) of the 1979 Act, went some way towards helping the judges; but the Court of Appeal has held that the only effect of the section was to adopt one of the previous judicial definitions (s8 SGA 1979). Although this limited the permissible approaches to questions of merchantability, it did not, and cannot, provide a sufficiently detailed definition to cover every possible case.

Any code of commercial law will have to state principles in a way which has defined the judges. Even the codification which has taken place has done little to ease their task because of the different ways in which the statutes have defined the law. The 1979 Act states specific rules in some instances, for example in relation to ascertainment of the price (s35 SGA 1979), and in others gives a general principle which has to be defined further by the courts. A classic example of this is the concept of an 'act inconsistent with the ownership of the seller' in the doctrine of acceptance (s35 SGA

1979). The 1974 Act, on the other hand, leaves very little for the courts to do because the Act and the many statutory instruments under it are extremely detailed. Any code would have to choose which method of codification to follow.

Undoubtedly the Consumer Credit Act 1974 is a masterly piece of legislative draftsmanship in providing for a code of consumer credit law which has few holes. But a comparison of that Act and the Sale of Goods Act 1979 shows the principal problem which the codifier would face. Much of the subject matter of the 1974 Act is regulatory and is suited to detailed codification. There is little scope for judicial interpretation of the formalities provisions, because whether or not the correct copies of documents have been given to the debtor is a simple matter of fact. By contrast any statement of principle about such concepts as merchantable quality must be qualified by the judges from case to case. This, indeed, has already happened to the definition in s14(6) of the Sale of Goods Act 1979.

This does not mean that a codification would be a waste of time because it cannot sensibly be argued that the Sale of Goods Act 1893 was anything other than a success in bringing the previously opaque caselaw into some sort of coherent shape. But it should not be expected that codification would simplify the law in areas which frequently give rise to very difficult questions of fact.

Certain limited codification would simplify the law enormously. In this regard, without doubt an amalgamation of the Sale of Goods Act 1979 and the Supply of Goods (Implied Terms) Act 1973 would be a useful start, because the terms about the goods implied into sale and hire purchase contracts are the same. But it would not necessarily be wise to go one step further and involve the Unfair Contract Terms Act 1977 in such an amalgamated statute, because the 1977 Act applies to almost all contracts whether they involve a sale of goods or not.

A significant hurdle in the way of a codification of commercial law generally would be the inevitable difficulty of stating any principles about authority of agents. The question when someone should be responsible for the acts of another whom he has not expressly authorised to act in a particular way is one which has caused the courts immense difficulties and which could not properly be answered by a statute. Apparent authority causes enough problems, and if Parliament attempted to simplify the law it would undoubtedly be seen to have passed an unfair Act. The flexibility of the common law is essential if all cases are to be adjudicated properly.

Furthermore the advance of equitable concepts into commercial law in recent years makes codification undesirable unless those concepts are to be omitted from the code and left to develop by themselves. Any Act which allowed for the present state of the law on retention of title, tracing and constructive trusts, would undoubtedly soon be overtaken by equity's advance in other areas of the law. To stifle the development of equity by enshrining the 1988 rules in a statute would be to defeat the whole purpose of those rules, and to codify commercial law without considering equity may lead to the code quickly becoming outdated in many important areas.

Question 3

'Modern commercial law is essentially obsessed with two competing policies: on the one hand, affording protection to contracting parties and, on the other, controlling the ways in which parties, in particular sellers and other creditors, can protect themselves.'

To what extent is this statement true?

University of London LLB Examination
(for External Students) Commercial Law June 1990 Q1

Skeleton solution

- Definition of commercial law; scope, eg consumer law, credit sales, etc, sale of goods; international trade
- Origins of law
- Origins and development of policy in commercial law. Basic contractual principles
- Protection afforded to contracting parties especially consumers
- Controls with special reference to protection afforded to sellers and creditors
- Comparison with protection for consumers/sellers/creditors
- Conclusion - recent development

Suggested solution

The candidate is required to comment on the truth of the widely drawn quotation 'modern commercial law is essentially obsessed with two competing policies: on the one hand, affording protection to contracting parties and, on the other, controlling the ways in which parties, in particular sellers and other creditors, can protect themselves.

This statement is widely drawn and requires analysis of the origins of commercial law to the present time and the basic contractual principles which underlie all the disparate elements which make up the various relationships between consumers and debtors and their opposite numbers, namely sellers and creditors.

It is well nigh impossible to set out all the categories of contract that make up the generic term 'commercial law' - the law itself is derived from many different sources and is constantly developing to meet the requirements of the increasingly complicated 'consumer society'. Even the term consumer can be ambiguous in this context because, for example, goods (eg a micro-computer) bought for use in a business or in the home may still be 'consumer goods'.

There are common themes that have developed in commercial law over the years but it appears that English Law has developed no comprehensive 'commercial law'; rather developments have been derived in piecemeal fashion from disparate categories of law. For example, common law doctrines, statutory codes, administrative remedies and even some criminal law sanctions.

The proposition herein is that 'modern commercial law' is 'essentially obsessed' with the competing interests of consumers/debtors and those of sellers/creditors. Initially therefore, one must look at some of the categories of individuals and trading entities that the law recognises before one can fully explore the nature of these competing interests. If one accepts the simple proposition that modern commercial law is concerned with two basic forms of contractual arrangement - namely the transfer of ownership title and risks in property for the consideration known as the price or the provision of finance for the purchase of goods and/or services, then one can explore more readily the nature of the competing interests and the development of commercial law. One can then properly assess the competing interests of buyer/debtors and sellers/creditors.

Many common law doctrines and maxims underpin the modern commercial law; but they have been overlain with statute law, precedents and various principles and doctrines from civil and criminal law. Take for example the maxim of caveat emptor (buyer beware); essentially this remains the basis of a commercial contract, the responsibility is placed on the buyer to properly investigate and assess the goods offered and to discharge the onus placed upon him in this respect. The consumer has had statutory protection since the Sale of Goods Act 1893 (as amended by the Sale of Goods Act 1979) of certain inalienable rights with regard to consumer contracts; in particular title of the seller, fitness for purpose merchantable quality, corresponding with description etc have been and still remain, the subject of implied terms. The protection afforded by the 'implied terms' of the Sale of Goods Act 1979 has been enhanced by precedents and other supporting statutes derived from civil and criminal law.

Thus, for example, the maxim caveat emptor appears to have been in some respects effectively reversed by s3 of the Misrepresentation Act 1967 and the trader must beware of committing himself to any statement that may amount to a misrepresentation. Section 51(2) Sale of Goods Act 1979 contains a codification of the principles established in the case of *Hadley* v *Baxendale* (1854) to enable the better assessment of the measure of damages under a breach of a contract for the sale of goods: "the measure of damages is the estimated loss directly and naturally resulting in the ordinary course of events from the seller's breach of contract".

Consumer protection is further enhanced by, for example, the statutes controlling the extent to which sellers of goods/services can impose and exercise exclusion clauses over liability for their products and services. Thus the Unfair Contract Terms Act 1977 replaced the controls first contained in the Supply of Goods (Implied Terms) Act 1973. Persons 'dealing as a consumer' (s12(1) UCTA 1977) can claim the protection of the UCTA and the courts will apply the test of 'reasonableness' (s2 and s11 UCTA) to any disputed exclusion clause. The consumer, furthermore, has the benefit of the long succession of precedents developed in the consumer's favour in respect of exclusion clauses under the 'contra proferentum' principles. (Some of the notable examples being *Olley* v *Marlborough Court* (1949) and *Thornton* v *Shoe Lane Parking* (1971). Protection does not end at the UCTA; some further recourse may be had to the control by the criminal law of exemption clauses under the Consumer Transactions

(Restrictions on Statements) Order 1976 (amended by CT(RS)O 1978) which introduces criminal offences for breaches of s6 UCTA and the Trading Stamps Act 1964.

It is obvious that no coherent code has been developed and that as previously stated the law has developed in a piecemeal fashion. Sales and purchases of goods are not the only form of the modern commercial law; the provision of finance by hire purchase and the various methods of credit are another important aspect that fall to be considered under the main proposition. There are obviously policies that have developed in relation to modern commercial law and their obvious aim is to control the relationships between sellers/buyers and debtors/creditors. To what extent it is true to say that commercial law is 'obsessed' with these competing policies is difficult to ascertain. It may be fairer to state that the commercial law is developing 'pendulum' fashion in response to the changing needs and requirements of the opposing parties in commercial transactions, rather than as a result of deliberate and effective policy making. That, for example, consumer interests will be perceived as being in need of protection in some respect; that protection may be afforded as the result of new legislation; too much bias in favour of the consumer will result and the pendulum will then 'swing' in favour of the creditor/seller (for example through precedent, amending legislation or failure to effect new legislation favourable to the consumer, but prejudicial to sellers) to redress the bias and restore the equilibrium.

As a result of the way in which commercial law has developed, the lack of direction and discernible policy has presented many difficulties. An examination of the law relating to credit and the provision of credit seems to indicate that present policy is directed at establishing a firm position where both parties to a transaction are adequately (but not overly) protected and can lawfully and commercially pursue their bargain. This development appears to be mirrored by recent developments in the law relating to the sale of goods, consumer protection and product liability.

Both parties to a commercial transaction require some protection and remedies to redress any injustices against them; this applies to credit and sale of goods contracts alike. Both parties have obligations and rights; the key policy objective should be equality of treatment and not an 'obsessive' interest in propagating the conflicts that arise. Credit transactions and the provision of credit should afford both creditor and debtor ample commercial scope to make agreements and to terminate such agreements. The 1971 Crowther Committee (Cmnd 4596) expressed concern about 'the serious anomalies arising from the division of credit transactions into legally distinct compartments and from failure to accord a uniform treatment to a range of security devices all designed to achieve the same objective'. The recommendations of the Crowther Committee favoured a policy of 'uniformity' and rationalisation of the law of security; in order to license and regulate credit provision and protect both debtor and creditor's interest.

The result of the Report of the Crowther Committee was the White Paper 'Reform of the Law on Consumer Credit' and the much acclaimed piece of legal draftsmanship, the Consumer Credit Act 1974 (CCA 1974). The key concept in the CCA is that of

'Regulated Agreements' (ie Consumer credit agreements or consumer hire agreements, other than exempt agreements - s189 CCA). The Act came into force gradually and was finally fully in force by 19th May 1985. The Act has proven itself to be forward looking and versatile and still regulates credit agreements even those of more recent origin (cash-point dispenser cards for example).

In conclusion, whilst the modern consumer law does contain, by its very nature competing interests, the policy regulating its present form seeks to balance out the respective interests and to maintain the equilibrium that has long been striven for. The law has developed in a rather 'hotch-potch' fashion, but at present it is not true to regard the equilibrium created by statutes, precedents, private, civil and criminal law as 'obsessive' or 'divisive'. Both parties to a commercial transaction have adequate safeguards and remedies to enable equitable and profitable commerce.

Question 4

'The Sale of Goods Act codifies cases concerning certain types of dealings which regularly came before the courts in the nineteenth century. It has not proved adequate to deal with the variety of transactions in different types of goods which have come before the courts this century.' Discuss.

University of London LLB Examination
(for External Students) Commercial Law June 1991 Q2

Skeleton solution

- 1893 SGA, codification, 1979 consolidating.
- UCTA.
- Consumer Protection Act 1987.
- Supply of Goods (Implied Terms) Act 1973.
- Supply of Goods and Services Act 1982.
- Whether all the defects of and gaps in SGA are now covered.

Suggested solution

Before 1893 the law relating to the sale of goods had no special features. In theory at least, it was governed by ordinary contractual law. But already much of the law was governed by tradition, custom and usage; the day to day backdrop to the regulation of mercantile law. Much of these traditional rules ended up incorporated into the Sale of Goods Act (SGA) along with the more mundane rules of contractual law.

The overall effect of the SGA 1893 was to set up a code of law; the primary function of which was to imply certain terms, where the contract between the parties was silent and, in some cases even imply terms over and above the wishes of the parties. It was certainly possible for most of these implied terms to be excluded, if the parties thought to do so, but with the advent of the Unfair Contract Terms Act 1977 (UCTA) this became much more difficult.

The SGA 1893 was consolidated into the SGA 1979 with a presumption that no alteration in the previous law was intended: *Bank of England* v *Vagliano Bros* (1891).

One gets the impression from this that the 1893 Act had worked so well, and been so comprehensive, that no defects in it were seen, and no changes necessary in the succeeding Act. In fact there were a number of shortcomings and problems. The first of these has already been mentioned, the fact that the provisions of the Act were quite easily sidestepped by judicious use of exclusion clauses.

The courts attempted to control the use of excessive exclusion clauses, but without much success. It was not until the advent of UCTA in 1977 that the position with regard to contracts for sale of goods was brought under control. It should be remembered that when the SGA 1893 was first drafted most contracts for sale of goods were between individual merchants, negotiating on a more or less equal footing. It was not until after the Second World War that modern standard form contracts began to be introduced to any great degree. Standard form contracts are a great boon to traders, but of course as far as individual consumers are concerned they are very much at a disadvantage. If exclusion clauses were incorporated into sale of goods contracts the trader could offer such terms to the consumer on a 'take it or leave it' basis; especially if he had a monopolistic position in the industry. UCTA operates alongside ordinary common law and either bans completely, or limits the effect of, exclusion clauses. Protection is given in varying degrees to different types of contract, with consumers dealing with businesses enjoying the most stringent protection.

The original SGA in 1893 assumed, as noted earlier, that a typical sale of goods transaction was a commercial sale, with both parties on an equal footing. Consumers are a fairly recent phenomenon. The Consumer Protection Act (CPA) of 1987 is a major piece of legislation, containing several innovations. Under the old SGAs 1893 and 1979, although a purchaser of a defective product was protected to some degree under the implied terms (especially ss13-15); the whole law was riddled with anomalies. This was in part due to the contractual law of privity - what happened if the party injured was not the purchaser? - and partly because of the very nature of today's commercial practices. The seller of the goods is rarely the manufacturer, goods are imported from all over the world, there may be a whole chain of people caught up in the production and marketing of goods. In *Lambert* v *Lewis* (1982) for example a distributor was unable to identify the wholesaler of products and thus could not bring an action under the SGA. Without going into detail as to the provisions of the CPA it should be noted that the key provision is s2(1) which provides in part:

'Subject to the following provisions of this Act, where any damage is caused wholly or partly by a defect in a product, every person to whom subsection (2) applies shall be liable ...'

and subsection (2) goes on to list everyone from manufacturers, importers, packagers etc up to and including the final supplier.

This and other consumer protection legislation (the Food Act 1984, Medicines Act 1968, Trade Descriptions Act 1968, Fair Trading Act 1973 etc, etc) have been made necessary by the shortcomings of the SGA. In particular, because no contractual relationship existed between the last link in the chain, the consumer, and the earliest links such as manufacturer or importer, contractual redress was not always available.

Also when someone other than the consumer, say a member of his family, was injured problems occurred. Consumer protection legislation does not in any way alter or detract from SGA, it reinforces it.

One final problem should be mentioned, the definition of 'goods' in the context of SGA. The old Act was very limited in its application, because the definition was strictly applied. In 1973 the Supply of Goods (Implied Terms) Act extended the provisions of the then 1893 SGA to hire purchase contracts; thereby defeating the proviso that there had to be a cash sale. But the problem of situations in which the subject of the sale was not goods, but some sort of service, remained until 1982, when the Supply of Goods and Services Act was introduced. The problem of cases such as the provision of certain skilled services was often made more complex by the fact that goods were involved; thus an artist who is commissioned to paint a portrait will be selling primarily his skill, but also canvas and paints. A tradesman who supplies a fitted kitchen is supplying along with his own skills, the timber and other materials that go to make up the kitchen units. Until 1982 such a contract would be outside the SGA (*Robinson* v *Graves* (1935)) but since the introduction of the SGSA, contracts for skill and labour and materials will come within this Act. Contracts for things like installation of central heating, electrical and plumbing work will fall within this Act, which would never have been covered by the SGA.

In cases where the contract concerns some work and the passing of property in goods, the test as to which Act applies is what, on balance, constitutes the essence of the contract. To take the earlier example: if a person buys electrical goods which require some work to install them, despite the labour this is basically a contract for the sale of goods. But if a person orders a fitted kitchen, into which will be installed certain kitchen units, electrical goods and plumbing, then the contract is, on balance, not one for the goods themselves but for skill and labour; the passing of property is incidental and the contract will be governed by the SGSA. The Act is based largely on the SGA but unlike that Act there is little or no statute-related case law and it has, on the whole, a narrower sphere of control.

Thus while it is true to say that originally the SGA was limited in application, recent statutes based on the model of SGA have to a large degree filled the earlier lacunae, and taken together cover in one form or another most of the transactions that come before the courts today.

Question 5

How far does modern commercial law reconcile giving effect to voluntary concluded agreements with protecting the interests of the weaker party?

University of London LLB Examination
(for External Students) Commercial Law June 1991 Q3

Skeleton solution

- Normal contractual rules eg duress.
- Definition of scope of 'modern commercial law'.

- Consumer as the weaker party.
- Caveat emptor - inroads on this maxim.
- SGA 1979, UCTA 1977.
- Consumer Credit Act 1974.
- Consumer protection - product liability.

Suggested solution

The twin doctrines of freedom of contract and laissez faire are now to a large extent becoming obsolete in commercial law. There are so many statutory provisions which control the form and content of contracts that it is just not true any longer to say that the parties are free to make whatever contracts they wish, on whatever terms they wish.

Commercial law is of course governed by the ordinary rules of contract save where these may be specifically excluded by statute. Thus the rules as to duress, undue influence and inequality of bargaining power apply as much to contracts for sale of goods, or hire purchase contracts and so on, as to any other contract. However because of the extra statutory controls which give added protection to the weaker party in many typical commercial contracts, it may not be necessary to seek to invalidate a contract by pleading duress or undue influence. It remains true however that commercial pressures amounting to duress will vitiate a contract (*Atlas Express* v *Kafco* (1989)). But note that the pressures must be improper; the presence of what might be called normal commercial competition is not sufficient to constitute duress (*Pao On* v *Lau Yiu Long* (1980); *Universe Tankships* v *ITWF* (1982)). Thus the law will give relief to a party to any contract, including commercial contracts, where the contract into which he entered has been obtained by some form of improper pressure. The pressure must be such that the party subjected to it cannot be said to have acted freely and voluntarily (see *Dimskal Shipping* v *ITWF* (1991)).

It may be a useful exercise to try to define the term 'modern commercial law', so as to assess the potential terms of reference for this answer. It is almost impossible to define the term 'commercial law' in any generic way - English law has never developed and codified any comprehensive commercial law as such. Instead it is constantly developing to meet the needs of an increasingly complex consumer-orientated society. Developments are added in a piecemeal fashion as and when needed and no two experts in the subject seem to define the subject in the same terms. There are however certain basic principles which underlie commercial law which may be studied to give some idea of the scope of this area of law. The sale of goods (and to a lesser extent services), that is, the transfer of ownership, title and risks in property for a monetary consideration known as the price; and the financing of such sale or supply contracts, comprise in one form or another the two basic forms of commercial contract. Almost all commercial law, as it stands at present, is concerned with one or other of these two types of contractual arrangement.

Most of the contracts thus negotiated will be between a party supplying goods or services by way of business and a 'consumer'. Commercial law is largely concerned to protect the consumer. While it is true that commercial contracts may very well be negotiated between two companies (or to a lesser extent between two individuals), it is to the protection of the weaker individual party, the consumer, that commercial law largely addresses itself. It may equally be true that even where two businesses deal together, they may not be on an equal footing; one business may be near bankruptcy or have some other disability, but when commercial law talks of protecting the weaker party, it is usually the individual consumer that is so designated. As has already been stated, if the commercial pressures exerted by one company on another become 'improper', then duress will destroy the reality of the weaker party's consent and the contract may in certain circumstances be considered invalid. But this is a common feature to all contracts, not peculiar to commercial law.

The consumer has had some form of statutory protection since the first Sale of Goods Act 1893 and the list of statutes has grown ever since. The maxim for commercial contracts has always been 'caveat emptor' - let the buyer beware. Assuming both parties to be free to negotiate and agree their contractual terms to their mutual satisfaction, the law has always placed the responsibility on the buyer to properly investigate and assess the goods offered to him, before completing negotiations. This maxim has been steadily lessened in its effect by various statutory provisions. The Sale of Goods Act 1979 grants considerable protection by way of implied terms in consumer contracts, particularly as to title of the seller, fitness for purpose, merchantable quality, correspondence with description and so on. These implied statutory terms have in their turn been further enhanced by case law. (See for example, the recent case of *Harlingdon & Leinster Enterprises Ltd* v *Christopher Hull Fine Art* (1990) as to protection for consumers in transactions concerning paintings, and in particular the attribution and authentication of paintings.)

The maxim of caveat emptor appears to be effectively reversed by s3 of the Misrepresentation Act 1967, and the trader must beware of committing himself to any statement that might amount to a misrepresentation. The role played by the Unfair Contract Terms Act 1977 should also be included in this list. This Act limits the extent to which sellers of goods and services can limit or exclude their obligations to the consumer by incorporating exclusion or limitation clauses. In some instances such exclusions are not permitted at all (for example s6(2) provides that liability for breach of the implied conditions arising from SGA 1979 cannot be excluded at all as between supplier and consumer); in other cases the exclusion clause will be subjected to a 'reasonableness' test (ss2 and 11 UCTA). Furthermore, the Consumer Transactions (Restrictions on Statements) Order 1976, amended 1978, introduced a criminal offence for certain breaches of UCTA, especially of s6. Thus not only may an exclusion clause be ineffective, the seller or supplier may commit a criminal offence in incorporating it into the contract in the first place.

Just as 'caveat emptor' is being slowly eroded by various statutory measures designed to protect the consumer, so too are other basic rules of law being systematically 'altered' to give effect to such protection. It always used to be the case that once a party had, with full knowledge of all the relevant facts, entered into a contract, he was bound. No matter what his argument, no matter how harsh that rule appeared, having made his 'bargain' he was stuck with it. The Consumer Credit Act 1974 with its 'cooling off' period is an exception to the general rule. Sections 67-73 of CCA cover cancellation and thus depart from normal common law rules, because revocation is normally not possible once acceptance has taken place. Similarly the CCA makes provision (ss137-140) for judicial control of 'extortionate' credit bargains. The courts' jurisdiction is extremely wide, the aim being to protect the debtor (or sometimes the debtor's surety). Under the CCA, even agreements not regulated by the Act are subject to the courts' right to re-open extortionate credit bargains and either set aside the contract completely or virtually re-write the terms. The courts have always had of course, by virtue of common law, the right to imply terms into a contract, but this right has been limited in the case of 'ordinary' (that is, as opposed to those covered by CCA) contracts, to terms implied by virtue of statute or of custom or trade usage or simply those required to give 'reasonable efficacy' to the contract. In other words, at common law the courts are concerned to give effect to the parties' wishes whereas in the case of 'extortionate' credit bargains, the new terms are imposed by the courts. The creditor, at any rate, presumably will not welcome such implications by the court, but they will be imposed to protect the debtor. Before concluding, one other area should be briefly mentioned, that of consumer protection. In a sense this goes back to the maxim 'caveat emptor', mentioned earlier. In a normal contract, it is assumed that, because each party freely and voluntarily enters into the contract, negotiating whatever terms seem to him most appropriate, then if the outcome of the contract is that one party ends up with inferior goods, or not quite what he bargained for, then this is his problem and not in itself grounds for invalidating the contract. (This is of course discounting such truly vitiating elements as illegality or misrepresentation.) Much of the earlier commercial law follows this policy. The Sale of Goods Act, for example when first drafted in 1893, was worded on the assumption that most commercial transactions were between merchants, where the parties had equal status and bargaining power. Nowadays much more attention is paid to the rights of the consumer buyer, and he is given special protection in a number of ways. The Consumer Protection Act 1987 incorporates not only the common law as to contractual liability, but also tortious liability. Additionally because the liability for defective products is strict, many of the difficulties in bringing an action are removed. Consumers injured by defective products may therefore bring an action at law more easily and quickly. There are other statutes which wholly or partly seek to protect the consumer (Trade Descriptions Act, Fair Trading Act, etc). The overall effect of Acts like these and the CPA is that terms as to product safety, compliance with description and so on, are effectively implied into consumer contracts without the consumer having to negotiate them specifically. As the weaker party he would be unlikely to be able to negotiate such advantageous terms in any event.

Thus it is true that the weaker party, in the form of the individual consumer, is given special protection in a number of ways in the field of commercial law. Freedom of contract, with the stronger party imposing terms on a reluctant weaker party, is not possible with the level of statutory protection a consumer now enjoys. But it should not be forgotten that if, by weaker party, one means simply one merchant as compared to another, or one company and another; then there is little similar protection for the weaker party here. Duress, as applied in common law, or the possibilities as afforded by the 'reasonableness test' insofar as it may be applied to exclusion clauses in the light of UCTA: these are about the limits of the protection the law will grant to a 'weaker party' who is not a consumer. Otherwise freedom of contract still survives to this extent and in this area of commercial law.

36 UNIVERSITY OF LONDON LLB (EXTERNAL) 1993 QUESTIONS AND SUGGESTED SOLUTIONS

UNIVERSITY OF LONDON
LLB EXAMINATIONS 1993
for External Students
PARTS I & II EXAMINATIONS (SCHEME A) and
THIRD AND FOURTH YEAR EXAMINATIONS (SCHEME B)

COMMERCIAL LAW

Friday, 11 June: 10am to 1pm

Answer *FOUR* of the following EIGHT questions.

(Assume that all contracts are governed by English law.)

1 'The first thing you learn about the law of sale of goods is that there are various classifications for goods - as specific, ascertained, future and so on. No doubt these classifications are not perfect, but usually the classification doesn't matter anyway.'

When does it and why?

2 'The obligations imposed by a sale of goods contract depend on what is negotiated. A seller who says little incurs minimal liability. But the content of his obligation will be increased where the buyer makes clear his expectations of the goods and of the seller.'

Discuss.

3 'Far better to enter into a simple contract of sale than to incur all the problems you get when you supply goods under a secured transaction.'

To what extent do you agree?

4 Annie is the Despatch Manager for Prince Plc. Her job is to pack and post goods sold by Prince. Sale agreements are basically the responsibility of Queenie, Prince's Sales Manager, but Annie is permitted to sell goods for up to £100 without consulting Queenie and she has received no complaints when she has occasionally exceeded that amount.

Tim makes enquiries of Annie about 100 Windsor word processors (which Prince sells at five per cent above the normal trade price) and 100 Squidgy printers (which Prince does not sell but which are sold by Annie's friend Marcus). Marcus offers to supply the printers to Annie for sale to Tim at 15 per cent below the trade price and tells Annie that she can keep ten per cent of any money received for them as a present. Annie quotes separate prices for the word processors and printers. Tim offers to buy only the printers, as he can get the word processors more cheaply elsewhere. Annie tells him that the printers are only available at that price if he orders the word processors too, so Tim orders both.

That evening Tim meets Queenie at a party and tells her that he is surprised that someone like Annie is handling such important business. Queenie tells Tim that the firm has complete confidence in Annie. The following morning, a messenger delivers to Annie full payment for the goods in cash.

Advise Prince.

5 In 1900, the Noreuropean Post Office issued a commemorative set of stamps, most of which are generally on the market except the Danish Pink and the Norwegian Blue. Scando, a dealer in rare stamps, obtains a Danish Pink and two Norwegian Blues. He agrees to sell the Danish Pink and a Norwegian Blue to Balt and the other Norwegian Blue to Perot. The contracts provide for free insurance to destination, a returnable ten per cent deposit and any outstanding sums to be paid on delivery. By mistake, Scando places the two Norwegian Blues in the envelope addressed to Balt and the Danish Pink in the envelope addressed to Perot. He hands the envelopes to Easyrider for delivery. On his way, Easyrider swerves into a canal. The envelope addressed to Perot is lost and one of the stamps in the envelope addressed to Balt is damaged by canal water.

Advise Scando, Balt and Perot.

6 a) Slimbo agrees to sell a motor car and a caravan to Bilbo cif Melbourne. Bilbo contracts to resell the goods to Tex. Bilbo becomes insolvent. The car is washed overboard in a storm and the caravan is damaged by seawater. Slimbo's neighbour Wilma, who is working in Melbourne for a few months, asks Slimbo whether she can have the caravan delivered to her for temporary accommodation.

Advise Slimbo.

b) Boris wishes to buy a mare for breeding and agrees to buy one from Selina for £2,000. Unfortunately the mare supplied is unable to conceive: if it had been able to Boris would have expected to earn £15,000 from foals which he could have sold. Xerxes offers to buy it from Boris for dogmeat for £175, which he says is £100 more than Boris would get if Xerxes bought her at the end of her breeding life. However, since Boris had also intended to hire a horse for £600 for giving rides in the summer season around his animal sanctuary, he decides to use the mare instead of hiring the other horse. During the summer, it becomes clear that the mare's condition is due to a disease, which infects other animals in the sanctuary, which have to be destroyed.

Advise Boris.

7 a) Delia is a car dealer who keeps a vintage motor car in her window for show. Roger offers to buy the car. Delia says that she does not want to sell it but that she will only be able to afford the rent for the premises on which she runs her business if she can increase her profits, so she agrees to sell the car to Roger for fifteen per cent more than his original offer, the sum to be paid in ten monthly instalments. Roger defaults on the third instalment, so Delia loses the premises and her business suffers substantial losses.

Advise Delia.

b) Sugrav advertises for sale a foreign car for £8,000. Blibbip wishes to acquire it on hire-purchase terms, so Sugrav sells it to Finkco Ltd, which agrees to supply it to Blibbip for 20 monthly instalments of £500. Four months later, the government bans the import of foreign cars, as a result of which Blibbip is able to sell the car to Trumo for £20,000.

Advise Finkco.

8 Barny inspects a sample of zgwerchmeit seed in Sadsack's New York storehouse. Thereafter, Sadsack contracts to sell to Barny 'US $50,000 worth of zgwerchmeit as per sample cif London, payment cash against documents.' On Barny's instructions, the Karkey Bank is to open a letter of credit in favour of Sadsack for payment 'as per terms of sale contract.'

Sadsack ships the goods and presents the shipping documents to the bank and tenders a bill of exchange for US $50,000. The bank states that it will accept the shipping documents but (as it believes that sterling is about to be devalued) will only accept a bill of exchange for the current sterling equivalent of US $50,000. Sadsack objects but, in case he cannot resell the goods elsewhere, gives in to the bank's terms. The following day, sterling is devalued and the bill of exchange loses 10 per cent of its value. Sadsack wishes to recover this loss.

On the voyage, a heatwave causes the temperature in the hold to rise. This stimulates the growth of a fungus which was not detected when Barny inspected the sample at New York. The fungus makes the seed sterile, although on a visual examination it appears to be in the same condition as when Barny first saw it.

Advise Sadsack and Barny.

Question 1

'The first thing you learn about the law of sale of goods is that there are various classifications for goods - as specific, ascertained, future and so on. No doubt these classifications are not perfect, but usually the classification doesn't matter anyway.'

When does it and why?

University of London LLB Examination
(for External Students) Commercial Law June 1993 Q1

General comment

A question which many students might rush to answer as being easy. It is not. It is the sort of question which many students will answer in a sufficiently adequate manner as to score a bare pass mark, if that, but very few students will score high marks.

It is all too easy to leap head-first into the classification part of the question and forget the rest. Students should make sure they allocate time equally between the twin problems of classifications of goods and whether these classifications are important. It would be all too easy to get so wrapped up in the first question as to forget the second completely.

Skeleton solution

- Classifications of goods under SGA 1979.
- Importance of classification.
- Consequences of classification.
- Determination of validity or otherwise of contract.
- Sale or agreement to sell.
- When does property pass?
- Doctrine of frustration.
- Remedies, especially decree of specific performance.

Suggested solution

It is true that, as the question makes clear, the classification of 'goods' under the Sale of Goods Act is an area with which most students of commercial law quickly become familiar. To most, the question of existing or future? Specific or unascertained?, when categorising goods is a fairly straightforward matter and one easy to resolve. It is equally true, however that these classifications, superficially so clear and precise, do in fact conflict on occasion: a matter to which we shall return later in this answer.

Firstly, though, it may be useful to run quickly through the various accepted classifications of goods. These classifications may be 'the first thing you learn' but it is always a useful exercise to recapitulate even the most elementary information.

Goods may be either existing or future, that is to say that they may be owned or possessed by the seller, or they may be about to be manufactured or acquired by the seller. The statutory definition of future goods (s61(1) SGA 1979) provides that such goods are to be 'manufactured or acquired by the seller after the making of the contract of sale'. The concept of existing or future goods is to a large extent echoed by the classification of goods into the classes of either specific or unascertained. Specific goods are defined by s61(1) SGA which lays down that, subject to contrary intention this means goods 'identified and agreed upon at the time ... of sale'. Unascertained goods are, however, nowhere to be found defined in the SGA 1979. The Act uses the phrase, but only as a contrast to specific goods. It is reasonable to assume, by a process of analogy, that unascertained goods will be those either to be manufactured or grown by the seller, or to be separated out from a larger unit, or to be in some way prepared (ie weighed, measured, packaged etc). Section 16 of SGA provides that when the contract is for unascertained goods, 'no property will pass ... unless or until the goods are ascertained', thereby making it clear that unascertained goods may change to ascertained. The actual procedure of ascertainment may differ depending on the type of goods.

The question remarks that the classifications are 'not perfect'. One weakness has already been noted: the fact that 'unascertained' has no statutory definition and must be resolved by a process of analogy. A second problem is that the concepts of existing/future and specific/unascertained are not exactly matching; they cover, in fact, rather different categories. Note firstly that specific goods are those in existence and identified at the time the contract was made (s61(1) SGA) whereas ascertained goods are those which were unidentified when the contract was made, but which have subsequently become ascertained/identified. To this extent specific and ascertained goods can *never* be considered to be in the same category. Yet while goods which are existing and goods which are specific may be considered to be roughly equivalent, goods which are future normally would not seem to include ascertained goods. The definition of future goods, however, both at common law and under the SGA, anticipates that such a category as specific future goods might exist. For example specific crops to be grown, or animals to be bred. Such specific goods would be those identified at the time of the contract (eg the result of a match between two named racehorses) but which are not actually in existence at that time. Ascertained goods are, as already stated, quite a different category. While unidentified at the time of the contract, they become identified subsequently at some point (ss16 and 61(1) SGA 1979) by some act of ascertainment.

While the categories of goods are fairly well established - in that regard the question is accurate - it is *not* correct to say that the classification of goods does not matter. It is true that for practical convenience specific and ascertained goods are often treated in the same way and future and unascertained goods are considered to have broad similarities. This is really only feasible in cases which present no problems. When something goes wrong with a contract for the sale of goods it may be of the utmost importance to clarify at an early stage into exactly what category the goods fall. Broadly speaking, the exact nature of the goods may resolve a number of issues including:

a) whether the transaction is a true sale of goods or an agreement to sell;

b) when property in the goods passes from seller to buyer;

c) whether there is a valid contract of sale;

d) whether the doctrine of frustration will apply;

e) whether the remedy of specific performance is available.

For example, the goods forming the subject matter of the sale may be either existing or future goods. A contract for the sale of future goods can only be, by its very nature, an agreement to sell. It is clear from s12 SGA that it is not necessary for the seller to be the absolute owner, however, subject to the implied statutory condition that he has a 'right' to sell the goods. It is quite common to have sales in which the seller offers goods which he anticipates acquiring in the near future (see *Varley* v *Whipp* (1990)). The mere possession of such goods is enough to classify them as existing goods. But obviously if the seller offers goods which are to be manufactured or grown etc, then because the goods are future, the deal can only be an agreement to sell.

The second factor; the passing of property is all important. The distinction between specific and unascertained goods is, as s16 SGA makes clear, particularly problematic in sale of part of a bulk consignment. The normal rules may be stated briefly thus:

a) property in specific goods passes only when the parties intend (s17); and

b) property in unascertained goods is postponed until such time as the ascertainment occurs.

Leaving aside the problem of deciding the intention of the parties, which is not properly a topic for this answer, it is apparent that it is all-important to categorise the goods as either specific or unascertained from the outset. The counter-problem, exactly when ascertainment occurs, is of course another indication of how important it is to classify goods correctly. The leading case of *Re London Wine Co (Shippers) Ltd* (1986) is a useful illustration of the rules relating to ascertainment. To some extent commercial dealers have attempted to overcome the problems posed by bulk consignments by issuing separate delivery orders, or other documents of title to show symbolic ascertainment. At such a point, of course, title would pass. Nevertheless it is not a very satisfactory solution (witness cases like *Colin & Sheilds* v *Weddell & Co* (1952), *Inglis* v *Robertson & Baxter* (1913) and *Wardar's Import & Export Co Ltd* v *W Norwood & Sons Ltd* (1968)), but at the same time it may be appreciated that s16 SGA specifying that property cannot pass until the goods are ascertained, has to a large extent forced this symbolic ascertainment in commercial circles.

The actual classification of the goods in the most literal sense ie that they *are* goods, whether existing or future, will be a guide-line as to the validity of the contract. The SGA is precise in its (s2) definition as to the requirements of a valid sale. Most notable in this context is that it must be a contract for sale of goods. The property cannot pass unless or until the goods are identifiable. It is also to be recalled (see above) that the nature of the goods will determine whether the transaction is a sale or an agreement to sell.

As with all contracts the doctrine of frustration will normally apply. Yet ss6 and 7

SGA make it clear that only contracts for specific goods are capable of being frustrated. Unascertained goods, consequently can never form the basis for any action to seek redress for frustration of contract.

Finally, when considering remedies available it should be noted that specific performance will only be decreed (see *Re Wait* (1927)) when the goods, 'identified and agreed upon at the time of the sale', can be classified as specific. It is worth remembering though that this and other similar decisions have been heavily criticised as being more of a policy decision than a strict interpretation of the SGA. The intention is clearly to avoid third party hardship by refusing to grant specific performance in any but the most exceptional cases. Closer examination of earlier Sale of Goods Acts, especially s52 of the 1893 Act, reveals the fact that it was clearly intended that specific performance should be available in a wider range of cases including specific *and* subsequently ascertained goods. Yet given the present attitude of the courts it is clearly of considerable importance to be able to say that goods come into the 'specific' category.

From the foregoing, therefore, it will be apparent that the classification of the goods is all important in a number of different ways. It may help to determine whether there is a valid contract at all and if so whether it is covered by the SGA 1979. It will determine when property passes and whether or not the contract is capable of being considered frustrated and finally, if the contract has failed, whether specific performance is likely to be available.

Question 2

'The obligations imposed by a sale of goods contract depend on what is negotiated. A seller who says little incurs minimal liability. But the content of his obligation will be increased where the buyer makes clear his expectations of the goods and of the seller.'

Discuss.

University of London LLB Examination
(for External Students) Commercial Law June 1993 Q2

General comment

On the face of it this is a very straightforward question, easily answered. Certainly almost any student with the slightest knowledge of sale of goods could make a reasonable showing on preliminary information (eg implied conditions). But what the question actually asks for - an assessment of the seller's obligations if his skill and knowledge is relied upon by the buyer - is more difficult to provide.

And running through the question is the suggestion that the less a seller says, the better, which true or not, needs some discussion. Altogether a question which, if it is desired to score high marks, needs to be approached with care.

Skeleton solution

- Implied conditions as to description, fitness and quality; ss13-14 SGA.

- Misrepresentation in sale of goods contracts.
- Inclusion of express clauses conveying more than minimum rights.
- Concept of reliance.
- Skill and knowledge of the seller or his agents.
- Additional duties imposed on the seller by the SGA where there is reliance by the buyer.

Suggested solution

The Sale of Goods Act 1979 (SGA) contains a number of implied conditions as to fitness and quality. Section 13 relates to sales by description, s14 to fitness and merchantable quality, and s15 to sales by sample. The only other conditions or warranties which might be included by implication are those incorporated into the contract by a particular trade or usage (s14(4) SGA). Otherwise the normal rule of caveat emptor applies. These implied conditions represent the bare minimum of protection afforded to a buyer by the sale of goods legislation. It is, of course, always open to the parties to incorporate additional terms expressly.

These minimum standards are of course subject to various forms of exception. The supply of goods must be in the course of a business sale, in other words a consumer sale. Sales between, for example, two private individuals would not be so protected. Similarly if the seller specifically draws a defect to the attention of the buyer, there will be no conditions as to merchantability; or if the buyer examines the goods beforehand, any defects which he ought reasonably to have discovered in his examination will not be covered by the implied conditions as to merchantability.

These are, as stated, *minimum* standards. Many contracts of sale will have express terms incorporated giving the buyer additional protection. A seller who says nothing at all during the making of a contract (a truly difficult feat if one remembers that 'saying something' about the goods will include written advertising, signs, packaging, and so on) will still incur liability if the goods are in some way not in accord with the requirements of ss13-15 of SGA. But contracts for sale of goods are as much likely to be affected by misrepresentation as any other contract. Whether or not any statement can be construed as a representation or contractual term is a question of fact for the courts to decide in each case; but if misrepresentation is present, the effect on the contract will be the same for sale of goods as any other transactions. Remedies will largely be governed by the Misrepresentation Act 1967.

Misrepresentation of course will only occur if the seller volunteers information. What if, although he says nothing, does nothing (but supply the goods), but the buyer makes it clear to him that he requires the goods for some particular purpose? Immediately the duties of the seller under SGA become more onerous. Yet there are certain criteria which must be satisfied before these additional obligations will become operative.

If goods are sold by description for example (s13) it is clear, from *Harlingdon & Leinster Enterprises Ltd* v *Christopher Hull Fine Art Ltd* (1991) that the buyer must make clear to the seller that he has seen/read/heard the description and is relying on it.

It is this reliance which is crucial. If goods are sold under a description, but the buyer does not rely on it, the situation will be very different. Similarly the implied undertakings in s14 as to quality, fitness and merchantability (they all overlap in this context) are much affected by the state of knowledge on the part of the seller or his agent(s) and the degree of reliance on this skill or knowledge by the buyer. Note that the above refers to the seller OR his agent(s). This is particularly important where goods are purchased on credit. In credit sales, in antecedent negotiations the supplier is deemed to act as agent for the creditor (s56(4) Consumer Credit Act 1974).

We should now examine the concept of reliance in more detail. It is not sufficient that the seller is aware of the particular purpose intended for the goods sold; the buyer must have relied on the seller's (or agent's) skill and knowledge at the time of the contract. There has been, of recent years, a shift in the burden of proof: the seller must now prove that the buyer did *not* rely on him, hereby transferring the onus of proof. In most cases, in all practical terms, this really means reliance will be assumed unless the seller can prove to the contrary. This reliance must, in the circumstances, be reasonable. Thus in *Ashington Piggeries Ltd* v *Christopher Hill* (1972), it was held that where both seller and buyer have their own areas of expertise, it would be reasonable for the buyer to rely on the seller if those areas of expertise are different. If both seller and buyer have the same field of expertise then it would be unreasonable to anticipate reliance. If the goods are sold under a trade name the courts' normal approach is that it would be unreasonable to say the buyer relied on the seller's skill and judgment (*Wilson* v *Rickett, Cockerell & Co Ltd* (1954)). One other factor which should be considered is whether if the goods, or their packaging, contain or are marked with instructions or warnings then it may be argued that it is unreasonable to place reliance on the seller's skill and judgment. In *Wormell* v *RHM Agriculture* (1987) for example, where the sellers recommended, contrary to instructions on the pack, a weedkiller which proved to be not so much damaging as totally ineffective. One line of argument was that it could not be said that the plaintiff relied on the seller; it would be unreasonable to do so in view of the fact that instructions on the can clearly contradicted the seller's advice. (It is incidentally, worth noting that the Court of Appeal stated that packaging, especially instructions, are governed by the same provisions of the SGA as to fitness for purpose as the goods themselves).

So much for the reliance factor. We should also look briefly at the question of the knowledge possessed by the seller or his agents. We have already seen that in credit sales and the like, knowledge possessed by one is imputed to the other. Thus if the buyer explains his special requirements to a supplier, who in turn contacts others in the chain right back to the manufacturer, then usually the buyer can be said to have communicated his purpose to all of them. However, note that if the purpose for which the goods are required is not a common one, or if the goods are suitable for several different things and the buyer wants the goods for one of the less common purposes, the duty is correspondingly greater on him to communicate exactly what purpose he wishes to use the goods for (*Ashington Piggeries*).

So to sum up, how far can one say that a seller who is told exactly what the goods are required for, by a buyer who is clearly relying on the seller's skill and judgment, is under a greater duty than the seller who has not had this information conveyed to him?

All goods are required to comply with description (s13(1) SGA). However, it would be wrong to assume that all statements as to description automatically become contractual terms (*Harlingdon & Leinster*). It is, however, true that if the buyer makes it clear that his reliance on the description is what governs his agreement to the contract, then this will place the seller under a greater burden, especially with regard to misrepresentation.

Section 14(6) SGA requires that all goods be of merchantable quality. This means that the goods be ' ... as fit for the purpose ... for which goods of that kind are commonly bought as is reasonable to expect.' This implied duty has thus little to do with the state of the seller's knowledge, or the buyer's reliance on that knowledge. It is enough that the goods be suitable for whatever purpose or purposes such goods are usually put to. Section 14(3) of SGA however supplements the concept of merchantability with a statutory requirement that the goods be 'reasonably fit' for any normal purpose or special purpose as 'communicated to the seller'. It is this subsection of course, in which the state of the seller's knowledge and the buyer's reliance are all important. However, it should be borne in mind that these two subsections do overlap - the statute requires all goods to be reasonably 'fit for purpose' irrespective of whether the supplier himself has exercised due care and skill. In effect liability is strict: *Frost* v *Aylesbury Dairy* (1905). Sellers of goods will always have a general liability under s14(6), and may have some degree of liability under s14(3) if the criteria of knowledge and reliance are satisfied. They are not alternative duties; the latter is superimposed on the former.

Question 3

'Far better to enter into a simple contract of sale than to incur all the problems you get when you supply goods under a secured transaction.'

To what extent do you agree?

University of London LLB Examination
(for External Students) Commercial Law June 1993 Q3

General comment

A difficult question, not least because the student might spend so long trying to define the highly ambiguous 'secured transaction' that he loses sight of the actual question. 'Secured transaction' could mean a whole series of different things, none of which would make the slightest sense in the context of the question. The sense of the question is all-important and once the examiner's intention is pinned down the question itself is fairly straightforward.

Skeleton solution

- Meaning of the term 'secured transaction'.
- Reservation of title clauses.
- Effects of inclusion of a Romalpa clause.
- To whom is there any advantage/disadvantage?

- Is a straightforward sale of goods contract with no Romalpa clause actually advantageous: (a) to the seller; and (b) to the buyer?

Suggested solution

The first matter which is to be addressed is to decide just what is meant by 'secured transaction' as used in the context of the question. This phrase is capable of possessing a number of meanings: firstly it may be that the financing of the transaction is secured, secondly the goods in question may be bailed or hired, the transaction may be governed by consumer credit legislation, or fourthly, a contract of guarantee may exist to support the main transaction. We need to look at all of these briefly. It is however most likely that the 'secured transaction' to which the question refers is concerned with more unconventional security provisions such as retention of title clauses. But before we turn to this aspect, we must look at some of the less likely possibilities.

Firstly in certain debtor-creditor contracts the lending of the money is secured by lending against a mortgage of either land or chattels perhaps reinforced by the use of covenants, for example as to how the money may or may not be used. Such contracts *may* be used to finance sale of goods contracts, but it is unlikely.

When goods are supplied on bailment or hire, the purpose of the contract is different from that of sale, because it is not usually intended that property in the goods will pass to the bailor or hirer. Nevertheless commercial hire contracts, leasing arrangements and the like, (governed largely by the Supply of Goods and Services Act 1982 (SGSA)) are more akin to sale of goods contracts in that, for all practical purposes, the goods are transferred on a more or less permanent basis to the hirer/leaser. This is seen even more clearly in hire purchase contracts and conditional sale agreements. Currently the provisions relating to sale of goods contracts under the Sale of Goods Act 1979 (SGA) and the hire/hire purchase/lease of goods under the SGSA are now more or less identical save for the issue of passing of property and limited exceptions to the nemo dat rule. Implied terms as to the title, quality, fitness, etc are all virtually the same and the wording of the question could thus not really be said to be applicable.

Consumer credit sales and guarantees, though entirely different concepts, can equally be dismissed in a few words. Though each is in its own way an example of security, it seems unlikely that it is either one of these to which the question refers. Consumer credit legislation in particular is as complex as any part of the SGA; but it could not be said that a simple contract of sale is any less likely to incur problems.

What seems most likely is that the examiner refers to contracts in which goods are supplied subject to some sort of reservation of title clause. What needs to be done therefore is to examine the forms that such clauses may take and then, secondly, ascertain whether or not it is true that contracts secured in such a way do in fact make for such problems that it would be better to have 'a simple contract of sale' as the question describes it.

The best known case is of course *Aluminium Industrie* v *Romalpa* (1976), but there are a whole string of cases in which retention of title is in issue. These include: *Re*

Bond Worth (1980) and *Armour* v *Thyssen Edelstahlwerke AG* (1990), though there are numerous others. It is clear from a thorough examination of the leading cases that reservation of title clauses can fall into one of several categories, eg:

a) a *simple* clause; when the seller retains ownership until the full purchase price is paid;

b) an *all liabilities* clause, when the property in goods supplied does not pass until all debts outstanding between buyer and seller are satisfied;

c) an *extended* clause, when the seller retains ownership in goods supplied, not only against the buyer but against any sub-buyers too, until full purchase price is paid;

d) a *prolonged* clause, which is similar to the above but when the seller not only reserves ownership against any sub-buyers but also reserves the right to sue sub-buyers should the primary buyer not pay in full.

There are also clauses which are an aggregate of one or more of the variations listed above, but which go further and make claims against manufactured property made from goods supplied, possibly on a proportionate basis.

The courts' attitude to reservation of title clauses has been mixed. They have in the past placed great emphasis on agreement between the parties to the insertion of such clauses. They prefer to base the rationale of allowing reservation of title clauses on an analogy with the concept of bailment: see *Borden (UK)* v *Scottish Timber Products* (1981) and *Re Andrabell* (1984). In certain instances (for example the *Romalpa* case itself) the courts looked at the relationship between the seller or supplier of goods and the sub-purchasers as one of agency; treating the seller as an undisclosed principal and the main buyer as agent. The concept of retention of title has also led the courts into the fields of equity, particularly the law of sale through a trust instrument. This in turn involves the doctrine of 'tracing' (an equitable remedy hitherto linked to trusts). It may be seen even from this brief and hurried survey that the courts' attitude to retention of title clauses has been one of reserve. They have applied by a process of analogy doctrines more applicable to bailment, or to agency, or to the equitable doctrine of trusts. The overall policy has obviously been wherever possible to limit the effectiveness of such clauses.

It remains to be seen whether the inclusion of a retention of title clause does, in fact, create numerous problems. The primary purpose of *Romalpa* clauses is to secure payment. The effect of the clause is such that if payment is not made in full the goods should be returned to the seller. Quite apart from the purely practical problem of how this may be achieved if the goods supplied were to be raw materials in some manufacturing process, the question arises as to whether this is *legally* possible.

Under the SGA and SGSA the situation is the same; property passes, according to the type of goods, either on delivery or on payment. Often these are simultaneous. Once property passes, the seller may have certain rights against the buyer if he remains unpaid, but because the buyer now has title and can convey that title to others, the unpaid seller will have no rights against sub-buyers. In particular he will certainly not have the right to retrieve the goods themselves. There are of course exceptions to the rule that property passes on delivery and/or payment. One of these, with particular reference to specific goods, is that property passes when the parties intend it to (s17 SGA). It is this provision that has opened the way to reservation of title clauses, though it is true to say that the common law also recognises the possibility of a condition precedent (ie full payment before property passes to the buyer).

By reserving title to the goods the seller may adversely affect the rights of others, especially the buyer's creditors. By inserting such a clause into the contract of sale the seller will enjoy a status equivalent to that of a secured creditor. The SGA 1979 makes it clear that though there may be very limited remedies (such as that of lien and/or stoppage in transit) the seller's only remedy following delivery is normally restricted to an action against the buyer for the purchase price. He will of course be in competition with any other unsecured creditors. So, to sum up, is there any truth in the statement that a 'simple contract of sale' is far better than incurring problems in a secured transaction? There are, admittedly, some complications. Seller and buyer must, for example, consciously agree a reservation of title clause, otherwise the normal presumptions of the SGA will apply as to passing of title. Whether or not a potential buyer can be persuaded to agree to the insertion of a *Romalpa* clause, depends presumably on the state of commerce ... it is not a clause which a buyer would favour, for obvious reasons. Secondly, note that the courts' attitude to such clauses is on the whole one of reserve. There is no fixed rule as to whether such a clause will be deemed valid by the courts; most of the cases have depended on individual facts and a stringent interpretation of the express wording of the clause. In particular the courts will always look for freely given consent of both parties. The existence of some fiduciary relationships between the parties has also been regarded as necessary, at least until recently.

But, assuming a reservation of title clause is used, then the seller will be infinitely better off in the case of the buyer's insolvency. And since such insolvency may be all too common nowadays, it may be well worthwhile to the seller at least to insist on the inclusion of such a clause, rather than supply goods under a 'normal' contract of sale governed by the SGA.

Question 4

Annie is the Despatch Manager for Prince Plc. Her job is to pack and post goods sold by Prince. Sale agreements are basically the responsibility of Queenie, Prince's Sales Manager, but Annie is permitted to sell goods for up to £100 without consulting Queenie and she has received no complaints when she has occasionally exceeded that amount.

Tim makes enquiries of Annie about 100 Windsor word processors (which Prince sells at five per cent above the normal trade price) and 100 Squidgy printers (which Prince does not sell but which are sold by Annie's friend Marcus). Marcus offers to supply the printers to Annie for sale to Tim at 15 per cent below the trade price and tells Annie that she can keep ten per cent of any money received for them as a present. Annie quotes separate prices for the word processors and printers. Tim offers to buy only the printers, as he can get the word processors more cheaply elsewhere. Annie tells him that the printers are only available at that price if he orders the word processors too, so Tim orders both.

That evening Tim meets Queenie at a party and tells her that he is surprised that someone like Annie is handling such important business. Queenie tells Tim that the firm has complete confidence in Annie. The following morning, a messenger delivers to Annie full payment for the goods in cash.

Advise Prince.

University of London LLB Examination
(for External Students) Commercial Law June 1993 Q4

General comment

There is always at least one fairly general question on aspects of agency and this question is fairly typical of its kind. The depth of detail required is fairly superficial because it covers so much ground. Any student reasonably well acquainted with agency law should be able to complete this question and score high marks on it.

Skeleton solution

- Forms of agency, methods of creation, modes of authority.
- Misconduct by an agent.
- Liability of a principal regardless of misconduct.
- Personal liability of agent.
- Remedies:

  by principal against agent for misconduct;

  by third party against either agent or principal.
- Disclosed and undisclosed principals.

Suggested solution

Annie's (A's) position as despatch manager for Prince Plc (P) would appear to create a form of express agency. It may be that such a form of agency was originally created by a written contract drawn up specifically for the purpose; though the relationship does in fact seem to be undergoing a gradual change. We are told that Annie has specific authority to sell goods up to the value of £100, but we are also told that she must consult with the sales manager for sales over that amount and that she has on occasions sold goods valued at more than £100 without consulting the sales manager and the firm have honoured those transactions. In short, although the precise relationship between A and P may have been defined expressly, her authority has in the interval apparently changed and increased with the acquiescence of P.

When agency is created by agreement, the agent has actual authority. If there is a specific contract, it may be possible to ascertain the agent's exact powers (*Hely-Hutchinson* v *Brayhead* (1968); *Biggar* v *Rock Life Insurance* (1902)). In this case, though, it is likely that A's powers have in fact changed and increased since the original agreement between her and P was made. It is possible to have a form of implied actual authority (*Freeman and Lockyer* v *Buckhurst Park Properties* (1964)) in which by looking at the agreement between A and P one can ascertain all the implied terms which are common in such a form of agency. In the present case, it may present problems that A's official function is described as despatch manager; close examination of the normal contractual duties of a despatch manager would not seem likely to include sales work. Yet A is clearly given a power to sell, at least small items, on her own initiative and that power would seem to be increasing.

Can she then be described as a general agent? Provided the principal has not specifically excluded them, such an agent will have all the normal powers that go with the job to which the agent has been appointed (*Hely-Hutchinson*). This is known as usual authority. Leaving aside for the moment the problem of defining the exact jurisdiction of a despatch manager, has A been given specific instructions not to make contracts of the type she apparently enters into with Tim (T)? There is obviously a vast difference between selling goods at over £100 on occasion and expecting P to similarly condone a transaction which must at the very least involve several thousands of pounds. A can be in no doubt that this is contrary to P's specific instructions. But is T aware of this also?

A general agent may have, as well as usual authority, what may be termed apparent (or ostensible) authority to bind the principal in any act in the course of the agent's business. This is the case, even if the act has been specifically forbidden, unless the third party knows or ought to know of it (*Watteau* v *Fenwick* (1893)). Two things might alert T; firstly that the function of despatch manager is not normally to conclude sales, especially sales of this magnitude; there is after all a sales manager; secondly, half the goods he wishes to buy are not sold by P but by A's friend M. But does T *know* that A's function is that of despatch manager and that some of the goods are being supplied from M rather than P? He obviously has doubts, because of his comment to Queenie the sales manager. There is, it is true, a form of agency known as agency created by estoppel. It is not really a form of appointment at all, but involves a representation by P to T that makes T believe P has appointed A his agent. If T acts on that representation, P will be estopped from denying the agency relationship. Had P made the statement that the firm had every confidence in A there is no doubt but that A's act in selling the word processors/printers would be quite validly considered by T as part of her normal duties as an agent. *But* the representation is not made by P; it is made by Q, his sales manager. It would therefore be necessary to prove, either that Q made the remark with the knowledge of and on behalf of P or alternatively that Q has full rights as an agent to create other agencies for P. The only evidence that can be adduced in support of this latter argument is the fact that A is told that if she wishes to make sales of more than £100 she must consult with Q, the implication being that Q has power in her own role as agent to confirm such sales.

Finally in discussing modes of creation of agency P should be advised that he may, should he wish, retrospectively confirm the transaction between A and T, a process known as ratification. The main stumbling block here is that the subject of at least half the sale is not the product of P's firm, but of Marcus. In order for ratification to be effective it must be of the whole contract. P cannot ratify A's deal with T for sale of the Windsor word processors and ignore the sale of the Squidgy printers.

So, to sum up, before turning to other matters A cannot be said to have actual authority, nor may it be said she has usual authority. Her clearly defined status as despatch manager precludes this. She will have apparent or ostensible authority only if T did not know, nor had reason to suspect she was acting in defiance of P's instructions. It is not clear whether T did know, but he certainly seems to have been suspicious - as his remark to Q shows. Whether or not A could be deemed to have authority conveyed by Q's 'holding her out' to be an agent is dubious (see above).

The next question we must turn to concerns the extent to which P may be held liable on the contract even if A has exceeded her authority or even has no authority at all, and correspondingly, the extent to which A may be personally liable on the contract.

Firstly, it should be stated that given certain circumstances, a principal may be liable, even though he has specifically given the agent instructions which do not cover the contract actually made. Does that apply here? Where an agency is disclosed, whether the principal is named or not any contract made with apparent authority will bind the principal. Bearing in mind the fact that apparent authority may be negatived if the third party has any reason to believe that the agent is not acting in the normal course of business, which is a problem we examined earlier in this answer, it is worth remembering also that A while acting as agent for a disclosed principal P, also has an undisclosed one, Marcus. While it is true that this would perhaps present fewer problems were each transaction to be treated differently, A has systematically insisted that word processors and typewriters be sold in one contract.

So, is A personally liable on the contract? If A indicates to T that she is contracting only as agent, whether she names the principal or not, she will not normally be liable on the contract. But there are important exceptions to this rule; two of the most likely to apply here are when the agent is in fact contracting on her own behalf, or when the agent assumes liability personally. The courts will look to the intention of both parties (see *Foalquest Ltd* v *Roberts* (1990)) and in A's case might very well decide that A had decided to go into business on her own. The transaction is so different in value from her normal dealings, and she is dealing not only with P's goods, but also with M's. Obviously in reality a great deal would depend on what she did after receiving payment for the goods. If for example she then supplied word processors and printers, it might be said she was assuming personal liability for the contract and should, for example, the goods prove faulty,Tim might find he had an action against A personally. It should be borne in mind that in cases where the agent may have personal liability, whether or not the fact of the agency is concealed, T will usually have an alternative. He can sue *either* the agent *or* the principal but not both (*Clarkson, Booker Ltd* v *Andjel* (1964)). In this case, remember there are two: the disclosed, P, and the undisclosed, Marcus.

Assuming that there *is* an agency situation still extant between A and P; is A guilty of any misconduct? Misconduct by an agent will not necessarily terminate the agency, it should be noted, but it may mean that the principal has certain remedies against the agent. The agent's duties are both express and implied. Obviously the actual mode of appointment and purpose of the agency will govern what express terms exist. Implied duties include: disclosure of any personal interest in the contract, especially conflict of interest, to P; and not to take any bribe or make any secret profit from the agency.

We are told that P does not sell printers so it is unlikely that there is a conflict of interests. Indeed the contrary may be said to apply - T is most interested in the printers and actually prepared to acquire the word processors elsewhere and is only constrained to buy them because they come as a 'package' with the printers. Effectively A might be said to be securing extra trade for P. So, no conflict of interest here, but might A be said to be taking a bribe or making a secret profit? The problem here is that it is usually anticipated that it will be a third party who finds it necessary to bribe his way to a contract. In this case the offer to A to allow her to keep 10 per cent of money made from sale of the printers comes from Marcus not T. However it might be said that A has failed to reveal to P the fact that she has a financial stake in the transaction (*Armstrong* v *Jackson* (1917)). A principal is entitled to repudiate a contract if it is the third party's bribery, but it is not: if there *is* bribery (which is doubtful) it is Marcus who is responsible. Consequently if there is misconduct P may be entitled to recover the secret profit from A and end the agency. He may also be entitled to withold her remuneration/commission. As a result of the foregoing P might be advised thus:

- while it is true that there may be misconduct on A's part, it will not necessarily relieve P of liability on the contract - the misconduct will not always end the agency;
- while A has exceeded any express authority she may have (sales under £100 only!) she may have apparent authority (though T's question to Q makes it clear that he has suspicions that this is not so);
- even if she has no apparent/ostensible authority Q's remark to T may be constructively imputed to P and amount to estoppel;
- P may have certain remedies, as discussed against A;
- P cannot ratify the contract because it cannot be ratified in its entirety ... the goods are not all his;
- P may have some liability in the contract but effectively the transaction will have to be treated as two transactions with two principals (P as the disclosed principal) and A as the common agent.

Question 5

In 1900, the Noreuropean Post Office issued a commemorative set of stamps, most of which are generally on the market except the Danish Pink and the Norwegian Blue. Scando, a dealer in rare stamps, obtains a Danish Pink and two Norwegian Blues. He agrees to sell the Danish Pink and a Norwegian Blue to Balt and the other Norwegian Blue to Perot. The contracts provide for free insurance to destination, a returnable ten per cent deposit and any outstanding sums to be paid on delivery. By mistake, Scando places the two Norwegian Blues in the envelope addressed to Balt and the Danish Pink in the envelope addressed to Perot. He hands the envelopes to Easyrider for delivery. On his way, Easyrider swerves into a canal. The envelope addressed to Perot is lost and one of the stamps in the envelope addressed to Balt is damaged by canal water.

Advise Scando, Balt and Perot.

University of London LLB Examination
(for External Students) Commercial Law June 1993 Q5

General comment

Delivery has often cropped up in past questions but usually only as a small part of an answer. It is therefore unusual to find a whole question devoted to the topic.

While this question is a gift to those students who 'just happen' to be familiar with the buyer's duty to deliver, it is a fairly specialised area. Many students might be hard put to rake together sufficiently detailed information to answer this question in the depth and at the length needed in such a way as to score high marks.

Skeleton solution

- Delivery, definition.
- Place of delivery.
- Passing of property.
- Risk in transit.
- Buyer's right to sue for non-delivery.
- Delivery of faulty goods; buyer's right to reject, rights under s53 SGA.

Suggested solution

The duty of the seller in a contract for sale of goods includes the duty to deliver. The term 'deliver' is defined in s61(1) Sale of Goods Act 1979 (SGA) as 'a voluntary transfer of possession from one party to another'. Delivery may be actual eg physically handing over the goods, or constructive eg by handing over a document of title. Which applies here? Scando (S) obviously intends to send the stamps to Balt (B) and Perot (P) by courier; which would amount to physical delivery. At the same time however, the question mentions contract documents providing for free insurance, a 10 per cent deposit and outstanding sums to be paid on delivery. Can these contracts then be said to amount to constructive delivery? This is very doubtful, partly because the deposit is said to be returnable, and partly because cash is to be paid apparently on the actual delivery of the stamps rather than, for example, a bill of exchange or a bill of lading. So, what, if any, is the significance of the contracts referred to? It is suggested that it may have some relevance in determining the place of delivery. Section 29(2) provides that unless the parties indicate otherwise, the place of delivery will be the seller's normal place of business. *But* s29(2) only comes into operation if the parties make no provision to the contrary. It should be noted also that cases such as *Wiskin* v *Terdich Bros* (1928) make clear that place of delivery will be inferred from such phrases as 'please send us ...'. Thus the question refers to contracts stipulating payment on delivery, thereby implying the parties' intention that place of delivery be elsewhere than the seller's place of business. Place of delivery may be important for a number of reasons, not least because it will indicate whether the seller has properly delivered the goods.

When goods are sent from seller to buyer the question often arises as to who must bear the liability if goods are lost (as with P's stamp) or deteriorate (as with B's) in transit. The seller may be in breach of s14(2) as to implied conditions on merchantability and fitness for purpose if the goods fail to withstand a normal journey. Also s32(2) of SGA makes it clear that if the damage, loss or deterioration is because the seller has failed to make adequate arrangements for carriage he will be responsible. Cases like *Thomas Young & Sons* v *Hobson & Partners* (1949) make it clear that negligent arrangements for carriage will render the seller responsible for any loss. Is S responsible for choosing Easyrider (E) who hardly seems the most capable of despatch riders? Unless S is aware of some problem with E then usually he is not negligent. Obviously if E's rates were very cheap, or S knew he regularly lost goods entrusted to him, or kept crashing, then the situation might be different.

Risk in transit may be affected by insurance. We are told that the contracts cover insurance to destination at the seller's expense. This may very well be taken as an indication that the fact that S is offering free insurance means that the goods remain his responsibility while in transit. Note for example that in cases of doubt the loss or any damage or deterioration will remain with the seller until such time as property passes. Property will normally pass on delivery. By virtue of s33 if there is some risk inherent in the method of transit, then the buyer must take that risk, even though delivery is agreed to be at seller's risk. But presumably that will not apply here - P and B do not seem to want the stamps especially quickly, or specifically delivered by E.

So, if place of delivery is to be at P's and B's homes or offices (the question merely talks of addresses without specifically saying which) then the first thing to note is that delivery is never effected at all to P. His remedies will thus differ from those of B who receives the goods, but in a damaged condition.

To look at P's situation first. By virtue of s51 SGA P has the right to sue for non-delivery of the goods. The measure of damages is the estimated loss directly and naturally resulting in the ordinary course of events, from the seller's breach of contract. The stamps are, we are told, rare. How can the value of them be estimated? The concept of 'available market' is a useful one here, (see cases such as *Esteve Trading Corporation* v *Agropec International, The Golden Rio* (1990) and *Williams* v *Agius* (1914) for more details on assessing contract prices and available market).

Does it make a difference that in packing up the stamps S sends not goods that P has ordered, but other goods which he has not? Effectively not, because property never passed anyway; it is still non-delivery. But it may make a difference to B who receives goods not only damaged, but in part, not what he ordered. B has ordered a Pink and a Blue stamp. What he gets is two Blues, one damaged. It is not clear whether all stamps have the same value, but they are all said to be rare. Delivery of the wrong goods is covered by s30(4) which states that when goods which were contracted to be sold and delivered mixed with other goods the buyer may accept the goods which are in accordance with the contract and reject the rest. However when goods are delivered mixed with other goods of defective quality, as opposed to goods of a different description; then s30(4) will apply. What B wanted was a Blue and a Pink stamp. What he has are two Blues, one damaged. Can he accept the undamaged Blue, arguing that the Blue and the Pink are quite different goods and that by sending a pair of Blues these are quite different from a Blue and a Pink? Or will they be considered to be all generically just 'stamps' in which case s30(4) will not apply?

In practical terms it may not be all that important. If s30(4) does apply B will be able to keep the perfect Blue and reject the other as being different from the Pink he ordered. If it does not he will be able to sue for damages, only instead of damages for non-delivery like P, B will be suing under s53 SGA for breach of condition or warranty. If B seeks to reject which is presumably the case, he must make no move which might be construed as acceptance. Obviously if no delivery is effected at all, as in P's case, no rejection is necessary. But B does receive stamps and must decide as already discussed whether according to s30(4) to reject both or only the imperfect Blue. Section 53 permits the buyer to sue for breach of warranty as to merchantability and fitness. The measure of damages will be, prima facie, the difference between the value of the goods at the time of delivery and the value they would have had had they fulfilled the warranty. It should not be forgotten that S imposed a 10 per cent deposit which is, of course, recoverable.

One final point to remember is that in the case of unusual items like paintings or, in this case rare stamps, merchantability may be a difficult concept to establish (*Harlingdon & Leinster Enterprises Ltd* v *Christopher Hull Fine Art* (1990)). A painting for example might be said to be merchantable even if it is not by an attributed artist. But in this case the non-compliance with s14(3) does not consist in a quibble about the value of a rare stamp, but involves water-damage. No stamp, rare or otherwise, could be said to be merchantable following immersion in a canal.

Question 6

a) Slimbo agrees to sell a motor car and a caravan to Bilbo cif Melbourne. Bilbo contracts to resell the goods to Tex. Bilbo becomes insolvent. The car is washed overboard in a storm and the caravan is damaged by seawater. Slimbo's neighbour Wilma, who is working in Melbourne for a few months, asks Slimbo whether she can have the caravan delivered to her for temporary accommodation.

   Advise Slimbo.

b) Boris wishes to buy a mare for breeding and agrees to buy one from Selina for £2,000. Unfortunately the mare supplied is unable to conceive: if it had been able to Boris would have expected to earn £15,000 from foals which he could have sold. Xerxes offers to buy it from Boris for dogmeat for £175, which he says is £100 more than Boris would get if Xerxes bought her at the end of her breeding life. However, since Boris had also intended to hire a horse for £600 for giving rides in the summer season around his animal sanctuary, he decides to use the mare instead of hiring the other horse. During the summer, it becomes clear that the mare's condition is due to a disease, which infects other animals in the sanctuary, which have to be destroyed.

Advise Boris.

University of London LLB Examination
(for External Students) Commercial Law June 1993 Q6

General comment

With two very similar questions (see also Q8) a student who is well acquainted with the general area of cif contracts might be spoiled for choice. The second part of the question is perhaps less usual, but still well within the reach of most students. Remedies generally are always a popular topic for questions and most students will have anticipated something similar.

Because of the two sections it needs a fairly lengthy answer though, and anyone running short of time would be advised to steer clear of this one.

Skeleton solution

a)
- Cif contracts: main features.
- Passing of risk and title.
- Insolvency and the unpaid seller.
- Rights of the unpaid seller and especially the unpaid seller in possession.

b)
- Fitness for purpose and merchantability under s14 of SGA.
- Breach of implied terms covered by s14.
- Measure of damages.

Suggested solution

a) A cif contract (the initials stand for cost, insurance, freight) is a form of international sale contract in which the seller undertakes to ship the goods, insure and deliver them to the buyer. The price quoted by the seller will include all necessary expenditure incurred in the shipment/insurance of the goods.

Payment on a cif contract is normally cash in exchange for documents, and property in the goods is usually deemed to pass on the handing over of the documents. The responsibilities of buyer and seller under a cif contract are often scrutinised in cases which come before the courts, but the International Chamber of Commerce has also produced a sort of standardised set of conditions known as Incoterms. It should be stated from the outset that the parties are free to vary a standard cif contract (for example as to passing of property), but there is no indication that this has been done here.

We are told that Bilbo (B) becomes insolvent, the implication being that he has not paid cash nor have the documents been exchanged. In this case, of course, the goods, at least such as have survived, are still the property of Slimbo (S) the seller.

Of course if B paid cash against documents *before* going insolvent, the situation would be very different. The fact that payment has been made in no way affects the buyer's right to reject the goods. The implied terms of the SGA 1979 are of particular importance here, the main question being whether the caravan has been so badly damaged as to be unmerchantable or unfit for purpose. If it was sold on description, it may no longer comply with the description (ss13-14 SGA). The car of course has in any event been lost overboard.

If B has paid, he will of course be able to convey title to the goods to Tex (T) and S will have no right to retain the property and (most especially) no right to allow Wilma (W) to use the caravan. Similarly if B has paid, he will have a right of action against S for the lost and damaged goods. He may lose the right to reject on acceptance; however, s53 SGA in particular covers cases when the seller has delivered the goods in such a condition that it amounts to a breach of contract (or of course failed to deliver at all.)

Will the situation be different if B goes bankrupt *before* he can pay cash against documents? The major difference will of course be that since property is not normally assumed to pass until payment against documents, B will have no property in the goods and S will retain it. On the basis of the 'nemo dat' rule no title can be conveyed to T whose only right will be to sue B on the contract of resale. Certainly T will not have any 'right' (in the sense of title) to the goods. If S still has the goods and property in them, he is of course perfectly entitled to allow W to use the caravan by way of accommodation. Two main problems will no doubt be troubling S. At whose risk are the goods? And secondly, if he has not been paid, can he secure payment from B and (since B has become insolvent) how?

Section 20(1) SGA provides that unless the parties state otherwise the goods remain at the seller's risk until property passes. Can it be said that in entering into a cif contract the parties have stated otherwise? Cif contracts usually have the effect that the seller has to arrange carriage of the goods and insurance at his (the seller's) expense, but not at his risk. Risk usually ceases when the seller places the goods on board ships. The parties can vary these arrangements but there is no indication that S and B have done so.

Can the contract be said to be frustrated? Section 7 provides that if specific goods are lost before risk passes to the buyer then the contract is frustrated. But risk will almost certainly have passed to B the moment the goods went on board; whereas the car was not washed overboard until some time into the voyage, consequently it is extremely unlikely that the doctrine of frustration will apply.

As an unpaid seller S will have certain rights but of course since B has become insolvent, S may have to compete with other creditors. Effectively S will be looking for the full price. It has been held (*Manbre Saccharine* v *Corn Products*

(1919)) that even though goods may be lost or damaged, if the contract is cif the seller still has a right to present documents of title and claim the price. Loss to the buyer should of course be covered by insurance.

But if B is insolvent, obviously to claim the price is going to be difficult or well nigh impossible. Has S any other potential remedies apart from suing for the price of the goods? As an unpaid seller in possession of (at least a part of) the goods he may under s48(2) have a right of resale. He also (ss39 and 41-43) has a right of lien over the goods. Finally, he may have a right of stoppage in transit (ss39 and 44-46). If S were to allow W to use the van for temporary accommodation however, though he might recoup some of his expenses he would not really achieve a full remedy. If property has not passed it is up to him to do what he wishes with the goods, but once he presents documents against payment property passes and he is no longer the owner. The various rights (of resale, lien, stoppage in transit) must then be exercised in accordance with the strict tenets of the SGA. Temporary leasing would not seem to be within the ambit of the Act, though there is, of course, a common law duty to mitigate loss. S might argue that this is his sole reason for leasing.

b) In deciding how to advise Boris (B) it is assumed that he will be suing Selina (S) for breach of condition or warranty under SGA 1979. Clearly the right of rejection may be dismissed out of hand since acceptance presumably took place when the mare was first received by B and sent for mating.

If a horse, as with any other goods, is sold for a specific purpose (in this case, breeding purposes) the various sections, in particular s14(3) of the SGA, as to fitness for purpose, apply. S was presumably made aware very early on in the proceedings of this purpose and reliance will undoubtedly have been placed by B on her skill and judgment in selecting the mare as being appropriate to B's purpose. It remains only to advise B as to how damages will be assessed.

There are a number of factors to take into account:

- what B would have earned by breeding and selling of foals;
- what X would have paid for the horse for dog-meat (which amount is according to X more than normal);
- what B has saved by using the mare to give rides at the animal sanctuary instead of hiring a horse;
- what the cost is to B of having to have the other animals put down.

It remains to be seen how these various factors can be reconciled. Had the horse been able to breed B anticipated receiving £15,000. It is not clear whether this sum is arrived at before or after expenses. Obviously if feed and vet's bills and stud fees etc were to be taken into account the £15,000 might be reduced considerably. Before we go on to consider any other factor - could B claim this amount from S? Section 53(3) provides that if the breach is a defect in the goods (as opposed to, for example, late delivery) then the measure of damages will be the value of the goods as delivered and the value they would have had, had the condition or warranty been fulfilled. Loss of profit from goods which are defective is an acceptable measure of damages, but obviously the burden of proof is on the buyer to establish the exact lost profits with certainty. Potential prices for foals not yet bred might be difficult to establish! The normal contractual rules, as to remoteness will apply here.

Consequential damage and loss is recoverable under normal contractual rules. The actual value of the goods might be minimal (X offers £175 and remarks that this is really £100 more than it should be) but consequential loss may be considerable (*Godley* v *Perry* (1960)). It remains to be seen of course whether the value of the animals in the sanctuary amounts to much. Of their very nature such sanctuaries do not normally house animals of any substantial value. But B will have incurred vet's bills and the loss (perhaps) of revenue and contributions to the sanctuary.

So, on the face of it, B will be entitled not only to his £15,000 lost profits from his frustrated breeding plan, but also the cost of all the expense caused by the fact that disease spreads from the mare to other animals in the sanctuary. But there is one final question that should be asked - is it relevant that B turned down X's offer, kept the mare, and thereby suffered all the consequences of the animal's disease spreading? All plaintiffs are under a duty to mitigate loss. The fact that, as it turned out, the plaintiff's action was the wrong one is irrelevant, provided he acted reasonably in the circumstances. B's refusal of X's offer, thinking to save himself £600 on the hire of a riding horse, would seem quite reasonable in the circumstances. It is not incidentally clear just at what point 'during the summer' that the mare's condition becomes clear. Whether or not B actually saved himself the full £600 is unclear; certainly if he did this could be offset against the damages he claims from S.

B should be advised therefore, that he will be entitled to sue S for £15,000 anticipated profits, provided the normal rules as to remoteness of damage mean his potential earning from the mare can be established. Also B will entitled to compensation for damage caused to the animals in his sanctuary. If he saved £600 though or a proportion of it, this must be offset against the total, as must any money he obtains from X if the mare did go for dogmeat in the end.

It should be added as a post-script that of course if there were any suggestion of misrepresentation on the part of S (which there is not) then B will have additional redress under the Misrepresentation Act 1967.

Question 7

a) Delia is a car dealer who keeps a vintage motor car in her window for show. Roger offers to buy the car. Delia says that she does not want to sell it but that she will only be able to afford the rent for the premises on which she runs her business if she can increase her profits, so she agrees to sell the car to Roger for fifteen per cent more than his original offer, the sum to be paid in ten monthly instalments. Roger defaults on the third instalment, so Delia loses the premises and her business suffers substantial losses.

Advise Delia.

b) Sugrav advertises for sale a foreign car for £8,000. Blibbip wishes to acquire it on hire-purchase terms, so Sugrav sells it to Finkco Ltd, which agrees to supply it to Blibbip for 20 monthly instalments of £500. Four months later, the government bans the import of foreign cars, as a result of which Blibbip is able to sell the car to Trumo for £20,000.

Advise Finkco.

University of London LLB Examination
(for External Students) Commercial Law June 1993 Q7

General comment

Consumer credit and hire purchase contracts, alone or in tandem, have occurred several times in questions over the past few years.

The main difficulty lies in the fact that since this is a two-part question it makes a fairly lengthy question to tackle. The reverse of this is however the advantageous fact that not very much depth of knowledge is required. A student with even a superficial knowledge of consumer credit transactions should find this a fairly untaxing question to attempt. One aspect that it might be easy to overlook is the possibility that the transaction in part a) might not be covered by the consumer credit legislation at all.

Because of the time factor, it is not a question for those running short of time.

Skeleton solution

a)

- Credit sales and the Consumer Credit Act 1974.
- Is this transaction in the normal course of business and thus a regulated transaction?
- 'Default'. Meaning?
- Repudiatory breaches, minor defaults.
- Repossession.
- Other remedies, especially damages.
- Measure of damages.
- Common law remedies if the transaction is not regulated by CCA.

b)

- Hire purchase contracts; main characteristics.
- Passing of title.
- Nemo dat rule; does T have good title?
- Exceptions especially under s27 Hire Purchase Act 1964.
- Possibility that B has arranged early settlement.
- F's other remedies against B.

Suggested solution

a) If a person is supplied with goods on condition that he pays for them in instalments then it will be one of a number of transactions collectively known as credit sales. Not enough is known about the exact terms of the contract between Delia (D) and Roger (R) to say with any certainty whether the transaction is a credit sale specifically, or one of the close 'cousins', a hire purchase agreement or a conditional sale. Whatever its exact category the contract will be governed by the Consumer Credit Act 1974 and it is to this Act that D must look for her remedy when R defaults.

Firstly however it should briefly be mentioned that this transaction may be a non-commercial agreement (s189(1) CCA), that is to say, an agreement made by the creditor otherwise than in the normal course of business. While it is true that D keeps the antique car for show only, and does not really wish to sell it, she IS a car dealer. Of course, if the transaction is outside the provisions of the CCA D will still have remedies available to her, under the ordinary law of contract; we shall turn to this later in the answer.

In assessing R's position as under the CCA a primary question to decide is just what is meant by the word 'defaults' as used in the question. Is it, in fact a complete failure to pay, linked with an obvious intention to pay nothing in the future? Or is it simply a late payment? In the first case the default may be so serious as to amount to a repudiatory breach - one so serious that it is made obvious that R intends to go no further with the contract. In such a situation D may choose to treat the contract as at an end and proceed to look for a remedy under the CCA. It should be noted that since *Lombard North Central plc* v *Butterworth* (1987) if the creditor makes it clear that time of payments are 'of the essence' then failure to pay on time will be a repudiatory breach. In view of D's remarks to R about her financial problems, she might be considered to have made it clear to R that time of payment was 'of the essence'. Otherwise late payment is not treated as being of any great importance unless it is obvious that, as discussed earlier, the late payment is an obvious prelude to a complete breakdown in the contract.

Under the CCA D will have a number of possible remedies including re-possession. However, quite apart from the obvious fact that the return of the car (unless she can sell it elsewhere) will not help D's financial problems much, there are other problems. Section 90 covers the process of repossession and lays down fixed rules as to how repossession may be carried out. It should be borne in mind however that if D does repossess, her only entitlement will be those instalments due; interest will only be payable on missing instalments if the contract so provides. Goods are, it should be noted, protected goods (ie they cannot be recovered without a court order) once one-third of the total price has been paid (s90(1)). That does not seem likely to apply here (unless the payments are unequal in amount) because R has defaulted at the third of ten payments. In any event, because of D's financial problems repossession is unlikely to be much of a solution for her. Are there other remedies she might pursue? If the creditor's losses exceed the value of the missing payments, it is possible to sue for damages for loss of future benefits from the contract. This is only the case where the debtor's breach is a repudiatory one, so it is obviously important to consider early in the proceedings whether R's default *is* repudiatory. The creditor should be compensated in such a way as to place him in the same position as he would have been had the contract been performed properly (see *Overstone* v *Shipway* (1962) and *Yeoman Credit Ltd* v *Waragowski* (1961), etc, on the measure of damages). Note that if D wishes to repossess the goods she must serve a default notice, s87(1), but if she merely wishes to sue for damages or missing instalments she may do this without giving R any formal notification under s87(1).

Finally to revert back to the possibility mentioned earlier: what if the sale of this vintage car is not 'in the normal course of business' and D has no protection under the CCA? Even without statutory protection of course, common law offers redress to those involved in 'ordinary' contracts which are breached. In this instance since D spells out to R exactly what her financial problems are, damages will be assessed not only under the first, but also the second rule in *Hadley* v *Baxendale* (1854), the 'special circumstances', ie that she will be unable to pay the rent without the profits from the sale of the car. R therefore is aware, or ought reasonably to realise, that failure to pay on time may be enough to make it probable that D will be unable to pay the rent and her business will be placed in peril.

b) Hire purchase contracts are characterised by the fact that property is bailed to a person in return for periodic payments. Title in the goods does not pass until such time as the provisions of the contract are fully complied with (eg all payments made in full, interest paid etc) and the party to whom the goods are bailed has exercised an option to purchase. Therein lies the problem. Under the provisions of the CCA 1974 title in the goods will remain with the bailor until such time as the contract has been completed. In selling the car to Trumo (T) only four months into the contract Blibbip (B) is in default of his contract. In particular he would have no title to convey to T.

Several different problems arise. First of all, assuming this to be a regulated agreement under s8 of CCA, the first question is whether B can 'speed up' the contract in order to conclude it prematurely and vest title in himself. It should be noted, of course, that it does *not* say in the question that he does this; but it would be a convenient solution.

The right to settle early is given by s94. No particular form of words is needed. If the debtor wishes to exercise this right he should write to the creditor Finkco (F) and ask how much he must pay in order to be released from the agreement and F must give this information to B (s97(1) CCA). If the creditor gives no reply within one month he will be in default of the agreement and commit a criminal offence (s97(3)). Section 95 CCA provides that the debtor is entitled to a rebate for settling early. Normally of course it can only be in the creditor's interest to accept early settlement, but in this case the reasons for B's desire to settle early will not have escaped F and they may be reluctant to provide figures. But by s97 they must do so, and on payment of the requisite amount B should exercise his option to buy, thereby completing the contract.

He would then, quite legitimately, be able to sell to T. That could, of course be the ideal solution. But what if B simply purports to sell the car to T? Can he convey any title to T and secondly, does F have rights (and if so what) against T and against B?

The normal nemo dat rule means that no-one can convey title he does not possess. As a party to an HP contract B will have no title until he exercises his option to buy. Yet the problem of motor vehicles subject to HP contracts being sold on is so acute that there are special rules to protect those who buy in such circumstances. Part III of the Hire Purchase Act 1964 (as amended by CCA 1974) make certain important exceptions to the nemo dat rule. A bona fide purchaser for value from a person in possession under a HP contract will obtain good title. The purchaser must be a private purchaser, must take in good faith, and must have no notice of the existing HP contract. We know nothing about T. If he were, for example, a car dealer himself he would receive no title in the goods (though if he then disposed of the goods to a private purchaser that individual would receive title (s27(3) HPA 1964). The only doubtful aspect might be as to T's good faith and lack of notice. In view of the sudden increase in the value of foreign cars might it be argued that T ought to verify that there is no HP agreement outstanding? Cases such as *Barker* v *Bell* (1971) make it clear that constructive knowledge is not sufficient - actual notice is needed. Good faith does not involve a duty to actively seek out and investigate the seller's title. So, on the face of it T will have good title to the car and F will be unable to repossess it from him. What remedies do they then have against B? B has presumably paid four months of 20 projected monthly payments. In claiming damages for what will presumably be a repudiatory breach the debtor will have to compensate F not only for the missing instalments but any other amount necessary to put the creditor in the position he would have been in had the contract been performed. This will include interest of course, but not the sudden enormous increase in the value of foreign cars. The transaction and price were already completed and agreed and F would not in any event have stood to gain had B carried out the contract in the orthodox way.

Question 8

Barny inspects a sample of zgwerchmeit seed in Sadsack's New York storehouse. Thereafter, Sadsack contracts to sell to Barny 'US $50,000 worth of zgwerchmeit as per sample cif London, payment cash against documents.' On Barny's instructions, the Karkey Bank is to open a letter of credit in favour of Sadsack for payment 'as per terms of sale contract.'

Sadsack ships the goods and presents the shipping documents to the bank and tenders a bill of exchange for US $50,000. The bank states that it will accept the shipping documents but (as it believes that sterling is about to be devalued) will only accept a bill of exchange for the current sterling equivalent of US $50,000. Sadsack objects but, in case he cannot resell the goods elsewhere, gives in to the bank's terms. The following day, sterling is devalued and the bill of exchange loses 10 per cent of its value. Sadsack wishes to recover this loss.

On the voyage, a heatwave causes the temperature in the hold to rise. This stimulates the growth of a fungus which was not detected when Barny inspected the sample at New York. The fungus makes the seed sterile, although on a visual examination it appears to be in the same condition as when Barny first saw it.

Advise Sadsack and Barny.

University of London LLB Examination
(for External Students) Commercial Law June 1993 Q8

General comment

This sort of combination of sale of goods and international sales is a common one. Because of the ambiguity of the phrase 'was not detected' (deliberate or accidental on the part of the examiner?) this is not an easy question to answer, because so many assumptions have to be made. Provided the student can keep track of all the alternatives so as to give a comprehensive answer, then there should be no great problem. But all the different permutations do make this a long answer.

Skeleton solution

- Goods sold by sample, by description, implied conditions under ss13-15 SGA.
- Merchantable quality.
- Correspondence of the sample to the bulk; what constitutes a 'reasonable examination'.
- Cif contracts.
- Passing of risk.
- Passing of property in the goods.
- Duties of the bank; their dual role.
- Unpaid seller; rights and duties.
- Right to reject, when lost.
- Other remedies especially rights under s53 SGA.

Suggested solution

Goods sold in bulk present special problems with regard to implied terms as to fitness and also on the question of the passing of risk and of title from seller to buyer. Those problems are compounded in this instance because the goods are sold by sample.

Where goods are sold by description as well as by sample then, in accordance with ss13-15 SGA, goods must correspond with description and sample, and if sold in the course of a business they must be merchantable under the provisions of s14. Goods sold by description include goods sold under a trade name (*Azemer* v *Casella* (1867)) though it is not clear whether 'zgwerchmeit' is a trade name. Goods sold by sample must correspond with that sample - as indeed is the case here. The only problem is that the defect in the seed is not visually apparent; s15(2)(c) excludes the implied condition that the goods should be merchantable where the defect rendering them so could have been ascertained on a reasonable example of the sample. In s14(2) the implied term of merchantability is only excluded if an actual examination has been made. It is assumed that a buyer in a sale by sample will examine the sample - if he does not do so he will have no remedy for defects he could have discovered on examination.

There is a problem in the wording of the question which makes it unclear as to whether the fungus was not detected on Barny's (B's) inspection because it was not then present or whether it was present but undetected in a reasonable examination. In this respect the wording is ambiguous. Obviously if the fungus was not present in the sample, the bulk does not correspond to sample. If it was present even in the sample a good deal depends on what constitutes a reasonable examination. Remember that B inspects the sample in the warehouse, where laboratory tests and microscopic examination would be impossible. For further discussion of what constitutes a reasonable examination, see *Godley* v *Perry* (1960) and *Wren* v *Holt* (1903). Ultimately it boils down to the fact that if the defect is latent the buyer may reject goods, whether or not they correspond with the sample, whereas if the defect is patent and could have been detected on examination he will have no right to reject.

There is, however a further complication in that it is the heat on board ship which causes the fungus to grow making the seed sterile. Is the condition of the hold ... poor loading, lack of ventilation ... the fault of the shipper or his agents? Could it be argued that the seed, even if affected by the fungus, was perfectly merchantable until adversely affected by the heat? This is obviously of considerable importance to Sadsack (S) and B alike.

The next question to look at therefore is exactly when risk would have passed in such a contract. The agreement between S and B is a cif contract, the seller arranges insurance and freight and places the goods on board ship. Seller's risk normally ceases and passes to the buyer when the goods are placed on board ship. This will be the case unless S and B have re-allocated risk and there is no indication that they have. Consequently, if the seed has been adversely affected by the heat and would have been merchantable (with or without the fungus) had it not been for the heatwave, B may not have the right to reject the goods or consider the contract breached. (This is of course the sort of eventuality insurance is arranged to cover.)

Property in goods (as opposed to risk) normally passes in cif contracts on presentation of the documents of title against payment. Here again there are problems. S presents the bill of exchange to the K Bank but is told that the bank will only pay out a sterling equivalent. Under pressure S caves in and loses $5,000 on the transaction. Two distinct questions arise. Does the bank's action in any way affect the passing of property to B and secondly will S have any right of action against B as an unpaid seller?

The normal rule is that the bank has a dual role when accepting cif documents; firstly it acts as agent for the buyer, and secondly it acts on its own account and is contractually liable to pay the seller on presentation of the correct documents. If the bank have executed improper pressure or behave improperly in instigating their own 'condition' that the bill of exchange be for current sterling values, they will of course be liable on their own account. Though, as is normal, they act as agents for B, there is no suggestion that he has so instructed them. Nevertheless in any agency situation where the agent has apparent/ostensible authority, the principal, B in this case, will be liable for the agent bank's action regardless of whether they have disregarded his instructions. Effectively 10 per cent of S's payment is still owing and S will qualify as an unpaid seller with all the rights that status carries. B may of course have a right of action separately against his agent, the bank, for not following his instructions.

Note that S may have a right against the bank to sue for the 10 per cent loss as equally he may have a right against B, but these are alternative courses of action; he may not pursue both. Should he decide to sue he must elect, as is usual in agency situations, to sue one or the other and is then bound by that choice.

Thus S may be able to recover, either from the bank or from B, the difference in sterling values. But what of B's rights? As already stated, if the fungus is harmless and has only mutated because of the heatwave on board ship, then since the goods are travelling (presumably) under normal cif rules at the buyer's risk, B will have to rely on insurance of the goods to make good the loss he has suffered.

If on the other hand the defect in the seed ie the presence of the fungus would sooner or later have rendered the seed sterile and thus unmerchantable then B will have the right to reject the goods and/or compensation. We have already discussed the problem of latent/patent defects and the assumption is that the presence of the fungus could not, at the point B examined it in New York, have been detected. Of course if it was apparent and B missed it, he loses his protection under the SGA.

Transfer of property in the goods takes place in cif contracts (unless the parties indicate to the contrary) on payment of cash against documents. Two questions arise in this case. S has lost about 10 per cent of the total price - does this count as 'payment'? And secondly, if property has been transferred, does this mean B has lost his right to reject?

Unless a seller is paid in full the assumption would normally be that no property has passed. This will be of considerable significance to S. It is only after property has passed that a seller can maintain an action against the buyer for the purchase price (or part of it). While the property lies in the buyer this remedy can only lie in damages. This means that he must try and mitigate his loss by selling elsewhere and the question notes that S anticipates he might have difficulty doing this. In any case the goods are now known to be unmerchantable; to try to re-sell them would of necessity involve a degree of deception on S's part. For convenience, even if because of some financial hiccup payment is not made, or not made in full, property is normally assumed to pass when the seller tenders the documents of title. This is the case even if for some reason cash payment is not made (*Arnold Karlberg* v *Blythe* (1916)).

But if property has passed to B, will it avail S to begin an action for the 10 per cent unpaid? B will have far greater rights, he has after all received a ship-load of seed which is unmerchantable.

If a buyer exercises his right to reject the goods as being in breach of ss13, 14 and 15 SGA, then he can either decline to pay the price, or if he has paid he may recover it as being paid for a total failure of consideration by the seller. He is not required to return the goods to the seller (s36 SGA). In certain circumstances, however, the buyer may lose the right to reject - has this happened to B? The passing of property no longer affects the right to reject, but acceptance of the goods by B may mean he loses his right to reject. What would constitute acceptance? Sections 34-35 SGA govern the rules as to when acceptance will be deemed to have occurred. Section 34 in particular provides that until such time as the buyer has had a reasonable opportunity to examine the goods, he cannot be deemed to have accepted. It is not clear whether B has yet had such an opportunity. Section 35 says that if the buyer intimates acceptance or otherwise performs some act consistent with ownership (eg selling on goods) then acceptance will have occurred. Section 34 however takes priority; a buyer will sometimes sell-on goods before having an opportunity to examine them. Obviously if a buyer has such an opportunity to inspect and does not avail himself of it then he will lose the protection of s34. It is not clear whether B has either inspected the goods or acted in a way indicating acceptance. It may be in any event that discovery of the defect would be considerably delayed, because we are told that visually the seed looks perfect, but its sterility would presumably be only discovered after being sown.

Merely because B accepts the goods, thereby losing the right of rejection, does not mean that he is bereft of any other means of redress. Section 53 of the SGA provides that, in the event of a breach of warranty (such as a defect in the quality of the goods) the dissatisfied buyer may sue for damages. The measure of damages is the difference in the value of the goods as they presently are (presumably nil in this case!) and the value they would have had if they had fulfilled the warranty. Particularly in the case of seeds etc, a breach of s14(2) as to merchantable quality means that the potential gain from the seeds if they had grown properly can be taken into account. But, it should be noted that sub-sales to other buyers are generally not included in these damages (*Slater* v *Hoyle and Smith* (1920)).

So even should S, in the interval before the defect in the seeds is noted, be able to recover the amount still outstanding, once the sterility of the seeds becomes apparent B will have a corresponding right either to reject (if it is not too late and it probably is) or to sue under s53. The limitation period of course starts to run from the period when the defect giving rise to the cause of action first becomes apparent.

APPENDIX I

Questions from University of London LLB (External) Commercial Law papers (June 1983-1992) shown by **year and chapter**.

1983	Question	1	Ch 34
		2	Ch 26
		4	Ch 30
1984	Question	2	Ch 29
		3	Ch 10
		4	Ch 14
		5	Ch 17
1985	Question	1	Ch 23
		2	Ch 13
		4	Ch 12
1986	Question	1	Ch 27
		2	Ch 4
		3	Ch 34
		4(b)	Ch 16
		5	Ch 19
1987	Question	1	Ch 7
		2	Ch 1
		5	Ch 11
		6	Ch 31
		7	Ch 22
		8	Ch 21
1988	Question	1	Ch 35
		2	Ch 28
		3	Ch 5
		5	Ch 15
		8	Ch 18
1989	Question	1	Ch 24
		2	Ch 8
		3	Ch 35
		6	Ch 32
		7	Ch 20

1990	Question	1	Ch 35
		2	Ch 26
		3	Ch 3
		4	Ch 24
		5	Ch 4
		6	Ch 31
		7	Ch 18
		8	Ch 17
1991	Question	1	Ch 23
		2	Ch 35
		3	Ch 35
		4	Ch 24
		5	Ch 10
		6	Ch 5
		7	Ch 30
		8	Ch 18
1992	Question	2	Ch 8
		3	Ch 17
		4	Ch 28
		5	Ch 8
		6	Ch 15
		8	Ch 20

Note also Elements of Law of the Contract Paper 1983 - Q4 - Ch 3.

APPENDIX II

Questions from University of London LLB (External) Commercial Law papers (June 1983-1993) shown in combination with others by **year, topic and format**.

KEY

- * denotes that the relevant question is quoted in full in this Revision WorkBook. See Appendix I for details.
- E denotes an essay question.
- P denotes a problem question.
- E/P denotes a combination, usually a straight divided question, sometimes in more than two sections.

Year	Format	Question	Topic
1983			
	*E	1	Documentary credits in export sales
	*P	2	General agency: effects of an agent acting outside his authority
	P	3	NEMO DAT rule & exceptions with particular reference to motor cars under Pt III of Hire Purchase Act 1964
	*P	4	Passing of property in CIF/FOB contracts, possible breach of condition(s) implied by SGA 1979, exclusion clauses, remedies of buyer
	P	5	Types of consumer credit agreements, rights of debtor under CCA 1974
1984			
	E	1	Personal liability of the agent specifically
	*P	2	Agency relationship's generally, types of agent
	*P	3	Sale of goods, sale or return, NEMO DAT & exceptions especially Pt III of HP Act 1964 Consumer Credit agreements
	*E/P	4	Law relating to damages especially under ss50-51 SGA 1979, concept of 'available market'
	*P	5	Hire purchase law as governed by Consumer Credit Act 74, especially formalities of hire-purchase agreements

1985

*E	1	Discussion of various authorities' definitions of agency, nature of agency
*P	2	Sale of Goods, NEMO DAT & exceptions, implied terms of SGA 1979, remedies
P	3	Agency relationships generally, definition of terminology
*E/P	4	Damages, including wider issues of general law of contract. Problem relates specifically to statutory damages under ss50-51 SGA 1979
P	5	Sale of Goods, especially implied terms as to fitness/merchantability, consumer credit regulations especially cancellation, licensing of credit brokers

1986

*E	1	General discussion of agency especially as to agents liability (personal liability for torts)
*P	2	Sale of goods, implied terms as to fitness etc, NEMO DAT & exceptions, exclusion clauses, remedies
*P	3	Export sales, rights & duties of parties to CIF/FOB contracts, documentary credits. Remedies.
*E/P	4	Agency, sale of goods, implied terms, consumer credit agreements, Supply of Goods & Services Act 1982 on hire contracts.
*P	5	Rules in CCA 1974 relating to repossession, protected goods, court orders. Also liability of a company for torts/crimes of employees.

1987

*P	1	Sale of goods, implied terms as to fitness/merchantability. Exclusion clauses. Remedies.
*E	2	Concepts of risk, property, title in the context of sale of goods
E	3	Satutory remedy of damages in context of the SGA 1979 - applicable both as to buyer and seller
P	4	Insurance contracts - agency - misrepresentation
*E/P	5	Sellers real remedies especially under s28 and ss38-48 SGA

(1987 continued)

*P	6	FOB/CIF contracts, SGA implied terms as to quality, bills of lading/documentary credits remedies
*E	7	Consumer credit law, especially concept of credit, CCA '74 as applicable to credit cards
*E/P	8	Extortionate credit bargains, relief to debtor, judicial controls

1988

*E	1	Codification of commercial law, arguments for and against
*E	2	Relationship between principal and agent, personal liability of agent
*E	3	Terminology, present law on merchantability, common law SGA, defects, Law Commission's recommendations
P	4	NEMO DAT rule and exceptions especially as to agency and Factors Act
*P	5	Sale of Goods, implied terms of SGA as to quality, exclusion clauses remedies. Negligence. Consumer Protection Act 1987.
P	6	CIF contracts, documentary credits UCP
E/P	7	Differences between running account credit and fixed sum credit. Effect of Act on overdrafts
*P	8	Formation of consumer credit agreements, CCA 1974, cancellability, withdrawal, cooling off, termination

1989

*E	1	Analysis of concept of agency, types of agent methods of creation
*E	2	Comparison of the concepts of 'passing of property' and 'transfer of title' in the context of sale of goods.
*E	3	Consumer Credit Act, approach of act, criticisms, controls imposed
P	4	Duties and liability of bailees; similarity with trustees, estoppel by negligence
P	5	Sale of goods, implied conditions under s14, SGA passing of property, risk. Exclusion clauses
*P	6	Rights, duties & liabilities of parties to a CIF contract

(1989 continued)

*P	7	Consumer credit agreements, cancellability and termination
P	8	Acceleration clauses - penalties? - validity of such clauses under CCA 1974

1990

*E	1	Commercial law - origins & scope - controls with special reference to sellers & creditors - recent developments
*E	2	Origins of agency - exception to privity of contract rule - a warrantable exception?
*E	3	Terms, conditions and warranties - caveat emptor - 1979 SGA - implied terms
*P	4	Agency - duties of agents - bribes and secret profits
*P	5	Sale of goods contracts - passing of property - risk - delivery to carrier
*P	6	C + F contracts - documents and title ex-ship contracts - defective product. Consumer Protection Act 1987
*P	7	HP contracts - passing of title - exclusion clauses
*P	8	HP contracts - DCS/DC agreements - cancellation - repossession - protected goods - default

1991

*E	1	Agency, general account of principal - agent - third party relationships
*E	2	Sale of Goods - limitations of SGA - other legislation with a similar purpose
*E	3	Discussion of overall effect of commercial law in protecting weaker party
*P	4	Agency - effects of agent acting outside his authority - agent's misconduct
*P	5	Nemo dat rule - exceptions
*P	6	Sale of goods - implied terms as to fitness
*P	7	International sales contracts and sale of goods
*P	8	Consumer credit, hire purchase especially formalities of HP contracts

1992

E	1	Doctrine of the undisclosed principal
*E	2	Passing of title and right to reject

(1992 continued)

*E	3	Hire purchase and sale of goods contracts contrasted
*P	4	Agency: especially creation by estoppel and misconduct
*P	5	Reservation of title clauses
*P	6	Sale of Goods - Consumer Protection Act 1987 - common law aspects including doctrine of privity and negligence
P	7	Fob and cif contracts, especially passing of title and risk
*P	8	Consumer Credit Act 1974 - various aspects

1993

***Note: all questions from this paper (and solutions) are included in Chapter 36**

P	1	Classification of goods in the context of Sale of Goods Act
P	2	Formation of sale of goods contract - especially reliance by buyer on the vendor's skill and knowledge
P	3	Secured transactions - especially reservation of title clauses
P	4	Agency, especially appointment, authority and misconduct
P	5	Sale of goods contracts especially duty to deliver, risk and title
P	6	Cif contracts, risk and property. Breach of contract. Remedies
P	7	Regulated payments under Consumer Credit Act 1974. Default by debtor. Exceptions to the nemo dat rule with especial reference to cars
P	8	Cif and fob contracts - documentary credits - defective product - risk and title.